RELIGION AND PERSONAL LAW
IN SECULAR INDIA

Religion and Personal Law in Secular India

A Call to Judgment

Edited by Gerald James Larson

INDIANA UNIVERSITY PRESS

Bloomington and Indianapolis

This book is a publication of
Indiana University Press
601 North Morton Street
Bloomington, IN 47404-3797 USA

http://iupress.indiana.edu

Telephone orders 800-842-6796
Fax orders 812-855-7931
Orders by e-mail iuporder@indiana.edu

© 2001 by Indiana University Press

The paper used in this publication meets the minimum requirements of American National Standard for Information Sciences—Permanence of Paper for Printed Library Materials, ANSI Z39.48-1984.

Manufactured in the United States of America

Library of Congress Cataloging-in-Publication Data

Religion and personal law in secular India : a call to judgment / edited by Gerald James Larson.
p. cm.
Includes bibliographical references and index.
ISBN 0-253-33990-1 (cloth : alk. paper) — ISBN 0-253-21480-7 (pbk. : alk. paper)
1. Legal polycentricity—India. 2. Religion and state—India. 3. Religious minorities—Legal status, laws, etc.—India. 4. Domestic relations—India.   I. Larson, Gerald James.
KNS479 .R45 2001
344.54′096—dc21
2001002122

1 2 3 4 5 06 05 04 03 02 01

Contents

Contents

vi

Preface

In spring of 1999, Indiana University, Bloomington, hosted a scholarly conference entitled "Religion and Personal Law in Modern India: A Colloquium." The colloquium was co-sponsored by the India Studies Program and the School of Law and was supported also by the College of Arts and Sciences, the Office of International Programs, the Office of the Chancellor at IU, Bloomington, and the United States Department of Education.

Article 44 of the "Directive Principles of State Policy" of the Constitution of India calls for the development of a uniform civil code: "The State shall endeavour to secure for the citizens a uniform civil code throughout the territory of India." Such a uniform code has not yet been achieved in India after fifty years of independence. Systems of "personal law" (in contrast to territorial law) regarding marriage, dowry, divorce, parentage, legitimacy, guardianship, religious and charitable endowments, wills, inheritance, succession, and so forth, continue to operate for Hindus, Muslims, Parsees, and Christians. The purpose of the colloquium was to examine all aspects of the personal law issue: the desirability of a uniform civil code, the current political situation in India in terms of the development of a uniform civil code, and the attitudes among various social groups (Muslims, Hindus, Christians, young married couples, older religious leaders, women and minorities, and so forth) toward the development of a uniform civil code. A wide range of scholars from the United States and India took part in the conference, and this collection of essays is the result of that scholarly gathering.

In addition to the articles submitted to the colloquium, two other articles have been included because they are directly pertinent to the colloquium theme. They are Lloyd I. Rudolph and Susanne Hoeber Rudolph's "Living with Difference in India: Legal Pluralism and Legal Universalism in Historical Context," and Rajeev Dhavan's "The Road to Xanadu: India's Quest for Secularism." The former was first given at the Mansfield College Political Quarterly Conference on Religion and Democracy in September 1999, and is to be published by Blackwell in a collection edited by David Marquand and Ron Nettler entitled *Religion and Democracy*. The latter is an essay included in a volume edited by K. N. Panikkar entitled *The Concerned Indian's Guide to Communalism* and published by Viking in 1999. Our thanks to the Rudolphs, Rajeev Dhavan, and the respective publishers for permission to include these articles in our collection.

Gerald James Larson
Bloomington, Indiana, USA

RELIGION AND PERSONAL LAW
IN SECULAR INDIA

Introduction

The Secular State in a Religious Society

Gerald James Larson

The subtitle of the present collection of essays, *A Call to Judgment*, is deliberately ambiguous, or perhaps a double entendre, evoking on one level the challenge to the Indian legal system to treat all citizens fairly, but evoking on another level the challenge to be responsive to the many varying communities of faith in India. As the Honorable Ruma Pal, Supreme Court Justice of India, points out in her essay in this volume: "India is a land of religions. Hindus, Buddhists, Jains, Christians, Muslims, Parsees, and Sikhs form the nation." At the same time, of course, the preamble to the Constitution of India describes the modern nation-state of India as a "sovereign socialist secular democratic republic." Balancing, negotiating, and mediating the claims of secularism and the claims of the various communities of faith in India represent some of the most difficult and frequently intractable problems in maintaining the viability of India as a modern nation-state.

There are two well-known passages in the secondary literature on religion and law in India that are especially salient in highlighting the basic issues that are being addressed in this collection of essays. The first is the rather direct assertion of Donald Eugene Smith in his important book, *India as a Secular State*. Says Smith:

> [a] major problem is the position of religious personal law in the legal structure of present-day India. That a Hindu, a Muslim, and a Christian, all citizens of the same country, should be governed by different inheritance laws is an anachronism indeed in modern India and diametrically opposed to the fundamental principles of

1

secularism. The Constitution declares that the state must strive for a uniform civil code. . . .

. . . The conception of the secular state both presupposes a uniform civil law, and requires that the religious beliefs of a minority be respected. Probably 90 per cent of the Indian Muslims feel that their law is of the very essence of Islam. This is the dilemma which must one day be faced.[1]

The second passage is the equally direct assertion of T. N. Madan in his plenary address to the Association for Asian Studies entitled "Secularism in Its Place." Says Madan:

Now, I submit that in the prevailing circumstances secularism in South Asia as a generally held credo of life is impossible, as a basis for state action impracticable, and as a blueprint for the foreseeable future impotent. . . . Secularism is the dream of a minority which wants to shape the majority in its own image. . . .

From the point of view of the majority, "secularism" is a vacuous word, a phantom concept, for such people do not know whether it is desirable to privatize religion, and if it is, how this may be done, unless they be Protestant Christians but not if they are Buddhists, Hindus, Muslims or Sikhs.[2]

Madan continues:

While society seethes with . . . a vibrant religiosity, the feeble character of the Indian policy of state secularism is exposed. At best, Indian secularism has been an inadequately defined "attitude" . . . of "goodwill towards all religions" . . . ; in a narrower formulation it has been a negative or defensive policy of "religious neutrality" . . . on the part of the state. In either formulation, Indian secularism achieves the opposite of its stated intentions; it trivializes religious difference as well as the notion of the unity of religions.[3]

These two passages nicely frame the limits within which the modern Indian nation-state has been struggling to deal with the incredibly difficult but important issues of religious pluralism and what might be called legal pluralism. D. E. Smith argues the secularist position of individual citizenship, freedom of religion as private belief, and the need for a uniform civil code for all citizens regardless of their religious heritage. T. N. Madan argues what might be called an empirical, "on the ground" position. He points out that a secular mind-set is characteristic of a small elite minority, that large numbers of people in India are deeply committed to their religious traditions and follow the personal law of their respective traditions, that the "privatization of religion" is not at all desirable or even practically workable, and that the state policy of secularism, expressed either as "goodwill towards all religions" or "religious neutrality," is utterly vacuous and has only trivialized the issues of religion and law in modern India.

The Constitution of India is, of course, for the most part on the side of D. E. Smith and the secular minority, with its protection of the fundamental rights of equality before the law (Article 14), non-discrimination in terms of employment and political participation (Article 16), freedom to profess, practice, and propagate religion (Article 25), lack of state support for any "particular religion or religious denomination" (Article 27), and the absence of religious instruction of any kind in "any educational institution wholly maintained out of State funds" (Article 28).

On the other hand, the Constitution, both implicitly and explicitly, appears to be aware of the sorts of realities "on the ground" to which T. N. Madan points, and therefore recognizes the great disparities and inequities in Indian life and makes provisions for a great variety of remediation, both in terms of reservation policies based on group identities and in terms of compensatory discrimination or affirmative action based on group identities (Articles 46, 325, 330, 334, 338, 340, and so forth). The Constitution also recognizes the validity of the system of personal laws. Article 44, which, on one level as a "Directive Principle" of state policy, calls for the establishment of a uniform civil code ("The State shall endeavour to secure for the citizens a uniform civil code throughout the territory of India"), on another level recognizes the continuing validity of the system of personal laws.

The Constitution, in other words, is something of a "both-and" compromise or what Galanter has called a "principled eclecticism" between the hard-core, highly individualist-cum-secularist proposals of a D. E. Smith and the more empirically based, group identities orientation of a T. N. Madan.[4] Or, as Granville Austin has put it (in *The Indian Constitution: Cornerstone of a Nation,* Oxford, 1966): "India's original contributions to constitution-making [include] . . . accommodation . . . the ability to reconcile, to harmonize, and to make work without changing their content, apparently incompatible concepts. . . ."[5] Lloyd I. and Susanne H. Rudolph, however, have not seen a "principled eclecticism" or an "accommodation" so much as a contradiction. Say the Rudolphs: "The contradiction in India's concept of secularism [and, one might add, implicitly, its attitude toward the relation between religion and personal law in particular] was its simultaneous commitment to communities and to equal citizenship."[6]

4

Turning now specifically to some of the basic issues that are taken up in this collection of essays, let me offer a few brief historical comments, and then a set of questions that the essays in this collection seek to answer.

The criminal and procedural law in India has been, of course, long codified by the British Raj with the passing of the Code of Civil Procedure (1859), the Penal Code (1860), and the Code of Criminal Procedure (1861), but the British held back from codifying the so-called "personal law" (involving marriage, dowry, dissolution of marriage, parentage and legitimacy, guardianship, adoption, maintenance, gifts, wills, inheritance, succession, and so forth) of Hindus and Muslims. These matters were, in the judgment of the British administrators and legal experts, inextricably intertwined with the customs and laws of specific religious communities. J. Duncan M. Derrett quotes a passage from the Privy Council in 1871 which nicely characterizes this notion of "personal law":

> While Brahmin, Buddhist, Christian, Mahomedan, Parsee, and Sikh are one nation, enjoying equal political rights and having perfect equality before the Tribunals, they co-exist as separate and very distinct communities, having distinct laws, affecting every relation of life. The law of Husband and Wife, parent and child, the descent, devolution, and disposition of property are all different, depending, in each case, on the body to which the individual is deemed to belong; and the difference of religion pervades and governs all domestic usages and social relations.[7]

The Hindu traditions of law were based on the old *smriti* literature, especially the *Dharmashastras,* and on such later digests as the eleventh century compilation by Vijnaneshvara, called *Mitakshara* (meaning something like "well crafted"), which came to be authoritative regarding issues of personal law in south India and much of north India as well, with local sub-schools in four areas, including Dravida (south India), Mithila, Bombay, and Banaras. The compilation of the thirteenth- or fourteenth-century writer Jimutavahana, called *Dharmaratna* and with a section on personal law known as *Dayabhaga* (meaning something like "portions for inheritance"), came to be authoritative in the region of Bengal.[8] The Muslim traditions of law were dominantly Sunni and of the Hanafite type, that is, followers of the tradition founded by Abu Hanifa. For both Hindu and Muslim traditions, however, there was great variance depending upon sectarian divisions (Sunnis and Shi'as among Muslims, for example), specific region, and local custom. Moreover, the traditions of Hindu *dharma* and the traditions of Muslim

Shari'at were totalistic, covering all aspects of life and making little differentiation between moral, customary, and legal matters. Most important of all, these traditional systems of custom and law had little if anything resembling the notion of equality before the law. Hence, Muslim and Hindu communities, at least with respect to what we identify as civil law, operated quite separately from one another from region to region and with respect to different status groups. Even during centuries of Muslim control, so long as Hindus paid the required taxes, they were permitted to be ruled by their own local customs and personal laws.

When the British first came to the subcontinent they did not concern themselves with local or regional law, and it was not until 1772 that the East India Company decided to "stand forth as Diwan" (that is, as "civil administrators"). Warren Hastings introduced a uniform criminal law (based largely on Muslim criminal law) together with the notion of equality before the law for both Hindus and Muslims, but he also provided that "in all suits regarding marriage, inheritance, the laws of the Koran with respect to Mohammedans, and those of the Shastras with respect to Gentus (Hindus) shall be invariably adhered to." Thereafter Brahmin pandits and Muslim jurists were regularly appointed and consulted to administer and develop the Anglo-Hindu and Anglo-Islamic "personal law." In 1864, the court pandits and Muslim jurists were eliminated, mainly because of disparate interpretations of the various texts as well as suspicions of corruption. Thereafter judges interpreted the personal laws without the aid of pandits and jurists. Anglo-Hindu "personal law" was based largely on the *Dayabhaga* digest for the region of Bengal and on the *Mitakshara* digest (with its four sub-traditions) for other regions of India, together with customs and usages that could be traced back to at least 1772. Anglo-Islamic "personal law" was based on interpretations of the *Shari'at* by Sunni, Shi'a, and other sectarian traditions, together with some acceptance of local customs. There have been various changes, reforms, law commissions, and so forth, through the years, and of course a growing accumulation of case law, but the basic systems of "personal law" as briefly outlined continued to be in operation up until the time of independence.

A first attempt at the development of a uniform civil code came shortly after independence in 1948 with the introduction of the Hindu Code Bill, a bill designed to codify the myriad of regional Hindu customs and laws as a first step toward a uniform civil code for all. There was much Hindu opposition, and the bill was set aside without passage in 1951, thereby triggering the resignation of the distinguished law minister and untouchable leader B. R. Ambedkar, who had led the fight for the bill. The Hindu Code was later introduced piecemeal in the mid-1950s, when Nehru had a more pliant Parliament, and was passed as the Hindu Marriage Act (1955), the Hindu Succession Act (1956), the Hindu Minority and Guardianship Act (1956), and the Hindu Adoptions and Maintenance Act (1956). This provided a basic codification, at least for Hindu communities, and a possible model for codification for other communities. As already mentioned there was also, of course, the "Directive Principle" (Article 44) in the Constitution, calling for a "uniform civil code throughout the territory of India," but no action in that direction has been taken. It is widely feared, with probably more than a little justification, that any such attempt to establish a uniform civil code would lead to widespread violence among the various religious groups.

But let me move on to articulate some of the basic questions that the essays in this collection raise. I have identified six such questions.

1. What is the relation between a "religion" and a "system of personal law"?

Is the relation necessary or is it simply contingent? In other words, is the relation so necessary that if the system of personal law is removed or significantly altered, a given religious tradition can no longer maintain its identity or meaning, or is the relation such that it is quite possible to maintain one's religious identity and sense of meaning with or without a system of personal law?

A liberal Protestant would probably argue for a contingent relation. Also, most secularists would so argue. Most Muslims, on the other hand, and probably many Hindus, Christians, Sikhs, Parsees, and Jews as well, would tend to see a necessary relation between a "religion" and a "system of personal law." How can such an issue be decided one way or the other? Clearly good arguments can be mounted on all sides, depending on how one wishes to construe the notion of religion. In other words, it is not a matter of "either-or," but rather a matter of "both-and." It is quite possible that "religions" may differ in their interpretations of such issues and that there is no simple answer that fits all cases. Does this mean that we are equivocating in our use of the terms "religion" and "system of personal law"?

2. Regarding the notion of "religion," is what T. N. Madan has called the largely "Protestant" and "late Christian idea" of the "privatization of religion" (together with the corollaries of individualism, secularization, and the secular state) possible or even desirable in south Asia (or elsewhere) for religious communities such as Hindus, Buddhists, Sikhs, Muslims, Parsees, Jews, or Catholics (both Roman and Orthodox)?

J. Duncan M. Derrett has called attention to the "unattractive" realization that the privatization of religion really means that religious formulations function only on the level of ideas and ideals but impinge hardly at all on the larger social reality. One is entitled to believe whatever one wishes so long as it makes no difference on the level of social reality. One thereby gains a tolerant pluralism on the level of thought but at the price of detaching religious interpretations from social behavior. As Derrett puts it:

> The unattractive compromise became a fact, and no amount of religion enables an individual to contravene his country's laws, whatever they are. This naturally comforts those who do not think too deeply . . .[9]

Here again, "either-or" dichotomies can be seriously misleading. Many devout believers find fulfillment in their spiritual lives through personal meditation and have little or no need for the support of a religious community. Others find their deepest spiritual longings met in the life of community and ritual performance. Still others maintain a balance between private devotion and communal involvement.

I have argued elsewhere that just as we have a notion of "citizenship" in terms of understanding individual rights, equality before the law, equal opportunity, and individual freedom of religion, we can perhaps learn something of value from India's serious attempt for many years to take seriously the claims of group-based identities, something I have called "community-ship."[10] In contrast to "communalism," which is the selfish and separatist efforts of a particular religious group to act in ways contrary to the larger community or nation, "community-ship" is a nation's attempt to deal equitably with the well-being of all its constitutive communities. Just as the notion of slavery or human bondage contrasts with the notion of the free "citizen," so "communalism" contrasts with "community-ship" on a social level.

3. Regarding the notion of a "system of personal law," is such a system inherently discriminatory, or is it possible to reform a system of personal law so that minorities, women, lower castes, Scheduled Castes and Scheduled Tribes, and Other Backward Classes, and so forth, are treated equitably?

As Tahir Mahmood has shown in his *Personal Law in Islamic Countries,* as many as twenty-two Arab countries and some eighteen non-Arab Muslim countries have systems of personal law that have been codified and reformed in a variety of ways, some of which are not discriminatory against women, outsiders, and so forth.[11] Asghar Ali Engineer has argued in a similar way in his article "A Model for Change in

Personal Law," in *The Times of India,* 25 July 1995. Is this a realistic possibility for India, and if so, how might one proceed? On the other hand, Swapna Mukhopadhyay, in her book *In the Name of Justice: Women and Law in Society,* has argued that the law in general in India, whether criminal, civil, or "personal" has been inherently discriminatory against women.[12]

4. Regarding the issue of reform, either of "religion" or any "system of personal law," should the initiative for reform come from within the religious community involved or may it emerge from general considerations of public policy by the state?

The standard in India has been not to introduce any change with respect to the rights and privileges of minorities unless there is substantial support for change within the minority community itself. This has led to the charge of "pampering" or "pandering" to minorities in India. Is it the case that "one must give the minorities what they want?" As D. E. Smith has pointed out, it was relatively easy to push through the Hindu Code, even though there was massive opposition all over India among Hindus, since after all the majority in Parliament was overwhelmingly Hindu. Doing the same thing for a minority community is a dramatically different task.

5. Regarding issues of law, whether "personal law" or a uniform civil code, what is the relation between theory and practice? Given the digests of "personal law," for example, how are these laws applied in actual cases in various parts of India? Even if there were a uniform civil code fashioned for India, how would it be applied and administered? Would the fashioning of a uniform civil code really make a difference in cases of marriage, divorce, inheritance, and so forth, in village communities all over India which have little awareness of the larger social reality in their immediate region, not to mention any kind of all-India national awareness? Would changes in the theory of the law really make a difference in such contexts?

From the opposite point of view, is reliance on judicial activism, and this or that legal decision, really an adequate way of changing the civil law in India over a long period of time? Is it practical to believe that communities will really change and reform from within? Is not the retention of the system of personal laws with occasional tinkering on this or that issue really only a conservative status-quo posture that will never succeed in overcoming the problems of casteism and gender discrimination that are so prevalent in India?

6. Finally, what is the significance of our subject, namely, "religion and

personal law in modern India," for contemporary American social reality and for the social reality of the global network of civilizations emerging at the end of our twentieth century?

I have in mind here Samuel P. Huntington's *The Clash of Civilizations and the Remaking of World Order* wherein he argues that we are moving into what might be called a post–nation-state world in which conflicts will occur more and more among ethnic groups within a particular nation and between world-class civilizations that transcend national boundaries.[13] In many ways the clashes currently occurring in India between "religions" and between "systems of personal law" (Hindu, Muslim, Sikh, Christian) may well be diagnostically significant for identifying similar conflicts beginning to occur elsewhere in the world and possibly in America.

Finally, a brief word about the individual essays in the volume. The essays are divided into four parts. Part I, "The Secular State and Legal Pluralism: The Current Debate and Its Historical Antecedents," features two introductory essays about some of the current issues being debated, the first by Granville Austin, the well-known authority on the Indian Constitution, and the second by the Honorable Ruma Pal, who currently sits on the Supreme Court of India. This first part also includes a longer essay by Susanne H. and Lloyd I. Rudolph on the historical background of the notion of a uniform civil code, suggesting that the notion is best thought of in terms of an ongoing historical process. The Rudolphs argue, in other words, that a uniform civil code has no single meaning over time but represents various levels of meaning in differing historical contexts.

Part II, "Religious Endowments, Reservations Law, and Criminal Law," looks at specific areas within the personal law and the possibilities for a uniform civil code. John H. Mansfield examines religious and charitable endowments and argues that a general Indian law of endowments appears to be emerging over time. Laura Dudley Jenkins looks at two recent court cases that show how personal law interacts with group-based reservations law. Arvind Verma looks at India's uniform criminal law and its administration as a possible analogue to the administration of a uniform civil code. Verma argues that the administration of criminal law is corrupt and inefficient and that a uniform civil code would have similar problems in terms of practical implementation.

Part III, "Personal Law and Issues of Gender," includes four essays on women and the personal law. Robert D. Baird argues that most of the issues related to personal law are really about issues of gender. Regarding Muslim personal law, Baird suggests that there is a definite gap be-

tween the ideal theory of Muslim personal law and its practical implementation in local contexts. He also argues that although the Constitution is clearly sensitive to gender issues, gender equity has not been
achieved in India. Srimati Basu looks at issues of inheritance. She shows
that even though women are often aware of the law, they are dissuaded
in practice from making use of it. Kunal M. Parker looks at what he
calls "gendered legal subjectivities" in India, arguing that whereas male
"legal subjectivities" have both "personal" and "impersonal" applications, more often than not, female "legal subjectivities" are limited only
to areas of "personal" applications. Paul B. Courtright and Namita Goswami take up the famous case of self-immolation, or the ritual of *sati*,
of Roop Kanwar on the funeral pyre of her husband in the village of
Deorala in Rajasthan in 1987. They look at the cultural and legal implications of the revival of *sati* among Rajputs and Marwaris, both in terms
of understanding the religious significance of the act and in terms of
the manner in which feminist scholarship has dealt with the issue. They
conclude their essay with "personal epilogues" about their own reactions to the *sati* of Roop Kanwar. This part concludes with an essay by
Sylvia Vatuk about the application of Muslim personal law in cases of
marriage and divorce in Chennai (formerly Madras) in south India. She
argues that there is an all-pervasive paternalism that operates in family
law courts.

Part IV, "Cross-Cultural Perspectives," contains two specifically
comparative essays, the first by Kevin Brown comparing the reservation
system in India with affirmative action programs in the United States,
and the second by Marc Galanter and Jayanth Krishnan comparing personal law regimes in India and Israel. Brown's essay on reservations and
affirmative action argues that there is a dramatically different valuation
of the notion of "selfhood" in India and the United States which helps
to explain the difference between reservation quotas in Indian court
cases and affirmative action programs in the United States.

Galanter and Krishnan's essay makes the interesting comparative
point that controversies over personal law tend to be intra-communal in
Israel (that is, within and between various Jewish groups) but inter-
communal in India (that is, between Hindu, Muslim, Sikh, and Christian groups). Rajeev Dhavan's essay, "The Road to Xanadu: India's
Quest for Secularism," provides a concluding overview in this fourth
part regarding the future of the secular state and the possibility of a
uniform civil code.

Finally, William D. Popkin presents a summary paper highlighting
some of the more important issues that remain for future consideration.

Notes

1. D. E. Smith, *India as a Secular State* (Princeton: Princeton University Press, 1963), pp. 497–498.

2. T. N. Madan, "Secularism in Its Place," *Journal of Asian Studies* 46, no. 4 (November 1987): 748–49.

3. Ibid., p. 750.

4. Marc Galanter, *Competing Equalities* (Berkeley: University of California Press, 1984), p. 567.

5. Cited in Galanter, ibid., p. 561. See also the new "Classic Reissue" of Granville Austin's *The Indian Constitution: Cornerstone of a Nation* (Delhi: Oxford University Press, 2000), especially pp. 317ff.

6. Lloyd I. Rudolph and Susanne H. Rudolph, *In Pursuit of Lakshmi* (Chicago: University of Chicago Press, 1987), p. 39.

7. Quoted in J. Duncan M. Derrett, *Religion, Law and the State in India* (New York: Free Press, 1968), p. 39.

8. For a fuller discussion together with notes, see Gerald J. Larson, *India's Agony over Religion* (Albany: State University New York Press, 1995), pp. 220–221, but also pp. 209, 212, 214, 219, 227, 256–61, and 266.

9. Derrett, *Religion, Law and State in India*, pp. 556–57.

10. Larson, *India's Agony over Religion*, pp. 285–288.

11. Tahir Mahmood, *Personal Law in Islamic Countries* (New Delhi: Academy of Law and Religion, 1987), p. 1 and pp. 268–310.

12. Swapna Mukhopadhyay, ed., *In the Name of Justice: Women and Law in Society* (Delhi: Manohar, 1998), pp. 9–14.

13. Samuel B. Huntington, *The Clash of Civilizations and the Remaking of World Order* (New York: Simon and Schuster, 1996), see especially pp. 301–321.

PART I

THE SECULAR STATE AND LEGAL PLURALISM: THE CURRENT DEBATE AND ITS HISTORICAL ANTECEDENTS

One

Religion, Personal Law, and Identity in India

Granville Austin

Religion and personal law in India are more or less closely intertwined. When analyzing their relationship for society as a whole and for individuals, both participants and observers must think in theological, sociological, cultural, and political terms as well as in terms of personal predilection. "Religion," as broadly defined and popularly understood, is ever-present in the country's public affairs and in individual, private lives. The communities most concerned with the connection between religion and personal law are the Hindus and the Muslims. For Hindus, since the incorporation of much of their personal law in the national civil code in the 1950s, the relationship of their religion to their personal law has become attenuated, which frees certain Hindus to focus on Muslim personal law. For Muslims, the connection between the two is very strong. Their personal laws were not incorporated into the common civil code, as were the Hindus', and as was called for in Article 44 of the Constitution's non-justiciable Directive Principles of State Policy.

The discrepancy between the two religions regarding the importance of the personal law to their adherents would be of little matter in public affairs were it not for the desire of some militantly Hindu groups to employ it for political purposes—such as for winning elections and for discrediting the Muslim community for not being truly "Indian," indeed for being a foreign substance within the Hindu body that constitutes the "true" India. Under this stimulus, Muslims' identification of themselves with Islam and the personal law accompanying it has been greatly intensified.

15

Before proceeding, several comments need to be made about terms. Both "Hindu" and "Muslim" are broad terms used for convenience, but they can be misleading. It should be understood that neither "religion" is monolithic—any more than are religions elsewhere. Each has internal faiths with their customary practices. Custom and tradition may carry as much weight for individual and group conduct as does religious "law," of which each religion has several schools. (Hindu schools of law continue to be relevant despite the incorporation of elements of personal law in the common civil code.)[1] "Hinduism" is a conglomeration of a multitude of closely related faiths and practices, for which the well-known trinity of Brahma, Shiva, and Vishnu are the wellsprings. The Sikh community also has internal belief divisions, has its own strong customs and practices, and, so far as personal law is concerned, functions under the civil code into which Hindu personal law was secularized. The Parsi and Christian communities, although also maintaining traditional customs and practices, function largely under the nation's civil code. Yet these are only the beginnings of compartmentalization of Indian society. Division according to language, region, clan, caste, and class, to mention only the most important, must be added to the list.

To use the term "ethnic" as a means of description in these circumstances is misleading because it is inadequate. Much more satisfactory, it seems to me, is to identify the individual according to how he or she identifies himself or herself and the groups to which he or she owes primary allegiance—and perhaps secondary and tertiary allegiance. For example, how in uncomplicated daily life do I identify myself: as a Hindu, as a Brahmin or a Yadav, as a Hindi or a Tamil speaker, as a Shaivite or a Vaishnavite; as a Muslim, as a Sunni or a Shi'a or a Sufi, as an Urdu speaker or a Gujarati speaker, as a follower of Hanafi or Hanbali law? Or as a follower of a particular religious or political personality?

Moreover, identifiers and allegiances may change according to circumstances. Who am I when reacting to a threat or a promise from within or outside my primary or secondary allegiance group? Who am I when the actions or interests of my allegiance groups conflict? Who am I when I have to seek allies in a quest for a personal goal or a goal of my group?

Governments in the country have had to contend with these matters for years. The British found that they had to increasingly administer personal laws in addition to British law as their empire spread across the country—although much law and custom continued to be administered by authorities within the various communities. When matters involving personal law came to British courts, religious authorities from the faith concerned sat beside and advised the British magistrate—Pandits (Brahmins) for Hindu law and Maulvis for Islamic law. As Marc Galanter has pointed out, this produced a body of idiosyncratic decisions. The British largely left the content of Hindu and Islamic law alone—although they did attempt to ban practices they thought offensive, for example, *sati* among the Hindus and certain punishments administered under Muslim law. They eventually did abolish Kazi courts, presided over by Muslim judges. Hindus' reactions to British administration of personal law, and to the implementation in the mid-nineteenth century of modified British codes, were ambivalent. There was resistance to this foreign intrusion into ages-old judicial systems along with welcome for a parallel judicial system that could be used for adjudication of commercial disputes and for the pursuit of personal rights and social reforms unhampered by the canons of tradition and the oppressions of hierarchy.

With the independence movement, a demand grew for secular law along European and American lines to protect the fundamental social and economic rights both of individuals and communities. This was seen as both desirable in itself and as contributing to unity among the society's communities and compartments in order to present a common front against British domination. Sensitivity to the concerns of the various communities and minorities in the name of unity and fairness appeared in independence-movement pronouncements from the twenties onward. As the 1928 Nehru Report put it, a declaration of rights was needed due to the country's communal differences. "Certain safeguards are necessary to create and establish a sense of security among those who look upon each other with distrust and suspicion. We could not better secure the full enjoyment of religious and communal rights to all communities than by including them among the basic principles of the Constitution."[2]

In the Constituent Assembly (1946–1949), members had to resolve the issues of religion and minority rights in the immediate context of partition and its accompanying communal slaughter. Protecting communal rights, restoring communal harmony, while unifying the new nation of India after the subcontinent's vivisection over religious difference, became the pre-eminent goal. When the issue of providing for a uniform civil code for the country came up in 1947 in the assembly's Advisory Committee, opponents criticized it as striking at the orthodoxy of all faiths. Conversely, Minoo Masani, a Parsi and at that time a socialist, plus a few others, wanted the country rid of these "watertight compartments." Later, when the Fundamental Rights Subcommittee of the Advisory Committee decided to divide the negative and positive rights into the Fundamental Rights and the Directive Principles of

State Policy, Nehru insisted, in deference to the Sikhs and Muslims, that the framing of a uniform civil code be a goal set out in the Directive Principles, the implementation of whose provisions was neither mandatory nor justiciable. The nationalist Muslims in the assembly, having chosen to remain in India instead of joining Pakistan, opposed even this. Nevertheless, Article 44 of the Directive Principles became part of the Constitution: "The State shall endeavor to secure for the citizens a uniform civil code throughout the territory of India."

Religious rights for individuals and communities appear in six articles in the Fundamental Rights. Religion appears in other articles, assuming—as one should—that caste is a manifestation of religion. Caste is one of the most prominent and certainly the most enduring practice of "Hinduism," arching over the sub-faiths within it. Indeed, a residual awareness of caste is an unspoken, comparatively minor element in the Sikh, Muslim, and Christian communities, although their adherents typically deny this. Separate protections for the Scheduled Tribes include those for their religions. Amendments to the Constitution would specifically protect the religious rights of the Nagas and the Mizos when the peoples in these areas were granted statehood under the Constitution.

That the many compartments existing in society, including religions and their sub-faiths, might endanger the new nation's unity and integrity aroused much anxiety in the minds of Nehru and other members of the national leadership. Time has shown these fears largely to have been unwarranted, but they were very real during the first two decades of independence. The epithet applied to the compartments was that they were "communal." Undue loyalty to and identification with any of these compartments—as distinct from overriding loyalty to India—was thought "communalist," and "communalism" endangered unity and integrity and was anti-national.

"Secularism," communalism's antithesis, led toward national unity, or at least did not impede progress toward it. Countless public pronouncements emphasized these views. Caste loyalties were a negation of nationalism, said Nehru. Many have argued that casteism is separatism, and many have said that the national goal of socialism could not walk hand in hand with sectarianism. In an attempt to eliminate one compartment, Hindu personal law, Nehru's government introduced the Hindu Code Bill in Parliament in 1951. Resistance to this omnibus bill brought its defeat, but later in the decade Parliament enacted several separate bills incorporating much Hindu personal law into the uniform civil code.

Communalism in its most frequently used sense—that is, enmity between Hindus and Muslims—arguably could have posed a threat to national security. Doubts about Muslim "loyalty" were to be expected, even if unjustified, in the few years after partition. And other "communal" dangers were seen. Hindu Mahasabha leader S. P. Mookerjee's oft-proclaimed rejection of partition in the early fifties and his avowals to undo it could have provoked hostilities with Pakistan. Nehru and his colleagues so feared this that Mookerjee was preventively detained to silence him. In recent times, of course, Hindu-Muslim enmity has played its part in the disastrous Kashmir situation, which, one regrets to say, arose initially from New Delhi's flawed policies toward Srinagar. To a lesser extent, communal (Hindu-Sikh) conflicts have appeared in the Punjab.

Yet Nehru's and others' genuine fears that society's compartments threatened unity and integrity were considerably misguided and apparently arose from a lack of understanding of Indians' ability to accommodate seeming contradictions, in this case strong subordinate loyalties, with an overall allegiance to country. Nehru seems to have been thinking of national *integration*, defined as a large degree of homogenization of society's compartments, as distinct from national integrity, defined as firmly established national frontiers and as individuals' and groups' loyalty both to nation and to their niche in society. By postulating India's unity and integrity, indeed its very survival as a nation, as dependent upon the homogenization of its society's compartments, Nehru was envisaging the impossible. An unrealistic definition of national unity and integrity resulted in unwarranted fear that it was in danger. One of the several products of this confusion was the centralization of government to protect against national disintegration. During the years after Nehru's death, political leaders from time to time would revive these fears, either because they genuinely shared them or because they served personal or partisan purposes.

Religion and religious custom long have been staples of Indian public affairs. They still are, as the news from India daily reminds us, because religion and custom are the first and principal identifiers by which individuals and groups distinguish themselves from others. Although thoroughly aware of what their religious identification is, Indians, for their silent satisfaction, do not go around telling themselves, I am a Hindu— or a Muslim or a Sikh or of this or that community within a religion. But to distinguish themselves from others, they will assert their religious identity: an aspect of themselves called upon when needed. In this fashion, devotees of one religion may think themselves superior to members of another. Christians and Sikhs think their religion gives them status superior to Hindus', for they or their forebears "escaped" from under the Hindu banner. Sikhs also added a scriptural and liturgical language, Gurmukhi, and items of dress to their religious identity. For Muslims, religion constitutes an especial singularity—a subject to which we shall return.

In "ordinary" circumstances, where the customary routines of daily life obtain, the religious identities of individuals and groups do not come into conflict. Individuals and groups live in harmony or mutual indifference. An event or occurrence may arouse enmities between religious communities or caste groups, but their provocation into riots and bloodshed is done by individuals, or their hirelings, who have a personal stake in violence as a means to enhance their power and position, or to satisfy their ideology or psychology.

These instigators and their ruffians, the "professional" religionists, employ apocalyptic language in their political pronouncements and in their violence against the other communities. "Islam in danger"; "Hinduism in danger," are the cries. The most absurd claim by Hindu agitators is that Muslims are outbreeding Hindus and that Hinduism is bound for extinction. They bolster this claim of being a minority in the country with arithmetic that includes among Hindus only the three upper varnas of the twice-born and the shudra varna. In this formulation, "untouchables," the Scheduled Castes, are not included among Hindus. On different occasions, the agitators reverse their arithmetic and, unblushingly, attempt to recruit Scheduled Caste members to join the "Hindu" political parties to resist the Muslim menace. The ex-untouchables who have converted to Islam or Christianity or, in greater numbers, to neo-Buddhism are, in contradictory fashion, vilified both for their previous untouchable status and because they have endangered Hinduism by deserting it. Those who have done or have been accused of doing the converting are similarly attacked. As we know, Christian missionaries have recently been murdered in Orissa.

Religion and caste are used as identifiers to motivate communities to act against each other. Although violence may be incited primarily on religious grounds, economic competition is more frequently the cause of confrontations. Typically, Muslims keep their heads down to avoid attracting adverse attention, although they often have acted in concert during elections. The predictable exception is whenever the topic of a common civil code is broached, with its obvious implications for Muslim personal law. Then secular and religious Muslim leaders, with few exceptions, unite to cry that Islam is in danger.

The impatience, the intolerance even, of some Hindu individuals and organizations toward Muslims' having their own personal law seems to arise from the conviction, which is common among even more rational

Hindus, that theirs is a syncretistic religion. It is tolerant, absorptive; in its house, many mansions may flourish. Yet, well over one hundred million Indian Muslims clinging steadfastly to their own religion and personal law disprove the myth. Moreover, for the rigidly righteous among Hindus, Islam and Christianity are foreign in origin. They have their principal holy places outside of India. The congregants of each therefore are seen to have extra-territorial connections, even extra-territorial loyalties, perhaps even loyalty to Pakistan. Conspiracy theories blossom easily in a country so sensitive to its colonial past—during which, as we know well, the conquerors were Muslims and Christians. Muslims, particularly, are an undigested lump in the throat of Hindu professionals. They must be absorbed—that is, Hinduized—or coughed up. One might say that Hindu professionals' attitude toward Muslims (and Christians) is *swadeshi* applied to religion.

Whereas, for such Hindus, Hinduism is indigenous. The very soil of India, its rivers and mountains, are sacred to Hinduism. To be a "true" Indian, therefore, one must be a Hindu. Hindu and India, in this school of thought, are synonymous. A peculiarity of this complex of attitudes is that it appears to be much less prevalent in the south—particularly its anti-Christian manifestations. Nevertheless, in Hindu-Muslim relations, religion is the identifier of primary allegiance in the south as well as in the north. Sikhism and Jainism largely escape this prejudice because, although deviants from Hinduism, they are indigenous to India. Buddhism is much-respected and mostly absent from the country.

The Muslims' reaction to their position and condition in Indian society in general, and *vis-à-vis* the professional Hindus in particular, is defensive. Muslims feel themselves a community under pressure— whose votes are courted but whose interests are ignored, and sometimes attacked. In addition to their social-economic agendas, Muslims wish to strengthen the society's secular character under the Constitution as a protection against Hindus while preserving their last line of defense, Muslim personal law, which is Shari'at law, derived directly from the Prophet, the Qur'an, and the Sunna. For them, their monotheism is superior to the Hindus' idolatry, and their personal law is its expression. An attack on it, or perceived designs on it, is an attack on Islam, the religion of submission, and thus threatening to the community's core identifier. Only among the most sophisticated and secular Muslims is this not the situation.

The rigidity of this position is assured by its being in the hands of those least likely to dilute it: the 'ulama', the Muslim Personal Law Board, and those in politics who agree with them. For these Muslim professionals the personal law is not only sacred but is also their job security and the source of their power, religious and political. Conservative theologians also fear how the ideas of liberals in their own community might affect the law and their own positions.

Muslim personal law in today's India is interpreted in and applied by the Constitution's secular courts. Why, then, the fear of its codification in a common civil code? There are two fears. First, Hindus would be legislating on Islam, and second, the law likely would be "reformed" in the process of codification, as was Hindu law to some extent. The Muslims believe they had a foretaste of this in the Shah Bano case, when the Supreme Court granted a divorced woman a greater maintenance allowance than that provided for in the Shari'at. Also, if personal law were codified, the 'ulama' and the Muslim Personal Law Board would lose much—perhaps all—of their authority to interpret the law, for it no longer would be the province solely of the Muslim community.

There should be little doubt that Muslims of all ranks and persuasions would exhibit greater flexibility in matters of personal law reform —even, perhaps, to accepting the law's incorporation in a common civil code—if they did not believe they live in an environment where their individual and collective religious identity is under threat. Among the examples they cite are:

- Economic progress by Indian Muslims is often met with hostility and sometimes with repression.
- Muslims in the Vale of Kashmir are under siege and their loyalty to India is being questioned.
- Urdu (the primary language of Muslims in north India) has had a continuing battle for recognition as a language in schools and in the wider society, although it is recognized in the Constitution's Eighth Schedule as one of the country's languages.
- Hindustani, with its Persian and Arabic connections, fell victim to the breakaway of Muslims that was partition. Hindi written in the Devanagari script, with its Sanskrit connections, became the primary language of government communication along with English.
- Shari'at law was attacked by the Supreme Court in the Shah Bano case.
- The Babri Masjid was destroyed by Hindu extremists, who have threatened to demolish several other of Indian Islam's holy places.
- The Bharatiya Janata Party (BJP) government is perceived as being actively hostile to Muslims.

Modernization, economic progress, and education, especially for women, are likely to decrease the Muslims' sense of isolation in society and their consequently tenacious grip on their personal law as an essential identifier—while, quite reasonably, not diminishing their Islamic faith. But the opportunity to make Muslims equal partners in building the new India rests in the hands of the Hindus. Modernization already has diminished the force of religious considerations—whether toward Muslims or otherwise—among professional Hindus, just as it has done to caste as an identifier and as an attractor of allegiance within the Hindu community.

Within the breadth of the Muslim community, and even within the Muslim Personal Law Board, according to several insiders, there is talk in favor of reform. Support for reform, as might be expected, exceeds agreement on details, and these internal discussions are very private. Meanwhile, other developments are taking place. Liberal and modernist Muslims, among them women, are lobbying the 'ulama' publicly and privately to interpret the Shari'at liberally. And, it is said, persons of this persuasion are making other approaches to the country's high court justices to educate them about Muslim issues that might come before them and to encourage them toward judicial activism where Muslim law is involved.

A decline in Muslims' adherence and allegiance to Shari'at law as a principal personal and group identifier will materialize only from within the community, if and when it comes. And this will occur considerably in reverse proportion to pressures from outside—read from Hindus—to accept a uniform civil code. Nor, in this writer's view, are India's national unity and integrity and its future as a "secular democracy" dependent on the Muslims doing so.

Notes

1. For example, Mitakshara law, Dayabhaga law, and so on. See Alladi Kuppaswami, editor and reviser, *Mayne's Hindu Law and Usage*, 13th ed. (New Delhi: Bharat Law House, 1993).

2. All Parties Conference, *Report of a Committee to Determine Principles of the Constitution for India* (Allahabad: Indian National Congress, 1928), pp. 89–90. This was the so-called Nehru Report, named for Jawaharlal Nehru's father, Motilal.

Two

Religious Minorities and the Law

Ruma Pal

India is a land of religions. Hindus, Buddhists, Jains, Christians, Muslims, Parsees, and Sikhs form the nation. They coexist as separate and distinct communities. Each community has its own laws governing marriage and divorce, infants and minors, adoption, wills, intestacy, and succession. These personal laws go with an individual across the states of India where they are part of the law of the land, and the individual is entitled to have that individual's own personal law applied and not the law which would be applied in the local territory.[1] The idea of a uniform civil code, therefore, strikes at the heart of custom and orthodoxy.

Under the Indian Constitution, the state has distanced itself from religion. In 1976, the word "secular" was added to the preamble of the Indian Constitution to emphasize that no particular religion in the state will receive any state patronage whatsoever and no citizen in the state will have any preferential treatment or will be discriminated against simply on the ground that he or she professes a particular form of religion. In other words, in the affairs of the state the professing of any particular religion will not be taken into consideration.

But the Constitution itself gives protection to the different religions and religious groups by including religious rights as fundamental rights. Under Article 25 of the Constitution, all persons are equally entitled to freedom of conscience and the right to freely profess, practice, and propagate religion subject to public order, morality, and health. Article 26 gives to every religious denomination a fundamental right to manage its own affairs in matters of religion. This cannot be abrogated in any way. Article 29 gives the absolute and unqualified right to minorities to

24

conserve their distinct language, script, and culture. Article 30 gives the fundamental right to all minorities, whether based on religion or language, to establish and administer educational institutions of their choice, but the religious denomination's right to manage its own affairs is restricted to "matters of religion" which are "subject to public order, morality and health." The only rights that are absolute and unfettered are the right to freedom of conscience under Article 25 and the right of minorities to conserve their distinct language, script, and culture under Article 29.

Under the Constitution religion is not equated with freedom of conscience, and the freedom of religion (defined as embracing the propagation, practice, and public expression of it) is not an absolute one and is subject to regulation by the state. In the context of the Indian Constitution, religion has been defined as having "its basis in a system of beliefs and directives which are regarded by those who profess that religion to be conducive to their spiritual well-being."[2] In a number of cases the Supreme Court has also held that religion was not merely a matter of faith and belief, but also included rituals, ceremonies, and religious practices according to the tenets of a religion. Courts are called on to determine not only whether a practice of a religion is an essential part of the religion, but also to scrutinize governmental restrictions on the practice and propagation of religion to determine whether the restrictions pass the test of public order, morality, and health. If not, they are not to be upheld.

Thus when a group of Muslims in the state of Gujarat claimed that a law prohibiting the slaughter of cows, bulls, and bullocks in public violated the religious and cultural rights of Muslims under Article 29, the Gujarat High Court held that the right claimed formed no part of the Muslim religion or culture.[3] Again, when children belonging to the sect of Jehovah's Witnesses were expelled from school for refusing to sing the national anthem, the Supreme Court held that saluting and joining in the singing of the national anthem were forbidden by their religion and the expulsions were set aside.[4] In 1990 when the police sought to prohibit a procession of Ananda Margis (a Hindu sect) in which they performed an erotic ritual dance, it was held that the public performance of the dance was a matter of religion of the Ananda Margis and that they could not be prohibited from practicing it in public.[5]

The controversy with regard to the right to propagation of religion has always existed and is a particularly live issue in our country now. Does the freedom to propagate one's religion impinge upon the freedom of another to practice his? In 1968, the state of Orissa enacted the Orissa Freedom of Religions Act. It said that "no person shall convert or attempt to convert either directly or otherwise any person from one religious faith to another by the use of force or by inducement or by any fraudulent means nor shall any person abet any such conversion."[6] Punishment for contravention of the prohibition was imprisonment of up to one year and/or a fine of up to Rs 5,000. In the case of a minor, a woman, or a person belonging to a Scheduled Caste or Tribe, the punishment was up to two years of imprisonment and the limit of the fine raised to Rs 10,000.[7]

Many Roman Catholics protested. They said that propagation of the Christian faith was an essential part of Christianity. The High Court in Orissa accepted this but said that Article 25 did not protect conversion by force or fraud since this would be contrary to public order. Nevertheless the right to convert by inducement was affirmed because "the definition of the term 'inducement' is vague and many proselytizing activities may be covered by the definition." The Act itself was struck down as a whole, however, on the ground that the state legislature did not have the right to legislate matters of religion.[8] At about the same time another state, Madhya Pradesh, enacted the *Madhya Pradesh Dharma Swatantra Adhiniyam, 1968*,[9] which also sought to restrain conversion by "force, fraud and allurement." The challenge by some Christians to the Act that the provisions violated their fundamental right under Article 25 was negated by the Madhya Pradesh High Court.[10] The decisions of the two High Courts were challenged before the Supreme Court.[11] The Supreme Court upheld the decision of the Madhya Pradesh High Court and reversed the decision of the Orissa High Court. It was said "what is freedom for one, is freedom for the other, in equal measure, and there can, therefore, be no such thing as a fundamental right to convert any person to one's own religion" and that the state legislatures were competent to enact such laws.

The decision of the Supreme Court has been justifiably criticized,[12] not only because it ignored the legislative history of Article 25 but also because the Supreme Court did not draw a distinction between conversion by force and conversion by persuasion:

Art. 25(1) confers freedom of religion—a freedom not limited to the religion in which a person is born. Freedom of conscience harmonizes with this, for its presence in Art. 25(1) shows that our Constitution has adopted a "system which allows free choice of religion." The right to propagate religion gives a meaning to freedom of choice, for choice involves not only knowledge but an act of will. A person cannot choose if he does not know what choices are open to him. To propagate religion is not to impart knowledge and to spread it more widely, but to produce intellectual and moral conviction leading to action, namely, the adoption of that religion.[13]

While recognizing the need of ethnic and religious groups to affirm their distinctive religious identities, the Constitution does not treat personal laws as religion though they may have been derived from it. Article 44 of the Constitution mandates the state to "endeavour to secure for the citizens a uniform civil code throughout the territory of India." The underlying assumption of Article 44 is that a uniform civil code would create a sense of "Indianness" and strengthen national unity. Article 44 is one of the principles which have been described as "fundamental in the governance of the country," but is not directly enforceable by any court. By making Article 44 a directive principle, the Constitution guaranteed that a uniform civil code can only be brought about by Parliament, although the seeds of a uniform civil code are sown in the very articles of the Constitution which protect religion.

Article 25 itself does not speak of the personal laws of any religious denomination and a citizen cannot claim a fundamental right to follow the personal law of the group or the community to which he belongs or professes to belong. Article 25 contains a clause giving power to the state to regulate and restrict economic, financial, political, or other secular activity that may be associated with religious practice. The freedom of religion, therefore, does not include social and economic practices, and in certain matters relating to civil laws that do not form part of the essence of religion but are secular practices or usages connected or associated with religion, the legislature would be competent to make a uniform law relating to such secular activities and thereby implement Article 44 of the Constitution.[14]

According to Derrett, the whole course of Indian legal history evinces a tendency to manipulate the sources of law. The systems of which the present personal laws are remnants have in the past been "vigorously truncated and surreptitiously modified without any outcry from those who now feel that their religion has been endangered. . . ."[15] Significantly, during the Constituent Assembly debates, an amendment was sought by a member who wanted the House to accept that the regulatory power of the state did not empower it to do anything with reference to the personal law. The suggested amendment was not accepted.

In fact, soon after the Constitution was drafted, in violent break with the past as far as Hindus were concerned, the Hindu Marriage Act was enacted in May 1955, the Hindu Succession Act in June 1956, the Hindu Minority and Guardianship Act in August 1956, and the Hindu

Adoption and Maintenance Act in December 1956. According to some, this was contrary to the *Dharmashastra*, which incorporates classical Hindu jurisprudence. For example, polygamy, which was practiced by Hindus, was made illegal. Among Hindus, marriage is not a contract but a sacrament, and divorce was not recognized. The law now provides for divorce on stated grounds. Child marriages were forbidden by raising the age of marriage, and women who would not inherit property earlier were brought on par with men as heirs. The acts on Adoption and Guardianship also elevated the status of women to a certain extent, for example, by allowing a widow to adopt a child and by allowing a girl to be adopted.

As far as Indians as a whole were concerned, the Special Marriage Act of 1954 provides a special form of marriage that any person in India and all Indian nationals in foreign countries can take advantage of, irrespective of the faith either party may profess. Persons who are married under this Act enjoy the benefits conferred by it and are subject to its prohibitions. Even if one is permitted to have more than one spouse under one's personal law, once the marriage is under the Act, one cannot. Bigamy is punishable and the second marriage is void. Again irrespective of the personal laws on maintenance, the divorced wife is entitled to permanent maintenance. Submission to the Act, however, is optional.

After this burst of legislative activity in the mid-fifties there was no further move to have more uniformity on a national basis. For India, codifying the Hindu law was only a partial step toward a uniform code.[16] As a result, India continues to have local institutions and concepts which are unique to particular religious groups and their ways of life.

The Hindu Undivided Family is one such institution. It was and perhaps still is to a large extent the normal condition of Hindu society. It consists of persons lineally descended from a common ancestor. They are joint in estate, food, and worship. The ancestral property is held by the family. A Hindu Undivided Family can carry on business, can initiate legal action, and is subject to tax. The only impact on this concept by the Hindu Succession Act since 1956 is that the female members of the family have been given an equal right to the self-acquired property of their father, a right which they did not have earlier.

Another unique legal concept is the provision for a religious endowment to a deity, which is represented by a particular image among Hindus in India. There are strict rules traditionally followed before an image becomes a deity.

Before the image can be used for worship it has to be properly consecrated. On an auspicious day a ceremony is held known as the *prana-pratishtha*, "life-implacing," in which the *murti* or gross form of the deity is infused with life by the chanting of "mantras, ... besprinkling with water from holy places, and anointing with ghee, to the sound of trumpets and conches." Thereafter the deity is believed to reside within the form (*vigraha*) of the image, which is thus a symbolical reflection (*pratima*) of the deity and becomes worshipful (*archa*). The image is now treated as a living being, either permanently residing in the clay, or occupying the clay when summoned by the welcome (*avahana*), and then honoured by the other services of *upachara* or worship. The daily routine of life is gone through, with minute accuracy; the vivified image is regaled with necessaries and luxuries of life in due succession even to the changing of clothes, the offering of cooked and uncooked food and the retirement to rest.[17]

When property is given absolutely by a pious Hindu for worship of an idol, the property vests in the idol itself as a juristic person. It is a sacred entity, an ideal personality possessing proprietary rights,[18] and it can sue for protection of its property through the *shebait* or manager.[19]

In the midst of all this continued diversity, the sporadic attempts of either the legislatures or the courts to achieve greater uniformity have not met with much success. The government's attempt at cultural uniformity at the cost of distinctiveness has not been allowed by the courts. The state of Karnataka's attempt to introduce Kannada (the language spoken by the inhabitants of Karnataka) as the medium of instruction in all educational institutions in the state was disallowed by the courts on the ground that it violated the rights of the minorities not only under Article 29 but also under Article 14, which guarantees the right of equality.[20]

At the same time, when the courts have sought to effect uniformity in personal laws, the move has been firmly upset by Parliament because of political considerations. Attempts by judges to inject uniformity in the laws of maintenance of deserted or divorced wives have met a similar fate. The Supreme Court's first step toward creating this uniformity was in 1979 when it granted maintenance to Bai Tahira[21] under Section 125 of the Code of Criminal Procedure. Section 125 gives a wife, including a divorced wife, a right to maintenance from her husband. The right is limited by Section 127 of the Code, which provides that a woman would not be entitled to maintenance if she received sums under any customary or personal law applicable to the parties which were payable on divorce.

"Mahr" in Muslim law is regarded as consideration for the marriage and is in theory payable by the husband to the wife before consummation. The Muslim law allows its division in two parts. One of these is "prompt" and is payable before the wife can be called upon to enter the conjugal domicile. The other is "deferred," which is payable on the dissolution of the contract of marriage by either of the parties or by divorce.[22] "Iddat," on the other hand, is maintenance that is payable after divorce and that is intended to provide for the divorced wife during her pregnancy if she is pregnant, or for a period of three months to exclude the possibility of pregnancy. In Tahira's case, the "mahr" which had been agreed to between the parties at the time of marriage was Rs 5,000. The Court said that the amount was unreasonable. It said:

> If the first payment by way of *mehar* [mahr] or ordained by custom has a reasonable relation to the object and is a capitalized substitute for the order under Section 125—not mathematically but fairly—then Section 127 (3)(b) subserves the goal and relieves the obligor, not *pro tanto* but wholly. The purpose of the payment 'under any customary or personal law' must be to obviate destitution of the divorcée and to provide her with wherewithal to maintain herself. The whole scheme of section 127(3)(b) is manifestly to recognize the substitute maintenance arrangement by lump sum payment organized by the custom of the community or the personal law of the parties. There must be a rational relation between the sum so paid and its potential as provision for maintenance; to interpret otherwise is to stultify the project. Law is dynamic and its meaning cannot be pedantic but purposeful. The proposition, therefore, is that no husband can claim under Section 127 (3)(b) absolution from his obligation under Section 125 towards a divorced wife except on proof of payment of a sum stipulated by customary or personal law whose quantum is more or less sufficient to do duty for maintenance allowance.[23]

In other words, the Supreme Court construed the provisions of Muslim law and gave Tahira the relief she wanted.

In 1980 the Supreme Court restated the Muslim personal law on the subject in the case of *Fazlunbi v. K. Khaded Bali*[24] but also said:

> Neither personal law nor other salvationary plea will hold against the policy of public law pervading S.127(3)(b) as much as it does

S.125. So a farthing is no substitute for a fortune nor naïve consent equivalent to intelligent acceptance.

This reasoning was followed and expounded even further and somewhat intensively in *Mohd. Ahmed Khan v. Shah Bano Begum and Ors.*[25] The only justification for such judicial insensitivity was perhaps the appalling facts of the case. Mohammad Ahmed, who was a reasonably successful lawyer, was married to Shah Bano in 1932. Three sons and two daughters were born. In 1975, after forty-three years of married life, Mohammad Ahmed drove Shah Bano out of the matrimonial home. Shah Bano filed a petition against her husband under Section 125 of the Code of Criminal Procedure in the court of the Judicial Magistrate, Indore, asking for maintenance. Ahmed's defense was that she had ceased to be his wife by reason of the divorce, that he was therefore under no obligation to provide maintenance for her, that he had already paid maintenance to her at the rate of Rs 200 per month for about two years covering the period of "iddat" and that he had deposited a sum of Rs 3,000 with the court by way of dower or "mahr." The magistrate directed Ahmed to pay the princely sum of Rs 25 per month to his wife as maintenance. Shah Bano appealed. The High Court of Madhya Pradesh increased the amount of maintenance to Rs 179.20 per month. Mohammad Ahmed appealed to the Supreme Court.

The matter should probably have been dealt with by the Supreme Court as a question of interpretation limited to the parties to the litigation. Instead, the Muslim Personal Law Board and the Jami'at al-'ulama'-i-Hind were allowed to intervene in the matter. The five judges of the Supreme Court were all Hindus. Whereas this has never posed a problem in India even in questions of interpretation of personal law other than those of the judge's faith, the issue took on an "us" versus "them" color. The Supreme Court commented on the extreme stands that were taken in the case:

It is a matter of deep regret that some of the interveners who supported the appellant took up an extreme position by displaying an unwarranted zeal to defeat the right to maintenance of women who are unable to maintain themselves. The written submission of the All Indian Muslim Personal Law Board has gone to the length of asserting that it is irrelevant to inquire as to how a Muslim divorcée should maintain herself. The facile answer of the Board is that the Personal Law Board has devised the system of Mahr to meet the requirements of women and if a woman is indigent, she must look to her relations, including nephews and cousins, to support her. This is a most unreasonable view of law as well as life.[26]

32

The Supreme Court held that as a matter of interpretation there was no conflict between the provisions of Section 125 and those of Muslim personal law on the question of the Muslim husband's obligation to maintain his divorced wife who is unable to maintain herself. The Supreme Court then took upon itself the decision regarding the priority between the right to maintenance under Section 125 of the Code of Criminal Procedure and the Muslim personal law on the assumption that there *was* a conflict between the two laws. They said they wanted to set the question of priority to rest once and for all. They took upon themselves the task of giving effect to the objective of Article 44. They said:

> It is also a matter of regret that Article 44 of our Constitution has remained a dead letter. It provides that "The State shall endeavour to secure for the citizens a uniform civil code throughout the territory of India." There is not evidence of any official activity for framing a common civil code for the country. A belief seems to have gained ground that it is for the Muslim community to take a lead in the matter of reforms of their personal law. A common civil code will help the cause of national integration by removing disparate loyalties to law which have conflicting ideologies. No community is likely to bell the cat by making gratuitous concessions on this issue. It is the state which is charged with the duty of securing a uniform civil code for the citizens of the country and, unquestionably, it has the legislative competence to do so. A counsel in the case whispered, somewhat audibly, that legislative competence is one thing, the political courage to use that competence is quite another. We understand the difficulties involved in bringing persons of different faiths and persuasion on a common platform. But, a beginning has to be made if the Constitution is to have any meaning. Inevitably, the role of the reformer has to be assumed by the courts because it is beyond the endurance of sensitive minds to allow injustice to be suffered when it is so palpable.[27]

The Supreme Court reached the conclusion that the right conferred by Section 125 can be exercised irrespective of the personal law of the parties.[28] This decision was not necessary at all and led to an uproar among a certain section of the Muslim community which the government then in power sought to control by promptly enacting the Muslim Women (Protection of Rights on Divorce) Act, 1986, which is not only contrary to the mandate of Article 44 but which contains precisely those provisions the Supreme Court had condemned as a "most unreasonable view of law as well as life."

While laws may be derived from religion, they do not form part of it, and the need for a uniform civil code cannot be overstated. It would not impinge on the freedom of an individual's conscience, nor on the expression of it. It has been suggested that "their (the minorities) anxiety about their personal law does not relate to the laws themselves but rather to their privileged position as minorities in a country."[29] Successive governments have acquiesced in this argument either for political gains, fear of political loss, or from a misunderstanding of the words "religious tolerance." They have not sufficiently realized that differences in the law create a feeling of disparity and, inevitably, resentment. Given this "inertia of timidity," the task of unification has been indefinitely postponed.

Jurists have suggested legal solutions out of this impasse. One is to legislate more common personal laws which would be optional in their application.[30] For example, Section 5 of the Muslim Women (Protection of Rights on Divorce) Act, 1986, allows the application of Sections 125–128 of the Code of Criminal Procedure if the divorced woman and her former husband declare by affidavit or at least in writing that they would prefer to be governed by the provisions of the Code. The Special Marriage Act, 1954, is also seen as the first step in introducing uniformity. Derrett has suggested a legislative blueprint for the contents of a Code of Family Law, for example, by introduction of legislation making financial injury to a wife a tortious act so that she could sue for damages when she is injured by divorce or desertion.[31]

Given the legislative silence, the Supreme Court has cast judges in the role of activists to take the country toward uniformity. In *Fazhinabi v. Khaleda Bibi* (see note 24) the court said:

> Law does not stand still. It moves continually. Once this is recognized, then the task of the Judge is put on a higher plane. He must consciously seek to mould the law so as to serve the needs of the time. He must not be a mere machine, a mere working mason, laying brick on brick, without thought to the overall design. He must be an architect—thinking of the structure as a whole—building for society a system of law which is strong, durable and just. It is on his work that civilized society itself depends.

Piecemeal attempts by courts, however, to bridge the gap between personal laws cannot take the place of a uniform civil code. Justice for all is a far more satisfactory way of dispensing justice than is justice from case to case.[32] It is also doubtful that the goal of uniformity can be left to ideas and interpretations of judges where varying attitudes may dictate the outcome.

Ultimately the people of India themselves, through education, open

34

debate, and responsible political action, will have to elect a government that will finally move Article 44 from a Directive Principle to a fundamental right for all citizens of modern India.

Notes

1. J. Duncan M. Derrett, *Religion, Law and the State in India* (New York: The Free Press, 1968).
2. *Ratilal Panachand Gandhi v. State of Bombay:* AIR 1954 SC 388.
3. *Usmanbhai Hasanbhai v. State:* AIR 1981 Guj. 40.
4. *Bijoe Emmanuel v. State of Kerala:* AIR 1987 SC 748.
5. *Commissioner of Police v. Jagadiswarananda:* AIR 1991 Cal. 263 (DB).
6. Section 3 of the Orissa Freedom of Religions Act, 1968.
7. Section 4 of the Orissa Freedom of Religions Act, 1968.
8. *Yulitha Hyde v. State:* AIR 1973 Orissa 116.
9. This translates into "Madhya Pradesh Freedom of Religion Act."
10. *Rev. Stanislaus v. State:* Unreported Judgment 23.4.74 in C. R. No. 159/91.
11. *Rev. Stanislaus v. State:* AIR 1977 SC 908.
12. H. M. Seervai, *Constitutional Law of India* (4th ed.) (Bombay: N. M. Tripathi Pvt. Ltd., 1978), p. 1287.
13. Ibid.
14. *Basu's Commentary on the Constitution of India* (7th ed.), vol. E, p. 139.
15. Derrett, *Religion, Law and the State in India*, p. 439.
16. Ibid., p. 321.
17. *Thackersey v. Hurbhum:* ILR 8 Bom. 432, 456.
18. Ibid.
19. J. Mukherjea, *Hindu Law of Religious and Charitable Trusts* (4th ed.) (Bombay: N. M. Tripathi, 1968).
20. General Secretary, *Linguistic Minorities Protection Committee v. State of Karnataka:* AIR 1989 Karnataka 226 (FB).
21. *Union of India v. Prafulla Kumar Samal and Anr.:* AIR 1979 SC 366.
22. G. J. Larson, *India's Agony Over Religion* (Albany: State University of New York Press, 1995), pp. 257–258.
23. B. Tyabji, *Muslim Law* (Lucknow: Eastern Books, 1980), p. 366.
24. *Fazlund v. K. Khaded Bali*, AIR 1980 SC 1730, 1731.
25. *Mohd. Ahmed Khan v. Shah Bano Begum and Ors.*, AIR 1985 SC 945.
26. Ibid., para 31, p. 954.
27. Ibid., para 32, p. 954.

28. Ibid., para 10, p. 949.

29. Derrett, *Religion, Law and the State in India*, p. 546.

30. John H. Mansfield, "The Personal Laws or a Uniform Civil Code?" in *Religion and Law in Independent India*, ed. R. P. Baird (Delhi: Manohar, 1993).

31. Derrett, *Religion, Law and the State in India*, p. 541.

32. *Md. Ahmed v. Shah Bano* (note 25).

Three

Living with Difference in India
Legal Pluralism and Legal Universalism in Historical Context

Susanne Hoeber Rudolph and Lloyd I. Rudolph

Modern India has provided a setting for the contest between legal pluralism and legal universalism. Legal pluralism recognized and legitimized the personal law of India's religious communities. Legal universalism engenders calls for a uniform civil code. By modern India, we mean the India of the East India Company (ca. 1757–1857), the British Raj (1858–1947), Congress nationalism (1885–1947), and independent India (1947–present). We will visit times, places, and events in search of discourses and practices that shaped legal recognition of personal law and the debate over instituting a uniform civil code.

In particular we will visit the contest, mainly in Bengal but in memory and discourse standing for "India," between the particularistic Orientalists and the universalistic Utilitarians during the East India Company era; the trauma of the 1857 rebellion and its aftermath, Queen Victoria's 1858 proclamation accepting difference; the fracture of partition as it was foreshadowed in Sir Sayyid Ahmad Khan's many-nations doctrine; Muhammad Ali Jinnah's two-nation doctrine; the Indian National Congress's universalist one-nation doctrine; the cohabitation in Congress's secularism between equal recognition of all religions and special privileging of minority religion, particularly Islam; and the rise (and faltering?) of the Hindu nationalist ideology of homogeneity in the 1980s.

Splitting the Difference: Between
Uniformity and Pluralism

Legal pluralism has been one way to give expression to India's continuously and variously constructed multi-cultural society. Legal universalism has been associated with liberal and nationalist ideas about equal, uniform citizenship. Speaking analytically, legal pluralism posits corporate groups as the basic units, the building blocks, of a multi-cultural society and state. Particular legal rights and obligations attach to collective identities such as Hindu, Muslim, Christian, Sikh, Jain, Buddhist, and Parsi, and to *sampradayas* (sects) and *quoms* (communities) such as Dadupanthis, Kabirpanthis, Sunnis, Shi'as, etc. Legal universalism treats individuals as the basic unit of society and the state and imagines homogenous citizens with uniform legal rights and obligations.

Indian law and politics have vacillated between these two positions. The Supreme Court, in the landmark case of *Balaji v. State of Mysore* (1963), tried to quantify the proportionate weight that should be accorded to each.[1] The case involved group rights in the form of quotas in university admissions and government jobs for Dalits (ex-untouchables) and for OBCs (Other Backward Classes, an administrative euphemism for lower castes). Article 16(4) of the Constitution on the one hand guarantees the "equality of opportunity in matters of public employment." On the other hand, it provides that

> nothing in this article shall prevent the State from making any provision for the reservation of appointments or posts in favour of any backward class of citizens which, in the opinion of the State, is not adequately represented in the services under the State.

The Court split the difference; it limited permissible reservations to 49 percent. Beyond 49 percent the Court held would be a *fraud on the Constitution* (emphasis in the original) because it would impinge upon the constitutional mandates providing for equality before the law (Article 14) and prohibiting discrimination (Article 15). In other words, *Balaji* in 1963 weighted legal pluralism in the form of group rights at 49 percent and legal universalism in the form of equal citizenship at 51 percent.

The institutional progenitors and philosophical lineages of legal pluralism and legal universalism were differentially mobilized and reinforced by company, colonial, nationalist, and post-colonial political actors. The rise of Hindu nationalism and the articulation of *hindutva* (Hinduness) ideology in the 1980s and 1990s lent new meaning and urgency to the tension between pluralism and universalism. The tension is likely to continue for the foreseeable future in a multi-cultural society and state that has to accommodate on a daily basis the contrasting imperatives of integration and diversity. Neither is likely to drive out the other.

Legal pluralism is not simply a question of values. It is also a question of power, of who gets what when and where. "Universality" in the law is not only valued by enlightenment liberals and Fabian socialists, it is also the strategy of centralizing modern states. Pluralism in the law is both a norm and the strategy of those who favor dividing, limiting, and sharing sovereignty in federal and pluralist states that allow for diversified geographically and culturally defined communities.[2]

The Company Discovers and Legitimizes Difference: Cultural Federalism and Legal Pluralism

Cultural federalism is a term we have coined to suggest that India has dealt with diversity in ways that recognize legal identities on the basis of cultural as well as territorial boundaries. The Ottoman millet "system," under which leaders of the Greek Orthodox and of Christian, Armenian, Jewish, and other communities were given civil as well as religious authority over their respective flocks, represents a significant historical example of cultural federalism. As we shall see, early East India Company doctrine and practice followed similar principles. In independent India, cultural federalism is given expression in Article 29 of the Constitution, what might be called the multi-cultural clause, which protects the interests of minorities by granting them the right to "conserve" their "language, script and culture," and Article 30, which gives minorities the "right to establish and administer education institutions."[3] These provisions are in tension with the universalistic proposals of Article 44, a non-justiciable Directive Principle of State Policy that enjoins the state to "endeavour to secure for the citizens a uniform civil code throughout the territory of India."

So why did Warren Hastings, who in 1774 became the East India Company's first Governor-General; Sir William Jones,[4] a company judge in Bengal and one of the first Englishmen to master Sanskrit; and the stellar scholars, also servants of the company, who made up the founding generations of the Asiatic Society of Bengal, adopt a policy of cultural federalism and legal pluralism? Why did they decide to apply "the laws of the Koran with respect to Mohammedans and that of the Shaster with respect to Hindus"? Why did Jones construct a world composed of Hindus and Muslims? Why and how did he construct the categories "Hindu" and "Muslim," categories that, in changing guises and with changing meaning and consequences, are present today at the close of the twentieth century?

A post-colonial perspective leads to reading nineteenth- and twentieth-century categories and outcomes into the mentalities and intentions of eighteenth-century actors. The motive becomes imperial power, the tactic religious division. Power becomes as unsubtle a determinant of thought as is control of the means of production.

We read the ideas and actions of Hastings and his Asiatic Society colleagues, including their construction of Hindu and Mohammedan, as shaped by two concerns: the sources and meaning of "civilization" conceived of within the framework of eighteenth-century European understandings of world history; and, for Hastings in particular, a powerful sense of being a *local* ruler. Hastings, Jones, and their Asiatic Society colleagues, all trained in European classical traditions, developed a "civilizational eye." They came to understand legal pluralism in terms of large, coherent cultural wholes defined by great languages and their classic texts. In their cultural imaginations, Hastings and Jones treated Sanskritic and Persian civilizations as equivalent to those of Greece and Rome. Their sense of being local rulers led them to do what they thought local rulers did, rely on the laws of the peoples under their authority to administer justice. Anachronistic efforts to read divide-and-rule communal politics into company policy need to be modified by attention to the civilizational perspective and the self-understanding of company servants as local rulers.

English eighteenth-century representatives of the East India Company acted as agents of the Mughal emperor. At least nominally, they understood themselves as agents, not principals. At this state of the British relationship to India, their mentality, as Uday Mehta, writing about "liberalism and empire," might have put it, was more Burkean than Lockean,[5] more attuned to pluralist multi-culturalism than to liberal universalism. Hence they recognized and accepted the existence and value of different civilizations on the Indian subcontinent. A "Burkean" consciousness accounts for what we characterize as Warren Hastings's policy of cultural federalism, a policy which made each group subject to its own laws. In a much-quoted memorandum Hastings ordered that

> in all suits regarding inheritance, marriage, caste and other religious usages and institutions, the laws of the Koran with respect to the Mohammedans and those of the shaster with respect to the Gentoos [Hindus] shall be invariably adhered to; on all such occasions the Moulvies or Brahmins shall respectively attend to expound the law, and they shall sign the report and assist in passing the decree.[6]

Recent scholarship on the eighteenth century questions the company's emphasis in the Hastings era on religious and caste groups to construct Indian society. The result entrenched the categories religion and caste in the mentalities and practices of succeeding generations.[7] For the purposes of our argument, which groups are featured is less important than that self-regulating groups[8] with cultural markings, rather than unmarked standardized individuals, were thought to constitute society.

An Indian Theory of Self-Regulating Groups

Henry Thomas Colebrooke, leader of the second generation of Asiatic Society of Bengal Orientalists, distinguished Sanskritist, author of *Digest of Hindu Law* [1798], and founder of the Royal Asiatic Society, joined other scholars in the belief that in India the laws of groups pre-existed the state. He cites an injunction from Bhrigu, a mythical lawgiver, that calls on each category of person to litigate controversies according to its own law:

> The frequenters of forests should cause their differences to be determined by one of their own order; members of a society, by persons belonging to that society; people appertaining to an army, by such as belong to the army . . . husbandmen, mechanics, artists . . . robbers or irregular soldiers, should adjust their controversies according to their own particular laws.[9]

Sanskrit law texts held that the king should oversee the self-regulating society rather than create laws for society. The *Manusmriti*, initially translated from Sanskrit into English by Sir William Jones, holds that "the king [was] created as the protector of the classes and the stages of life, that are appointed each to its own particular duty, in proper order." Nor were such injunctions found solely in the Hindu texts favored by the early British Orientalists such as Jones and Colebrooke. Richard Eaton shows numerous exemplars of legal understandings in sixteenth-century, Mughal-ruled Bengal, where Muslim administrators enforced laws particular to specific communities.[10] Such an understanding of Indian society supported the view that Indian society was constituted by groups.

Legal Uniformity and Individual Rights
Enter the Contest

Group concepts flourished under company rule as long as Jones and his Orientalist brethren held sway. Their view of the value of Indian civilizations and social formations and practices was challenged and largely overturned with the arrival in 1828 of Lord William Bentinck, the first of a series of liberal and utilitarian Governors-General. Liberal individualist themes now competed with earlier Orientalist constructions of India as a society constituted of groups. Liberal utilitarians in the era of Bentinck and Thomas Macaulay strove to liberate Indians from domination by groups, to unravel individuals from the grip of family, caste, and religious community, to strengthen individual choice against collective decision. Until Victoria's 1858 proclamation reversed its course, the Benthamite thrust posited that individualism and universalism were a requirement for progress and civilized living.

It was Governor-General Dalhousie's egalitarian policy of "treating all natives in much the same manner" that helped bring on the 1857-58 rebellion.[11] Corporate structures, James Fitzjames Stephen observed, would "decay because they represent a crude form of socialism, paralyzing the individual energy and inconsistent with the fundamental principles of our rule."[12] A series of legislative acts, none of them very consequential outside a small circle of urban-based cosmopolitan elites, advanced this individualist vision. Several were designed to establish rights independent of the joint family, the customary holder of property: the Freedom of Religion Act of 1850 saved converts, upon conversion, from losing their identity as Hindus, an identity they needed to secure property rights in the joint family;[13] the Widow Remarriage Act of 1856 asserted a woman's rights in the face of customary demands of the joint family in many upper castes; the Gains of Learning Act made it possible for a son educated by his joint family to appropriate the subsequent income to himself instead of having to share it with the family.[14] The introduction of wills substituted choice, by means of a legal instrument, for the prescriptive claims of the joint family.[15]

Individualism and legal universalism gained a formidable ally when in 1835 Thomas Babbington Macaulay joined Bentinck's government as law member of the council. Macaulay, who unashamedly admitted having "no knowledge of either Sanskrit or Arabic," alleged in a rightly notorious passage

> that all the historical information which has been collected from all the books written in the Sanskrit language is less valuable than what may be found in the most paltry abridgements used at preparatory schools in England.

He wrote a minute on education that convinced a majority of Bentinck's council to overturn the Orientalist support for Indian learning and languages. Macaulay's vision was to assimilate all mankind into the higher civilization of the educated Victorian. His goal was to form "a class of persons, Indian in blood and colour, but English in taste, in opinions, in morals, and in intellect."[16] In 1835 Bentinck's council agreed to allocate its educational funds to teaching Western learning to young Indians in the English language. Macaulay's project of anglicized uniformity was deepened in 1857 when Sir Charles Wood's 1854 Education Dispatch recommending inter alia the establishment of English medium universities in the three presidency cities—Bengal, Madras, and Bombay—was acted upon. By 1885 English higher education had produced a national Indian elite who had "studied the classics of English literature and . . . followed . . . the course of politics in Europe [including] the rise of nationalism. . . ."[17] They were on the road to liberal universalism. In 1885, seventy-two of them met in Bombay to form the Indian National Congress. They imagined, or most of them did, that India would be *a* nation, constituted by individuals acting on majoritarian principles.

The Reaction against Liberal Universalism

A new discourse began after the 1857–58 revolt. The revolt had destroyed British confidence; loss of control, not only military but also cultural, was unexpected and sudden. "Henceforth, the British in India would always walk in fear. . . . [n]ow the British stepped back permanently into their neat little compound, fenced and right-angled, of facts and rules."[18]

Queen Victoria's 1858 proclamation repudiated and reversed the utilitarian and evangelical-inspired liberal universalism of company policy, a policy that extended from Bentinck and Macaulay in the 1830s through Dalhousie in the 1850s. But the retreat functioned to moderate rather than eliminate the processes of rationalization and universalization already set in motion.

Non-intervention was thought an appropriate remedy for the causes believed to have led to the 1857 revolt, utilitarian and evangelical-inspired "reforms" and "annexations" under the doctrine of "lapse."[19] The Queen, who in 1877 was made Queen-Empress of the British Empire in India, pledged to respect and protect India's alien diversity, including its religious practices. The proclamation declared "it to be our royal will and pleasure that none be in anywise favoured, none molested or disquieted, by reason of their religious faith or observances, but that all shall alike enjoy the equal and impartial protection of the law; and we do strictly charge and enjoin all those who may be in authority under us that they abstain from all interference with religious belief or worship of any of our subjects on pain of our highest displeasure."[20]

Queen Victoria's 1858 non-interference proclamation was, of course, a doctrine, not a practice. Gordon Johnson argues that Henry Maine's cautious, conservative approach to legal reform can be taken to epitomize the way post-1858 British rule in India managed change while pursuing a doctrine of non-intervention.

> As Law Member [1862–69], Maine passed no striking laws. . . . Although . . . responsible for over two hundred separate Acts, his colleagues are remarkably unanimous in their welcome of his low key approach. Sir Richard Strachey found that Maine's virtue lay in that "he limited itself to the actual requirements of his time" while Courtney Ilbert . . . praised Maine for abstaining "from passing a great many measures of doubtful utility." Here was no adventurous law-giver as Macaulay had been thirty years before.[21]

> While Maine was nominally complying with the non-intervention order, his Acts gave legislative form to civil usages and religious practices of particular groups of Indians, and here, while there were some notable exceptions as regards marriage, the overall tendency was to put into statute form customary laws and to do so in ways which were prevalent at the time. . . .

The effect of his tinkering was to universalize and standardize the law's relationship to society, and to move legal pluralism outward and upward from the diversely constituted periphery toward a more uniform national level. It set the stage for the struggle in the 1990s between minority rights based on legal pluralism and the various perceived requirements of the Directive Principle's Article 44 "to secure a uniform civil code for the citizens" of India. Victoria's retreat from the utilitarians' efforts to rationalize Indian administration and to codify Indian law left Indian society with a viable group life, but stood in tension with an incompatible universalizing discourse.

Group Rights as Defense against Majoritarianism

Sir Sayyid Ahmad Khan, the pre-eminent Muslim modernist reformer, contributed mightily to the British resurrection of a corporate theory of Indian society. He found the formal creation of Indian nationalism in 1885 by anglicized liberal universalists a threat and a challenge. From his perspective Muslims had much to fear from claims that there was *an* Indian nation. Few Muslims had responded to Macaulay's call to become "English in taste, in opinions, in morals, and in intellect," or to Sir Charles Wood's call to be educated in English language learning. Sir Sayyid typified the ambivalence of his time as he encouraged Muslims to join Anglo-Victorian universalism on the one hand while creating a protective arena for Muslim group rights on the other.

Muslim "backwardness" had many causes, one of which was that the British, having wrested power from the Mughals in whose name the East India Company had ruled India, feared and distrusted (even while emulating) their former Muslim masters. The 1857–58 rebellion was in part an effort by Indian Muslims and others to oust the British and to place Bahadur Shah II, a Mughal emperor, back on the throne. Sir Sayyid tried to deal with a debilitating psychology of past greatness and with the nostalgia and inertia that marked the downward mobility of Muslim lineages and families who remembered being the rulers of India. His goal was "to lure his community from its tents of Perso-Arabic mourning for the demise of Mughal glory into the market place of vigorous competition with Hindus, Parsis, Christians for ICS [Indian Civil Service] positions and the privileges of Anglo-Indian power."[22]

To that end, on Queen Victoria's birthday in 1875, two years before she was declared Queen-Empress of India, Sir Sayyid established the Muhammadan Anglo-Oriental College at Aligarh.[23] The young Tory from Cambridge who became the college's second principal, Theodore Beck, modeled it on the British public school—games, little magazines, a liberal curriculum. Sir Sayyid hoped to create an alternative anglicized elite that could hold its ground with, even best, the elite that Macaulay's and Wood's educational reforms had brought into being. By gaining positions in the ICS, the "steel frame" that governed India for the British crown, Muslims too would have seats at the table.

Sir Sayyid found it difficult to accept Congress's one-nation theory. For him India was "inhabited by different nationalities." In 1883 in a debate in the Governor-General's Council on the Central Provinces [now Madhya Pradesh] Local Self Government Bill, he warned the Council that

> in borrowing from England the system of representative institutions, it is of the greatest importance to remember the socio-political matters in which India is distinguishable from England. . . . India . . . is inhabited by vast populations of different races and creeds. . . . The community of race and creed makes the people one and the same nation . . . the whole of England forms but one community . . . in India . . . there is not fusion of the various races . . . religious distinctions are still violent. . . . education in its modern sense has not made an equal or proportionate progress among

all sections of the people. . . . So long as . . . [such] differences form an important element in the socio-political life of the country, the system of election, pure and simple [i.e., majority rule], cannot be adopted.

Without a homogenous nation, and India for the foreseeable future, in Sir Sayyid's view, could not be a homogenous nation, safeguards such as reserved seats, separate electorates, "weightage," and nominated members were necessary to insure "due and just balance in the representation of the various sections of the Indian population."[24]

Muhammad Ali Jinnah, the father of Pakistan and its Qaid-i-Azam (great leader), was a figurative son of Aligarh, i.e., the kind of anglicized, modern Muslim that Sir Sayyid Ahmad Khan sought to create. Like Sir Sayyid, he prospered under British policy and rule. And he too, fearing a Hindu majority, searched for mechanisms that would allow a Muslim community to have its fair share of seats in the chambers of government. Sir Sayyid had spoken of "many nations"; in 1937 Jinnah began speaking of two, Pakistan and India. With partition into two successor states in 1947, 10 percent (35 million then, 110 million now) of India's population were Muslims. How, without raj-like safeguards, was the new state to recognize and legitimize differences and protect minority rights in a parliamentary democracy with universal suffrage and majority rule?

Communal Reservation as
Group Entitlement

In pre-independence India, the answer to the question of how to reconcile minority rights with majority rule was communal reservations. Until the second half of the nineteenth century, the colonial government's policy had expressed the group principle mainly through legal practice in the arena of personal law. As representation of Indians was timidly and haltingly introduced into local and provincial governments in the 1880s, the principle took on political form. If India consisted of groups, groups would be the basis of representation.

The political expression of this vision was a policy of legislative reservations that emphasized the group nature of Indian society. From the first inclusion of Indians in governing councils at the state and national level after 1858, corporatist principles dictated the units: landowners, university bodies, municipalities, and eventually minority religious entities—Muslims, Christians, Sikhs.[25] In the south, the battle over representation took a different form. Because indigenous resistance to Brahminic dominance surfaced early in the twentieth century, caste rather than religious community became the contested group identity in politics and bureaucracy. The British introduced reservations for "forward" and "backward" non-Brahmin castes into legislatures, civil services, and educational institutions in south India beginning in the second decade of the twentieth century.[26]

The most important embodiment of the group principle before independence was a scheme to give "safeguards" to minority religious communities by providing them with separate electorates and reserved seats.[27] By privileging these categories for purposes of representation, the British both shaped and reflected the idea that religious identities trumped all others. In the process, they invented the principle that religious groups were homogeneous. Separate electorates had the effect of deterring appeals to cross-cutting cleavages, appeals which might allow individuals to escape corporatist domination and isolation. First institutionalized in the Morley-Minto constitutional reforms of 1909, reservations based on religious community, i.e., for Muslims, continued in the Montagu-Chelmsford reforms of 1919 and in the constitutional framework created by the Government of India Act of 1935.

Nationalists regarded "safeguards" which included both reservations of seats and "weightage," extra seats for minorities, as a policy designed to divide and rule Indians. The principle spread. During the negotiations preceding the Government of India Act of 1935, untouchables lobbied for similar group recognition, for separate electorates, and for reservations. They succeeded in having seats reserved for untouchables but failed to gain separate electorates after Gandhi's 1932 "fast unto death" against what he regarded as a British scheme to divide and weaken nationalism.[28] The potential for divisiveness of group reservations was realized in 1947 when India at independence was partitioned into two successor states, India and Pakistan.

The idea of group protection also infiltrated nationalist policy and practice. Paradoxically, it was the nationalist faction most wedded to equal citizenship grounded in territorially organized individuals, the rationalist modernists allied with Jawaharlal Nehru, who encouraged a decision-rule within the Congress Party and in Congress-controlled legislatures that gave groups the right to veto decisions affecting their interests. The rule was first adopted in the Congress Party's constitution, then incorporated in the Lucknow pact of 1916, which for a time united the Indian National Congress and the Muslim League on nationalist objectives. The rule provided that if three-fourths of the minority community, e.g., Muslim members, opposed a policy deemed to affect their interests, the policy could not go forward.[29] The decision-rule recognized the limits on majority rule in democracies. Minorities can threaten exit if denied voice.[30]

Between Group Identity and Individual Rights: The Constituent Assembly

We have tried to show how at independence in 1947 India's constitution makers had available alternative and competing norms stressing group particularism on the one hand and individualist universalism on the other. Historical processes and events had endowed these concepts with changing meaning and consequences over time. Independence in 1947 and the Constituent Assembly that sat until 1950 provided the high-water mark of liberal universalism. Since then, with the powerful exception of the rise of Hindu nationalism in the 1980s, difference and group identity expressed in the legitimation of legal pluralism, multicultural ideology and minority rights have gained ground.

In 1947, nationalist opinion held that group-based norms and practices, such as separate electorates, reserved seats, and weightage, found in British efforts to bring representative government to India in the reform acts of 1909, 1919, and 1935, were responsible for the partition of the subcontinent. The nationalists who ran the Constituent Assembly were likely to be socialists like Nehru, pluralist inclusivists like Gandhi, or liberal constructivists like Sapru and Rau, not primordialists or essentialists like raj officials or Hindu nationalist and Muslim nationalist politicians. Many nationalists believed that the religious and caste categories found in British censuses and official discourse and law were not natural or primordial, but the products of the raj's historical circumstances and fertile imaginations. The incentives offered by officially created groups and the reservations extended to them inhibited appeals to cross-cutting cleavages and cemented solidarities based on religion and caste. The many other identities and interests active and available on the subcontinent were marginalized by official raj sociology.

The Nehruvians, who were hegemonic in the Congress Party and in the Constituent Assembly, were doggedly determined to deny that religious identities trumped all others and to see to it that the 1935 Government of India Act, which served as the basic text for the new constitution, was purged of provisions recognizing and privileging group identity. Reserved seats and separate electorates for Muslims, Sikhs, Christians, and other minorities were eliminated. The only exception to the elimination of group rights was reservation by proportion of the population for the scheduled castes (ex-untouchables) and tribes.[31]

After independence, partition, and the departure of the British on 15

August 1947, the remaining Muslim members in the Constituent Assembly were uncertain about what to expect and what course to follow. Sixty percent of unpartitioned India's Muslims were now in Pakistan. Did the great vulnerability of the remainder require the continuation, even the strengthening, of minority safeguards, or did it suggest that the Muslims should ingratiate themselves with Congress leaders by offering to surrender to them? Vallabhbhai Patel, the deputy prime minister and home and states minister, who in retrospect appears as a Hindu nationalist, "quietly and privately put a great deal of pressure on the minorities to relinquish special privileges"[32] but "was too considerate of minority fears—and too much the strategist—to force the issue. . . . [Publicly he said that] the giving up of reservation should not be forced on any minority."[33] "The [Muslim] community," Granville Austin tells us, "was deeply split by the issue. Ultimately it would decide . . . to forego even reservations in the Legislature, hoping by its sacrifice to ensure fair treatment from the Hindu majority."[34]

It was not until May 1949 that the Constituent Assembly took its final decisions on the reservation of seats in legislatures. H. C. Mookerjee was a Christian member who, unlike others of his community in the Constituent Assembly, believed that the minorities, his own and others, should voluntarily give up reservations. It was Mookerjee who, on behalf of the relevant Advisory Committee, moved the resolution to abolish reservations for minorities. Scheduled castes and tribes were spared. All that minorities need, he urged, for protection from democratic majorities is the fundamental rights guaranteed to all citizens in Part III of the Constitution. Its Articles 14 through 29 provide inter alia for equality under the law, prohibiting discrimination, protecting freedom of speech, life, and personal liberty, and guaranteeing freedom of conscience and freedom to profess, practice, and propagate religion.

Mookerjee urged minorities to stop thinking in terms of sub-national minority groups. "I have all along held," he said, "that India is one nation." His resolution carried "with nearly everyone present agreeing or saying they did."[35]

Partition had taught not one, but two lessons. One was that minority safeguards, particularly reservations, can harden cleavages that lead to secession, the other that the Muslims in partitioned India would continue to feel endangered by what many perceived as a Hindu majority. They needed reassurance that their corporate identity was recognized and that their corporate life was secure. This second lesson of partition convinced Nehru and those he led in the dominant Congress Party that Muslims in partitioned India needed special guarantees. These took the form of allowing the Muslim community to preserve and practice their personal law.

Group Rights for Lower Castes

Looking back on the era of partition and constitution making from the perspective of the ideological excitement and political competition of the 1980s and 1990s, two kinds of groups continue to support legal pluralism against the constitutional injunction to implement legal universalism in a uniform civil code. Those groups are lower castes who seek reservations and religious communities who seek protection for their personal law.[36]

First, caste. As we have seen, reservations of legislative seats for scheduled castes and tribes survived in Articles 330 and 332 of the Constitution. These provisions had their progenitors in the British privileging of "backward" castes, expressed in their protection, via "communal awards," of non-Brahmin castes in the south beginning in the 1910s.[37] Positive or protective discrimination on behalf of "backward classes" that began with the Scheduled Castes and Tribes was extended nationally in the 1990s by wide-ranging reservations on behalf of "OBCs" (Other Backward Classes, an administrative euphemism for lower castes)[38] in the countryside where 75 percent of India's voting population lives. Their high levels of participation in national and state electoral politics have radically transformed the sociological profile of India's national Parliament, state assemblies, and their cabinets. The rise of the OBCs first in state and then in national politics has tended to marginalize the upper-caste, upper-class elites who dominated Congress Party politics in the Nehru/Indira Gandhi dynasty era.

A second "Backward Classes Commission"[39] chaired by B. P. Mandal was established to try to implement what the Constitution seemed to promise, reservations for "Other Backward Classes." Reporting in 1980, the Mandal Commission presented the country with an anthropological index organized by states specifying 3,743 backward castes. These were the castes said to qualify as beneficiaries under the constitutional clauses urging special care for "backward" citizens.[40] The Commission estimated that backward castes listed in its report constituted 52 percent of the population. It recommended, however, that only 27 percent reservations be set aside for the OBCs listed. Reservations totaling 52 percent when added to the 22.5 percent already reserved for scheduled castes and tribes would violate the Supreme Court's standard in *Balaji* that reservations totaling more than 50 percent would be a fraud on the Constitution, in part because exceeding 50 percent would violate the equal rights clauses of the Constitution.

Even before the Mandal Commission made its recommendations, many Indian states had already enacted legislation providing reservations in educational institutions and government jobs for "backwards." When Prime Minister V. P. Singh's government began to implement the Mandal Commission recommendations in 1990, the Bharatiya Janata Party withdrew its support from his coalition government and soon after launched a *padyatra* (national pilgrimage) on behalf of *hindutva* (Hinduness). There were riots and immolations mainly by disgruntled upper-caste, upper-class students, the government fell, and a mid-term election followed. In 1991, a Congress government under Prime Minister Narasimha Rao took office. It too began cautiously to implement the Mandal Commission's recommendation. Today OBC politics and reservations have been, if not fully normalized, at least accepted as part of the rules of the game. Legal pluralism in the form of reservations for particular lower castes seems well-established as the twentieth century gives way to the twenty-first.

Minority Rights for Religious Communities: The Uniform Civil Code

Religious collectivities also claimed exemption from universal rules. Having wiped out reservations of legislative seats on the basis of religion, the Constituent Assembly proceeded to write Article 29, which guarantees the right to maintain distinct cultures. "Any section of the citizens of India . . . having a distinct language, script [Gurmukhi was a script used by Sikhs; Urdu by Muslims] or culture [a euphemism for religion] shall have the right to preserve the same." Article 30 guaranteed the right of religious minorities to establish educational institutions and barred the state, which supports private educational institutions, including religious ones, from discriminating against them.[41] The Articles raise the question of whether it is constitutionally permissible to have different laws for different groups defined according to religion. Not really, the Constituent Assembly wanted to say. It almost said it. It almost asserted that a uniform civil code supersedes the varieties of personal law. But at the last minute, it held its hand.

At the urging of "liberals" such as Minoo Masani, Amrit Kaur, and Hansa Mehta, the Constituent Assembly considered including a uniform civil code in the justiciable provisions of the Constitution. Such a code, embodying general laws applicable to all individuals regardless of religion, would have been mandated to come into force over a five- to ten-year period.[42] By abolishing the differences in personal law it would "get rid of these watertight compartments . . . which keep the nation divided."[43]

The provision died in committee but was eventually included in the "Directive Principles of State Policy," non-justiciable Articles [36 through 51] included in Part IV of the Constitution. They articulate the imagined social revolution of the Nehruvian nationalist generation. It expresses purposes and goals but creates no rights. The hesitancy to include an actionable uniform civil code in the Constitution reflected the concern of the Nehruvian secular nationalists for the sensibilities and needs of India's religious minorities. They wanted to insure that Muslims particularly but also Sikhs, Christians, Parsis, Jains, and others in secular India would not only feel safe but at home. They were to be not only citizens with equal rights but also members of religious communities whose different cultures and identities would be secure and honored through the continued existence and viability of their personal law.

The Uniform Civil Code as Historical Process

One way to think about the uniform civil code is as a process that has gone on for more than 150 years and has been continually challenged. For much of that period, in the hands of British reformers before independence and nationalist secularists since independence, the tendency appeared to be in the direction of greater homogeneity. Since the 1970s, forces of difference and identity appear to have strengthened the heterogeneity of religiously based personal law.

Homogeneity was served powerfully in the nineteenth and twentieth centuries by three processes: changes in who administered the law; expansion of universal law by processes of codification; and the reformation and homogenization of personal law.

First, administration. The British began with a partial commitment to having the law interpreted by Hindu and Muslim religious adepts, attaching pandits and maulvis to their courts.[44] But these indigenous court advisors were dispensed with in 1864.[45] British magistrates or British-trained magistrates became the sole executors of personal law, soundlessly introducing principles of evidence and interpretation that smoothed out difference. The hierarchical organization that links all courts in India into a single system leading today to the Supreme Court also favored homogeneity.[46] The court *system* was universalized long before the law.[47]

The great wave of legal codification by the British in the nineteenth century swept away the particularities of criminal law (via the Penal Code of 1860), preserving neither Muslim nor Hindu penalties.[48] A series of civil law acts passed between 1865 and 1872 were based mainly on British civil law, exempting, however, the realm of personal law—marriage, divorce, succession, adoption, property, and definition of family.

Finally, the reformation of the personal law itself led toward uniformity within each of the compartments. To assert legally that there is one undifferentiated "Hindu" and "Muslim" personal law was itself a significant act of homogenization. The personal law of Hindu lower and upper castes differs markedly, as does law between regions which have different kinship systems. "Muslims" too is an amalgam of sectarian identities with different rules and practices.[49] When the Shari'at Act was passed in 1937 to regularize and rationalize Muslim law, it wiped out the particular personal laws of several Muslim communities that constituted minorities within Indian Islam: the Khojas and Cutchi Memons of Gujarat and the Muslims of North West Frontier Province, all of whom followed Hindu laws of inheritance, and the Malsan Muslims, who followed matriarchal laws of inheritance.[50]

Just as the practice of the British courts narrowed the number of precepts accepted as Muslim or Muhammadan law, Muslim hierarchical organization gave a kind of finality to *Shari'at* which it could not attain when authority was localized and distributed among many *madrasas* as well as individuals.[51]

If we understand the uniform legal code as a historical process instead of a one-time legal enactment, this is the story of the homogenization process. But there is a parallel story of the survival and reassertion of legal pluralism. The sensational 1985 Shah Bano case encapsulates the intense contemporary tension between the uniformity-making process and the pluralist counterforce.

Shah Bano, a divorced Muslim woman, sued her husband for maintenance. The court held her entitled to maintenance under Article 125 of the Code of Criminal Procedure, which had often been previously invoked, including in cases of Muslim women, to prevent female vagrancy by forcing husbands to support wives whom they had divorced. The Supreme Court decision was rooted in cases dating back to the raj that had not occasioned Muslim challenge. This point matters, suggesting that the acceptance of the homogenizing process is premised on the trust and distrust prevailing among contesting groups at particular moments in historical time. The decision was welcomed with jubilation by women's groups and was seen as a step in the direction of a uniform civil code. But the Muslim community *in this instance,* at a historical moment that saw a rising spiral of Hindu nationalism, interpreted the court's decision in favor of Shah Bano as violating Muslim personal law, which mandates that when the marriage contract is terminated by divorce, the husband's financial obligations cease and are to be taken up by blood relatives or Muslim religious bodies.[52] Muslim protests and electoral reaction were sufficiently strong that the Rajiv Gandhi government, which had originally welcomed the decision, reversed course and passed legislation protecting the Muslim personal law in cases of Muslim divorce.

The Shah Bano case highlights the fact that the uniform civil code arena is likely to represent a process rather than an enactment, a continual negotiation more than a unilinear progression. Much of that process is likely to consist of the gradual accumulation of court decisions and particular pieces of legislation pointing in contradictory directions. In a careful review of cases litigated since the reform of the Hindu Code in the 1950s, Vasudha Dhagamwar, an activist legal scholar, traced a process of accumulation through the debates and litigation surrounding the Bombay Hindu Bigamous Marriages Act, the Hindu Marriage Act of 1955 (an element of the "Hindu Code"), the Bombay Excommunications Act, the various versions of the Indian Adoption Bill, and the cases arising out of the Code of Criminal Procedure of 1973 which led to the Shah Bano case. Dhagamwar believes that the process since independence has been to erode the forces promoting uniformity.[53]

Legal Pluralism as Multiculturalism: A Uniform Civil Code vs. Minority Rights

When Rajiv Gandhi's Congress government in 1986 gave support to Muslim personal law by passing a Muslim Women (Protection of Rights on Divorce) Act, his action raised a political storm.[54] Sections of the Hindu nationalist Bharatiya Janata Party asserted that minorities were being pampered and privileged at the expense of the "majority community," a euphemism for Hindus. The Bharatiya Janata Party's post–Shah Bano advocacy of a uniform civil code had placed the contest between legal uniformity and legal pluralism at the center of Indian political debate. It was a contest which fanned the flames of Hindu nationalism that leaped ever higher between 1985 and 1992. On 6 December 1992, thousands of Hindu nationalist youths wearing saffron headbands and wielding pickaxes destroyed the sixteenth-century Babri Masjid (mosque built by the Mughal emperor Babur) while the prime minister of India stood helplessly by. They did so on the ground that it dese-

crated the site on which a temple to Lord Ram had stood. The interna-
tionally televised event became the symbol of a monumental crisis in
India's self-definition as a secular state.

These events raise a number of questions. One is, how did Indian
public discourse about difference move from the harmony of civilizations to the "clash of civilizations"? Was the shift occasioned by the rise
of Hindu nationalism an aberration or is it likely to endure?

As we write, the flames of Hindu nationalism appear banked. In its
quest to become the dominant party in a diverse multi-cultural land,
the Hindu nationalist Bharatiya Janata Party has responded to the 1996
and 1999 elections by off-loading its communal, anti-minority planks.[55]

Advocacy of a uniform civil code has been abandoned. The party has
attempted to distance itself from extremist fringes. It has shown movement toward the policies that governments in a multi-cultural society
find prudent to embrace, recognizing and valuing difference rather than
denigrating or eradicating it.

Representative of a new discourse that makes a uniform civil code
compatible with the continuing existence and integrity of personal law
is S. P. Sathe's argument that "the Constitution doubtless visualizes
the emergence of a uniform civil code but does it mean a single law for
all? . . . Within one nation there can exist a number of legal systems.
In fact federal government," he continues, "means the coexistence of
such multiple laws. . . . This means that Maharashtra may have its own
family law different from that of Karnataka. In the U.S. each state has
its own matrimonial law."

A uniform law, Sathe argues, "does not necessarily mean a common
law but different personal laws based on uniform principles of equality
of sexes and liberty for the individual. . . ."[56]

The struggle between legal uniformity and legal pluralism remains
at the center of public debate. We see the contest as an open-ended story
about balancing the uniformity of a civil code that protects individual
rights with the diversity of personal laws that protects minority rights.
Hopefully it will be the story of an unstable but viable equilibrium that
combines the legal equality of human rights with a post-civilizational
"multi-culturalism." The language of multi-culturalism exhibits a family resemblance to the language of India's eighteenth-century Orientalists, in their common belief that difference would be recognized and
valued rather than denigrated or eradicated.

The idea of a uniform civil code carries no single meaning over historical time. Its advocates change, and change sides. Semioticists might

call it a multivalent signifier. We identify five possible meanings for the uniform civil code.

One. The British implicitly moved toward a uniform civil code without calling it that. At the cultural level, making the law more uniform, standardizing it, was an expression of rationalization and modernization. Uniformity of rules and regulations made it easier for those in charge of the "steel frame" to administer justice, provide law and order, and collect the revenue. Legal uniformity was in keeping with the formal organizations of the raj's administrative state. It made the law more legible for bureaucrats who were strangers to India's diversity and villages. And it was believed to facilitate control. These rationales were equally congenial to those charged with ruling the post-colonial state.

Two. For modernist, rationalist nationalists a uniform civil code seemed to promise national integration. It would do for twentieth-century India what nineteenth-century nationalism was thought to have done for European states, dissolve or erase differences. It would help bring into being a nation whose people shared an identity congruent with state boundaries.

Three. For civil rights activists, those speaking for the marginalized and powerless, women, children, cultural and ethnic minorities, and lower classes, a uniform civil code signified the expansion of rights to categories of persons oppressed by patriarchal, gerontocratic, collective, and oligarchic forms of social domination and control.

Four. For religious minorities, the uniform civil code signified an effort to erase the personal law of diverse communities. It posed a threat to their cultural identity, even to their cultural survival.

Five. For Hindu nationalists, a uniform civil code promised a legal means to eliminate cultural differences and the "special privileges" accorded to "pampered minorities." It would also have rectified what they perceived as an injustice, the reform in the 1950s of Hindu personal law (the "Hindu Code Bills")[57] without reforming the Muslim personal law,[58] making it possible in principle (but rarely in practice) for Muslim men to have four wives and to divorce at will.

At independence, about 1947–1950, the first three meanings of the uniform civil code were dominant. In the last decade, especially since the destruction of the Babri Masjid in December 1992, the last two meanings have come to the fore, seeing the uniform civil code as a means to diminish if not eradicate cultural pluralism. The foregrounding of these two meanings has changed the politics surrounding the uniform civil code by problematizing prior alignments. In contemporary Indian politics, civil and human rights activists who favor legal uniformity are accustomed to opposing the anti-Muslim *hindutva* politics of Hindu nationalist politicians. Yet they find themselves on the same side with respect to a uniform civil code. They think of a uniform civil code as protecting and promoting the fundamental rights found in the Indian Constitution and human rights found in international law. Feminists who typically oppose Muslim patriarchal controls are obliged to recognize that wiping out a repressive Muslim personal law is also an act of identity destruction. How to be pro-civil and human rights and pro-feminist without being anti-Muslim? Where to go?

We have suggested that a uniform civil code can be conceptualized as a process rather than as a specific outcome, a process in which legal uniformity and legal pluralism jockey for dominance, not for the whole field. The liberal and progressive dream that it is the fate of difference to fade and for humanity increasingly to repair to a common mold,[59] and the additional dream of rationalists that it is the fate particularly of religion to fade away in face of the triumph of modern science, have receded in the last two decades not only in India but the wider world. In India, the opposition between legal pluralism and legal uniformity is not likely to yield a smooth progressive historical narrative in which society moves inexorably from the first to the second. Whether regarded as benign or malign, identity formation, in the form of religiously based personal law, seems to be alive and well.

The debate about the uniform civil code versus personal law need not be a zero-sum conflict. "To put the choice as one between the personal law system and a uniform civil code is to pose the issue too sharply," John Mansfield argues. He holds that it may be sensible to make distinctions and to adopt a "particularizing approach," such as "has been going on since 1772."[60] He bases his prescription on the importance of preserving difference, preserving, that is, the identity of ethnic or religious groups within a territorial state even while moving toward greater uniformity of rights.

Notes

1. The Supreme Court in *Balaji v. State of Mysore*, AIR 1963 S.C. 649 (664) stated that "There can be no doubt that the Constitution-makers assumed . . . that while making adequate reservation under article 16 (4) [which permits reservations in government employment or government funded institutions such as universities for 'any backward class of citizens'] care would be taken not to provide for unreasonable, excessive or extravagant reservation—therefore . . . reservations made under article 16 (4) beyond

the permissible and legitimate limits would be liable to be challenged *as a fraud on the Constitution* (underlining in the original)." Durga Das Basu, *Introduction to the Constitution of India*, 16th ed. (New Delhi: Prentice Hall of India, 1994), p. 93. For constitutional provisions and detailed commentary on them based on case law, including a discussion of percentages, see Durga Das Basu's humorously named *Shortage Constitution of India*, 11th ed. (New Delhi: Prentice Hall of India, 1994), p. 81.

The limits have been generally interpreted as meaning that reservation should not exceed 50 percent, although, at the time of this writing, Tamilnadu state legislation setting higher limits was protected from judicial review by being placed in the ninth schedule of the Constitution, a schedule that immunizes legislation from court intervention. However, the judiciary under the Keshavananda rules [*Keshavananda v. State of Kerala*, AIR 1973 S.C. 1641], which give the Court jurisdiction in cases where the "basic principles" of the Constitution are threatened, could, presumably, intervene against Tamilnadu.

The Report of the Backward Classes Commission in 1980 estimated that Other Backward Classes deserving of reservations constituted 52 percent of the population, but recommended only 27 percent reservations because, together with the 22 percent already reserved for Scheduled Castes [ex-untouchables or Dalits] by the Supreme Tribes, the total would be just under the limit set by the Supreme Court in *Balaji*. Government of India, *Report of the Backward Classes Commission*, vol. 1 (New Delhi, 1980), pp. 63 and 92.

2. This is an argument that Partha Chatterjee advances and problematizes in "Secularism and Toleration," *Economic and Political Weekly*, 9 July 1994, pp. 1768–77. Many of the issues he raises there were examined in the context of legal decisions by John H. Mansfield, "The Personal Laws or a Uniform Civil Code?" in Robert D. Baird, ed., *Religion and Law in Independent India* (Delhi: Manohar, 1993), pp. 139–177.

For a wide-ranging comparative study of pluralism and democracy, particularly in Islamic countries, see Alfred Stepan, "The World's Religious Systems and Democracy: Crafting the Twin Tolerations," paper delivered at the Mansfield College/Political Quarterly Conference on Religion and Democracy, Oxford, 10–12 Sept. 1999.

Conflict among multi-culturalism framed as minority rights; popular sovereignty framed as democratic majoritarianism; and equal citizenship framed as individual rights and legal equality, were featured in papers prepared for The Second International Liechtenstein Research Program on Self-Determination held at the Woodrow Wilson School of Public and International Affairs, Princeton University, 10 June 1995. See particularly papers by Daniel A. Bell, "Comments on Min Xin Pei's . . . A Strategy for Improving Minority Rights in China" [where he argues that "*a priori* there is no reason to believe that representatives of majority interests will respect the rights of minorities," and cites the murder by the Chinese government of one-fifth of the Buddhist population of Tibet as evidence], and Michele Lamon's "Cultural Dynamics of Exclusion of Community in France, the United States, and Quebec." Conference papers were published in Wolfgang Danspeckgruber and John Waterbury, eds., *Self-Determination in Our World* (New York: Oxford University Press, 1998).

3. Article 29 provides that "any section of the citizens of India . . . having a distinct language, script [read Gurmukhi for Sikhs and Urdu for many Muslims] or culture [the identity and way of life, the 'ethnicity,' inter alia of Muslims, Sikhs, Christians] shall have the right to conserve the same." According to Durga Das Basu, Article 29 protects "the cultural, linguistic and similar rights of any section of the community who might constitute a 'minority' from the . . . democratic machine . . . being used as an engine of oppression by the numerical majority." D. D. Basu, *Introduction,* p. 367. Article 25 guarantees to "any denomination and any section thereof" the right to "manage its own affairs in matters of religion," which of course leaves the question, relevant to the Shah Bano case (below), of what is religion.

4. We use the "Sir" in identifying William Jones to recognize the somewhat "miraculous" moment in his life, on the eve of his departure to India to take up a judgeship in Bengal, when he acquired the title. He would serve the East India Company under the Bengal presidency of Governor Warren Hastings, soon [1784] to become the company's first Governor-General in India. After Jones had been impatiently and anxiously waiting for three years, King George III, thought by some to be mad, personally intervened on his behalf to secure his appointment.

See Garland Cannon, *Letters of Sir William Jones,* 2 vols. (London: Oxford University Press, 1970), vol. II, pp. 515–517, as quoted in O. P. Kejariwal, *Asiatic Society of Bengal and the Discovery of India's Past* (Delhi: Oxford University Press, 1970), pp. 32–33.

5. See Uday Singh Mehta, *Liberalism and Empire: A Study in Nineteenth-Century British Liberal Thought* (Chicago: University of Chicago Press, 1999). According to Mehta, "Burke reflected on and wrote about various major sites of the empire—Ireland, America, and India . . . [he saw that] the British empire was neither predominantly Protestant nor Anglophone. [After the Seven Years' War, 1756–63] it . . . included French Catholics in Quebec and millions of Asians who were neither Christian nor white. . . . Burke's writings make it undeniably clear that he reflected with great seriousness on the situation in which the exercise of power and authority was implicated with considerations of cultural and racial diversity, contrasting civilizational unities, the absence of . . . consensual government, and alternative norms of political identity and legitimacy" (pp. 154–155).

If difference was all for Burke, if persons were always and inevitably marked, for Locke sameness was all. Human nature was the same everywhere and always. For Mehta, Locke's ideas in *Two Treatises on Government* capture "liberal universalism," a world of "transhistorical, transcultural, and most certainly transracial" principles and persons. "The declared and ostensible referent of liberal principles is quite literally a constituency with no delimiting boundaries: that is all humankind. The political rights that it articulates and defends, the institutions such as laws, representation, contract all have their justification in a characterization of human beings that eschews names, social status, ethnic background, gender and race . . . liberal universalism stems from . . . what one might call a philosophical anthropology . . . the universal claims can be made because they derive from certain characteristics that are common to all human beings" (pp. 51–52).

Timothy Shah used his paper "The Religious Origins of Liberalism, 1604–1704" as the takeoff point for a similar critique of liberal universalism. Mansfield College/Political Quarterly Conference.

6. From *Proceedings of the Committee of Circuit at Kasimbazaar,* 15 August 1772, quoted in Bharatiya Vidya Bhaven, *History and Culture of the Indian People,* vol. 8, p. 361. For a longer discussion of Warren Hastings's role in the initial defining of difference, see Lloyd I. Rudolph and Susanne Hoeber Rudolph, "Occidentalism and Orientalism: Perspectives on Legal Pluralism," in Sally Humphreys, ed., *Cultures of Scholarship* (Ann Arbor: University of Michigan Press, 1997), pp. 219–251.

7. For alternative categories that mattered in the seventeenth and eighteenth centuries, notably regional lineages, see the work of Christopher Bayly, e.g., *Rulers, Townsmen and Bazaars; North Indian society in the age of British expansion, 1770–1870* (Cambridge: Cambridge University Press, 1983).

For categories more generally see J. C. Masselos, "The Khojas of Bombay: The Defining of Formal Membership Criteria during the Nineteenth Century," in Imtiaz Ahmed, ed., *Caste and Social Stratification among Muslims in India* (Delhi: Manohar, 1978), pp. 97–116, and Harjot Oberoi, *The Construction of Religious Boundaries* (Delhi: Oxford University Press, 1994).

Amrita Shodan shows how Bombay province's law collectors moved in the 1820s from looking at a variety of legal sources—court cases, Shastris, heads of castes, common people, others knowledgeable about the law—to concentrating mainly on castes as the units of legal practices. The form of inquiry in turn intensified the propensity for courts to treat caste as *the* form of community that generated law. ("Legal Representation of Khojas and Pushtimarga Vaishnavas," Ph.D. dissertation, Department of South Asian Languages and Civilizations, University of Chicago, 1995, p. 15.)

For a critique of categories from a Saidean perspective, see also Ronald Inden, *Imagining India* (Oxford: Basil Blackwell, 1990). In the introduction of our *Modernity of Tradition: Political Development in India* (Chicago: University of Chicago Press, 1998), we speak of the "imperialism of categories" to critique Western scholars' imposition of "home" concepts on Indian civilizational experiences (p. 7).

8. For the centrality of self-regulating social groups in defining state–society

relations in Indian historical experience and thought, see Lloyd I. Rudolph and Susanne Hoeber Rudolph, "The Subcontinental Empire and the Regional Kingdom in Indian State Formation," in Paul Wallace, ed., *Region and Nation in India* (New Delhi: Oxford University Press and IBH Publishing Co., 1985).

9. Henry Thomas Colebrooke, "On Hindu Courts of Justice," in *Transactions of the Royal Asiatic Society of Great Britain and Ireland*, vol. 2 (London: Parbury, Allen, 1830), 174, 177.

10. Richard Eaton, *The Rise of Islam and the Bengal Frontier* (Berkeley: University of California Press, 1993).

11. Stanley Wolpert, *A New History of India* (New York: Oxford University Press, 1992), p. 242.

12. Leslie Stephen summarizing his brother's views in the *Life of Sir James Fitzjames Stephen* (London: Smith, Elder, 1895), p. 285.

13. Ibid.

14. Gains of Learning Act was brought before provincial legislatures but was not passed until 1930.

15. Wills began to be effective as early as 1792 in Bengal, in Bombay in 1860, and in Madras in 1862. See Sir Francis Dúpre Oldfield, "Law Reform," in H. H. Dodwell, ed., *Cambridge History of India* (1st Indian reprint, no date), vol. VI.

16. Macaulay as quoted in Wolpert, *India*, p. 215.

    The high point of the Bentinck era's liberal universalism was probably Article 47 of the East India Charter Act of 1833, which was more honored in the breach. It proclaimed: "No Native of said Territories . . . shall, by reason of only his religion, place of birth, descent, colour, or any of them be disabled from holding any place, Office, or Employment under the said Company." Wolpert, *India*, p. 213.

17. Reginald Coupland, *The Indian Problem; Report on the Constitutional Problem in India*, 3 vols. in 1 (New York: Oxford University Press, 1994), vol. 1, p. 23.

18. Marian Fowler, *Below the Peacock Fan: First Ladies of the Raj* (New York: Penguin Books, 1988), p. 150. Fowler's romantic pen contrasts Lord Auckland's (George Eden, Governor-General 1836–42) sister Emily Eden's easy familiarity and admiration for Indians and things Indian with Charlotte Canning's (wife of Lord Canning, Governor-General before and during the 1857 revolt and Viceroy from 1858 until 1862) alienation from and fear of India. Emily Eden's connections to India were not precisely subalternate, but she "had played chess with Dost Mahomed and taught English to Pertab Singh. . . . The Eden sisters [Fanny as well as Emily] had caught glimpses of Mughal magic and magnificence, of Peacock Thrones ablaze with light, enough to fire their imaginations, enough to see by. . . ." After 1857 such "easy conviviality between Indian ruler and English was

... gone forever. . . . They sensed that the Indians hated them; and so they ruled with an iron hand, but one which trembled a little" (p. 150).

19. The classic text for "reform" is the late Eric Stokes's *The English Utilitarians in India* (Oxford: Clarendon Press, 1959). Part III, "Law and Government," and the "The Penal Code" are specially relevant to our theme.

   "Lapse" was a doctrine practiced particularly by Governor-General Dalhousie [1848–1856], barring succession in princely states of adopted heirs. It rationalized even if it did not legitimize an East India Company policy of "annexation," a de facto resort to war, against estates without natural heirs. Narratives of the 1857 rebellion feature the "annexations" of Jhansi and Oudh, thought to be triggering events. For a comprehensive and insightful account of the motives and consequences of annexation, see Michael H. Fisher, ed., *The Politics of the British Annexation of India, 1757–1857* (Delhi: Oxford University Press, 1993).

20. As quoted in Wolpert, *India,* pp. 240–241.

21. Gordon Johnson, "India and Henry Maine," in Mushirul Hasan and Narauani Gupta, eds., *India's Colonial Encounter: Essays in Memory of Eric Stokes* (Delhi: Manohar, 1993), p. 31.

   Johnson makes clear that "Maine's contemporaries recognized that his influence spread far beyond the making of laws. His serious writing—particularly *Ancient Law and Village Communities East and West*—had a profound effect on how Indian society was observed and understood." Among other things, Maine saw India with an ethnographic eye, arguing ". . . strongly against there being any uniform or clearly stated set of Indian law: rather the whole was a mess of shifting customs which varied from place to place and over time" (pp. 33 and 34).

22. Narrative based on and quotes from Wolpert, *India,* p. 264.

23. See the late Irene A. Gilbert's essay on Aligarh's founding, operation, and consequences, "Autonomy and Consensus under the Raj: Presidency (Calcutta); Muir (Allahabad); M.A.O. (Aligarh)," in Lloyd I. Rudolph and Susanne Hoeber Rudolph, eds., *Education and Politics in India* (Cambridge, Mass.: Harvard University Press, 1973), pp. 171–206.

24. Coupland, *Indian Problem,* vol. 1, pp. 155–156.

25. Ibid.

26. Eugene Irshick, *Politics and Social Conflict in South India: The Non-Brahman Movement and Tamil Separatism* (New Delhi: Oxford University Press, 1969).

27. For an account of the gradual expansion of representation, see Coupland, *Indian Problem,* vol. 1, pp. 47, 128, 138, 151.

28. The fast was seen by Dr. B. R. Ambedkar, leader of the untouchables and subsequently the law minister who guided the drafting of free India's Constitution, as an attempt by conservative Hinduism to deny autonomy to untouchables. The fast was the opening drama for Gandhi's extended campaign throughout the 1930s against the practice of untouchability—a cam-

paign that is seen by today's radical *Dalits* as paternalistic and demeaning, but which led to the special privileges for "scheduled castes" in the Constitution. For some aspects of the debate, see Rudolph and Rudolph, "Traditional Structures and Modern Politics: Caste" in *The Modernity of Tradition*, pp. 136–145.

29. Coupland, *Indian Problem*, vol. 1, p. 48.

30. See Albert Hirshman's *Exit, Voice and Loyalty* (Cambridge, Mass.: Harvard University Press, 1970) for more on these concepts and how they can be applied.

31. See Articles 330 and 332 reserving seats in national and state legislature for scheduled tribes and scheduled castes. Unless renewed and extended, the reservations were to expire in ten years after the coming into force of the Constitution in 1950. (They have been renewed by amendment in each ten-year period since 1950.)

32. Granville Austin, *The Indian Constitution* (New York: Oxford University Press, 1966), p. 151.

33. Ibid., p. 152.

34. Ibid., p. 151. See pages 151–154 for a discussion of the ambivalent quality of some of this support.

35. Ibid., p. 154.

36. Another voice in support of legal pluralism is regionally dominant linguistic groups ("sons of the soil") who have demanded to be privileged in employment as against immigrants from other regional linguistic areas. The most notorious example is that of the Shiv Sena in Maharashtra, who began by attacking Tamils and of late has been attacking Muslims from Bengal and Bangladesh. We will not deal with this form of legal pluralism here.

37. See Irshick, *Politics and Social Conflict*.

38. For a careful account of the history of reservations and their legal standing see Marc Galanter, *Competing Equalities: Law and the Backward Classes in India* (New Delhi: Oxford University Press, 1984). See also our *Modernity of Tradition*, notably pp. 137–154. A codicil to the universalizing language of Article 16, "Equality of opportunity in matters of public employment," states that "Nothing in this article shall prevent the State from making any provision for the reservation of appointments or posts in favour of any backward class of citizens which, in the opinion of the State, is not adequately represented in the services under the State" [Article 16 (4)]. A similar codicil envisioning protections to "socially and educationally backward classes of citizens or for the Scheduled Castes and the Scheduled Tribes" attaches to Article 15, which prohibits "discrimination on grounds of religion, race, caste, sex or place of birth." 15 (1).

39. The first Backward Classes Commission was chaired by Kaka Kalelkar, who concluded that "backwardness could be tackled on the basis or a number of bases other than that of caste." Transmittal letter, in Government

of India, Backward Classes Commission, *Report of the Backward Classes Commission* (Delhi: Manager of Publications, 1955), vol. 1.

40. The Constitution avoids using the term *caste*, and refers rather to "backward classes," evidence of the founders' interest in privileging criteria other than caste. Special provisions for "socially and educationally backward classes" are exempted from the prohibition, under Article 15, of discrimination on grounds of religion, race, caste, sex, and place of birth. These provisions are again exempted from the guarantee, in Article 16, of equality of opportunity in public employment. Article 340 provides for the appointment of a commission to investigate the conditions of the backward classes and recommend remedies. See also Government of India, *Report of the Backward Classes Commission* ("Mandal Report"), vol. 1 (New Delhi, 1980), pp. 63 and 92. The Supreme Court declared the Mandal reservations valid in 1993.

41. The high bar, sometimes referred to as "a wall of separation," between the state religious institutions including educational institutions that characterizes U.S. practice does not govern Indian law and practice, nor did it British, which includes grants-in-aid to religious institutions subject to certain standards.

42. For a detailed discussion of the Constituent Assembly debate see Vasudha Dhagamwar, "Women, Children and the Constitution," in Robert D. Baird, ed., *Religion and Law in Independent India* (New Delhi: Manohar, 1993), pp. 218–221.

43. Minoo Masani, cited in Granville Austin, *The Indian Constitution*, p. 80.

44. These adepts were messengers of the written texts of high culture law, in the case of Hindus of "Brahmanic" law. They disprivileged the local usage and customs of the lower castes who constituted the vast bulk of the population. Rudolph and Rudolph, "Legal Cultures and Social Change," in *Modernity of Tradition*, pp. 274–279.

45. W. H. Mcnaghten, *Principles and Precedents of Hindu Law* (Calcutta: University of Calcutta Press, 1829), vol. I, p. vi.

46. See Gregory C. Kozlowski, "Muslim Personal Law and Political Identity in Independent India," in Baird, *Religion and Law in Independent India*, p. 81.

47. However, it is important to recognize that the official court system accounts for only a part of adjudication of disputes under personal law. Much adjudication still takes place in caste councils among Hindus and by the decision of religious scholars among Muslims. See, for example, Gregory C. Kozlowski's account of the cases handled by the *mufti* of a Hyderabadi *madrasa*, "Muslim Personal Law," pp. 82–85.

48. Although elements of excommunication as a penalty survived.

49. See inter alia Katherine Ewing's "Introduction: Ambiguity and Shari'at—A Perspective on the Problem of Moral Principles in Tension"; David Gilmartin, "Customary Law and the Shari'at in British Punjab," in Katherine

Ewing, ed., *Shari'at and Ambiguity in South Asian Islam* (Berkeley: University of California Press, 1988), pp. 1–24 and 43–62; and Kozlowski, "Muslim Personal Law," particularly "Creating Muslim Personal Law," pp. 79–82.

Special mention should be made of the essays in Asghar Ali Engineer, ed., *The Shah Bano Controversy* (Bombay: Orient Longman, 1987), and of Tahir Mahmood's study, *An Indian Civil Code and Islamic Law* (Bombay: N. M. Tripathi, 1976).

50. Dhagamwar, "Women, Children and the Constitution," p. 219.

51. Kozlowski, "Muslim Personal Law," p. 81. For similar discussion see Katherine Ewing, "Introduction: Ambiguity and Shari'at—A Perspective on the Problem of Moral Principles in Tension" and David Gilmartin, "Customary Law and the Shari'at in British Punjab," both in Ewing, ed., *Shari'at and Ambiguity*, pp. 43–62.

52. See a more detailed discussion of the case in its larger context in the struggle over secularism in Rudolph and Rudolph, *In Pursuit of Lakshmi: The Political Economy of the Indian State* (Chicago: University of Chicago Press, 1987), pp. 44–46.

53. Dhagamwar, "Women, Children and the Constitution," p. 255. For a recent discussion of a uniformity-promoting piece of legislation, see Mrinalini Sinha, "The Lineage of the 'Indian' Modern: Rhetoric, Agency, and the Sarda Act in Late Colonial India," forthcoming in Antoinette Burton, ed., *Unfinished Business: Gender, Sexualities, and Colonial Modernities*.

54. The immediate sign of a storm was the loss of a mid-term election in a Muslim constituency in Bihar. For details, see Rudolph and Rudolph, *Lakshmi*, end note 66, pp. 419–420.

55. By late 1995, with the eleventh Parliamentary election just three or four months away, strains began to appear within the Bharatiya Janata Party over its commitment to a uniform civil code. Not only were some in the party reluctant to drive away Muslim votes so vital for success in Uttar Pradesh, India's largest state, but also moderate and fundamentalist Hindus were having second thoughts about a uniform civil code. It had dawned on many of them that a uniform civil code was not the same thing as "their" Hindu Code and that its effects might not be confined to preventing Muslims from having several wives and from divorcing them at will. A uniform civil code could jeopardize, they realized, the Hindu undivided joint family, a legal fiction that can reduce tax liabilities and make it possible to discriminate against female members of the family by, inter alia, depriving them of equal property rights. The 1998 and 1999 elections, which made the Bharatiya Janata Party reliant on many secularist coalition partners, further made Hindu planks undesirable.

56. S. P. Sathe, "Uniform Civil Code: Implications of Supreme Court Intervention," *Economic and Political Weekly*, 2 September 1995. Imtiaz Ahmad's "Personal Laws: Promoting Reform from Within," *Economic and Po-*

litical Weekly, 11 November 1995, makes a similar argument. Ahmad has played a key role in bringing together Muslim intellectuals and 'ulama'. So has Mushirul Hasan, whose "Muslim Intellectuals, Institutions, and the Post-Colonial Predicament," *Economic and Political Weekly*, 25 November 1995, provides a learned and persuasive case for introducing laws and practices commensurate with "Indian Islam." Saabeeha Bano in "Muslim Women's Voices; Expanding Gender Justice under Muslim Law," *Economic and Political Weekly*, 25 November 1995, argues on the basis of results of an opinion survey among Muslim women in Delhi that the gender justice objectives that a uniform civil code might realize can be achieved by a process of reform of personal laws.

John H. Mansfield concludes his article "The Personal Laws or a Uniform Civil Code?" (in Baird, ed., *Religion and Law in Independent India*) with the observation that a uniform civil code should not entirely eliminate diverse personal law because of the importance of preserving the identity "of . . . ethnic or religious group[s] within a territorial state [and their] being able to maintain [their] distinctive identity and through this . . . members' sense of existing and having meaning" (pp. 175–176).

For versions of the debate about politics and of the battle over a uniform code, see "Uniform Civil Code; Striking Down a Right," *India Today*, 15 June 1995; Abida Samiuddin, "Status of Hindu and Muslim Women: A Comparative Study," *Mainstream*, 8 July 1995; and "Uniform Civil Code: A Calculated Gambit," *India Today*, 31 July 1995.

"Our Modern Hate: How Ancient Animosities Get Invented," *The New Republic*, 22 March 1993, dealt inter alia with the tension in India between multi-culturalism and Hindu nationalism.

57. See Harold Levy, "Indian Modernization."

58. For a relatively detailed discussion of the "Hindu Code," see Dhagamwar, "Women, Children and the Constitution," p. 234 ff.

59. For a debate along these lines see Martha Nussbaum, ed., "Patriotism or Cosmopolitanism," *Boston Review* XIX, no. 5 (October/November 1994). For an application of the debate to India see the contribution to the debate by Lloyd Rudolph, "The Occidental Tagore."

60. Mansfield, "The Personal Laws or a Uniform Civil Code?" in Baird, ed., *Religion and Law*, pp. 175–176.

PART II
RELIGIOUS ENDOWMENTS,
RESERVATIONS LAW,
AND CRIMINAL LAW

Four

Religious and Charitable Endowments and a Uniform Civil Code

John H. Mansfield

In discussing the sensitive subject of a uniform civil code, careful attention needs to be paid to the state of the law on each of the topics traditionally governed by the personal laws and the advantages and disadvantages of the present system with respect to each of these topics. To the
extent that there are disadvantages, it is necessary also to consider
whether the present case law contains trends tending to remove these
disadvantages, or opportunities that may be used to remove them, so
that legislative intervention through a uniform code or a uniform rule
on a particular topic may not be necessary. With respect to each topic
of the personal laws, it is important to assess the role the current system
plays in maintaining group identity and the importance of a uniform
rule on that particular topic for national unity. Application of the personal laws on a given topic may be seen by some groups as crucial to
their existence as religious or cultural entities, whereas on a different
topic, no such importance is attached to the personal law. At the same
time, having different laws on one topic may pose a substantial threat
to national unity or well-being, whereas on another it does not. In an
attempt to contribute to a particularized inquiry of this sort, in the
present paper I examine the law of religious and charitable endowments,
one of the topics traditionally governed by the personal laws, although,
as we shall see, not only by the personal laws.[1]

Questions Relating to the Personal Laws Generally

It is unnecessary to recite the well-known history of the decision by the
British at the beginning of colonial rule to apply the personal laws in

respect to certain topics, namely, "inheritance, marriage and caste and other religious usages and institutions."[2] The list of topics varied for the courts of the East India Company and the Supreme Courts established by royal charter in Bombay, Calcutta, and Madras.[3] The commitment to apply the personal laws to the listed topics was maintained throughout the colonial period in a series of regulations, acts of Parliament, court charters, and acts of Indian legislatures,[4] and independent India has continued the practice.

Religious and charitable endowments have from a very early date been recognized to be a topic to which the personal laws should be applied, either because it is a listed topic—under the Regulation of 1772, endowments might be considered a "religious usage or institution" and in some cases to involve "inheritance"—or because a direction to act in accordance with "justice, equity and good conscience," introduced into the regulations governing the Company's courts, required it.[5]

If originally it was envisaged that only the personal laws of the Muslims and Hindus would be applied, once the complexity of Indian society came to be appreciated, the laws and customs of other ethnic and religious groups were also applied.[6] This, of course, raised the question of what sort of group would be recognized, what sort of relationship among persons would be required to justify enforcing a group's laws or customs. Among groups lying along a spectrum between the purely contractual (usually referred to as voluntary associations) and the purely ascriptive (groups not constituted by their members' choices), which ones would qualify to have their laws enforced? If a convert would become subject to the law of the group to which he converts,[7] this suggested that the laws of voluntary associations would be enforced. At the same time, a certain comprehensiveness of relationship might be required, so that although a group constituted on the basis of race, religion, and language would have its laws or customs recognized, a group constituted on a more limited basis might not. For a group's law to be recognized, must the group be of a certain size? In some cases it is suggested that even a single family may be a cognizable group.[8] Is it required that the group have existed for a certain length of time?

Even if there is a cognizable group, does it have the sort of law, custom, or usage that warrants recognition? What must be the status of the norms in the life of the group? A group may have a body of law that is fundamental to its life, but this law does not address a particular matter, for instance religious and charitable endowments. If it is clear that both Hindu and Muslim laws speak to this topic, it is not clear, for example, that Christians have a law on the subject. What if, as might be true of Roman Catholics but not of Muslims and Hindus, a group's

law includes a method within the group for obtaining authoritative determinations of legal or factual questions? Will the state defer to this
authority? The cases seem to suggest that it will not.[9]

Assuming there is a cognizable group and that the group has a law
on the topic in issue, interesting and difficult questions arise as to the
circumstances under which this law should be applied. Sometimes the
question is one of a choice between the laws of two different cognizable
groups. Although each group's law has an answer to the question of
what law should be applied in the circumstances, and these answers may
be relevant to how the case should be decided, in the final analysis a
decision must be based on the state's own policy, not on that embodied
in either of the relevant personal laws. The choice of law question may
take the form of determining whether a person is indeed a "member"
of a particular cognizable group or whether he has ceased being a member and "converted" to another group, with the consequence that the
law of the second group is applicable.

The choice of law question may vary from topic to topic, so that even
though the same individual is involved, the Hindu law may apply for the
purpose of marriage and divorce, but the Muslim law for the purpose
of succession. The Supreme Court of India addressed such a situation
in *Sarla Mudgal v. Union of India*.[10] A man and a woman, both Hindus,
married under Hindu law. The husband then converted to Islam, and
without obtaining a divorce, married a second woman, a Muslim. The
question presented to the Court was whether the second marriage was
valid. The Court held that it was not. In reaching its decision, the Court
focused largely on the terms of the Hindu Marriage Act,[11] under which
the Hindu couple had married, the nature of the husband's undertaking
at that time, and the Hindu wife's interests and expectations. The
Court cited earlier cases that supported its position, but ignored or
overruled other cases in which the convert's interest in being able to
change his religion and live in accordance with his new beliefs was
stressed.[12] In focusing exclusively on the Hindu wife's interest, the
Court ignored the consequences to the Muslim woman and to the children of the second marriage, if there were any. The outcome of the case,
it seems, would have been no different if before marrying the Muslim
woman, the husband had divorced his Hindu wife under Muslim law, or
if under the Muslim law his conversion had effected an automatic divorce from her.[13] If at the time of the first marriage the Hindu wife had
agreed that the husband could take a second wife, that might have in-
validated the first marriage itself, leaving the way open for a second
marriage, under Muslim law, to the Muslim woman.

In the case of succession, it is usually held that the applicable law is that of the group to which the decedent belonged at the time of his death.[14] If the decedent had been converted, his property would be distributed in accordance with the law of his new religion. This situation does not differ entirely from a case involving marriage and divorce, such as *Sarla Mudgal,* for in both situations the interests of third persons may be affected and their expectations disappointed: relatives who would have inherited under the personal law of the old religion may receive nothing under the law of the new.

For endowments, in most cases it seems to be assumed that the governing law will be that of the group to which the creator of the endowment belonged, in the case of an inter vivos endowment at the time it was created, in the case of a testamentary endowment at the time of the creator's death. But, as we shall see, when an endowment involves members of more than one community, there are other possibilities.

The choice of law question in the context of the personal laws may be compared with problems that arise in other contexts. For instance, when it is a question of entitlement to a reserved place in government service or an educational institution, and membership in a particular group is required to qualify for the place, the policy of the law providing for the reservation might not be satisfied simply by following a classification made for the purpose of the personal laws, or a particular topic of the personal laws. Thus a person may be a member of a group and subject to its laws for the purpose of determining succession to property, but not for the purpose of a reservation.[15]

Matters Not to Be Considered

Before considering the different personal laws on the subject of endowments, it is necessary to sketch the limits of the present inquiry. It will be limited to the question of the validity of endowments and will not extend to other important questions. By validity I mean whether the endowment or dedication of property to a particular purpose will be recognized and supported by the state against adverse claims, such as those of the heirs or creditors of the creator of the endowment. The question of validity presents the issue of whether tying up resources in perpetuity for the purpose selected by the creator will be allowed in the face of other values and interests, for instance the interest of the living in having the power to direct resources to objects they deem important. In addition, validity may include questions regarding the formalities that must be observed in creating an endowment, the degree of permissible uncertainty in the objects to be supported, whether the creator of an endowment may retain a power of revocation, and finally, whether a will that creates an endowment must have been executed a certain time before death.[16]

Not included in the question of validity and not investigated in the present article is the rich and complex topic of the administrative and judicial regulation and enforcement of endowments, a topic that has both constitutional and non-constitutional dimensions. These regulatory laws are not addressed to validity, at least not directly; they assume validity and then speak to the matters of making sure that an endowment is put to its intended purpose, whether the original purpose may be fulfilled or it is justified to put the resources to another purpose (*cy pres*), and who should manage the endowment. Among the more important regulatory laws (regarding which there are a great number of judicial decisions) are the Central Wakf Act,[17] state laws governing Hindu religious and charitable endowments—that of Tamil Nadu being the oldest and best known[18]—the Bombay Public Trusts Act,[19] and Section 92 of the Code of Civil Procedure,[20] which concerns judicial rather than administrative supervision. At the same time, it would be misleading to suggest that a sharp line can be drawn between validity and regulation, between substance and procedure. Aspects of regulatory law often affect substantive rights and the extent to which the purposes of an endowment will be realized. Compare, for instance, the Bombay Public Trusts Act, under which uniform regulations are applied to all endowments regardless of religion, and the Tamil Nadu Hindu Religious and Charitable Endowments Act, whose enforcement rests in the hands of Hindus and necessarily reflects the values and attitudes of those appointed to office regarding that religion, including its true form and content.[21] But with these indirect effects on substantive law and validity, the present article is not concerned.

Likewise excluded from consideration are questions relating to the jurisdiction of particular administrative bodies. For example, under the Wakf Act, an endowment is a "wakf" for purposes of the jurisdiction of the wakf board only if it was created by a person professing Islam and for a purpose deemed pious under Muslim law.[22] Thus a mosque erected by a Hindu, although used by Muslims, may not be a wakf for purposes of the jurisdiction of the board,[23] although it may be a valid wakf nonetheless as an endowment under Muslim law.[24] Some cases hold that an endowment that will benefit both Muslims and non-Muslims is not under the jurisdiction of the wakf board;[25] if it is a religious endowment, it will not even be valid, whereas if it is a secular endowment, it may be.[26] The policy of the Wakf Act may be to centralize under the control of Muslims regulation of endowments created by Muslims and intended to benefit Muslims, whereas the policy underlying determinations of validity may be more broadly to assure protection by some means of properties that will be used to honor God and serve purposes considered pious under Muslim law. The question of regulatory jurisdiction also arises in connection with Hindu endowments.[27] Is the object of the endowment a "temple" for purposes of the Hindu religious endowments act? Here again the act may embody a policy of uniform supervision of properties dedicated to Hinduism, understood in a certain sense, in order that this religion may be integrated and strengthened. But even though an endowment does not fall within this policy, either because of the religion of the founder or the use to which the property is to be put, still it may be a valid endowment under Hindu law. In those states such as Maharashtra, where, rather than religion-specific agencies, there is a single administrative agency that deals with all public religious and charitable endowments, the policy determining the jurisdiction of this agency may indicate a different coverage than does the law governing validity. There may be valid religious or charitable endowments that do not fall under the jurisdiction of the agency and which are amenable to supervision only through judicial proceedings under Section 92 of the Code of Civil Procedure.

Finally, also not to be considered in the present article are tax questions. Sometimes the categories of "religious" and "charitable" when used in the tax laws have the same meaning as in the law relating to validity, so that, for example, if an endowment is valid under Hindu law it is exempt from taxation. But this is not always the case. In certain instances the tax laws embody a policy regarding what should be supported by means of tax exemption that may differ from the policy regarding what should be supported by protection from competing claims of heirs and creditors, or other claims by the state than for taxes.[28] However, the facts and analysis in some tax cases cast light on the question of validity,[29] as will be seen in some of the authorities discussed below.

The Validity of Endowments under the Personal Laws

Turning now to the law governing the validity of endowments, note may be taken of some of the differences among the personal laws. Under some of these laws, a particular purpose is a valid object of an endowment, while under others the same purpose is not. For example, under Hindu law an endowment to maintain and perform worship at the tomb or samadhi of an ordinary person is not valid;[30] under Muslim law it may be.[31] Under Muslim law an endowment that supports the rituals of another religion is not valid;[32] it is not clear whether the same is true under Hindu law.[33] Under Muslim law, an endowment of a mosque is valid only if the mosque is open to all Muslims;[34] under Hindu law it may be possible to restrict access to a temple to a particular class of Hindus.[35] Under Muslim law, a dedication of property to the support of the settlor's descendants from generation to generation with the income going to the poor or some other pious object if and when the family line runs out—a family wakf—is valid,[36] whereas under Hindu law it is not, nor under English law. Doubtless the influence of English law led the Privy Council to hold Muslim family wakfs invalid,[37] but the decision was overruled by legislation.[38] If under Hindu law it is not permissible to create a perpetual family endowment, it is permissible to dedicate property to a deity and constitute the settlor's descendants shebaits, in which capacity they may receive income to sustain them in the discharge of their functions.[39] Is it permissible under Hindu Law to endow property for the purpose of enabling devotees to live near their guru?[40] Different concepts resting upon different religious beliefs explain these differences among the personal laws regarding what may and what may not be supported by a perpetual endowment.[41] These concepts do not necessarily correspond to the English law notion of charity. Nor do the concepts of the different personal laws necessarily correspond to the English law notion of a charitable trust, under which a distinction is drawn between legal and equitable title. But both the Hindu and Muslim laws of endowments do contain ideas concerning fiduciary obligation. The formalities required to bring an endowment into existence differ from one personal law to another. Finally, the retention of a power to revoke may be invalid under one personal law, but not under another.

Earlier, in discussing the choice of law problem, it was stated that most authorities seem to assume that in the case of endowments, the law of the settlor should govern the question of validity. This view would be consistent with the approach taken to ordinary inter vivos gifts and testamentary bequests. Thus in the case of a Hindu who creates an endowment to support a mosque, the court would look exclusively to Hindu law to determine the validity of the endowment, even though the beneficiaries would be Muslims. Under Hindu law it is clear that a Hindu can create an endowment that confers secular benefits on non-Hindus,[42] but whether he can create an endowment that supports non-Hindu worship may not be so clear.[43] Possibly if the settlor holds some form of secular power or office, the endowment will be valid; it may be the settlor's dharma to support the religion of his subjects, whatever it may be.[44]

But why look to the law of the settlor rather than to the law of the beneficiaries? If enjoyment of the benefit would be permissible under the law of those who would receive it, why should the state not uphold the endowment? If in the case of marriage and divorce the interest of the unconverted spouse should be taken into account—as it was in *Sarla Mudgal*[45]—or in the case of succession the interests of those who would have benefited if the decedent had not converted are taken into account, why in the case of endowments should the interest of the intended beneficiaries not be given some consideration? It appears that under Muslim law, the endowment of a mosque by a Hindu is permissible if it is allowed by Hindu law.[46] But we are considering the situation where the endowment is prohibited by the law of the settlor, but allowed by the law of the beneficiaries in spite of this prohibition.[47] The answer would seem to lie in the state's policy in enforcing a system of personal laws. Is it to empower a settlor to accomplish his wishes within the limits permitted by his group's law, or is it to enable beneficiaries to receive benefits within the limits permitted by their group's law?[48]

If we are not dealing with endowments that cross community lines, but only with endowments limited to a single community, the case is clear. A donor who is a member of a community that has a personal law that addresses the subject of endowments cannot have the validity of his endowment judged under the law of another community. So long as the donor remains a member of the first community—the difficult question of whether he is a member has already been touched upon—if he may be advantaged by its law, so also he is limited by it. To allow him to create an endowment that would be valid under the law of another community can find no support in the rationale for a regime of personal laws. This explains the case referred to earlier of the widow who was not allowed to create an endowment to provide for worship at the tomb of her deceased husband. If she had been a Muslim, perhaps she could have, and as the court indicated, if she had been a member of a new group that observed this custom, the result might have been different. Similarly, a Hindu cannot create a family wakf. He must become a Muslim to do that. If he becomes a Muslim, he may be able to have the benefit of the Muslim law of endowments with an ease that he would not find if he attempted to divorce his Hindu wife or take a second wife. On the other hand, if a Muslim becomes a Hindu, he will not lose the power to create a family wakf if in converting to Hinduism he becomes a member of a class of Hindus that retains this feature of Muslim law.

The Indian Law of Religious and Charitable Endowments

It is now time to turn to what I shall call the Indian law of religious and charitable endowments. It is with hesitation that I use this term for fear of implying that such law has a claim to applicability superior to that of the personal laws, for such an implication is not necessarily correct. But the implication might be even stronger if I spoke of the general law of endowments, or the territorial law of endowments. Perhaps one could speak of the special law of endowments by way of analogy to the Special Marriage Act.[49] But that law's applicability depends on its being chosen by the parties, whereas, as will be seen, such is not necessarily the case with the Indian law of endowments. This law should not be referred to as a "personal law," for although its applicability may depend upon some fact about the settlor as a person—for instance that he took some action in India or was domiciled there—it does not depend upon his membership in a group or community, which ordinarily is implied by the term personal law.

One striking feature of this law is that, except for a qualification shortly to be noted regarding the Indian Succession Act[50] and possibly the Transfer of Property Act,[51] it is the product exclusively of judicial decisions.[52] Its only legislative foundation is the injunction to the courts, earlier noted, to act in accordance with "Equity, Justice and Good Conscience" or "Justice and Right." Although the law being referred to is not the English law of charitable trusts, it probably is similar in its general outlines, including the purposes that may be endowed. The fact that this body of law, to the extent that it exists, is predominantly if not entirely the product of judicial activity is particularly remarkable in view of the extensive legislation that has been adopted on closely related matters.[53]

The whole line of regulatory laws mentioned earlier, beginning with the Bengal and Madras Regulations of 1810 and 1817,[54] down to legislation of the mid-twentieth century, did not create a substantive law of religious and charitable endowments. It assumed the existence of substantive laws—the personal laws and possibly the Indian law of endowments that I am now discussing—and then erected regulatory systems to enforce endowments found valid under these laws.[55] The Bengal and Madras Regulations, and a later regulation in Bombay as well,[56] entrusted enforcement to the Boards of Revenue. The Religious Endowments Act of 1863,[57] still in effect in a few parts of India,[58] eliminated this jurisdiction and transferred supervisory power to committees of members of the religious or ethnic groups concerned with the endowments. Later Section 92 of the Civil Procedure Code[59] gave the courts jurisdiction over complaints brought by interested parties, with the consent of the Advocate General,[60] against these committees and other managers of endowments. In the early twentieth century, although no new administrative agencies were created to replicate the Boards of Revenue of the early nineteenth, the way was eased for interested persons to pursue civil actions for misconduct by committees and trus-tees, especially by increasing discovery opportunities.[61] A full return to nineteenth-century conditions was made when new administrative agencies dedicated to vigorous enforcement programs were created. This began with the Bombay Public Trusts Registration Act of 1935,[62] which as already remarked covered a range of public endowments in-stead of just those of a particular religion, followed by similar legisla-tion in other provinces. After independence, this development gained further strength. But, as already observed, in none of the legislation enacted in the course of this long story of regulation, de-regulation and re-regulation, was a substantive Indian law of religious and charitable endowments created or proclaimed.[63]

The Societies Registration Act of 1860[64] also would appear not to have created a substantive law of endowments. That act simply provides a mechanism for identifying endowments whose validity rests upon some other basis.[65] Furthermore, if a trust or other endowment already exists, registration does not have the effect of enabling the trustees to escape duties already imposed on them.[66] Although the text of the act speaks only of charitable societies, the Supreme Court has recently held that purely religious endowments may be registered as well.[67]

The Indian Trusts Act[68] does not create a substantive law of religious and charitable endowments. Its preamble refers to the purpose of the act as defining the law of private trusts, and Section 1 states that nothing in the act "affects the rules of Mohamedan Law as to *waqf* or the mu-tual relations of the members of an undivided family as determined by customary or personal law, or applies to public or private religious or charitable endowments. . . ." Before the act, under the direction to ob-serve justice, equity, and good conscience, the courts had developed a law of private trusts influenced by the English law of trusts, applicable when the personal laws did not apply. The Indian Trusts Act displaced this judge-created law and also probably certain aspects of the personal laws, other than Muslim law, that approximated the act's notion of a trust. But none of this touched religious and charitable endowments, which remained creatures of the personal laws or of what I have been calling the judicially created Indian law of religious and charitable en-dowments.[69]

An argument can be made that the Indian Succession Act[70] creates a statutory basis for religious and charitable endowments in the case of those established by will. Section 59 provides that anyone covered by the act (which does not include Muslims) may dispose of his property by will. If he may dispose of his property by will for any lawful pur-pose, perhaps this includes creating religious and charitable endowments. The provision in Section 118 of the act, which invalidates bequests to religious or charitable uses made by a will executed less than twelve months before death by a person who had a near relative living, seems to strengthen this inference. But even if the act does empower testators to create endowments, it is completely silent as to the extent of this power and the permissible objects of an endowment, so that it is necessary to go to the case law to determine the answers to these questions. In Section 114 of the act, there is a rule against perpetuities, and nowhere in the act is to be found an exception to this rule for religious and charitable endowments. Thus if it is held that Section 59 gives a power to create an endowment, an exception to the rule against perpetuities in Section 114 must be read into the act. It might be simpler to take the position that the omission of an expressed exception means that religious and charitable endowments were not intended to be affected by the act at all,[71] and that the power to create them, even by will, remains where it was before the act, in the personal laws and the judicially created Indian law of endowments.

If the Indian Succession Act could provide a statutory basis for an Indian law of testamentary endowments, so might the Transfer of Property Act[72] provide a basis for inter vivos endowments. Section 5 of that act defines a transfer of property as "an act by which a living person conveys property, in present or in future, to one or more other living persons, or to himself, and one or more other living persons. . . ." Section 122 states that a "'Gift' is the transfer of certain existing moveable or immoveable property made voluntarily and without consideration by one person, called the donor, to another, called the donee, and accepted by or on behalf of the donee." Though both these sections are stated as definitions, they could be read to create a power to make gifts, and if so a power to make gifts constituting endowments. But *Controller of Estate Duty v. Bhagwandas Velji Joshi*[73] says broadly that a charitable trust cannot be a gift under the Transfer of Property Act. If endowments do come under the act, they run into the rule against perpetuities contained in Section 14. But in this case the act, in Section 18, provides an exception for a transfer "for the benefit of the public in the advancement of religion, knowledge, commerce, health, safety, or any other object beneficial to mankind." As in the case of the Indian Succession Act, if these sections provide a statutory basis for the Indian law of inter vivos endowments, there is little guidance in the act as to the purposes for which endowments may be created, so the answer to this question must be found in the case law.

In some situations it seems clear that endowments cannot comfortably be located under the Transfer of Property Act. In *Suleman Isubji*

Dadabhai v. Naranbhai Dahyabhai,[74] the court held that when a property owner created a charitable trust, making himself the sole trustee, the endowment did not fall under the act. Either there was no transfer within the meaning of the act, or if there was a transfer, it was not a gift. But a valid endowment was created nonetheless.

What of inter vivos endowments under the personal laws? Are they within the Transfer of Property Act? It seems clear that in certain cases they are not. In *Shri Ram Kishan Mission v. Dogar Singh,*[75] where a Hindu created an endowment for a dharmashala, the court held that the endowment did not fall under the act because it was not a transfer to a living person, but to the dharmashala as a juridical entity. Likewise it is clear that a dedication to a Hindu deity is not within the act.[76] The act expressly excepts rules of Muslim law from its coverage.[77] Other personal laws that pertain to ordinary gifts rather than endowments, for instance the Hindu law of gifts, appear to have been replaced by the requirements of the act. Apparently it was thought that there was no significant difference between the Hindu law on this subject and the provisions of the act.[78]

Finally, the Companies Act[79] needs to be considered in its relation to the validity of endowments. Section 25 of that act provides: A company may be formed "for promoting commerce, art, science, religion, charity or any other useful object" as long as it is not authorized to distribute dividends to members and any profits must be devoted to the stated purposes of the company. Numerous charities, as well as some religious organizations, have taken advantage of this provision.[80] In discussing the Societies Registration Act, it was suggested that that act did not create a substantive law of endowments, or that if it did, it did not establish a test of validity independent of those found in the personal laws and the judicially created Indian law of endowments. The same view can be taken of Section 25 of the Companies Act: it simply provides for the creation of an incorporated entity with certain characteristics and powers, to carry out purposes independently approved by other laws. Although the language in Section 25 is broad, under this view the act does not create any substantive law of endowments. If to the contrary it is held that the act does create an independent test regarding permissible corporate purposes, taking into account the wording of the section and the broad powers conferred on government to authorize and revoke registration and to lay down conditions for a license, then indeed the Companies Act has brought into existence a substantive law of endowments, not to the exclusion of the judicially created Indian law of endowments, but alongside it. To date there are no cases that cast light on, much less settle, this question. Of course, if an endowment already exists under one of the personal laws or under the Indian law of endowments, its property may not be diverted from its original purposes to other religious or charitable purposes simply by the device of incorporation, any more than this can be done by registering under the Societies Registration Act. Incorporation under the Companies Act creates difficult jurisdictional questions regarding the Company Law Board and other administrative agencies that exist specifically to regulate charities.[81] It has been held that incorporation does not preclude a civil suit under Section 92 of the Code of Civil Procedure by a person interested in the charity.[82]

What evidence is there that a judicially created Indian law of endowments exists? The answer is that there does not exist conclusive evidence, but that strongly suggestive dictum can be found in a number of cases.

In *State of Uttar Pradesh v. Bansi Dhar,*[83] a case in which a settlor who had attempted to found a hospital tried to get his money back because the government failed to go ahead with the project (the validity of the endowment was not in question), the Supreme Court, through Krishna Iyer, J., observed:

> The law of gifts is, in a sense, a collection of equitable principles but crystallized for India under the British from Anglo-Saxon jurisprudence. . . . [W]hile these provisions [of the Indian Trusts Act] proprio vigore do not apply [because of the express exclusion from that act of charitable trusts], certainly there is a common area of legal principles which covers all trusts, private and public. . . . Care must certainly be exercised not to import by analogy what is not germane to the general law of trusts, but we need have no inhibitions in administering the law by invoking the universal rules of equity and good conscience. . . . [84]

In *Nawab Zain Yar Jung v. Director of Endowments,*[85] the question was whether an endowment created by the Nizam of Hyderabad was a wakf within the meaning of the Wakf Act, and so under the jurisdiction of the wakf board. The Supreme Court held that it was not. So far as validity under Muslim law was concerned, perhaps it was a wakf nevertheless, but Gajendragadkar, J. characterized it as "a trust of a public and religious character" and "a secular comprehensive public charitable trust."[86]

In *Kassimiah Charities Rajagiri v. Madras State Wakf Bd.,*[87] another case in which the question was whether the endowment was a wakf under the jurisdiction of the wakf board, the court contrasted wakfs with trusts "as recognized by modern jurisprudence" and trusts "under the ordinary law."[88] In some cases there may be a stretching of the personal law under the influence of the "modern" or "ordinary" law in order to find the validity of a religious or charitable endowment.[89]

The judicially created Indian law of endowments, assuming it exists, is neither in its concepts nor in the purposes it deems valid exactly the same as the English law of religious and charitable trusts,[90] just as the Indian Trusts Act is not exactly the same as the English law of ordinary trusts. Like the Trusts Act, the Indian law of endowments may not follow the English law in dividing title between legal and equitable. It was recognized that the English prohibition against trusts for superstitious uses, i.e., to support a religion other than the established religion, should not be applied in India.[91] Under Indian law, a trust can be established to support any religion the settlor wishes, provided it is not illegal. If the settlor had a connection with a particular religion, this fact might cast light on the object he intended to benefit, but such evidential use of a religious connection must be distinguished from using it to classify the settlor as a member of a community for purposes of applying its personal law.[92] Under the Indian law of religious and charitable endowments, a person can establish an endowment for purposes limited only by the policy of that law itself, not by the policy of any personal law. The Indian law may hold valid purposes prohibited by a particular personal law, or it may hold invalid purposes permitted by a personal law. The family wakf is an example: it is valid under Muslim law, but almost certainly invalid under the Indian law of endowments. The Indian law of endowments is not necessarily more or less liberal in the purposes it approves than are the personal laws; it is simply different.

When Does the Indian Law of Religious and Charitable Endowments Apply?

If there is good reason to believe that there does exist a judicially created Indian law of religious and charitable endowments, in what circumstances does it apply? Certainly it applies when the settlor does not belong to any group that has a personal law, or belongs to a group that has a personal law but that law does not cover the subject of endowments. An example would be the Parsis, who have no personal law on the subject.[93] Their law, such as it is, is neutral on the matter. Justice, equity, and good conscience probably require that persons in this class be able to make dedications for religious and charitable purposes.[94] Such a power would complement their power to make ordinary gifts under the Transfer of Property Act, ordinary testamentary dispositions under the Indian Succession Act, and to create private trusts under the Trusts Act. But what about persons who do have a personal law that speaks to the subject of endowments? May they in addition create endowments under the Indian law of endowments? This is a question to which at present there is no certain answer.

In *Saraswati Ammal v. Rajagopal Ammal*,[95] the case referred to earlier, in which a widow dedicated property to support rituals to be performed at the tomb of her deceased husband, the Supreme Court held that under its reading of the shastras, the specified rituals could gain no merit and so the endowment was invalid under Hindu law.[96] As noted earlier, the Court suggested that if there had been a showing that the widow's belief in the effectiveness of the rituals was shared by a substantial number of people—in my terminology a cognizable group—the result might have been different. But what about the possibility of sustaining the widow's dedication on the basis of the Indian law of endowments? Under that law, would not the validity of her dedication have been recognized, even if her beliefs were peculiar to herself alone? There is no mention of this possibility in the Court's judgment; perhaps it was not suggested by counsel.

If in *Saraswati Ammal* there is an implication that the Indian law of endowments is unavailable to one who has a personal law on the subject, in *State of Uttar Pradesh v. Bansi Dhar*,[97] a case already referred to, there is a strong implication to the contrary, although in dictum. The settlor in that case, a Hindu it would seem although his religion is not expressly stated, attempted to found a hospital for women, probably intended to be open to women of all communities. The case involved bureaucratic inefficiency and the failure of the government to go ahead with the project, even though it had accepted the settlor's money. The validity of the endowment was not in issue, but almost certainly the object would have been approved under Hindu law. Nevertheless, in the course of his judgment, Krishna Iyer, J. made an observation, earlier quoted in part, which could be read to suggest another basis:

> [Although the Indian Trusts Act does not apply to religious and charitable endowments], certainly there is a common area of legal principles which covers all trusts, private and public, and merely because they find a place in the Trusts Act, they cannot become 'untouchable' where public trusts are involved. Care must certainly be exercised not to import by analogy what is not germane to the general law of trusts, but we need have no inhibitions in administering the law by invoking the universal rules of equity and good conscience. . . .[98]

In a number of cases in which the jurisdiction of a regulatory body was in issue rather than the validity of an endowment, there is indirect support for the notion that an individual who has a personal law may in addition create an endowment under the Indian law of endowments. What is unclear in these cases is whether the Indian law of endowments will apply because the settlor has chosen it in place of his personal law, or simply because the Indian law of endowments would sustain the validity of the endowment, regardless of what law the settlor intended should apply. Under the first approach, the settlor is given the power to decide what law will apply; under the second the endowment will be sustained if it would be valid under either law, independently of the settlor's legal intention. At the same time perhaps it can be inferred from the fact that the settlor attempted to create the endowment, that he would wish to have applied any law that would sustain its validity.

In *Kassimiah Charities Rajagiri v. Madras State Wakf Bd.*,[99] already cited, the settlor, a Muslim, established a school that was to be open to both Muslims and non-Muslims, but with a reserved quota for Muslims, and a dispensary open to all. The court held that the charity did not fall under the jurisdiction of the wakf board because the beneficiaries included non-Muslims. Nevertheless, it stated in dictum that the endowment was valid under Muslim law. As mentioned earlier, although Muslim law may prohibit Muslims from supporting the worship of other religions, it does not forbid them from providing secular benefits, such as education and health care, to all persons. The court went on in dictum to observe: "[I]t is not essential that a Muslim in order to found a charity should necessarily adopt the form of a wakf. He may for example convey his properties to trustees in trust for the particular charitable objects specified by him."[100]

In *Nawab Zain Yar Jung v. Director of Endowments*,[101] as in *Kassimiah*, the issue was whether the endowment came under the jurisdiction of the wakf board. The endowment had been created by the Nizam of Hyderabad to support education and health, to relieve poverty, and to benefit religious institutions without distinction of caste or creed. The trustees included non-Muslims. In a judgment by Gajendragadkar, J., the Supreme Court held that under these circumstances the endowment was not a wakf within the jurisdiction of the wakf board. Validity was not in issue, but the Court seemed to think that the endowment would not be valid under Muslim law because it provided support for non-Muslim religious institutions. The fact that the donor was the former ruler of the state apparently made no difference in this regard. However, the Court also suggested that even though the endowment was not valid under Muslim law, it was valid nonetheless: "[A]mongst the objects for which the trust was created were included other charitable purposes without distinction of religion, caste or creed, and that obviously transgresses the limits prescribed by the requirements of a valid wakf."[102]

What the donor wanted, the Court thought, was "a trust for charitable purposes and objects in a secular and comprehensive sense."[103] The Court approved the breadth of the Nizam's purpose by remarking that his intention was "to help public charity in the best sense of the words. . . ."[104]

In *Ramanasramam v. Commissioner of Hindu Religious and Charitable Endowments*,[105] it was the Madras Commissioner of Hindu Endowments who sought to assert regulatory jurisdiction. The question was whether the property was a temple within the meaning of the Madras act. The court held that it was not because of the following characteristics: The property contained the tomb of Maharshi's mother, which had become an object of devotion and where puja and archanas were performed. (There was a linga near the tomb, but it was a sign of the goodness of the mother, not an object of devotion.) Also buried on the property were the remains of a cow, a monkey, and a dog. The teachings of Maharshi, whose samadhi and statue were nearby, transcended Hinduism, the court thought. It was not clear who had founded the endowment, whether Maharshi himself or others, but in any case those who managed it, used it, and contributed to it included non-Hindus. In these circumstances, the court held, the commissioner had no jurisdiction. It was not the purpose of the Madras act, the court noted, to bring under the jurisdiction of the commissioner those of religions other than Hinduism.[106] The validity of the endowment was not in issue, but it is fairly clear that the court thought the endowment was not valid under Hindu law. It is doubtful that those involved with the endowment constituted a cognizable group with its own personal law. Instead, one of the judgments in the case remarked simply that the endowment was a "religious public trust."[107] If some of the settlors were Hindus and remained Hindus notwithstanding their connection to Maharshi and his mother, the court's dictum must mean that an individual with a personal law of endowments may also create an endowment under the Indian law of endowments.[108]

Finally to be considered is *Controller of Estate Duty v. Bhagwandas Velji Joshi*,[109] which involved an inter vivos endowment to support needy brahmins of a certain caste, and under certain circumstances other Hindus. The deed of trust included a power of revocation in the settlor. The issue in the case was whether the property that had been dedicated should be included in the settlor's estate for tax purposes. Under the tax law, it was required to be included if a power of revocation existed at the time of the settlor's death. The court seems to have held that the Indian law of endowments was applicable with regard to the validity of the endowment.

Whether a Hindu, by a charitable act, wishes to dedicate property to God or not depends not upon whether he is a Hindu. It depends upon the mode which he selects for appropriating the property. If he selects a Hindu ceremonial mode, then he is dedicating property to God. If he selects a mode known to ordinary law, he is not dedicating property to God but he is executing a deed of trust and thereby creating a public charitable trust governed by the ordinary law of the land which would apply in this case both to Hindus and non-Hindus alike.

Marandas, having created all the above trusts by regular deeds of trust and not according to the ceremonies required under the Hindu law, the validity so far as the form of these deeds of trust is concerned cannot be judged by the principles of Hindu law but by the principles of the law of trusts.[110]

It would appear that the court embraced the first of the two possible approaches suggested above to the question of when the Indian law of endowments will apply: it will apply when the settlor has chosen that it should apply. At the same time, it cannot be said that the court is entirely clear about what action taken by the settlor constituted the making of that choice. Nor is it certain that the court is right that under Hindu law a particular ceremony is required.[111] In any case, after determining that the Indian law of endowments was applicable, the court went on to say that under that law, the inclusion of a power of revocation did not destroy validity.

Several aspects of the case may weaken the apparent holding, or perhaps even render it dictum. The court did not consider it necessary to inquire what the result would be under Hindu law. There was some basis for believing that under Hindu law, if a power of revocation is included in a dedication, the power is void and the endowment remains valid.[112] Thus the result might have been the same whether Hindu law or the Indian law of endowments governed the question of validity, so that there would have been no need to decide which law applied, and therefore no need to decide whether the Indian law of endowments was available to the settlor. Secondly, the court held that as a result of the settlor's merging administration of his trust with that of trusts created by others, he surrendered the power of revocation, so that it did not exist at the time of his death. The court could have interpreted the merger of administration as having the effect of creating a new trust, a trust that did not include a power of revocation, so that it was unnecessary to decide whether the original trust, which contained a power of revocation, was valid and what law governed that question.

Surprisingly, the court said that under the circumstances of the case, although the question of the effect of retaining a power of revocation was governed by the Indian law of endowments, the question of validity so far as concerns the permissible objects of the endowment would be governed by Hindu law, because the settlor was a Hindu.[113] It gave no reason why these different aspects of validity should be governed by different laws. In any case, the statement is dictum because the validity of the endowment so far as concerns permissible objects was not in dispute.

Would the language of some of the regulations, acts, and charters calling for the application of the personal laws[114] pose an obstacle to viewing the Indian law of endowments as an alternative to an individual's personal law? Does it make a difference whether the topic of endowments falls within the list of those topics to which government committed itself to apply the personal laws, or has had the personal laws applied to it in an exercise of discretion under the instruction to uphold justice, equity, and good conscience? Even if endowments come within the mandatory list, could this status be viewed as designed, in the case of endowments, only to have the effect of empowering a settlor, and not to prevent him from having the benefit of a law other than his personal law?

The conclusion to be drawn from the authorities just discussed must be that it is not settled whether a donor who has a personal law will have the validity of his endowment judged exclusively under that law, or whether he may choose between his personal law and the Indian law of endowments, or whether his endowment will be held valid if it would be valid under either law. The same uncertainty exists regarding the Companies Act: Can a non-profit corporation be created to carry out any purpose approved by the Indian law of endowments, or perhaps an even broader range of purposes, by an individual with a personal law, or can such a person only create a corporation to carry out purposes that are valid under his personal law? It is not surprising that uncertainty exists on these questions in view of the social policy that is at stake.

What is at stake may be appreciated by placing the question of endowments alongside other issues. We have already described the effect of conversion. If a person is converted and becomes a member of a new group, he loses the personal law of the old group and becomes subject to the law of the new group. The new group's law may have some features in common with that of the old group, but it is nevertheless the law of the new group that controls: it is not a situation in which an individual member of one group may invoke the law of another group, nor is it a situation in which the law of whichever group is favorable to a particular result may be invoked. One qualification must be made to this statement: by reason of the Caste Disabilities Removal Act,[115] the convert does not forfeit inheritance rights under his original personal law. If a person leaves his old group, but does not become a member of another cognizable group, he has no personal law and his property and relationships are governed by whatever laws of the state apply in such circumstances, for instance the Indian Succession Act. In the case of endowments, as we have seen, such a person almost certainly has the benefit and limitations of the Indian law of endowments.

In regard to ordinary inter vivos gifts that are not endowments, it is probable that their validity for all donors except Muslims is to be judged exclusively under the Transfer of Property Act. In the case of Muslims, perhaps the same question is presented as with endowments: if a Muslim's gift is invalid under Muslim law, can it be upheld under the gift provisions of the Transfer of Property Act? The act says only that it does not affect Muslim law, not that a Muslim may not make a gift under the act.

If a person marries under the Special Marriage Act,[116] the validity of the marriage and its incidents, as well as divorce, are governed exclusively by that act and not by any personal law.[117] It does not matter that he belongs to a cognizable group or converts to one after marrying.[118] Furthermore, except in the case of two Hindus marrying under the act, succession to the parties' property is governed by the Indian Succession Act,[119] not by any personal law. If two Hindus marry, succession continues to be governed by the Hindu Succession Act.[120]

Leaving aside situations involving conversion and the Special Marriage Act, if a couple marries under a personal law and the marriage is not valid under that law, it is clear that it cannot be saved by reference to another personal law, or to any claimed Indian law of marriage. In regard to testamentary succession, if a class of persons is excluded from the coverage of the Indian Succession Act, for instance Muslims,[121] and so remitted to their personal law, if a member of such a group executes a will that is invalid under his personal law, it cannot be saved by reference back to the Indian Succession Act. As to intestate succession, if a personal law is applicable, certainly recourse cannot be had to the Indian Succession Act, which might yield a conflicting designation of heirs. Thus from the perspective of certain other parts of the system, it may appear unusual to uphold under the judge-created Indian law of endowments an endowment determined to be invalid under a settlor's own personal law.

On the other hand, if in respect to endowments a person may choose between his personal law and the Indian law of endowments, or have an endowment upheld if it is valid under either, this bears a resemblance to procedures provided in the Shari'at Act[122] and the Muslim Women (Protection of Rights on Divorce) Act.[123] Under the former, a Muslim is permitted to choose to have the Shari'at applied to him and his descendants on certain topics otherwise exempt from the Shari'at (adoption, wills, and legacies),[124] while under the latter a Muslim couple may choose to be governed by the Code of Criminal Procedure on the subject of maintenance, rather than by the provisions of the act itself,[125] provisions that Parliament believed reflected Muslim law.

As already indicated, one way of viewing the suggestion contained in the endowment cases reviewed above is that an individual who has a personal law may elect between it and the Indian law of endowments. Election could be made before the creation of the endowment, a procedure similar to that provided by the Shari'at Act and the Special Marriage Act, or in the act of creating the endowment. Legal consequences would follow the settlor's choice of law. Evidence of the choice might be found in the objects sought to be advanced by the endowment or in extrinsic circumstances. Evidence of the choice also might be found in the characteristics of the settlor's personal law. Determining the settlor's choice of law would be different, however, from determining on the basis of available evidence, under whichever law is applicable, the objects the settlor intended to benefit. Whatever the result of the investigation into the settlor's choice of law, the law chosen would be the only law to govern the issue of validity. Perhaps it should be assumed under this analysis that if the settlor chooses the Indian law of endowments, he does not ipso facto exclude himself from his cognizable group and its personal law in respect to other topics, and perhaps even in regard to endowments could choose that personal law for another transaction.[126]

As earlier observed, another way of viewing the suggestion in the cases reviewed is that an endowment will be held valid if it would be valid under either the settlor's personal law or the Indian law of endowments. Under this analysis, the emphasis is not on the settlor's choice of law, but on finding a legal basis for upholding the validity of what he has done, which surely would be consonant with his wishes. This approach would expand settlors' power of disposition. It would favor validity over invalidity—it does not hold an endowment invalid if it would be invalid under either the personal law or the Indian law. It attaches importance to the judgment embodied in the Indian law of endowments as to when an endowment should be held valid—this law is the only recognized alternative to the settlor's personal law. It attaches importance to the settlor's connection with his group—that group's law is the only recognized alternative to the Indian law. Although the settlor's membership in the group is honored—for instance a Muslim because he is a Muslim may create a family wakf—the connection is weakened because the settlor can create an endowment not permitted by the law of his group—for instance, a Muslim can create an endowment to support non-Muslim worship. It is the looseness of this bond compared to what it would be if the donor were confined to his personal law that points up the fundamental policy issue the courts have yet to resolve clearly.[127] Of course, a factor in favor of permitting a loosening of the bond is that in many other areas of the law—contracts and torts for instance—the personal law has been completely replaced by the law of the state, and in the matters just referred to—the Shari'at Act, the Muslim Women Act, and the Special Marriage Act—the parties have been given the power to determine what law will apply.

A fully enforced system of personal laws might limit a member of a group to the law of his group and not even allow him to escape from the group and so change his law in that way. From early in the colonial period, this approach was rejected by the British because it conflicted with their notions of individual freedom, especially in matters of religion. A less thoroughgoing system might limit an individual to the law of the group so long as he remains a member of the group, but allow him to leave the group and so change the applicable law. Of course, as a practical matter, it may be costly for an individual to leave his group. A third way, which we have just been considering, would allow a member of a group, while continuing to be a member of the group, to choose to be governed by the law of the state instead of by the law of the group. A fourth way would be to uphold the validity of an individual's action if it would be valid under either the law of his group or under the law of the state. Finally, a system under which only one law is recognized—the law of the state, a uniform civil law—entirely rejects any idea of personal laws. In most Western countries, of course, this is the position in regard to all the topics, including endowments, that in India are governed by the personal laws in certain circumstances.

The alternatives listed reflect different values being attached to groups and individuals' connections with them. We have been considering in relation to endowments the second, third, and fourth alternatives: judging validity exclusively by the law of the group; allowing a settlor to choose the applicable law; and upholding an endowment if it would be valid under either the law of the group or the Indian law of endowments. The second approach reflects a high value being placed upon maintaining the group and the individual's connection with it, perhaps on the view that this ultimately is conducive to individual welfare and does not significantly jeopardize national unity. The third and fourth alternatives reflect less value being attached to maintaining the group and the individual's connection with it, and increased concern with national unity. The fifth alternative—a uniform code—of course entirely rejects the desirability of maintaining groups by enforcing their laws on the traditional topics of the personal laws. Among the judicial pronouncements that have been considered in this article, perhaps the one that points most strongly toward a uniform rule on endowments is that of the Supreme Court in *Nawab Zain Yar Jung v. Director of Endowments*,[128] where the Court went so far as to suggest that it favored endowments not restricted to supporting particular religions.[129]

We now may be in a position to summarize the foregoing discussion and take an overview of the whole subject of the validity of endowments. Under one sort of personal law regime, an individual can create an endowment only if it is validated by the law of the group to which he belongs. Theoretically, if he is dissatisfied with limitations imposed by that law, he may leave the group and join another with a more liberal law of endowments, if it will have him. If he leaves the group but does not become a member of another cognizable group, he cannot create an endowment, because on this topic, only the laws of cognizable groups are recognized; there is no state law of endowments.[130] Under this regime, the state attaches great importance to maintaining groups and individuals' connections with them, though not so much as under a regime that does not allow an individual to leave his group. Furthermore, regarding the question of maintaining the free disposition of wealth and not allowing it to be tied up indefinitely against the desirability of encouraging dedications of property to uses deemed particularly important, the state is willing to leave this question entirely to non-governmental groups.

As we have seen, it is certain that Indian law as it presently exists does not correspond to the system just described. Not only may an individual leave a group, he may leave it and, even though he does not become a member of another group, he may create endowments. He may do so under what I have been calling the Indian law of endowments. This law does embody a judgment by the state regarding the relative importance of maintaining the free disposition of wealth and encouraging individuals to dedicate property to the support of religion or other projects considered of special importance. An individual is both empowered and limited by this state judgment. That there is such an Indian law of endowments and that it is available to those who do not have a personal law on the subject of endowments is fairly clear, even though the content of that law has been little developed. This body of law probably approximates the English law of charitable trusts. The interesting question, as we have seen, is whether this law is also available to persons who are members of groups that have their own law of endowments. If it is, this is because the state, although it continues to attach importance to maintaining cognizable groups and individuals' connections with them, attaches less importance to these matters than under the system previously described; the state also attaches importance to individual freedom by giving a person the advantage of both his personal law and the Indian law of endowments.

What would be the meaning of taking the next step and moving to a uniform law of endowments? It should be understood that in accord with the limits set to this article, I am only speaking of a uniform law on the validity of endowments, not a uniform regulatory law.[131] This step would mean that the state now attaches such a value to wealth not being tied up indefinitely that it reserves to itself the decision as to what purposes are sufficient to justify a perpetuity. Doubtless such a uniform law would give wide room for individual choice, but it might disapprove purposes presently permitted under one or another of the personal laws. In addition, the adoption of a uniform law probably would reflect a judgment that even though group identities may be important, there is no persuasive argument for maintaining them through enforcement of their laws, at least on this particular topic, or even that it is not important to maintain these groups at all because they are deleterious to individual welfare and national unity. One element that might be seen as undermining national unity is resentment on the part of those who are not allowed to set up endowments of certain kinds—a family endowment for instance—toward those whose personal law permits them to do so. Of course, theoretically, under a regime of personal laws, there is no barrier to any group developing its own law to allow its members to create endowments for any purpose they desire, although it may take a long time for a change to be recognized by the state as applicable personal law.

In the area of endowments, we are not confronted with features of the personal laws that clash violently with the values of modern reformers and which are seen by some as inherently wrong, as in the area of marriage and divorce. Polygamy, divorce by talaq, the absence of a duty to provide maintenance, unequal treatment of men and women, possibly the inability to adopt, are examples where there is such a clash. Few would contend that endowments to support a settlor's descendants, with a dedication to the poor or some other pious object if the line runs out, should be placed in this category. Thus the desirability of a uniform law of endowments cannot be based upon its usefulness as a means to get rid of alleged evils of this sort. Rather, the argument for a uniform law of endowments must rest either on the belief, already referred to, that the importance of not tying up wealth is sufficiently great that the state must reserve to itself alone the judgment as to when this may be done, or on the belief that different laws for different groups is objectionable because it threatens national unity, even though the various personal laws on endowments do not contain any features that are seriously objectionable. This latter argument may see no difference among the various topics of the personal laws—between marriage and divorce and endowments for instance—so far as the desirability of a uniform law is concerned.

If value is attached to maintaining groups, group identity, and individuals' connections with groups, is there any difference between endowments and other topics of the personal laws, for instance marriage and divorce, in respect to this value? Probably generalization is impossible and what is needed is empirical study of different groups. It may be that with one group, ideas of marriage and divorce are powerfully expressive of the deepest meaning of the community, whereas with another, the permanent dedication of wealth to certain purposes serves that purpose.

If a uniform law on marriage and divorce were adopted, there is no doubt that its content would reflect closely the Hindu Marriage Act or the Special Marriage Act. These laws embody modern Western ideas. Some old-fashioned, albeit Western views in the Indian Divorce Act would have to give way. But the real burden of change would fall upon the Muslims. Because the Hindus already have had modern ideas applied to them in the Hindu Marriage Act, a uniform act would be seen primarily as aimed at the Muslims, and perhaps as an imposition of Hindu law on them. This would not be true in the case of a uniform law of endowments. On this subject, Hindus and Muslims would be more or less on an equal footing. Each group has continued to enjoy its personal law, as interpreted by the courts, relatively untouched by legislation.[132] The uniform law enacted would be the Indian law of endowments I have referred to, a law approximating the English law of charitable trusts. This law as the only law determining the validity of endowments could bring significant changes for some groups, and some of these changes might be seen as greatly undermining group identity. The uniform law would certainly abolish family wakfs, and earlier resistance to such a step demonstrates the importance of this particular institution to Muslims.[133] But at least a uniform law on endowments

John H. Mansfield

94

probably would not be seen as an effort by one group to impose its will on another, but rather as a law generally favoring individual choice over group solidarity.

Notes

1. Constitutional questions presented by the system of personal laws are not discussed in this article because I have considered them elsewhere. Mansfield, "The Personal Laws or a Uniform Civil Code?" in *Religion and Law in Independent India* 139 (R. D. Baird, ed., 1993). I would add to the authorities cited there, A. M. Battacharjee, *Hindu Law and the Constitution* (2nd ed. 1994), and *Muslim Law and the Constitution* (2nd ed. 1994). Some of the High Courts continue to assault the notion that different personal laws do not constitute prohibited discrimination on ground of religion in violation of Articles 14 and 15 of the Constitution (e.g., Preman v. Union of India, A.I.R. 1999 Ker. 93 [Division Bench (D.B.)] [holding § 118 of the Indian Succession Act, 39 of 1925 (originally 10 of 1865), which requires bequests to religion or charity, except by Hindus and Muslims, to be made by a will executed more than twelve months before death, impermissibly discriminates on the ground of religion in violation of Articles 14 and 15]), but so far the Supreme Court, while continuing to grumble about Parliament's failure to act on the direction contained in Article 44 to "endeavour to secure for the citizens a uniform civil code," continues to repel these assaults. For a recent example, see Ahmedabad Women Action Group v. Union of India, A.I.R. 1997 2d Supp. S.C. 3614 (Full Bench [F.B.]) (rejecting writ petition attacking constitutionality of provisions of personal laws that draw distinctions on grounds of religion, ethnicity, and sex).

   The respondent in a recent case before the Supreme Court, Abid Hatim Merchant v. Janab Salebhai Saheb Shaifuddin, 2000 S.C.C. 113, argued that a nineteenth-century endowment restricted in certain respects to members of a particular religious community (the Dawoodi Boras), should be reformed under the doctrine of *cy pres*, "so as to make it [the state] a true secular State, as professed in the Constitution," id. at 116, but the Court was allowed to escape deciding the question because of a settlement between the parties on which judgment was entered. (The Court's judgment was modified in minor respects by a subsequent order.) A question not addressed in my earlier discussion, which relates particularly to endowments, is whether it would be permissible under Articles 25 and 26 of the Constitution to forbid all perpetuities, even those established for religious purposes. See as possibly relevant, Article 26: "[e]very religious denomination or section thereof should have the right—(a) to establish and maintain institutions for religious and charitable purposes. . . ."

2. See G. C. Rankin, *Background to Indian Law* 2 (1946), quoting Article 27

of Regulation 2 of 1772, applicable to the courts of the East India Company.

3. Section 17 of the Act of Parliament of 1781, 21 Geo. 3, c. 70, called for the Supreme Court to apply the laws of the Hindus and Muslims in all cases involving "inheritance and succession to land rent and goods and all matters of contract and dealing between party and party." See G. C. Rankin, *Background to Indian Law* 9–10 (1946).

4. See, e.g., Government of India Act, 26 Geo. 5, c. 2, § 298 (2) (b) (1935).

5. See G. C. Rankin, *Background to Indian Law* 2 (1946). Justice, equity, and good conscience were found to require that the Muslim law of gifts be applied. See G. C. Rankin, *Background to Indian Law* 10 (1946). Endowments can be created either inter vivos or by will. In the former case they may in certain circumstances be part of the law of gifts, in the latter case part of the law of testamentary succession. See pp. 78–80 infra.

   For an example of the application of the personal laws to an unlisted topic, see Mt. Bibi Maniran v. Mohammad Ishaque, A.I.R. 1963 Pat. 229, 232–33 (D.B.) (Muslim law of gifts applicable by reason of justice, equity, and good conscience), and for a general discussion of the difference between the situations of the company courts and the Supreme Courts regarding unlisted topics, see Jacob v. Jacob, I.L.R. [1944] 2 Cal. 201, 214–15, 217 (Single Judge [S.J.]) (suit on separation agreement between Jewish husband and wife).

6. Abraham v. Abraham, 1863 9 Moore's Ind. App. 195, 239–49 (P.C.) (East Indians, i.e., Christians of mixed race); Jacob v. Jacob, I.L.R. [1944] 2 Cal. 201 (S.J.) (Jews); State of Rajasthan v. Sajjanlal Panjawat, A.I.R. 1975 S.C. 706, 713, 719 (F.B.) (Jains); Rev. Fr. Farcisus Mascarenhas v. State of Bombay, 1935 62 Bom. L.R. 790, 794 (S.J.) ("The Canon Law is not the law of the land. It can at best be regarded as the personal law applicable to those professing the Roman Catholic faith."). See also G. C. Rankin, *Background to Indian Law* 11 (1946); D. Pearl, *Interpersonal Conflict of Laws in India, Pakistan and Bangladesh* 34 n. 31 (1981); Tier, *The Evolution of Personal Laws in India and Sudan*, 26 J. Ind. L. Inst. 445, 449 n. 27, 462–63 (1984).

7. Abraham v. Abraham, 1863 9 Moore's Ind. App. 195 (P.C.) (Hindus who became Native Christians and then East Indians subject to law of East Indians).

8. See, e.g., Abraham v. Abraham, 1863 9 Moore's Ind. App. 195, 240 (P.C.).

9. E.g., Sally Joseph v. Baby Thomas, A.I.R. 1999 Ker. 66, 69 (D.B.) (court interpreting provision of Indian Divorce Act, 4 of 1869, authorizing decree of nullity on ground of fraud, as requiring reference to the personal law of the parties—the Canon Law of the Roman Catholic Church—but refusing to give weight to determination by church tribunal).

10. (1995) 3 S.C.C. 635 (D.B.).

11. 25 of 1955.

12. E.g., Ayesha Bibi v. Subodh Chandra Chakrabarti, I.L.R. [1945] 2 Cal. 405 (S.J.); Attorney-Gen. of Ceylon v. Reid, [1965] 1 All. E.R. 812 (P.C.), over-ruled, Abeysundere v. Abeysundere, Law & Society Trust Review, Jan. 1998, p. 3 (Sup. Ct. Sri Lanka, 1997).

13. If a couple marries under the Special Marriage Act, 43 of 1954, or has their marriage registered under that act, if one of the spouses changes his or her religion, divorce will still have to take place under that act before there can be another marriage.

14. E.g., Abraham v. Abraham, 1863 9 Moore's Ind.App. 195 (P.C.) (decedent East Indian at time of death, although earlier Native Christian).

15. See M. Galanter, *Competing Equalities* 301, 304 (1984).

16. Section 118 of the Indian Succession Act, discussed in Preman v. Union of India, A.I.R. 1999 Ker. 93 (D.B.), has such a requirement. See note 1 supra.

17. 43 of 1995, replacing 29 of 1954.

18. Tamil Nadu Hindu Religious and Charitable Endowments Act, 22 of 1959, originating in the Madras Acts 1 of 1925 and 2 of 1927. See C. Mudaliar, *State and Religious Endowments in Madra*s (1976).

19. 39 of 1950.

20. 5 of 1908.

21. An extreme example of procedure affecting substance is the Punjab Sikh Gurdwaras Act, 8 of 1925, in which the Punjab legislature created an entire politico-ecclesiastical structure to govern Sikh gurdwaras. See generally K. Singh, *Law of Religious Institutions: Sikh Gurdwaras* (1989); K. Singh, *Sikh Gurdwaras Legislation* (1991). See also Pannalal Bansilal Pitti v. State of A.P., (1996) 2 S.C.C. 498, 510 (D.B.) (not unconstitutional to enact regulatory regime limited to Hindu endowments).

22. Wakf Act, § 3.

23. See Punjab Wakf Bd. v. Gram Sabha, Basoli, A.I.R. 1986 H.P. 23 (D.B.) (no showing shrine dedicated by Muslim; no showing used for purpose recognized by Muslim law as pious); C. S. Peeran Sahib v. Madras State Wakf Bd., I.L.R. [1968] 1 Mad. 89 (D.B.) (dedication not by person professing Islam). However, a board does have jurisdiction over what are called "deemed wakfs," wakfs created by Muslims but contributed to by non-Muslims. Wakf Act, § 104.

24. See C. S. Peeran Sahib v. Madras State Wakf Bd., I.L.R. [1968] 1 Mad. 89, 96 (D.B.). But see H. S. Gour, *The Hindu Code* 659 (6th ed. 1992).

25. Kassimiah Charities Rajagiri v. Madras State Wakf Bd., A.I.R. 1964 Mad. 18 (D.B.); Nawab Zain Yar Jung v. Director of Endowments, A.I.R. 1963 S.C. 985, 991 (Constitution Bench (C.B.)); Karnataka State Bd. of Wakfs v. Mohamed Nazeer Ahmed, A.I.R. 1982 Kant. 309 (D.B.).

26. Kassimiah Charities Rajagiri v. Madras State Wakf Bd., A.I.R. 1964 Mad. 18 (D.B.) (dictum). See also P. Diwan, *Law of Endowments* 145 (1992);

G. C. Kozlowski, *Muslim Endowments and Society in British India* 14 (1985) (endowment of Christian church invalid; of hospital for Muslims and Christians valid).

27. E.g., Ramanasramam v. Comm'r for Hindu Religious and Charitable Endowments, A.I.R. 1961 Mad. 265 (D.B.).

28. See P. Diwan, *Law of Endowments* x–xi (1992).

29. See, e.g., Commissioner of Wealth-Tax v. Trustees of J. P. Pardiwala Charity Trust, I.L.R. [1965] Bom. 1040, 1044–45 (D.B.); Controller of Estate Duty v. Usha Kumar, A.I.R. 1980 S.C. 312 (D.B.).

30. Saraswathi Ammal v. Rajagopal Ammal, A.I.R. 1953 S.C. 491 (F.B.); Malayammal v. A. Malayalam Pillai, 1991 Supp. (2) S.C.C. 579 (F.B.).

31. But see G. C. Kozlowski, *Muslim Endowments and Society in British India* 144 (1985).

32. Kassimiah Charities Rajagiri v. Madras State Wakf Bd., A.I.R. 1964 Mad. 18, 21 (D.B.); P. Diwan, *Law of Endowments* 145 (1992).

33. See 1 H. S. Gour, *Hindu Code* 659 (6th ed. 1992).

34. Gupte & Dighe, *Bombay Public Trusts Act, 1950,* 153 (1995); P. Diwan, *Law of Endowments* 149 (1992).

35. So far as validity is concerned, leaving aside the effect of temple-entry legislation. See, e.g., Yagnapurushdasji v. Muldas, A.I.R. 1966 S.C. 119 (C.B.).

36. See, e.g., Trustees of Sahebzadi Oalia Kulsum Trust v. Controller of Estate Duty, (1998) 6 S.C.C. 267 (D.B.).

37. Abul Fata Mahomed Ishak v. Russomoy Dhur Chowdhry, (1894) 22 L.R.I.A. 76 (P.C.).

38. Mussalman Wakf Validating Act, 6 of 1913.

39. See J. D. M. Derrett, "The Reform of Religious Endowments," in *South Asian Politics and Religion* 311, 331 (D. E. Smith ed., 1966). Cf. Shiromani Gurudwara Prabandhak Committee v. Shri Som Nath Dass, A.I.R. 2000 S.C. 1421 (D.B.), (when Guru Granth Sahib installed in gurudwara, it becomes a "juristic person" and valid dedications may be made to it by Sikhs).

40. An issue implicated in, but not decided by, Shanti Sarup v. Radhaswami Satsang Sabha, A.I.R. 1969 All. 248 (D.B.). The purposes of a Sikh gurudwara cover a wide range of what would usually be considered secular needs, in addition to devotional ones. See K. Singh, *Law of Religious Institutions: Sikh Gurudwaras* 100 (1989).

41. In Shiromani Gurudwara Prabandhak Committee v. Shri Som Nath Dass, A.I.R. 2000 S.C. 1421 (D.B.), cited in n. 39 supra, holding that the Guru Granth Sahib is a juristic person and can receive valid gifts, the Court stated: "It is not necessary for 'Guru Granth Sahib' to be declared a juristic person that it should be equated with . . . [a Hindu] idol. Where beliefs and faith of the different religions are different, there is no question of

equating one with another." In this statement the Court appears to recognize a distinct Sikh law of endowments.

42. See Ramachandra Shukla v. Shree Mahadeoji, A.I.R. 1970 S.C. 458 (D.B.) (endowment by Hindu of wrestling ground invalid under Hindu law because wrestling not permissible object, but not suggested invalid because wrestlers included Muslims).

43. Mst. Mundaria v. Rai Shyam Sundar Prasad, A.I.R. 1963 Pat. 98 (D.B.) (gift by Hindu for imambara not valid under Hindu law); Fuzlur Rahaman v. Anath Bandhu Pal, 16 Cal. Wk. Notes 114 (1911) (D.B.) (refusal to enforce contract by Hindu to endow mosque, possibly because invalid under Hindu law).

44. See Venkatusubbarayudu v. Silar Sahib, A.I.R. 1930 Mad. 582, 584–85 (D.B.) (property given by Hindu rajah to provide lighting in mosque; validity not decided, but suggested significant donor a ruler). Cf. Kolandai v. Gnanavaram, A.I.R. 1944 Mad. 156 (S.J.) (manager of Hindu joint family has power to bind coparceners by gift to Catholic church). But see Mst. Mundaria v. Rai Shyam Sundar Prasad, A.I.R. 1963 Pat. 98 (D.B.) (gift by Hindu for imambara not valid under Hindu law).

45. (1995) 3 S.C.C. 635 (D.B.), p. 71 supra.

46. See Mst. Mundaria v. Rai Shyam Sundar Prasad, A.I.R. 1963 Pat. 98, 99 (D.B.). In Fuzlur Rahaman v. Anath Bandhu Pal, 16 Cal. Wk. Notes 114 (1911) (D.B.), it is unclear whether the court's refusal to enforce a promise by a Hindu to endow a mosque is on the ground that such an endowment would be invalid under Hindu law, or on the ground that it would be invalid under Muslim law regardless of the state of Hindu law, or because it would be invalid under Muslim law if it would be invalid under Hindu law, which it would be.

47. For discussions that touch on the question, see C. S. Peeran Sahib v. Madras State Wakf Bd., I.L.R. [1968] 1 Mad. 89, 96 (D.B.); Tamil Nadu Wakf Bd. v. S. Syed Imam Saheb, 1983 Mad. L. J. 299 (D.B.).

48. The Shari'at Act, 26 of 1937, provides: "[I]n all questions regarding . . . gifts, trusts, trust properties and wakfs (other than charities and charitable institutions and charitable and religious endowments), the rule of decision in cases where the parties are Muslims shall be the Muslim Personal Law (Shari'at)." As noted in C. Mohammed Yunus v. Syed Unissa, [1962] 1 S.C.R. 67, 73 (F.B.), Tamil Nadu has eliminated the exemption for endowments. This change presents the question of who are "the parties" for the purpose of deciding whether the Shari'at applies in determining the validity of an endowment?

49. 43 of 1954.

50. 39 of 1925.

51. 4 of 1882.

52. See Krishna Iyer, J. in Commissioner of Income Tax v. Sri Jagannath Jew,

(1976) I.T.R. 9, 18 (S.C.) (D.B.), noting the absence of legislation determining the validity of endowments, which has compelled the courts "to dive into hoary books and vintage case-law to ascertain the current law."

53. E.g., Indian Trusts Act, 2 of 1882; Transfer of Property Act, 4 of 1882; Indian Succession Act, 39 of 1925.

54. Regulation 19 of 1810; Regulation 7 of 1817.

55. See, e.g., T. Mahmood, *Statute Law Relating to Muslims in India* 382–83 (1995) (noting Wakf Act not addressed to substantive law).

56. Regulation 17 of 1827.

57. Act 20 of 1863.

58. Gurdwaras in Bihar are still governed by this act. K. Singh, *Law of Religious Institutions: Sikh Gurdwaras* 61 (1989).

59. 5 of 1908, formerly § 539, inserted by Act 20 of 1877.

60. Under present law by leave of court.

61. Charitable and Religious Trusts Act, 14 of 1920.

62. 25 of 1935, replaced by Bombay Public Trusts Act, 29 of 1950.

63. A qualification to this statement may be necessary so far as concerns the Bombay Public Trusts Act. Section 10 of that act provides that "a public trust shall not be void, only on the ground that the persons or objects for the benefit of whom or which it is created are unascertained or unascertainable." Sections 12 (disposition for religious or charitable purpose not void as public trust because no obligation annexed to hold for benefit of religious or charitable purpose) and 13 (not void on ground only that special object of trust has become impossible or particular institution has ceased to exist) also could be found to affect substantive law.

64. 21 of 1860.

65. It is unclear whether registration under the act should be viewed as bringing a corporation into being. See Shanti Sarup v. Radhaswami Satsang Sabha, A.I.R. 1969 All. 248, 257 (D.B.); Gupte & Dighe, *Bombay Public Trusts Act, 1950*, 201 (1995).

66. Sheikh Abdul Kayum v. Mulla Alibhai, A.I.R. 1963 S.C. 309 (D.B.). See also Shanti Sarup v. Radhaswami Satsang Sabha, A.I.R. 1969 All. 248 (D.B.).

67. Hindu Public v. Rajdhani Puja Samithee, A.I.R. 1999 S.C. 964, 967–68 (D.B.).

68. 2 of 1882.

69. See Tangilla Narasimha Swami v. Mamidi Venkatalingum, I.L.R. [1927] 50 Mad. 687, 695 (F.B.) (gift to deity not within Trusts Act). In Controller of Estate Duty v. Bhagwandas Velji Joshi, (1980) 139 I.T.R. 316, 327 (Bom.) (D.B.), although the court recognized that the Trusts Act does not apply to religious and charitable trusts, it noted that it contains language and concepts relevant to that subject.

70. 39 of 1925.

71. This is the position taken in B. K. Mukherjea, *Hindu Law of Religious and Charitable Trusts* 139 (5th ed. 1983).

72. 4 of 1882.

73. (1980) 139 I.T.R. 316, 326 (Bom.) (F.B.).

74. 1980 21 Guj. L.R. 232, 235–39 (D.B.).

75. A.I.R. 1984 All. 72, 75 (S.J.).

76. Ramalinga Chitti v. Sivachidambara Chetty, I.L.R. [1918] 42 Mad. 440, 442–43 (D.B.); Tangilla Narasimha Swami v. Mamidi Venkatalingum, I.L.R. [1927] 50 Mad. 687, 695 (D.B.).

77. See §§ 2, 129 and Mt. Bibi Maniran v. Mohammad Ishaque, A.I.R. 163 Pat. 229 (D.B.) (act's requirement of registration of gift of immovable property not applicable to Muslim gifts).

78. See 4 H. S. Gour, *Transfer of Property Act*, note to § 129, at 4446 (8th ed. 1974), referring to 1929 amendment; Mulla, *Transfer of Property Act*, 1882, 14 (8th ed. 1995).

79. 1 of 1956.

80. C. Mudaliar, *State and Religious Endowments in Madras* 380 (1976).

81. 81 See Gupte & Dighe, *The Bombay Public Trusts Act, 1950*, 113 (1995) (corporation must register under the Bombay Act).

82. M. Gomathinarayagam Pillai v. Sri Manthramurthi High School Committee, A.I.R. 1963 Mad. 387 (D.B.)

83. A.I.R. 1974 S.C. 1084 (D.B.).

84. Id. at 1089–90.

85. A.I.R. 1963 S.C. 985 (C.B.).

86. A.I.R. 1963 S.C. at 989, 992. See also the reference in *In re Halima Khatun*, I.L.R. [1910] 37 Cal. 870, 874 (S.J.), in connection with endowments, to the "ordinary local law," as contrasted with the personal laws.

87. A.I.R. 1964 Mad. 18 (D.B.).

88. Id. at 20.

89. Cf. id. at 20–23.

90. As pointed out earlier, p. 75 supra, the concepts and values embodied in the different personal laws do not correspond exactly to the English law notion of a charitable trust.

91. Jamshedji Cursetjee Tarachand v. Soonabai, I.L.R. [1907] Bom. 122, 188 (S.J.).

92. See Rev. Fr. Farcisus Mascarenhas v. State of Bombay, 1960 62 Bom. L.R. 790, 794 (D.B.) (suggesting question whether Canon Law of Catholic Church is a personal law or evidence of donors' intent when they gave money to Catholic parish).

93. Commissioner of Income Tax v. Bai Havajbai N. Gamadia, (1948) 16 I.T.R. 109, 115 (Bom.) (D.B.) (common law of England said to govern).

94. Whether they have a constitutional right to do so is a question not explored in this article. See n. 1 supra.

In Malvin v. Gonsalvis, A.I.R. 1999 Ker. 187 (S.J.), the question was whether members of a Roman Catholic Christian community could adopt. In an extremely unclear opinion, the court held that they could. It found that the law of the parties did not forbid adoption and that the Canon Law deferred to the civil law on the matter. The meaning of the decision would appear to be either that the parties' personal law, properly understood, did authorize adoption, or that although it did not, it did not forbid it, and that in these circumstances recourse could be had to a hitherto unknown Indian law of adoption. Does this mean that parties without any personal law also can adopt?

95. A.I.R. 1953 S.C. 491 (F.B.).

96. Reaffirmed in Malayammal v. A. Malayalam Pillai, 1991 Supp. (2) S.C.C. 579 (F.B.).

97. A.I.R. 1974 S.C. 1084 (D.B.), p. 81 supra.

98. Id. at 1090.

99. A.I.R. 1964 Mad. 18 (D.B.), p. 81 supra.

100. A.I.R. 1964 Mad. 18, 20 (D.B.).

101. A.I.R. 1963 S.C. 985 (C.B.).

102. Id. at 991.

103. Id.

104. Id.

105. A.I.R. 1961 Mad. 265 (D.B.).

106. But compare the broad understanding of Hinduism in the interpretation of statutes throwing open Hindu temples to all classes of Hindus, Yagnapurushdasji v. Muldas, A.I.R. 1966 S.C. 119 (C.B.), and in deciding whether a group is part of Hinduism for the purpose of determining whether its institutions are entitled to the protection afforded minority institutions. Bramchari Sidheswar Shai v. State of West Bengal, 1995 (4) SCALE 113, 198 (F.B.).

107. A.I.R. 1961 Mad. at 274.

108. See also Punjab Wakf Bd. v. Gram Sabha, Basoli, A.I.R. 1986 H.P. 23 (D.B.) (shrine erected by Hindus and Muslims at a place where holy man lived and probably died, used by members of both communities with rituals of both, not a wakf under the Wakf Act). In Shanti Sarup v. Radhaswami Satsang Sabha, A.I.R. 1969 All. 248 (D.B.), a case involving an endowment created by the guru of a branch of the Satsanghis, it is left unclear whether the validity of the endowment rested upon Hindu law, the law of the Satsangis as a separate cognizable group, or the Indian law of endowments, and whether if the settlor was a member of one of the first two groups, he could create an endowment under the Indian law of endowments.

109. (1980) 139 I.T.R. 316 (Bom.) (D.B.).

110. Id. at 334.

111. See Shukla v. Shree Mahadeoji, A.I.R. 1970 S.C. 458, 464 (F.B.); 1 H. S. Gour, *Hindu Code* 654–55 (6th ed. 1992); V. K. Varadachari, *The Law of Hindu Religious and Charitable Endowments* 96, 155 (3d ed. 1985); P. Diwan and B. K. Diwan, *Tax Planning for Public and Private Trust in the Conspectus of Tax Laws* 113–14 (1985). In State of Bihar v. Charusila Dasi, A.I.R. 1959 S.C. 1002, 1008 (C.B.), the Court treats the endowment involved there as based on Hindu law, although "the deed of trust in the present case is in the English form and the settlor has transferred the property to trustees."

112. See (1980) 139 I.T.R. at 324.

113. (1980) 139 I.T.R. at 334.

114. See p. 70 supra.

115. 21 of 1850.

116. 43 of 1954.

117. Except the act allows the application of certain customs regarding degrees of prohibited relationships. Section 4(d).

118. Because of the clear language of the act, this would seem to be the result even if the *Sarla Mudgal* case, see p. 71 supra, is wrong and a Hindu husband who becomes a Muslim should be able to take a second wife.

119. Section 21.

120. Special Marriage Act, §21A.

121. See Indian Succession Act, 39 of 1925, § 58 (1).

122. Muslim Personal Law (Shari'at) Application Act, 26 of 1937.

123. 25 of 1986.

124. Section 3c.

125. Section 5.

126. Election under the Shari'at Act may be irrevocable; under the Muslim Women Act, probably election of the Code of Criminal Procedure will pertain only to maintenance of the particular former spouse and in relation only to the particular former marriage.

127. The effect of loosening the bond is sometimes not fully recognized. See the expression of incredulity in Conrad, "The Personal Law Question and Hindu Nationalism," in *Representing Hinduism* 333–34 (V. Dalmia and H. von Stietencron, eds. [1995]), at a Muslim M.P.'s opposition to an Indian adoption bill on the ground that "there should be no such law to give any community, including Muslims, a liberty of abandoning their personal law." The suggestion, if intended, of a more or less inevitable movement from personal laws, to optional personal laws, to uniform law, made almost twenty years ago in D. Pearl, *Interpersonal Conflict of Laws in India, Pakistan and Bangladesh* 6 (1981), might be more open to question today.

128. A.I.R. 1963 S.C. 985, 991 (C.B.), p. 81 supra.

129. See also Rev. Kollandai v. Rev. Gnanavaram, A.I.R. 1944 Mad. 156, 157 (S.J.) (Hindu manager of joint family has power to donate family assets to Catholic Church):

> A fundamental unity underlies all living faiths. If we are to bring in religious and doctrinal differences in measuring pieties and charitable dispositions of people, we do more harm than good. I am not prepared to take a narrow view of the pious or charitable purposes for which a Hindu manager can within moderate and reasonable limits alienate joint family property. . . .

In Abid Hatim Merchant v. Janab Salebhai Shaifuddin, 2000 S.C.C. 113, cited in n. 1 supra, the respondent argued that the Constitution required that endowments not be restricted to members of a particular religious community.

130. This is the present situation in regard to adoption, except for the possibility noted in Malvin v. Gonsalvis, A.I.R. 1999 Ker. 187 (S.J.), cited in n. 94 supra.

131. Central regulatory legislation applicable to all communities was recommended in Report of the Hindu Religious Endowments Comm'n (Government of India, Ministry of Law, 1960–1962), but no action was taken.

132. A possible exception has already been referred to: Sections 10, 12 and 13 of the Bombay Public Trusts Act, n. 63 supra. See also the Punjab Sikh Gurdwaras Act, 8 of 1925, in which tests of orthodoxy are laid down for those who will control the endowments

133. For an account of this story, see G. Kozlowski, *Muslim Endowments and Society in British India* 131–91 (1985). The Privy Council held family wakfs invalid. Abul Fata Mahomed Ishak v. Russomoy Dhur Chowdhry (1894) 22 L.R.I.A. 76 (P.C.). This decision overturned existing family wakfs and prevented their creation in the future. The Mussalman Wakf Validating Act, 6 of 1913, reversed the decision, but was interpreted not to be retroactive. Further legislation, Mussalman Wakf Validating Act, 32 of 1930, then made the first act retroactive, thus validating all family wakfs, past and future. It is unthinkable that if a uniform law of endowments is enacted, it will be retroactive, so as to invalidate existing endowments established under the personal laws.

Five

Personal Law and Reservations
Volition and Religion in Contemporary India

Laura Dudley Jenkins

> State officials can often make their categories stick and
> impose their simplifications, because the state, of all
> institutions, is best equipped to insist on treating people
> according to its schemata.
> —James C. Scott, *Seeing Like a State*[1]

Who is a Hindu? This unanswerable question haunts both personal laws
and reservation laws because these group-based laws and policies neces-
sitate official social classifications. The continuing legal recognition of
personal law in India means that laws specific to different religious and
ethnic communities govern certain legal matters, including marriage,
divorce, maintenance, guardianship, adoption, inheritance, and succession.[2] Reservations are "compensatory discrimination" policies for the
so-called untouchables, officially known as the Scheduled Castes (SCs),
adivasi or Scheduled Tribes (STs), and the Other Backward Classes
(OBCs). These policies reserve a quota of government jobs and, in the
case of SCs and STs, university admissions and legislative seats for
these official categories of disadvantaged citizens.[3]

In India, the most culturally diverse country in the world, the
boundaries of religious and caste categories are often unclear. This is a
frequently classified, yet unclassifiable, society—one reason why personal laws and reservation laws have become among the most controversial issues in India today. In addition to the more frequently discussed
controversies over treating certain groups in society differently, further
dilemmas emerge when people do not fit neatly into the official religious
and caste categories necessitated by such policies. A far-reaching attempt to recognize and deal with cultural and religious differences and
group-based disparities, India's system of reservations and personal laws
often poses political and legal dilemmas.

Personal laws and reservations pose problems for both voluntary
and involuntary groups. In a legal context in which rights and benefits

are tied to group identities, how much room is there for self-defined identity as opposed to state identification, particularly for women, low castes, and other disadvantaged groups? Can they take advantage of these group-based policies if they want to? Can they escape them if they so desire? Ironically, for policies that purport to allow people to be true to their personal laws and to be uplifted beyond the strictures of caste, several recent court decisions squelch individuals who make personal decisions to break free from former identities. Due to rights and benefits associated with different identity claims, courts scrutinize conversions, marriages, and other ways of actively changing one's identity. Are these acts based on conviction or convenience? In the process of rooting out "spurious" claims, which courts have interpreted as something akin to identity fraud, the personal beliefs of the individuals in question are often lost in the effort to monitor official categories. The result is that personal law is anything but personal.

Individuals at times confound neat legal categorization. It is these liminal cases which highlight the dilemmas shared by personal law and reservation law. Issues of personal law enter into the debates over which individuals are eligible for reservations in a number of instances.[4] Recent litigants in court cases over reservation benefits include religious converts as well as the spouses and offspring of intercaste or interreligious marriages or adoptions. Personal law is integrally involved in these decisions about who should benefit from reservations. Recent court cases raise difficult questions: Should a woman who marries a "backward" caste man be eligible for reservations as a member of his community? Should the state recognize or scrutinize the reconversion of a child to the former religion of his parents? In these cases, both reservations and personal laws are involved in ongoing controversies about individual and group identities. These cases pose questions about the degree to which religious and caste identities (and the personal laws associated with them) can be at all "voluntary."

Compared to caste and race, religion, with its escape hatch of conversion, is often assumed to be a more voluntary form of identity. Donald Horowitz, in his broad comparison of types of ethnicity and ethnic conflict, argues that the notion of religion as "voluntary or affiliational, an act of faith" is a "modern Western" notion built on the Reformation, the Enlightenment, and the French Revolution.[5] Yet purportedly modern, Western colonial law tended to freeze the fluidity of prior legal systems and religious boundaries, in part because of assumptions that traditional systems were static to begin with. Thus colonial legal decisions offer prime examples of the denial of religious voluntarism, as converts are either shunted back into their original religious categories for legal purposes or declared "civilly dead." Such examples abound in Gauri Viswanathan's recent book on conversion. Says Viswanathan: "Subordinated to the legal and administrative will of the nation, religion in the modern secular state is less a marker of subjectivity of belief systems than a category of identification."[6] Sadly, the tendency of states to reduce religions to categories of external identification is not limited to colonial situations.

Laws which attach different rights and benefits to different religious "categories" cloud the act of conversion. They imbue what could be an act of personal conviction with official significance inasmuch as conversion can change the civil code to which one is subject and the benefits to which one is entitled. Courts struggle to distinguish between conversions of conviction and conversions of convenience. Another voluntary change of identity, marriage, faces similar legal scrutiny. The implementation of laws that depend on classifying members of society on the basis of religion tends to limit the convertibility of religious identities due to the state's need to distinguish genuine identity shifts from strategic ones. In many cases, this distinction would be difficult to draw even for a mind reader, let alone a court, since motives for conversion can be multiple and complex. State schema cannot completely squelch the fluid and complex nature of identity. Society will not simply be boxed up by the state. As Viswanathan comments, "the intransigent nature of such beliefs, reflecting inchoate ways of life and suggesting a different order of relationality, refuses to be made pliable by determined acts of classification."[7] Religiously liminal cases abound, involving conversions, reconversions, intergenerational reconversions, intermarriages, and offspring of intermarriages. Category-defying acts persist.

This essay builds on a wealth of literature critiquing colonial era classifications of religion and caste in India.[8] One legacy of these practices is the continuity of group-based laws, namely personal laws and reservation laws. Personal law means that certain civil matters are left to the laws of particular religious or ethnic communities. Reservations are a quota system in public employment, higher education, and legislative bodies to uplift certain disadvantaged communities. Through analysis of two recent court decisions, this article focuses on the contemporary intersection of these two bodies of law, the implications of personal law for questions of eligibility for group-based reservations in India. The first case deals with an intercaste marriage and the second with a religious conversion. In each of the cases to follow, three issues will be discussed—the use of personal law in reservations decisions, the official treatment of religion as a voluntary identity, and the implications of these practices for historically disadvantaged citizens.

Intercaste Marriage: Becoming Backward

A recent Supreme Court decision in the case of a Forward Class woman who had married a Backward Class man held that a wife became a member of her husband's caste, but that this did not entitle her to the benefits of reservations as a Backward Class person.[9] Valsamma Paul, described as "Syrian Catholic (a Forward Class)," married a man described as "Latin Catholic (Backward Class Fisherman)." Assuming her husband's status, she applied for and was appointed as a lecturer in the law department of Cochin University, in a position that was reserved for Latin Catholics. Although Christians are not eligible for reservations as Scheduled Castes (a critical point in the second case study on conversions), some Christian communities have been recognized as "Other Backward Classes" and thus are eligible for various central and state level reservations. The questions the court focused on in this case were whether she became a member of her husband's "caste" and, if so, whether she was a "Backward Class" person eligible for that reserved job. They concluded that she did join her husband's caste but did not become officially Backward.

Impact of Personal Law

In spite of the Christian marriage at the center of the case, the decision drew on Hindu law as well to determine that a woman joins her husband's "caste."

> Be it under the Canon law or the Hindu law, on marriage the wife becomes an integral part of her husband's home entitled to equal status of husband as a member of the family. Therefore, the lady, on marriage, becomes a member of the family and thereby she becomes a member of the caste to which she moved.[10]

The decision also drew on several texts on Hindu marriage law in a discussion of intercaste marriage, noting the historical distinction between the "*anuloma* form" in which "a male of superior caste marries a female of inferior caste" and the "*pratiloma* form" in which "a male of inferior caste marries a female of superior caste."[11] The court noted that historically the latter in particular were often considered "invalid," "obsolete," or unacceptable, but that the various current Marriage Acts (Hindu, Christian, and Special) permit some types of intermarriage. The use of the term caste rather than class is particularly striking in this discussion, given the Christian marriage in question and the current controversies over whether there is caste in Christianity and thus a ground for recognizing Scheduled Caste Christians—an issue pertinent to the case on conversion to be discussed next. The other striking aspect of this discussion is that in spite of the court's own recognition that the woman had been "transplanted" to her husband's caste and that her "*pratiloma*" marriage carries even more social stigma than other inter-caste marriages, they did not categorize her as Backward.

The decision dwelled on the diversity of laws regarding marriage and promoted intermarriage as one means toward national integration:

> The institution of marriage is one of the sound social institutions to bring harmony and integration in social fabric. Inter-caste marriages and adoption are two important social institutions through which secularism would find its fruitful and solid base for an egalitarian social order under the constitution. Therefore due recognition should be accorded for social mobility and integration and accordingly its recognition must be upheld as valid.[12]

Legal recognition of the validity of their marriage (which was never really at issue in the case) and verbal endorsement of intermarriage is as far as the court is willing to go; the court denies the woman the practical benefits of becoming Backward via marriage. In the context of the court's abstract discussion of the value of "inter-caste, inter-religion, and inter-region marriages" for "promoting national unity," the decision cited the Special Marriage Act of 1954, which can be used for such marriages, as well as the Hindu Marriage Act of 1955, which, by adopting a quite broad definition of "Hindu," can be used for marriages between Hindus, Buddhists, Jains, and Sikhs.[13]

The court also interpreted the Hindu Adoption and Maintenance Act of 1956 to mean that

> the balance is to be struck to maintain secularism and mobility of castes for national integration ensuring inter-caste marriages or adoption from one caste to another, allowing enough leeway for free mobility and integration of all sections of society as one homogeneous group. At the same time, the Court [is] required to construe the provisions of the Act and the Constitution to reconcile the right of the individual and society's right, namely, social justice.[14]

This is the dilemma the court faced. Mobility and voluntary changes of identity through intercommunity marriage or adoption are to be welcomed, yet the benefits aimed at those born Backward may be diluted by those who become Backward. Moreover, in some cases these marriages and adoptions might be strategic rather than starry-eyed. In addition to various personal laws of marriage, the decision made reference to adoption laws and cases in which Forward Caste members adopted by Backward Class families tried to get into medical school or other reserved positions on the grounds that they had become Backward.[15] Arguing that intercaste and interreligious adoption and marriage are both examples of "voluntary mobility to [a] reserved class," the court rejects identity by volition in favor of identity by birth as the basis for reservations.[16]

Issues of Volition

"Acquisition of the status of Scheduled Caste, etc. by voluntary mobility into these categories would play fraud on the constitution."[17] This statement summarizes the court's skepticism with identity claims not based on birth. Ironically, the very reservation policies which are supposed to get beyond a system of status associated with birth group have resulted in case law holding that birth is the only legitimate basis for an identity claim. The decision discussed the lack of volition that historically characterized the caste system: "Hindu social structure was erected by impregnable walls of separation with graded inequalities between different sections amongst Hindus. Caste became the result of birth and not volition."[18] The court went on to cite the discussion of caste in the famous "Mandal case," in which caste is described as a "socially homogeneous class": "One is born into it. Its membership is involuntary."[19] None of these descriptions of homogeneous and involuntary groups seem to fit the case of a woman acquiring her Backward status through marriage.

Yet, the assumption that caste is unchanging does not hold up under scrutiny. Historians and others studying caste have pointed out examples of voluntary caste mobility, both at the individual level, as in the case at hand, and at the group level, as in caste associations lobbying census commissioners for a higher official status.[20] Even if caste were as static as in the court's descriptions, the court's insistence on defining identity on the basis of one's birth group seems to defeat the purpose of policies designed to get beyond that mentality. Such a stance discourages any voluntary transgressions of community boundaries through intermarriage, since a decision to enter an intercaste marriage can entail social and economic costs yet can bring no benefit under the court's reasoning. A decision to encourage a change in one's caste identity seems more likely to undermine caste discrimination than using any evidence of volition to disqualify a candidate for a reserved post.

Given the stakes associated with identity claims, the court is justifiably wary of some attempts to get reservations. Problematically, however, in this case the court lumps together caste certificate fraud, adoption, and intermarriage, disqualifying all as a basis for receiving reservations because they are all ways of voluntarily being "transplanted" into a group eligible for reservations.[21] Caste certificates are used to prove one's social category in order to benefit from reservations. False certificates are certainly used for the purpose of illegitimately obtaining reserved positions, yet intercaste marriages occur for a variety of other reasons. Although it is possible that people might marry in order to receive reservations, to presume that a woman has become Backward in order to avail herself of a reserved job seems to be overly stringent scrutiny of such marriages. The court in effect accuses her of identity fraud by equating her case with that of someone trying to get a job with a false social status certificate. Note the way they phrase the question they are addressing in this case (the facts of which have nothing to do with certificate forgery or falsification): "The question, therefore, is: Whether a candidate, by marriage, adoption or obtaining a false certificate of social status, would be entitled to an identification as such member of the class for appointment to a [reserved] post?"[22] By including certificate fraud in the list, the conclusion seems foregone. On what basis does the court group such diverse cases together? All are examples of voluntarily taking on a caste status, as opposed to being born into it. After discussing several cases of attempting to get or use false certificates, the court comments: "It would be clear that there are attempts of transplantation of Forward Classes to Backward Classes. Instead of integrated forward march, it is a retrograde reverse march from forward to backward status to claim reservations."[23] To quell this trend toward claiming backwardness, the court does not recognize a personal decision to become Backward.

Implications for Disadvantaged Groups

In this case, a woman's changing definition of her own identity was rejected in favor of an official classification of her on the basis of her birth. Ranajit Guha's critique of statist discourse in historiography is applicable to the discourse of the state itself, in this case, the court:

> The small voice speaking in a certain undertone, as if in pain, is pitted, in this instance, against the privative mode of statist discourse, a commanding voice characteristically male in its "inability to *hear* what the women were saying."[24]

Ironically the decision includes long references to equality for women and even sings the praises of the UN Convention on the Elimination of Discrimination against Women (CEDAW).[25] Yet the court's substantive conclusions are disempowering for women who marry lower status men in several key respects. First, men's identities trump women's. Second, the court confirms all the costs and offers none of the benefits of marrying a man of lower status.

The woman takes on her husband's community and family. If she has children, they will not benefit from her status, but will take on the status of their father. In the case of women marrying "down," the degradation is often worse than if the genders were reversed. Drawing on commentaries on Hindu law, the decision even mentions that, historically, this type of "*pratiloma*" marriage in which "a male of inferior caste marries a female of superior caste" was singled out and considered invalid.[26] Ironically, the erasure of the woman's identity could in theory be the basis for advancement via her new identity and reservations—but no. Although the court recognizes that the woman takes on the caste and status of her husband, any benefits on the basis of this status are denied to her. In an attempt to protect the truly Backward, defined as those Backward by birth, the significant problems facing women who become Backward through marriage are discounted. Although the court sings the praises of intermarriage, rewarding women who transgress their community by marrying down is, it seems, out of the question.

Notably, women's loss of identity upon marriage can disadvantage them whether they marry up or down. In another case, a Backward woman marrying a higher status man was disqualified from the reservations benefits associated with her previous status.[27] The court attempted to protect those who are arguably more disadvantaged due to the cumulative problems they experienced from birth, yet the decision means that women in intercaste marriages and all those who "become" Backward are further disadvantaged.

Conversion: Convenience or Conviction?

Another recent Supreme Court case involved a man, S. Swvigaradoss, whose parents had been of the Adi-Dravida caste, a recognized Scheduled Caste in Tamil Nadu. Prior to his birth, his parents converted to Christianity. Swvigaradoss argued that he converted to Hinduism at age fourteen and became a member of his parents' former caste. Thus, he wanted to be recognized as a Scheduled Caste member, eligible for SC reservations. Since the Scheduled Caste category does not include

Christians, the act of conversion is a key element in this case. The court ruled that regardless of the conversion, "the petitioner was born of Christian parents"[28] and on this basis denied the suit.

Impact of Personal Law

The expansive yet bounded definition of "Hindus" found in Hindu personal laws set the stage for the current boundaries of the Scheduled Caste category. Originally only Hindus could be Scheduled Castes, but the category was gradually expanded to include Sikhs in 1956 and Buddhists in 1990.[29] Demands by some Christians and Muslims to also be included in the SC category have so far been rebuffed. A legal precedent for this broad categorization of religions seen as "Indian" or "Hindu"—as opposed to "foreign"—can be found in the Hindu Marriage Act of 1955. Given these official categorizations of religions and the current religious boundaries of the SC category, in the *Swvigaradoss* case the court concluded that "Christian is not a scheduled caste under the notification issued by the President."[30]

As an example of the politics of religious categorization, several Indian religions, with the notable exceptions of Islam and Christianity, have been subsumed under "Hinduism" for various legal purposes, including personal law. Buddhists, Jains, and Sikhs are considered "Hindus" in the 1955 Hindu Marriage Act. Such an inclusive view of Hinduism is also included in the Constitution itself, with regard to temple entry law, in Article 25 on the freedom of religion. In the clause allowing states to insist on opening Hindu religious institutions to all Hindus, "the reference to Hindus shall be construed as including a reference to persons professing the Sikh, Jaina or Buddhist religion."[31]

This legal categorization has entered into the debate over reservations. For example, an opponent of including Muslims or Christians in the SC category concludes that, "The Scheduled Castes have always been regarded as part of the Hindu community" and "for purposes of social welfare and reform the Hindus include the Sikhs, Jains and Buddhists" only.[32] Hindu nationalists are comfortable with a categorization that increases their numbers yet excludes Muslims; they draw on this broad Hindu category in their own political organization. For example, Aizaz Rizvi, National President of the Bharatiya Janata Party Minority Morcha, says Sikhs are governed by Hindu law and thus not part of the Minority Morcha, which includes only Muslims, Christians, and Zoroastrians.[33] Arguments drawing on religious categories used in Hindu personal law have been useful for those opposed to including Muslims and Christians in the SC category.

In addition to the personal law precedents for categorizing Hinduism, Sikhism, and Buddhism together and excluding Christianity and Islam, personal law comes into play in the *Swvigaradoss* case due to the question of categorizing an individual as a member of one of these religious categories. The legal category of Hinduism, developed to determine the relevant personal law for each case, has been quite inclusive. Marc Galanter notes that for personal law cases, the Hindu category "included all who did not openly renounce it or explicitly accept a hostile religion. The individual could venture as far as he wished on any doctrinal or behavioral borders; the gates would not shut behind him if he did not explicitly adhere to another communion."[34] In personal law cases, converts to Hinduism have been accepted with little question. In fact, it has been difficult in some cases *not* to be included in the Hindu category. In Swvigaradoss's case, however, the stakes associated with SC reservations forced the courts to look more skeptically at his reconversion to Hinduism. The at times contradictory relationship between converts' professed religious identities and the court's categorization of them bears on the issue of volition.

Issues of Volition

One of the challenges to reservations today is the growing demand from some Muslims and Christians to be included in the Scheduled Caste category on the grounds that conversion to these theoretically "caste-free" religions has not and does not spell the end of caste discrimination. Since Scheduled Castes can be Hindus, Sikhs, and Buddhists, some Christians have argued, unsuccessfully so far, that excluding them is religious discrimination.[35] The Swvigaradoss case poses a different argument. Rather than arguing that he should be free to convert to Christianity and that the SC category should be expanded to encompass him as a Christian SC, he argued that his reconversion to Hinduism be recognized so that he could fit into the existing category. Is he a Hindu and a Scheduled Caste member on the basis of his parents' former caste and his own religious conversion?

Characterized by historian Robert Frykenberg as "[t]his soft concept, this jumble of inner contradictions," Hinduism is particularly susceptible to open interpretations and porous boundaries.[36] In a reservations case that necessitated categorizing a Hindu-born convert to Buddhism, the Supreme Court of India commented: "Hinduism is so tolerant and Hindu religious practices so varied and eclectic that one would find it difficult to say whether one is practicing or professing the Hindu religion or not."[37] As mentioned above, there seems to be more scrutiny of conversion in reservations cases due to the possibility that the change of faith is motivated by material rather than spiritual factors. This case poses an additional challenge because the reconversion took place a generation after the conversion; the convert was born a Christian and so never was officially a Scheduled Caste member. Identity at birth became key in the decision, rather than identity choices made later.

In this case as well as in the previous case, decisions made by the individuals in question were discounted and their status at birth became the key to determining their official identity. The court concluded:

> Christian is not a scheduled caste under the notification issued by the President. In view of the admitted position that the petitioner was born of Christian parents and his parents were also converted prior to his birth and no longer remained to be Adi-Dravida, a Scheduled Caste for the purpose of Tirunelveli District in Tamil Nadu as notified by the President, petitioner cannot claim to be a Scheduled Caste.[38]

Individual decisions to become Hindu are more likely to be recognized by the court in personal law cases than in reservations cases, particularly in the ambiguous cases of intergeneration reconversions. In this regard, Galanter has commented:

> For the purposes of at least certain preferences, re-converts to Hinduism who were born in Scheduled Castes are deemed members of the Scheduled Castes. But those born in another religion (e.g., whose fathers were converts) are not treated as members of Scheduled Castes 'whatever may be their original family connections'. *Report of the Commission for Scheduled Castes and Scheduled Tribes*, 1953, p. 132. In the personal law cases, acceptance by the community was a measure of one's success in re-entering Hinduism; here, Hindu birth is the condition of enjoying the privileges devolving on the community.[39]

A Christian by birth, Swvigaradoss's claim to be a Hindu and a Scheduled Caste member in order to benefit from reservations was denied.

Implications for Disadvantaged Groups

Two aspects of this case have an impact on disadvantaged groups: (a) the disqualification of Muslims and Christian converts from SC benefits, and (b) the scrutiny of reconversions to Hinduism. The implications of the legal scrutiny of conversions are not clear-cut. Although troubling at first glance, the power of the state to decide on the validity of personal decisions to convert can also be used to protect the interests of some arguably disadvantaged groups. A striking example is a recent case involving personal law. In the 1995 *Sarla Mudgal* case, several women filed suit against their husbands for converting to Islam in order to marry second wives under Muslim personal law, an example of conversions of convenience. The court held that Hindu husbands can convert to Islam but cannot immediately be considered Muslims for all legal purposes; they need to end their Hindu marriages under Hindu law prior to marrying again, a decision protecting the first wives from polygamy or divorce under Muslim law.[40] This is an empowering decision for women, although the second wives in the case, now officially "invalid," were left in a difficult position. As John Mansfield has observed: "Of course all identities that are received, or even imposed, rather than individually chosen, are not for that reason automatically to be condemned."[41] A husband's individually chosen identity could have serious ramifications for his soon-to-be-ex-wife. Scrutiny of conversions to Islam for remarriage or quick divorces may take away an element of choice and could even be portrayed as a slight to a disadvantaged religious minority, yet it can protect women. In cases involving reservation benefits or personal law rights, trying to draw the line between conversions of conviction and convenience can be extremely difficult, but it may be necessary to protect those who can lose rights or privileges through unmonitored identity claims. In the *Sarla Mudgal* case, by limiting the rights associated with a convert's new religion, the court protected the converter's wife.

The other issue affecting disadvantaged groups is the legal categorization of religions in the definition of the Scheduled Castes. Given the finite opportunities associated with reservations, denying Scheduled Caste status to Christians and Muslims obviously helps disadvantaged Hindus, Sikhs, and Buddhists at the expense of disadvantaged Christians and Muslims. Many have pointed out the continuity of caste even in religious communities doctrinally opposed to caste.[42] On the other hand, Christians and Muslims do have the at least symbolic advantage of their caste-free doctrines, and some, particularly Christians, may benefit from community-based schools. Yet there is wide recognition, even in the courts, of the continuity of caste-based or caste-like discrimination and disadvantages in these religions. (Recall the matter-of-fact discussion of intercaste marriage in the above case involving two Christians!) Given the continuity of caste-based problems in other religions, the provision limiting SC status to Hindus, Sikhs, and Buddhists seems arbitrary at best. Dieter Conrad goes further: "The provision in the Scheduled Castes order can thus be understood only as a sanction against apostasy from Hinduism."[43] He argues that this is part of a worrisome trend toward what he calls legal Hindutva ("hinduness," i.e., a trend toward Hindu communalism).

Conversions in reservations and personal law cases raise similar dilemmas. Who is a Hindu (or a Scheduled Caste)? When should the court recognize conversions? The idea of a judge trying to determine which conversions are "genuine" is troubling, yet doing away with judicial scrutiny of conversions can also have detrimental effects on historically disadvantaged groups.

> [I]t would seem unavoidable that the state have its own criteria regarding what constitutes membership in a group for the purpose of imposition of group law on an individual, although these criteria may make some reference to the attitudes held by the individual and the group.[44]
> —John Mansfield, "The Personal Laws or a Uniform Civil Code?"

In recent court cases, self-defined or voluntary identities have been at odds with official identifications of individuals. To what degree have the courts taken people's attitudes into account when identifying those people for the purpose of group-based laws and policies? In the two cases discussed here, official categories outweighed individual attitudes and, ultimately, will shape those attitudes as people live with the effects of the decisions. James C. Scott comments:

> Categories that may have begun as the artificial inventions of cadastral surveyors, census takers, judges, or police officers can end by becoming categories that organize people's daily experience precisely because they are embedded in state-created institutions that structure that experience.[45]

Religious and caste categories are not simply artificial inventions of the courts or other state institutions, but judges' decisions regarding people's categories can have a major impact on their lives. Although religious and caste categories have not been constructed out of thin air, certainly the way states mediate identities must be taken into account when studying religion and caste in contemporary India. The most striking examples of state-mediated identity can be found in the area of reservations and personal law. State actions in the area of group-based law are not just responses to identity-based groups but contribute to the construction of these groups. The legal definition of "Hindu" in personal law, which is reflected in the categories used for reservations—as well as political organizations—is a case in point. Legal definitions of backwardness may factor into decisions about marriage or conversion.

State mediation of identity limits individual choices regarding identity. At times these limits hurt disadvantaged groups, but in other cases the scrutiny of identity claims protects them. The marriage case and especially the conversion case considered above raise some of the same issues of volition faced by converts grappling with personal law issues. Consider John Mansfield's perceptive comments on the issue of personal law and individual choice:

> The enforcement of the law of a voluntary association finds justification in the choice made by each individual member to accept the law of the association. In the case of ethnic and religious groups in India, however, the application of their laws can seldom be justified on any such voluntaristic basis. Although some consideration of individual choice may occasionally appear—here we touch on the complex subject of conversion—for the most part ascriptive elements are predominant.[46]

Reservations cases go even further away from voluntarism, since evidence of an individual choice to be in a Backward group is grounds to be disqualified from it. By saying certain marriages or conversions may not be used officially to change one's category, the court imposes an artificially static classification. Poor or otherwise disadvantaged groups may have fewer resources to challenge the courts in such cases, but imposed identities are not automatically disempowering for the weakest sections of society. As discussed above, in the *Sarla Mudgal* case, state scrutiny of a convert's decision empowered the convert's wife, who would have been hurt by his individual choice. The issue of the validity of religious conversion was at the heart of this case, a case in which encouraging volition and self-definition of identity could have been disempowering.

One disturbing trend in the state mediation of identities in India is the increasing dominance of the "Hindu" category. In reservations and personal law, Hinduism is at times all-encompassing and at times quite exclusive. In the first case, Hindu marriage laws and even caste rules were referred to in a case involving a Christian marriage. In the second, the convert from Christianity was still declared outside the fold of the increasingly expansive definitions of Hindus and Scheduled Castes. This flexibility in judicial interpretations of who is a Hindu may better reflect the inchoate nature of Hinduism than a more standardized approach; yet if the courts can be flexible in their use of the Hindu category and laws, perhaps people should also be given more options.

Rather than a rigid state definition of identities and corresponding laws, what are some ways, if any, to allow people to choose their own categories for legal purposes? Additional reservations for those who have intercaste marriages could benefit those who break down caste categories. To avoid penalizing women who take on the official status of their higher-caste husbands, the Ministry of Welfare has stated: "Intercaste marriage should be encouraged. To encourage non-SC male youth marrying unemployed SC girls, incentives of jobs outside the reserved quota may be considered."[47] Former government minister Ram Vilas Paswan has advocated such a step:

> In India you can change religion, you can change the party, you can become rich, rich can become poor, but you can't change your caste. So caste is just like a rock. So the only process where the caste system can be weakened is intercaste marriage. . . . If the reservation is made on that ground, intercaste marriage, then slowly, slowly the caste system will be abolished. And if there is not caste then there will be no reservation on the basis of caste.[48]

Paswan shares the assumption that religion is more convertible than caste, but the above cases illustrate the limitations of conversion. Clearly the religious classifications associated with personal laws can also be constricting.

Some have proposed optional personal law as a more flexible scheme than either a state-mandated common civil code or the existing personal laws.[49] The Special Marriage Act of 1954 is a precedent which allows people getting married to decline to categorize themselves or to subject themselves to a particular religious law of marriage. The question remains as to the degree of "choice" individuals, particularly women, actually have when electing a code for their marriage, given social or family pressures. Additional policies to empower women would be necessary to give many of them some a real say over their own identities. Yet if facilitating volition and flexibility in the area of religion is a desirable goal given India's history of cultural pluralism, optional personal and civil codes would offer the most choices. By starting to recognize more such choices, the state might get beyond the current ironies of its group-based policies, such as the preoccupation with birth groups and suspicion of any voluntary identity shifts. Legitimizing choices about identity may put the "personal" back into personal law.

Notes

1. James C. Scott, *Seeing Like a State: How Certain Schemes to Improve the Human Condition Have Failed* (New Haven, Conn.: Yale University Press, 1998), p. 82.

2. See John H. Mansfield, "The Personal Laws or a Uniform Civil Code?" in

Robert D. Baird, ed., *Religion and Law in Independent India* (New Delhi: Manohar, 1993), pp. 139–177.

3. Marc Galanter, *Competing Equalities: Law and the Backward Classes in India* (Delhi: Oxford University Press, 1991).

4. In addition to debates over which individuals are eligible for reservations, the question of which groups are eligible raises difficult questions about religious and caste identity, as some Christians and Muslims argue for official recognition of low caste status or backwardness in these doctrinally caste-free religions. See Galanter, *Competing Equalities,* and Theodore Wright, "A New Demand for Muslim Reservations in India," *Asian Survey* 37, no. 9 (Sept. 1997).

5. Donald Horowitz, *Ethnic Groups in Conflict* (Berkeley: University of California Press, 1985), p. 50.

6. Gauri Viswanathan, *Outside the Fold: Conversion, Modernity, and Belief* (Princeton, N.J.: Princeton University Press, 1998), p. xii.

7. Viswanathan, *Outside the Fold,* p. xii.

8. A few notable examples from this literature include Arjun Appadurai, "Number in the Colonial Imagination," in Carol A. Breckenridge and Peter van der Veer, eds., *Orientalism and the Post-Colonial Predicament* (Philadelphia: University of Pennsylvania Press, 1993); Kristin Bright, "Classified Ethnographies: The Production and Collection of Racial 'Evidence' in India, 1908–1915" (typescript); Bernard Cohn, *Colonialism and Its Forms of Knowledge* (Princeton, N.J.: Princeton University Press, 1996); Thomas Metcalf, *Ideologies of the Raj* (New Delhi: Cambridge University Press, 1995); Gyanendra Pandey, *The Construction of Communalism in Colonial North India* (Delhi: Oxford University Press, 1992).

9. *Valsamma Paul v. Cochin University and Others* (1996), 3 SCC pp. 545–568.

10. *Valsamma Paul v. Cochin University,* p. 546.

11. In this passage, the decision refers to Paras Diwan, *Law of Marriage and Divorce.* Other cited works on Hindu Law include Usha M. Apte, *The Sacrament of Marriage in Hindu Society from Vedic Period to Dharmasastras* (1978), and G. Banerjee, *In Hindu Law of Marriage and Stridhana* (1896).

12. *Valsamma Paul v. Cochin University,* p. 548.

13. *Valsamma Paul v. Cochin University,* p. 547. On the expansive definition of Hindu in the 1955 Hindu Marriage Act, see Dieter Conrad, "The Personal Law Question and Hindu Nationalism," in Vasudha Dalmia and Heinrich von Stietencron, eds., *Representing Hinduism: The Construction of Religious Traditions and National Identity* (New Delhi: Sage, 1995), p. 333.

14. *Valsamma Paul v. Cochin University,* p. 557.

15. *Valsamma Paul v. Cochin University,* p. 557.

16. *Valsamma Paul v. Cochin University,* p. 545.

17. *Valsamma Paul v. Cochin University,* p. 547.

18. *Valsamma Paul v. Cochin University*, p. 554.

19. *Valsamma Paul v. Cochin University*, p. 554, quoting from *Indra Sawhney v. Union of India* (Supreme Court 1992). Known as the "Mandal case," this is a major decision on the legality of reservations for Other Backward Classes. The case was in response to challenges to the Mandal Commission's recommendations to extend reservations to OBCs, recommendations supported by V. P. Singh.

20. Lloyd and Susanne Hoeber Rudolph, *The Modernity of Tradition: Political Development in India* (Chicago: University of Chicago Press, 1967).

21. *Valsamma Paul v. Cochin University*, p. 545.

22. *Valsamma Paul v. Cochin University*, p. 555.

23. *Valsamma Paul v. Cochin University*, p. 556.

24. Ranajit Guha, "The Small Voice of History," in Shahid Amin and Dipesh Chakrabarty, eds., *Subaltern Studies IX* (Delhi: Oxford University Press, 1996), p. 9. The internal quotation is from Vasantha Kannabiran and K. Lalit[h]a, "That Magic Time," in Kumkum Sangari and Suresh Vaid, eds., *Recasting Women* (New Brunswick, N.J.: Rutgers University Press, 1990), pp. 190–223.

25. *Valsamma Paul v. Cochin University*, p. 563. See also p. 549: "The full development of personality and fundamental freedoms and equal participation by women in political, social, economic and cultural life are concomitants for national development, social and family stability and growth—cultural, social and economical. All forms of discrimination on grounds of gender is violative of fundamental freedoms and human rights."

26. *Valsamma Paul v. Cochin University*, p. 560.

27. *Atul Chandra Adhikari v. State of Orissa*, Orissa, 1995.

28. *S. Swvigaradoss v. Zonal Manager, F.C.I.*, (1996) 3 SCC, p. 103.

29. A few specified communities of Sikhs were allowed to benefit prior to the decision to allow any SC professing Sikhism to qualify as an SC.

30. *Swvigaradoss v. Zonal Manager*, p. 103.

31. P. M. Bakshi, *The Constitution of India with Comments and Subject Index* (Delhi: Universal Law Publishing Co., 1996), p. 47.

32. V. S. Deshpande, "What Does SC Mean?" *Hindustan Times*, 28 May 1990.

33. Author's interview with Aizaz Rizvi, All India President of the BJP Minority Morcha (12 September 1996, BJP Central Offices, New Delhi).

34. Galanter, *Competing Equalities*, p. 120.

35. *Soosai v. Union of India*, (1986) AIR SC 733.

36. Robert Frykenberg, "Constructions of Hinduism at the Nexus of History and Religion" *Journal of Interdisciplinary History* 23, no. 3 (Winter 1993): 523.

37. AIR 1975 SC 420, quoted in Galanter, *Competing Equalities*, p. 309.

38. *Swvigaradoss v. Zonal Manager*, p. 103.

39. Galanter, *Competing Equalities*, p. 120 (fn. 60).

40. Viswanathan, *Outside the Fold*, pp. 270–272 (fn. 1). *Sarla Mudgal v. Union of India*, (1995) AIR SC 1531.

41. Mansfield, "The Personal Laws or a Uniform Civil Code?" p. 159.

42. Imtiaz Ahmad, "Ashraf-Ajlaf Dichotomy in Muslim Social Structure in India," *Indian Economic and Social History Review* 3 (1996): 344–50, and Imtiaz Ahmad, ed., *Caste and Social Stratification among Muslims in India* (Delhi: Manohar, 1978). Jose Kananaikil, *Scheduled Caste Converts and Social Disabilities: A Survey of Tamil Nadu* (New Delhi: Indian Social Institute, 1990). James Massey, "Scheduled Castes: A Special Reference to Christians of Scheduled Caste Origin," *Religion and Society* 38, no. 1 (March 1991): 26–36.

43. Conrad, "The Personal Law Question and Hindu Nationalism," p. 318.

44. Mansfield, "The Personal Laws or a Uniform Civil Code?" p. 162.

45. Scott, *Seeing Like a State*, pp. 82–83.

46. Mansfield, "The Personal Laws or a Uniform Civil Code?" p. 159

47. Ministry of Welfare, *Report of the Working Group on Development and Welfare of Scheduled Castes During Eighth Five Year Plan, 1990-1995* (New Delhi: Government of India, 1990), p. 75.

48. Author's interview with then Minister of Railways and General Secretary of SC/ST MPs Forum, Ram Vilas Paswan (20 December 1996, Railway Bhavan, New Delhi).

49. Conrad, "The Personal Law Question and Hindu Nationalism," pp. 334–35. Mansfield, "The Personal Laws or a Uniform Civil Code?" pp. 168–71.

Bibliography

Ahmad, Imtiaz. "Ashraf-Ajlaf Dichotomy in Muslim Social Structure in India." *Indian Economic and Social History Review* 3 (1996): 344–50.

Ahmad, Imtiaz, ed. *Caste and Social Stratification among Muslims in India.* Delhi: Manohar, 1978.

Appadurai, Arjun. "Number in the Colonial Imagination." In Carol A. Breckenridge and Peter van der Veer, eds., *Orientalism and the Post-Colonial Predicament.* Philadelphia: University of Pennsylvania Press, 1993.

Bakshi, P. M. *The Constitution of India with Comments and Subject Index.* Delhi: Universal Law Publishing Co., 1996.

Bright, Kristin. "Classified Ethnographies: The Production and Collection of Racial 'Evidence' in India, 1908-1915." Typescript.

Cohn, Bernard. *Colonialism and Its Forms of Knowledge.* Princeton, N.J.: Princeton University Press, 1996.

Conrad, Dieter. "The Personal Law Question and Hindu Nationalism." In

Vasudha Dalmia and Heinrich von Stietencron, eds., *Representing Hinduism: The Construction of Religious Traditions and National Identity.* New Delhi: Sage, 1995.

Deshpande, V. S. "What Does SC Mean?" *Hindustan Times,* 28 May 1990.

Frykenberg, Robert. "Constructions of Hinduism at the Nexus of History and Religion." *Journal of Interdisciplinary History* 23, no. 3 (Winter 1993): 523–50.

Galanter, Marc. *Competing Equalities: Law and the Backward Classes in India.* Delhi: Oxford University Press, 1991.

Guha, Ranajit. "The Small Voice of History." In Shahid Amin and Dipesh Chakrabarty, eds., *Subaltern Studies IX.* Delhi: Oxford University Press, 1996.

Horowitz, Donald. *Ethnic Groups in Conflict.* Berkeley: University of California Press, 1985.

Jenkins, Laura D. "Preferential Policies for Disadvantaged Ethnic Groups: Employment and Education." In Crawford Young, ed., *Ethnic Diversity and Public Policy: A Comparative Inquiry.* London: Macmillan, 1998.

Kananaikil, Jose. *Scheduled Caste Converts and Social Disabilities: A Survey of Tamil Nadu.* New Delhi: Indian Social Institute, 1990.

Mansfield, John H. "The Personal Laws or a Uniform Civil Code?" In Robert D. Baird, ed., *Religion and Law in Independent India,* pp. 139–177. New Delhi: Manohar, 1993.

Massey, James. "Scheduled Castes: A Special Reference to Christians of Scheduled Caste Origin." *Religion and Society* 38, no. 1 (March 1991): 26–36.

Metcalf, Thomas. *Ideologies of the Raj.* New Delhi: Cambridge University Press, 1995.

Ministry of Welfare. *Report of the Working Group on Development and Welfare of Scheduled Castes during Eighth Five Year Plan, 1990–1995.* New Delhi: Government of India, 1990.

Pandey, Gyanendra. *The Construction of Communalism in Colonial North India.* Delhi: Oxford University Press, 1992.

Rudolph, Lloyd, and Susanne Hoeber Rudolph. *The Modernity of Tradition: Political Development in India.* Chicago: University of Chicago Press, 1967.

Scott, James C. *Seeing Like a State: How Certain Schemes to Improve the Human Condition Have Failed.* New Haven, Conn.: Yale University Press, 1998.

Viswanathan, Gauri. *Outside the Fold: Conversion, Modernity, and Belief.* Princeton, N.J.: Princeton University Press, 1998.

Wright, Theodore. "A New Demand for Muslim Reservations in India." *Asian Survey* 37, no. 9 (Sept. 1997): 852–858.

Court Cases

Atul Chandra Adhikari v. State of Orissa, Orissa, 1995.
Indra Sawhney v. Union of India, Supreme Court, 1992.
Sarla Mudgal v. Union of India, AIR 1995 SC 1531.
Soosai v. Union of India, AIR 1986 SC 733.

S. Swvigaradoss v. Zonal Manager, F.C.I., 1996 3 SCC 100.
Valsamma Paul v. Cochin University and Others, 1996 3 SCC 545.

Interviews

Ram Vilas Paswan, Minister of Railways and General Secretary of SC/ST MPs Forum, 20 December 1996, Railway Bhavan, New Delhi.
Aizaz Rizvi, All India President of the BJP Minority Morcha, 12 September 1996, BJP Central Offices, New Delhi.

Six

The Uniform Civil Code Debate
Lessons from the Criminal Procedures

Arvind Verma

The discourse about personal laws in India is a sensitive issue. The argument *for* a uniform civil code (UCC) emphasizes the need to transcend communal, ethnic, and regional differences as a necessary condition for a modern nation. The argument *against* stresses the diversities and the need to preserve them. The debate is said to be bogged down by the strong opposition of Muslim *'ulama'* that will not tolerate any interference in its right to interpret the way of life for an Indian Muslim. The Islamic religious groups in India have vehemently opposed a secular court interpreting private and family matters governed by the Shari'at. On the other hand, most Hindu nationalist groups view Muslim opposition to a UCC as another example of the Muslims' loose attachment to the Indian nation and as a threat of further partitioning of the country.

In all this rhetoric, it is forgotten that the country has a uniform *criminal* code for everyone. The Indian Penal Code of 1860 (IPC) has been applicable for more than 140 years to all people living in India, including the different religious groups. The criminal justice system encompassing the police, the courts, and the prison system has been functioning without any distinction with regard to religion, ethnicity, caste, class, or gender. The Indian legislature too has implemented several "social" laws that again are neutral to religious beliefs. Furthermore, these criminal laws and the justice system touch a much wider section of the population than does the personal law. Whereas the personal laws are confined to disputes dealing with family, property, and inheritance matters, criminal laws intrude daily into everyday interactions. Accordingly, it is fruitful to study the introduction and implementation of these uniform criminal laws in the country. This may serve as an important learning experience to those considering the feasibility of a uniform civil code for India.

A Brief History of the Criminal Justice System in India

Before the advent of British rule, there were vast differences in legal practices across the country. The Mughal administrators had made a clear distinction between Hindu and Muslim populations. Although the Shari'at was the official law of the land, Hindus nevertheless were allowed to use their own religious texts for guidance when the two opposing parties in a dispute belonged to the same religious group. This was changed by the British authorities, who went ahead and introduced their own English legal practices on Indian soil after obtaining the Diwani rights at Calcutta, Bombay, and Madras.

The Elizabethan Charter of 1600 granted the East India Company the power to enact laws governing the Indian possessions of the company. This charter did not specify any territorial jurisdiction but ordained that customs and statutes of England would be followed in India. The Charter by Charles II in 1661 conferred legislative and judicial authority to the Presidency towns in all civil and criminal matters. These legal provisions covered all the people working for the company or those who chose to live under them. Again, the law of England was to be followed in these areas. It was only in 1726 that the charter by George I enabled the East India Company governors and councils to make independent laws for each of the Presidency towns of India. English principles and practices, however, were still the model followed in the justice systems that evolved in these areas.

The British were reluctant to impose their values on the different populations coming under their administrative jurisdiction. Warren Hastings initiated the Regulating Act of 1772 that stipulated that the Muslim and Hindu laws would be followed according to the usage and custom of respective persons in matters of inheritance, succession, and contract. The act of 1781 further guaranteed the protection of the personal laws administered according to the Qur'an and Shastras for Muslims and Hindus respectively. This was later extended to Madras in 1802 and Bombay in 1827. Warren Hastings wished to proceed slowly and felt it prudent to preserve the personal laws. He did not believe in letting the English legal system interfere in the common practices of the native people.

Yet in 1829, the English authorities did enact the Bengal Sati Regulation XVII Act that criminalized the practice of *sati* among the Hindu population. Of course, Raja Ram Mohan Roy's persistent efforts against the practice of *sati* were the catalyst that prompted Lord William Bentinck to enact this epochal legislation. Nevertheless, this initial approach was still hesitant, as the preamble to the law reveals:

> The Governor-General-in Council, without intending to depart from one of the first and most important principles of the system of Government of India, that all classes of people be secure in the observance of their religious usages so long as that system can be adhered to without violation of the paramount dictates of justice and humanity, has deemed the right to establish the following rules. (Preamble: Bengal Sati Regulation XVII Act, 1829)

The English also passed the Indian Slavery Act in 1843 that prevented any person from being coerced into compulsory labor or service on grounds that the person was a slave. Courts were forbidden to recognize any person as the property of another. The continuing objective of the company was to introduce as few modifications in the existing laws as possible. The English still did not feel confident imposing their will upon the vast multitude of the Indian population as they could in Canada, Australia, and other colonial possessions.

Some of the Shari'at practices, however, appeared too brutal for the liberal English officers to follow. For instance, it was impossible to enforce the law of retaliation for murder or stoning someone for sexual immorality and mutilating one for theft, as ordained in the Shari'at. The provision that non–believers of Shari'at cannot give evidence in cases involving Muslims was another problem. At the initiative of Lord Cornwallis, several proposals to modify these objectionable provisions of the Shari'at were gradually enacted as the law of the land. For instance, by the Regulation of 1790, Section 33, relatives of murder victims were debarred from giving pardon to the offender. By the resolution of 1791 the punishment of mutilation was removed, and in 1792, the Privy Council decreed that the courts will proceed against the accused even if the heirs refused to prosecute (Jois 1984: 54–55).

Thus, even before formal criminal laws were passed by the English in India, many intrusions were made that affected practices common to both Hindus and Muslims. There is little to suggest that the different religious groups offered significant opposition to these measures. In fact, a section of the elite, both amongst the Hindus and Muslims, welcomed them. The support of the orientalists for introducing reformatory legal measures was well-known. The measures were seen by Indian reform groups like Arya Samaj, Brahmo Samaj, and Prarthana Sabha as opportunities to learn from Western ideas and reform the degeneration that had crept into their culture (Callender 1987). Procedures applicable to both communities were also adopted in many other state matters before rule passed from the East India Company in 1857.

This process of repealing, amending, and introducing new laws in place of the Shari'at was a continual phenomenon until a new penal code superseded all existing laws in 1860. The adoption of the Criminal Procedure Code in 1862 and the Evidence Act in 1872 finally ensured that as far as criminal laws were concerned, everyone had to follow the same law of the land. Macaulay is said to have remarked that "our principle is uniformity when you can have it, diversity when you must have it; but in all cases certainty" (quoted in Jois 1984: 64).

These criminal laws have remained in force without major modifications until the present period, even after independence. It is worth examining the implementation of these laws since law in practice undoubtedly differs from law in theory. Is there any reason to believe that having a uniform set of criminal laws has brought about uniform justice for all the people? Is a uniform and centralized criminal justice system beneficial to the country?

I will attempt to answer some of these questions here. I make two arguments in support of the assertion that the criminal justice system is not being uniformly applied in India and is, in fact, a tool of repression against the common people. My main focus will be on the Indian police, since this group bears the responsibility for implementing the laws of the land. The first argument points out that the statutes provide considerable discretion to the enforcers. There is considerable scope for interpreting the legal provisions according to an individual officer's own prejudices or whims. This discretion ends up empowering the official machinery and provides the officers with extraordinary powers perhaps not intended in law. Secondly, I will give illustrative examples to suggest that this official machinery is corrupt, partisan, and unaccountable to the people for its actions. The discretion provided in law further enables police officers to abuse the powers for their own corrupt purposes. This vagueness in law and corrupt enforcement means there is little justice for the common people, especially the minority groups.

Finally, from these examples, I will extrapolate my arguments to the issue of a UCC and contend that rather than debating about the contents of the UCC, the more important need is to examine the system of law enforcement in the country. For irrespective of the nature of the law, corrupt, partisan, and ineffective enforcement machinery cannot be expected to provide uniform justice to the people even if there is the same set of rules for everyone.

Discretion in Law

The legal structure of the criminal law is such that it provides considerable discretion to those empowered to implement its provisions. As is well-known, any legislation leaves considerable room for interpretation (Bottomley 1973). The Indian law too has conferred vast, unbridled discretionary powers to the police. The Code of Criminal Procedure (C.Cr.P.), the guiding law which lays down procedures for police action, is a good example of such varying interpretations. Its language is structured to delegate considerable discretion to the police in matters of arrest, search, seizure, and other functions (Verma 1997).

Consider the provisions of arrest as spelled out in Sections 41 to 56 of the Indian Penal Code (Mitra 1960). These sections describe the situations in which a police officer may arrest a person without seeking the warrant from a magistrate. Section 54 C.Cr.P. states, "any police officer may arrest . . . without a warrant . . . such person . . . against whom . . . *reasonable* suspicion exists of his being so concerned . . . (fourthly) . . . in whose possession anything is found which may *reasonably be suspected* to be stolen property" (my italics). The italicized words are those that are vaguely defined and provide considerable latitude to the police officer. For what constitutes reasonable suspicion, even in subsequent clarifications, has not been spelled out and is said ". . . to depend upon circumstances of the particular case" (A.I.R. 1950 M.B. 83). Furthermore, clause four has extended this discretion and has stipulated that no formal citizen complaint is necessary for a police officer to arrest a person under this clause. Since it is the police officer who has to describe these factual details, there is ample room for misuse of the powers. The officer may attribute any behavior he wants to the suspect and make an arrest based on that behavior.

Furthermore, an arrest may also be made without the commission of a crime. Police have the power to arrest a suspect in order to prevent a crime. For example, Section 151 C.Cr.P. states: "a police officer knowing of a design to commit any cognizable offense may arrest . . . the person so designing, if it appears to the police officer that the commission of the offense cannot be otherwise prevented." Interestingly, judges have even acknowledged that "It is not open to the Honorable Court exercising jurisdiction . . . to go into the question whether in fact the police officer was justified in concluding that the necessity contemplated by this section really existed. The discretion is vested solely in the police officer and that discretion cannot be questioned" (Om Prakash, 51, Cr.L.J. 143 Mad.).

The decision that a person is likely to commit an offense is entirely that of the police officer, and moreover it is his discretionary judgment whether the arrest should be made without any questions being asked. In addition, Section 61 C.Cr.P. further permits the police to keep a suspect in custody for a maximum period of twenty-four hours, after which either the person has to be released or brought before a magistrate (Bose 1966). Using this provision, Indian police frequently arrest a suspect under Section 151 C.Cr.P. and then release him after some time. There is little relief against such arbitrary short-term detentions. For most people, it is virtually impossible to approach the courts or even senior police officers to seek redress against mala fide actions of police officers (Government of India [GOI] 1980). No wonder these legal provisions are often misused by police officers for pecuniary or other personal benefits.

Similarly, there is also considerable inherent discretion in the legal provisions for search. Section 165 C.Cr.P. states:

> whenever an investigating officer has reasonable grounds for believing that anything . . . may be found at any place . . . and that such thing cannot in his opinion be obtained without undue delay, . . . he may after recording the reasons . . . cause search to be made . . . even by a subordinate officer, duly authorized by him.

The use of the word "reasonable" provides unlimited powers to the officers. Moreover, the judgment that "the illegality of the search however does not make the evidence of seizure inadmissible" (A.I.R. 1965 Orissa 136–137) has given extraordinary powers to the officers. An illegal search does not vitiate a trial, since ". . . conviction on basis of discoveries made in such search can be made" (A.I.R. 1955 NUC M.B. 3862 DB).

Thus, in sharp contrast to the *Mapp vs. Ohio* (1961) exclusionary rule formulated by the American courts, Indian lawmakers have given considerable scope for discretionary judgment to the police officers in the investigation of criminal cases. Also, Section 166 C.Cr.P. extends the power to have such searches carried out even outside the jurisdiction, through another police officer of that area. Consequently, Indian police rarely attempt to obtain search warrants, for they can always search any place during any current ongoing investigation of a case

(Verma 1997). These legal powers are so extraordinary that the Indian police are able to make arrests and conduct a search of any premises without fear of interference from the courts.

Quite naturally, these powers are commonly abused. Police officers make threats by invoking the law against those who dare to oppose them or interfere with their actions. In reality, "the police in India have an unsavory reputation for extortion and at present, corruption is perhaps even more widespread and brazen than ever before" (Verma 1999). In the seventeen years of experience of the author, there has not been a single case in Bihar where a police officer has been held guilty by the courts for making a wrongful arrest or conducting an illegal search. Unlike in the U.S., there is absolutely no relief from the courts for misuse of police powers. The system of holding police departments responsible for the behavior of their members does not exist. No police department has ever been forced to pay compensation to the victims of excessive use of force, illegal detentions, or illegal searches, even though these are an almost daily phenomenon in the country.

How fairly has the Indian police been using its discretionary and other powers? It is difficult to answer this, since research on the Indian police is scant and has not examined the police behavior at the micro level (Bayley 1969; Das 1994; Gautam 1993; Ghosh 1988; Gupta 1979; Mitra and Mohanty 1992; Natarajan 1996; Philip 1996; Raghavan 1989; Subramanian 1992; Verma 1998). One way is to examine the implementation of the criminal laws and the people being targeted by the police officers. Unfortunately, there are no official documents that provide the socioeconomic, caste, and religious affiliations of the people arrested by the police. Thus, it is impossible to state if police action is selective or uniform when dealing with law violators.

Some idea about the state of insecurity and the process of justice, however, can be made out from published police statistics. According to the latest compilation of official police statistics by the National Crime Record Bureau (NCRB 1997), called "Crime In India," in 1995 there were 5,993,172 cognizable offenses registered in the country. This marks an increase of 33.7 percent over the 1985 figures when 4,481,212 crimes were registered. Violent crime during the last four decades has increased substantially from 8.2 percent of all crimes in 1953 (when nationwide records were first kept) to 14.5 percent in 1995. The frequency of rapes has almost doubled during the decade 1985–95 with an increase of more than 88.7 percent over the 1985 figures (NCRB 1997: 39).

Moreover, atrocities on the weaker sections have continued unabated.

In 1995, 32,996 cases were registered as crimes against Scheduled Castes, including 571 murders, 873 rapes, and 13,925 offenses under the recently legislated SC/ST Prevention of Atrocities Act, 1989. The corresponding figures in the case of Scheduled Tribes were 5,498 crimes, including 75 murders, 369 rapes, and 1,480 offenses under the SC/ST Prevention of Atrocities Act (NCRB 1997: 257–268). Crimes against children also show a disturbing trend. Altogether, 4,067 cases of child rape (up to sixteen years of age) were reported in 1995, which represented almost 30 percent of all the rapes reported in the country. Furthermore, there were 107 cases of procurement of minor girls and 36 cases involving buying or selling of girls for prostitution. Despite this rising trend and increasing victimization, the attempt by the police to prosecute the guilty has been dismal. The conviction rate in murder cases was 37 percent, rape 30 percent, and SC/ST Prevention of Atrocities Act 39.2 percent (NCRB 1997: 137–139).

Thus, even by official figures, criminal victimization in India has been increasing steadily and seriously affecting the weaker segments of the society. Moreover, these figures reflect only a portion of the crimes occurring in the country. Police minimization of offenses is a standard practice, as has been commented upon many times (GOI 1979; Saxena 1987; Verma 1993). Unfortunately, there are no alternative sources to study the nature of crime in the country. No victim surveys have been conducted and there is no standard procedure to verify the figures submitted by different police departments. Data management is in a dismal state in every organization and there is no external mechanism to verify the figures submitted by the police departments. Since these figures are frequently used by political parties as a measure of police performance (Verma 1999b), the tendency to keep the number of criminal incidents low is widespread.

The National Human Rights Commission's (NHRC) annual reports are perhaps more revealing about the state of police behavior in the country. The NHRC was set up as a statutory body with the responsibility of promoting and protecting human rights in the country. Even in the officially disapproving language of the commission one can detect the sorry state of rights violations in the nation. The commission writes:

In recent years, there has been growing concern in the country that the processes of governance have, on occasion, been corroded by a nexus between criminals, less than scrupulous political elements and members of executive lacking in integrity. The deleterious effect on human rights resulting from such a nexus can be gauged from the nature of petitions received by this commission, many of which complain of violations because the supposed protectors of rights have themselves turned predators. (NHRC 1998: 5)

The report also comments: "The Commission has observed that a majority of complaints that it has received relate to the conduct of the police, many questioning its integrity" (NHRC 1998: 22). This report lists altogether 1,332 custodial deaths between the period 1 April 1995 to 31 March 1997, with the states of Bihar, Maharastra, and Uttar Pradesh reporting the highest number of such police-inflicted deaths. Altogether, 20,514 complaints including complaints of custodial deaths and rapes involving police brutality were received by the commission during this period. Other complaints include charges of "disappearance," illegal detentions, false testimony, and police misuse of force. The National Police Commission too has remarked:

It is generally known that false criminal cases are sometimes engineered merely for the sake of making arrests to humiliate and embarrass some specified enemies of the complainant, in league with the police for corrupt reasons. (GOI 1980)

The NHRC reports reiterate the belief that the people do not have faith in the police department and generally fear approaching the police station for any kind of assistance. All this suggests that the Indian police are not an instrument that could be trusted for proper implementation of laws of any kind.

Another independent source about law enforcement is the newspapers, which are filled with reports about police atrocities, bias, improper procedures, and brutal behavior. A random survey of Indian newspapers for the year 1998 reveals that complaints of insecurity and fear of crime have been widespread (Kunwar 1997; Saxena 1997; Indian Express 1997; Sharma 1997; Sawant 1997). In many parts of Bihar, Uttar Pradesh, Andhra Pradesh, Madhya Pradesh, Rajasthan, and Assam, organized criminal groups appear to be firmly entrenched. Extortions, kidnappings, and killings have become common in many states (Ahmed and Baweja 1998). Media reports also suggest that police behavior toward minorities and females is less than exemplary (*Times of India* 1999a). Custodial deaths, rapes on police station premises, and abusive behavior are commonly reported in the national or vernacular press (*Times of India* 1999b; Prakash 1999). From my own experience in the police service, I can state with full confidence that an overwhelming majority of people arrested throughout the country come from the lower social and economic classes. Furthermore, the police departments are not impartial in their functions. There is clearly a class bias that manifests itself again and again (Balagopal and Reddy 1982; Setalvad 1998). The majority of people arrested or dealt with by the police are from the lower classes. Although the caste and class variables are not recorded officially, it is a common experience that a Mushar (scheduled caste person) or any other person belonging to some lower caste will be arrested on the faintest of suspicion while the police will wait for a direction from above to arrest any high-caste or wealthy person.

Even when abhorrent social behavior is criminalized as a means of controlling it, the legal provisions are so weak that little implementation occurs. The experience of implementing so-called progressive social legislation, such as the Civil Rights Act of 1976, the Bonded Labor Abolition Act, the Money Lending Control Act, the Anti-Dowry Act, and special provisions in the penal code covering offenses against women, has been disappointing. First, the enforcement has been left to the overburdened police departments, which are unable to cope adequately with the large number of criminal offenses. Second, few police officers are given legal training in these special kinds of social legislation, and most officers are unaware of their provisions. Third, the Civil Rights Act of 1976, the Bonded Labor Abolition Act, and the Money Lending Control Act have all been made bailable offenses with minor punishments. Trying to register these cases actually causes a loss of face since the culprits are released from custody immediately and the cases drag on in the courts for years. The punishments have been so minor that there can hardly be said to be any deterrent effect.

> In view of the trouble and expense, often accompanied by economic hazard and physical danger, the uncertainty of securing a conviction and the tiny effect of such a conviction, it is not difficult to see why few Untouchables would feel that there is anything to be gained by instituting a case. (Galanter 1989: 215)

A survey by the Bureau of Police Research and Development observed that ". . . most police investigations in these social law violations are superficial and there was general lack of interest in the conduct of such cases by the prosecuting agency" (Krishnamurthy 1983: 310). Undoubtedly, a clear lack of sympathy among police officers has also contributed to relegating this social legislation to a secondary level. Without a determined social mobilization, these laws will remain ineffective. The criminal justice system is simply not geared to bear this responsibility.

Indian jails further provide compelling evidence of class and caste bias on the part of the criminal justice system. The majority of people incarcerated in Indian prisons are from the lower classes. A sample of convicted prisoners of Tihar Jail in Delhi and Beur Jail at Patna has some very revealing data. Of the 482 people surveyed, 91 percent belong to the so-called backward or lower castes (Verma and Kumar 2000). Even though the main objective of this survey was not to determine the caste distribution amongst the arrestees, from this preliminary data the facts are revealing. There is a much greater likelihood of finding Paswans, Bhuyains, and Chamars (lower castes) than Trivedis, Sharmas, Vajpayees, or Khans (higher castes) in Indian prisons.

The implementation of the criminal law is also biased against women. Offenses against women are rising alarmingly in the country. Crimes like molestation, rape, dowry death, kidnapping for prostitution, and even honor killing are all increasing (NCRB 1997). Despite wide prevalence of rape, molestation, and domestic abuse, very few cases are actually registered and investigated properly. Police efforts to arrest and prosecute the guilty are largely ineffective. The conviction rates for rape are usually lower than for the non-serious cases of burglaries and thefts (NCRB 1997). In 1995, a total of 106,471 offenses nationwide were registered in which women alone were the victims. This marks an increase of almost 43.7 percent over the figures from 1991. There is also an alarming increase in cases of dowry death and torture or cruelty by the husband and his relatives (NCRB 1997: 225–227). The treatment of female complainants by the criminal justice system is, of course, notorious (Bhatnagar 1997; Kunwar 1997). The annual report from the Human Rights Watch for India is very revealing about this sorry state of affairs:

> In India, attacks on Dalit women during massacres, police raids, and caste clashes were on the rise in 1998. As untouchables, Dalit women constituted the majority of prostitutes and landless workers and thus came into frequent contact with law enforcement officials. In Tamil Nadu, for example, women were the primary targets during a February 26 police raid on Dalit villages in the aftermath of clashes between Dalit and middle-caste communities. Police also engaged in instances of "hostage-taking" wherein women were arrested and tortured as a means of punishing their absconding male relatives and forcing them to surrender. (Human Rights Watch 1999)

There is communal bias in the way criminal laws are implemented. The police continue to fail to protect minorities, whether religious, ethnic, or casteist. It is also frequently alleged that the police side with the majority Hindu community in most of the communal riots. Serious allegations of biased actions have been leveled against police forces such as the Provincial Armed Constabulary of Uttar Pradesh, the Bihar Military Police, and the Bombay police department. Justice Srikrishna, in his indictment of the police role during the Bombay riots of 1991, stated, "Built-in bias of the police force against the Muslims became more pronounced [during the riots]. . . . Bias was evident in active connivance of police constables with rioting Hindu mobs, in their role as passive onlookers" (Aiyar and Koppikar 1998).

Atrocities against the tribals and lower castes are common not only in Bihar but in Uttar Pradesh, Madhya Pradesh, Rajasthan, Haryana, Gujarat, and almost everywhere else (Human Rights Watch 1999). There was a notorious case in Bihar where a superintendent of police refused to register a case of arson when all the houses belonging to the Harijans were burned, on grounds that it would upset the high-caste groups and cause a law-and-order problem. Despite mass murders of lower castes, the number of offenders convicted has remained extremely low.

The police have been playing a role in matters concerning civil laws too. In a country where 45 percent of the people are illiterate, little distinction is made between the civil and criminal laws. Almost all disputes are first brought to the notice of local police officers. They have to decide if the matter is criminal or governed by the civil laws. If a criminal offense is committed, then under section 154 C.Cr.P., the subsequent action is to be taken by the police. Otherwise the dispute is sent to the court for resolution. However, this rarely happens in practice. Police officers first determine the possibility of extorting money from either of the parties, and wash their hands of the case only if this possibility is not lucrative enough. In many instances, the complainant too is interested in involving the police, not because of faith in the institution, but because of the nuisance value of reporting an incident. It is extremely easy for police officers to invoke a provision of the criminal law in addition to the civil dispute.

For instance, problems arising from marriage, inheritance, or property distribution—clearly part of personal law—are invariably taken first to the police station. Generally, the police direct the complainants to take the matter to the civil court, but there are occasions when such complaints are entered in the general diary. As mentioned above, by law police officers are required to register all complaints and, if they are non-cognizable, send a report to the magistrate to handle. During this period, there is sufficient time to threaten the opposite party with arrest, or solicit bribes to evade police action. It is easy to mix some criminal charge along with the civil dispute. In many cases, on the advice of more knowledgeable people, generally lawyers, complainants add allegations of theft or minor assault to involve the provisions of criminal law so that police can be involved in disputes that are obviously civil in nature.

Inheritance claims are similarly intertwined with criminal incidents to harass the other inheritors. In property distribution, allegations of theft or breach of trust are levied, and the onus of proof falls upon the opposite party. For instance, a statement such as "[the accused] also took away my part of the silver utensils that were given to me," a charge of theft, invokes Section 379 of the Indian Penal Code. This allegation makes the case cognizable and gives police the right to intervene in a matter that is clearly a civil dispute to be dealt with by the courts. Even subsequently, if a supervisor declares this charge to be false, the involvement of an investigator with consequent threats of arrest are strong incentives to the accused to make peace with the complainant. The legal process of prosecuting someone for making false allegations, Section 211 of the IPC, are so cumbersome that action is rarely possible through the courts. The difficulties of dealing with the police, dealing with the courts, and getting bail are so extensive that people are willing to make quick compromises rather than try to litigate.

Similarly, if a girl elopes against the wishes of her family, the dispute is not settled by negotiation or other private means. The family attempts to prevent the girl from marrying by registering a case of kidnapping against the boy and his family. To this charge is added the offense of stealing the family jewelry that the girl is said to have been wearing or that was in the house. This ensures that even if the girl denies that she was kidnapped, her missing jewelry can be used against her boyfriend and his family on a charge of theft. The girl is also declared a minor in most cases of elopement, since that would make it a clear case of kidnapping. In the absence of any proper birth records, the only way to ascertain a teenage girl's age is a dental checkup or some kind of medical examination. In such cases, the doctor could then be influenced to either deny that the girl is of age or make the report ambiguous. Furthermore, an unwanted physical examination the boy or girl may have to undergo becomes another strong deterrent. Thus, a matter that is a family dispute and that should be settled by personal laws becomes a problem involving the police. It is only a determined love that successfully transcends all these obstacles.

Police powers, despite the provisions of personal laws, also govern the celebration of religious festivities in the name of maintaining public order. Even at present, criminal justice agencies govern the observance of religious actions for all the citizens irrespective of their religious affiliations. This occurs because of the long-standing conflicts between Hindu and Muslim communities. Communal riots causing loss of property and life have been common in the country. The problem usually arises when members of one religion protest against the nature, time, or route of a religious procession organized by the other group, especially when it passes through or near their locality (Akbar 1988). Regulating crowds during such celebrations in order to avoid communal conflict is an important responsibility for the police. A disturbance during these celebrations could ignite large-scale rioting, since often thousands of people are involved. The police exercise considerable discretion in handling these situations, since the law provides little direction.

> The narrow lanes and crowded bazaars from where these processions pass makes crowd control in these settings an extremely challenging job. In order to control the physical setting, police attempt to regulate the *time* and *place* where the procession can be taken out by making use of section 24 of the Police Act 1861 which provides power to manage traffic on public roads. . . . It is through such a device that police insist on the time and route to be followed by the organizers . . . to ensure that the route does not pass through the localities of other communities, especially in front of temples or mosques, and further that police have space for their deployment and operations (Verma 1997).

Large communal riots have often occurred from such small matters as obstructing a procession, playing music when passing before a mosque, or shouting abusive or provocative slogans (Singh, Sharma, and Avasthy 1983). Every religious festival is a high-stress event for the police. Not surprisingly, police deployment is heavy and strategic. The objective is to prevent clashes, and in this role the police determine how a religious function will be celebrated. Thus, in the name of maintaining law and order, Indian police have been exercising considerable power and interfering directly in the religious affairs of almost every community.

It must be pointed out, of course, that police actions are not all negative. On many occasions, police powers are also put to social good. The threat of invoking the law and involving the police acts as a deterrent to most people in the country. Many times police officers use such threats to force an issue in the larger interests of a particular community, or to provide relief to an unfortunate victim. For instance, irrespective of the revision in the law following the Shah Bano case, police officers have intervened on behalf of poor Muslim women. In one case, an officer, whose sister was a Muslim lady, "persuaded" his sister's husband to provide money and shelter when the divorce was filed. The case did not go to any Shari'at or civil court but was reconciled by the individual police officer who was determined to safeguard the interest of his sister. Many such matters of inheritance and distribution of family property are similarly settled by individual officers who intervene beyond the procedures of law to ensure justice for the victims. They persuade concerned individuals to settle disputes within the family and sometimes act as impartial judges. Their involvement generally leads to an amicable solution and a settlement between the parties. Furthermore, police officers' involvement also ensures that both parties adhere to their promises for fear of antagonizing the powerful police establishment.

Another interesting phenomenon is the settlement of disputes concerning marriages between young people who find their parents opposing their choice of a mate. Many officers attempt to settle the dispute outside the purview of the law, and end up playing matchmakers or neutral mediators for lovers confronting parents who disapprove of their marrying outside their caste, religion, or class.

> There have been several instances of girls complaining of "wrongful confinement" by their parents when the police had gone to investigate cases of harassment by the boy or his family. . . . Very often, such complaints of "kidnapping" and "abduction" turn out to be simple cases of a couple eloping as a result of families opposing their union. Marriages have been arranged in police stations, at marriage registrar's offices and even in temples. . . . A police officer played the maternal uncle of a girl and performed the kanyadaan, even as some other colleagues became her brothers and cousins and ensured that all arrangements for the marriage were in place. (Chaudhuri and Prasad 1999)

The language of the criminal law or any kind of law will always be stated in general terms. It is next to impossible to specify a clear legal procedure that can cover all possible eventualities that may occur. Thus, discretionary judgments will always remain with the agency entrusted with the enforcement of the law. Police officers involved in the implementation of the law have the power to make an individual decision about the nature of the offense and the possible legal action to take in a case. As the above-mentioned examples suggest, this discretion is not being used uniformly or fairly. Police officers have acted and continue to act in ways that are not fair. The police personnel are poorly paid, ill-trained, and function under extremely difficult working conditions (Gautam 1993). Most officers, including magistrates, do not even know the law (Shourie 1999) and as a result make many improper decisions.

The only way to ensure that police officers do not misuse their powers is to improve the quality and training of police personnel. The selection, training, and working conditions for every officer must be such that an officer can be held accountable for performing at the requisite level. To achieve this, however, the present police organization has to be thoroughly reformed.

My argument is that even if a uniform civil code gets passed by Parliament, its implementation is altogether a different matter. Unless there is a qualitative change in the government and bureaucracy, especially the police department, laws will not be implemented faithfully. The present state of affairs hardly provides an indication that any kind of law, uniform or personal, would be implemented properly. There is little evidence to suggest that a uniform civil code will usher in uniformity amongst the citizens, for even if it is drafted as a sound legal document, it will be implemented by the same administrative machinery. It is, therefore, probably the better part of wisdom to leave the personal laws in place so that different identity groups can watch over their own communities without having to involve the generally corrupt policing system in modern India.

References

Ahmed, Farzand, and Harinder Baweja. 1998. "Making a Mockery of Democracy." *India Today*, 5 October.

Aiyar, V. Shankar, and Smrati Koppikar. 1998. "Tiger in Trouble." *India Today*, 17 August: 29–32.

Akbar, M. J. 1988. *Riot after Riot: A Report on Caste and Communal Violence in India*. New Delhi: Penguin Books.

Balagopal, K., and M. Kodandarama Reddy. 1982. "Forever Disturbed: Peasant Struggle of Sircilla-Vamulwada." *Economic and Political Weekly*, 27 November. Bombay: Sameeksha Publications, pp. 1897–1901.

Bayley, David H. 1969. *Police and Political Development In India*. Princeton, N.J.: Princeton University Press.

Bhatnagar, Rakesh. 1997. "Making Workplace Safe for Women." *Times of India*, Tuesday, 19 August.

Bose, S. K. 1966. *Indian Criminal Court Handbook*. Calcutta: Eastern Law House.

Bottomley, A. K. 1973. *Decision in the Penal Process.* London: Martin Robinson.

Callender, Ann B. 1987. *How Shall We Govern India? A Controversy among British Administrators, 1800–1882.* New York: Garland Publishing.

Chaudhuri, Sriranjan, and S. Sridhar Prasad. 1999. "They Play Matchmaker, and Also Catch Thieves." *Times of India,* Tuesday, 10 August.

Das, Dilip K. 1994. *Police Practices: An International Review.* Metuchen, N.J.: Scarecrow Press.

Galanter, Marc. 1989. *Law and Society in Modern India.* Delhi: Oxford University Press.

Gautam, D. N. 1993. *The Indian Police: A Study in Fundamentals.* New Delhi: Mittal Publications.

Ghosh, S. K. 1988. *Keeping the Peace: For Whom the Bell Tolls.* New Delhi: Ashish Publishing House.

Government of India. 1979–82. *Reports I–VIII of the National Police Commission.* New Delhi: Ministry of Home Affairs.

Gupta, Anandswarup. 1979. "The Police in British India 1861–1947." New Delhi: Concept Publishing Company.

Human Rights Watch. 1999. *Annual Report, 1999.* http://www.hrw.org/worldreport99/

Indian Express. 1997. *Innocents Held for Anti-Enron Stir.* Monday, 16 June.

Jois, Rama M. 1984. *Legal and Constitutional History of India.* Vol. II: *Modern, Legal, Judicial and Constitutional System.* Bombay: N. M. Tripathi. p. 64.

Krishnamurthy, S. 1983. *Impact of Social Legislation on the Criminal Law in India.* Bangalore: R.R. Publishers.

Kunwar, D. S. 1997. "Crime against Dalit Women Continues in UP despite BSP's Assurance." *Times of India,* Wednesday, 16 July.

Mitra, B. B. 1960. *The Code of Criminal Procedure.* 13th ed. Vols. 1 and 2. Calcutta: Eastern Law House.

Mitra, Rashmi, and Samarendra Mohanty. 1992. *Police and Social Change in India.* New Delhi: Ashish Publishing House.

Natarajan, Mangai. 1996. "Women Police Units in India: A New Direction." *Police Studies: The International Review Of Police* 19, no. 2: 63–75.

National Crime Records Bureau. 1997. *Crime in India—1995.* Faridabad: Government of India Press.

National Human Rights Commission. 1998. *Annual Report: 1996–1997.* New Delhi.

Philip, Prateep V. 1996. "The 'Friends of Police' Movement in India." *Police Journal* 69, no. 2: 126–130.

Prakash, Gyan. 1999. "Patna Cops Busy Fleecing Innocent People." *Times of India,* Saturday, 19 June.

Raghavan, R. K. 1989. *Indian Police: Problems, Planning and Perspectives.* New Delhi: Manohar Publications.

Sawant, Gaurav C. 1997. "Shoot Now, Think Later." *Indian Express,* Thursday, 24 May.

Saxena, N. S. 1987. *Law and Order in India.* New Delhi: Abhinav Publications.

Saxena, N. S. 1997. "Fake Encounters of the Official Kind." *Times of India,* Thursday, 19 June.

Setalvad, Teesta. 1998. "Communal Bias of Mumbai Police." *Hindustan Times,* 5 May.

Sharma, Rajnish. 1997. "Police Party Attacks Executive for Straying into PM's Route." *Times of India,* Tuesday, 13 May.

Shourie, Arun. 1999. *Consequences of Ignoring the Law.* www.indiaconnect.com /ashourie.htm

Singh, Balkar, R. S. Sharma, and S. C. Avasthy. 1983. "Policing a Major City: Pattern and Nature of Law and Order Problems Faced by the Police and How Handled." *Transactions* 37: 142–205. Hyderabad: SP National Police Academy.

Subramanian, S. 1992. *Human Rights and Police.* Hyderabad: Association for Advancement of Police and Security Sciences.

Times of India. 1999a. "Inhuman Bondage." Editorial, Monday, 15 March.

Times of India. 1999b. "Mystery Shrouds UT's Death." Sunday, 27 June.

Verma, Arvind. 1993. "The Problem of Measurement of Crime in India." *Indian Journal of Criminology* 21, no. 2: 51–58.

Verma, Arvind. 1997. "Maintaining Law & Order in India: An Exercise in Police Discretion." *International Criminal Justice Review* 7, no. 1: 65–80.

Verma, Arvind. 1998. "National Police Commission in India: Analysis of the Policy Failures." *Police Journal* LXXI, no. 3: 226–244.

Verma, Arvind. 1999a. "Police Corruption in India: Roots in Organizational Culture." *Police Studies: The International Review of Police Development and Management* 22, no. 3: 264–278.

Verma, Arvind. 1999b. "Lies, Damn Lies and Police Statistics." *Indian Police Journal* XLVI, no. 2–3: 29–36.

Verma, Arvind, and Manish Kumar. 2000. "Why People Commit Crime? An Exploration in India." Unpublished project report. New Delhi: Indian Council of Social Science Research.

PART III

PERSONAL LAW AND ISSUES OF GENDER

Seven

Gender Implications for a Uniform Civil Code

Robert D. Baird

It is a common indictment of many if not most traditional texts, religious and otherwise, that they were written by men for men, that they express a man's point of view, and that the perspectives of women and other marginalized persons are systematically if not consciously excluded. Judging from the list of persons credentialed to participate in the Constituent Assembly debates, it would appear that women were not excluded, but were a distinct minority.[1] This need not be taken as *prima facie* evidence that the Constituent Assembly debates is one more document engaged in gender hegemony. Throughout the discussion of the Constituent Assembly, an impressive number of men emerged in defense of rights for women. In an essay, "*Shakti* Ascending: Hindu Women, Politics, and Religious Leadership During the Nineteenth and Twentieth Centuries,"[2] Nancy Falk points out the important role that Indian men had in the Indian women's movement in general.

While the Indian scene is a platform for the types of discrimination found in other countries, it is also true that all Indian men should not be judged in such an *a priori* fashion. When the preamble to the Constitution of India resolves to secure justice, liberty, equality, and fraternity for "all its citizens," and to assure "the dignity of the individual," one can only interpret this to include women. Part II on citizenship is also gender-inclusive. At the time of the implementation of the Constitution, "every person" born in India, either of whose parents were born there, or anyone who has been a resident for not less than five years, is a citizen. Citizenship is gender-inclusive.

Moreover, equality before the law is gender-inclusive. Articles 14 and 15 of the Constitution state this explicitly.

14. *Equality before law.*—The State shall not deny to any person equality before the law or the equal protection of the laws within the territory of India.

15. *Prohibition of discrimination on grounds of religion, race, caste, sex or place of birth.*—(1) The State shall not discriminate on grounds of religion, race, caste, sex, or place of birth or any of them.

(2) No citizen shall, on the grounds only of religion, race, caste, sex, place of birth or any of them, be subject to any disability, liability, restriction or condition with regard to -

(a) access to shops, public restaurants, hotels and places of public entertainment; or

(b) the use of wells, tanks, bathing ghats, roads and places of public resort maintained wholly or partly out of State funds or dedicated to the use of the general public.

(3) Nothing in this article shall prevent the State from making any special provision for women and children.

The provisions of the Constitution of India are uniformly gender-inclusive, except in places where it provides for special conditions, presumably to correct unequal conditions inherited from the past.

Law in the Context of Social Setting

I have previously made the point that in the light of religio-historical analysis, the Constitution of India is, in addition to being a political, legal, and economic document, a religious document. It embodies a system of ultimate values which the state is intent on implementing.[3] One of those values is equality. I also pointed out that this system of religious values that embraces equality is in marked contrast with traditional religious models such as the one found in *The Laws of Manu*. There, both law and penalty are based on the principle of inequality, both as a principle for distinguishing men from women, and also as a principle for distinguishing men from men. The result is that for those who want to promote the principles of traditional systems of law, their systems of religious values are in a head-on collision with the system of values promoted in the Constitution of India. That is simply a matter of law and logic. Moreover, since the values deposited in the Constitution of India have supreme legal status, their implementation in the interest of gender equality requires the restriction of other religious values and practices which might otherwise also have constitutional protection.[4]

The conflict goes quite a bit deeper than that, however. Not only is the conflict a theoretical one, but the Constitution is also embedded in a social setting in which the inferior status of women is framed. Even among Indians who could not recite a single verse of Manu, and from whatever source this view received its impetus, it is widely held and practiced that women not only do but should have a place in society which is quite different from men. Upendra Baxi summarizes the extent to which the provisions of law which seek to implement equality are even known by Indians.[5] Commenting on the findings of B. B. Chatterjee's *Impact of Social Legislation on Social Change,*[6] he summarizes the following lack of knowledge on the part of inhabitants of four villages in Banaras District on matters of family law, issues most significantly affected by the concept of a uniform civil code.

> In the family law area, the findings indicate little or no knowledge of innovations in law. People do not know the minimum age of marriage, nor do they know that dowry is prohibited. There is also a near total lack of information concerning grounds of divorce. Knowledge of law against bigamy or polygamy is "very meager," though for economic and other reasons the practice appears to be on the decline. The Hindu adoption law, similarly, has made no impact since the rural mind is "totally indifferent due to lack of knowledge." As regards the Hindu Succession Act the position is no better. Only 12 out of 200 respondents claimed any knowledge of it! The only exception is here provided by the provision concerning daughter's right to inherit family property. Interestingly, while 78 per cent of other respondents viewed this provision favorably, about 68 per cent respondents, belonging to higher castes and relatively 'affluent' strata firmly opposed the position.[7]

In his volume *Secular Values for Secular India,* P. C. Chatterji addresses the implications of a uniform civil code for the issue of gender equality.[8] He discusses the place of women in "Hinduism," "Islam," "Buddhism," and "Sikhism." Rather than quoting from ancient texts such as Manu, Kautilya, and the Qur'an, as he does, and constructing a brief but reified picture of these "religions," I will move to an examination of certain gender issues in the so-called "Hindu Code Bill."

Gender and the "Hindu Code Bill"

In "Uniform Civil Code and the Secularization of Law" (1981),[9] I argued what should be obvious. Since both Hindus and Muslims consider their codes of family law sacred and part of their religion, the implementation of a uniform civil code would require the secularization of law. I also pointed out that the religious model embodied in the Constitution of India involved the interpretation of life through two large categories: the secular and the religious. This I labeled a "New Great Tradition." It was a tradition that was in conflict with traditional ways of thinking for which religion was a way of life and included virtually every dimension of life. It was also a dominant tradition that required that if the more traditional ways of thinking were to survive at all they would have to survive in a significantly modified form. That is, they could not continue to exist as they had in the past. The Supreme Court had already decided that the appointment of temple priests in Tamil Nadu is a secular matter.[10] It had decided that the determination of what rituals should be performed in a temple is a secular matter.[11] And, even if temple entry was a religious matter, it had to give way to the constitutional model since the opening of all Hindu temples of a public nature to all Hindus was also a constitutional provision.[12] All conflicts between the constitutional religious model and traditional religious models were inevitably resolved in terms of the categories and values of the constitutional model.

I would like to suggest as a corollary to my thesis that the secularization of law is basic to a uniform civil code. While seeing law as either religious or secular is surely basic, *in terms of content* this conflict is encapsulated in issues relating to gender. Since the attempt to pass a "Hindu Code Bill" has been seen by both Indian legislators as well as scholars such as J. D. M. Derrett as the first step toward a uniform civil code, it is a likely place to begin such an examination.[13]

It would seem, then, that although the basic issue was the secularization of law, when it came to specific points on which the two religious models were in conflict, it was frequently a gender-related issue.

One pamphlet published and distributed during the debates over the Hindu Code Bill by Shastra Dharma Prachar Sabha was titled *Why Hindu Code Is Detestable*. Along with its view that when such a code is passed, Indian society will become as corrupt as Western societies, the real issues centered on gender.

> Yet these vicious bills are directed to (1) provide for intercaste marriage, (2) Sagotra marriage, (3) Introduce divorce, (4) make bigamy punishable by law, and (5) give a married daughter a share in her father's property. The bills go against fundamental principles of the Hindu Shastras, God's Spoken Words, on which the Society is based.[14]

Although the Constitutional Changes Committee was forced to admit that opposition to its recommendations was widespread, it forged ahead on the principle that it was not a matter of numbers but of right. Furthermore, basic to the proposals was a principle that had no place in earlier law codes, namely, the principle of equality. The former Chief Justice of the Supreme Court of India, in two lectures delivered at Karnataka University in 1951, made the point clear.

> It seems to me that it is the preemptor requirement of the present age that we must have a Hindu Code, which is based on absolute equality among all Hindus, irrespective of their caste, creed, or sex. If we are all agreed on this elementary proposition, there must be unanimity amongst us all in bringing about this reform.[15]

Once it was determined that the new code was to be based not on textual exegeses, but on social utility, logic, and modern values, one could appeal to gender equity.[16] And it is that appeal to gender equity that is comfortable in the constitutional model but is not at home in traditional texts nor in the lived experience of many modern "Hindus."

In discussing the right of a woman to inherit when a father dies intestate, logic left no resting place until daughters were given a right similar to sons.

> For example, we put to some of the witnesses the case of a Mitakshara father dying leaving a daughter and a brother; his interest in the coparcenary property goes to the brother by survivorship and if the brother subsequently dies leaving a daughter, the interest goes to the brother's daughter, the original owner's own daughter being thus ousted. No one desired such a result, but it could only be prevented by a further inroad upon the existing Mitakshara Law; e.g. by giving the daughter a right by birth similar to that of a son or by giving the father a right to dispose of his coparcenary interest by will or by some such device. Again, if the daughter is to have an absolute estate in the property which she gets from her father, how can we consistently refuse a similar estate to the son by insisting on the Mitakshara rule that his son, grandson and great-grandson shall have a right by birth in such property?[17]

While the practice of dowry placed heavy economic burdens on a family on behalf of its daughters, and although other issues also arose to complicate the implementation of equity, there is little doubt that equity was the goal of the framers of the Code. Women witnesses before the Committee were taken seriously. They reported that "Most of the women witnesses consider it inequitable to deny to the daughter the same share as the son, but practically all of them accept the half-a-share as a compromise."[18]

When the Committee proposed monogamy in place of polygamy, it was argued that monogamy could not be sustained without divorce, which was contrary to the Hindu notion that marriage was a sacrament. Moreover, there were those who argued that many Hindus would convert to Islam in order to benefit from permission to have more than one wife. The Committee, however, held that monogamy and divorce were two separate issues and that monogamy could be sustained either with or without divorce. There were witnesses who both favored and did not favor divorce who wanted to insist on monogamy. One of the arguments to surface in favor of monogamy was the weight of world opinion. The Committee found compelling the argument that monogamy merely gives to women the position that men already have. "In fact, this corresponds to the position now occupied by Hindu men, and these witnesses therefore only wanted Hindu men to be put in the same position as Hindu women."[19]

Those who opposed divorce argued that marriage was a sacrament, which created a bond between husband and wife that carried throughout life and even into death. Widowers were free to remarry, but widows were to treat their husbands as gods even after death. The Committee recounted the destitute situation of widows. When traditionalists argued that in such instances women might well exemplify patient suffering, the Committee responded that they were not willing to demand the same for men, for whom they desired the possibility of remarriage.[20] There was considerable discussion as to whether a man's keeping of a concubine should be sufficient grounds for divorce. While the committee held that many wives would not file for divorce on this ground alone, it should be a valid ground. If the woman were to become the concubine of another man, the sacramental bond of marriage would presumably be broken and divorce would be possible. If that is the case with the woman, it must also be the case for the man.[21]

Although the Committee recommended that both monogamy and divorce be part of the Hindu Code, it made it clear that monogamy was so important that it should be enacted even if there were no provision for divorce. Some had argued that with polygamy, provision was made whereby a man could, if his wife contracted some serious disease or were barren, marry a second wife while maintaining the security of the first wife. But the principle of gender equality could not be ignored.

Again, Hindu women are now bound by the rule of monogamy, although they are not entitled to divorce except where their communities allow it.[22]

If, then, the broader principle under dispute was whether family law was religious or secular, one of the most compelling concrete areas of dispute was the area of gender equity. It was the admission of the *Report of the Hindu Law Committee* that "The primary aim of most of the alterations in the existing Hindu Law proposed in the draft code . . . [was] to effect an improvement in the status of women."[23]

From time to time when specific issues were being discussed, statements which affirmed the general principle of gender equity were made. While discussing the issue of concubines, the Committee stated, "As far as possible the law should operate equally between man and woman, and public opinion will not, in our opinion, tolerate differential standards in this respect at the present day."[24] And in the context of discussing monogamy with or without divorce, the Committee stated, "It is not after all unreasonable to require that men should be subjected to the same rules and restrictions as women are at present."[25]

In spite of the Committee's frequent appeal to gender equity in framing its laws, complete equality escaped their grasp. Many of the issues were too complex to be resolved easily. As Tahir Mahmood has pointed out,[26] the Hindu Marriage Act of 1955 allows the marriage of a girl at eighteen, but not a boy until the age of twenty-one [sec. 5(iii)]. In spite of its efforts to create equity, the Hindu Succession Act prescribes different schemes of intestate succession for male and female intestates. The Hindu Minority and Guardianship Act of 1956 does not permit a mother to act as a child's natural guardian unless the father is dead or otherwise disqualified (sec. 6). And under the Hindu Adoptions and Maintenance Act of 1956, a natural mother would not be allowed to give her child in adoption unless the father is dead or otherwise disqualified (sec. 9).

While these differences show that complete equality has not been embodied in these bills, they should not be allowed to minimize the effort of the Committee in the direction of gender equity nor do they weaken my contention that the substantive issues of debate are issues of gender equity. Although the bills that were finally enacted may have fallen short of perfect equality, and although in the society at large they may be far from fully implemented, it is fair to say that the intention was gender equity and it was on issues of gender equity that the debate frequently hinged.

Issues for Indian Muslims

The bills of 1955–1956, which constituted the "Hindu Code," apply to the vast majority of Indians.[27] Those defined as "Hindus" in these bills include Jains, Buddhists, and Sikhs, as well as some agnostics and atheists. Moreover, it was a "Code" that was not only a unification, but also a modernization of Hindu law on the basis of reason, equality, modernity, and public opinion. Those who argued for it conceived it as a first step toward a unified civil code. The next step would be to accommodate the Muslims, Parsis, Christians, and Jews, the minorities not included in it. The bills of 1955–1956 constituted a Hindu bill for Hindus even though in the process of unifying family law for Hindus, traditional Hindu law was reconfigured in the light of modern values. Most of the minorities have been rather silent about the uniform civil code. And the government has taken the approach that it will avoid reforming the family law of minorities unless they request it. As Kiran Deshta puts it,

> The minority communities have, by and large, been maintaining a silence on the subject. This is because they feel they are too small to matter and in any case the Muslims will prevent the Uniform Civil Code from becoming a reality, so there is hardly any point in wasting energy over it.[28]

Muslims, with notable exceptions, have been strongly opposed to a uniform civil code into the present. They continue to argue the religious nature of the *Shari'at*, and champion the view that by modifying it the government would be interfering with their religion. Furthermore, according to Articles 25 and 26 of the Constitution of India, they claim the right to freedom in that area. We have noted that the Hindus argued the same thing but were overruled. But the majority in Parliament at the time was Hindu of one sort or another and was more willing to impose something on themselves than they would be to impose it on a minority. Voting blocks also influence these issues, since Members of Parliament are aware that arguing for a uniform civil code will cost them a significant Muslim vote.

The result is that the Muslims continue to argue the basic premise of a uniform civil code. They are opposed to the secularization of their law. Tahir Mahmood has stated that the Supreme Court judgment in the Sarla Mudgal case makes it clear that in judicial opinion the guiding spirit and ultimate object of Article 44 is secularity in family law—"the call for uniformity is merely the means."[29] I would put it in reverse. The call is for uniformity, the basis for that is the secularization of law. But Mahmood's statement reinforces my observation that the continuing issue that agitates Muslims is the prospect of the secularization of something they consider sacred, i.e., Muslim personal law.

Having said that, I would like to point out that when one does arrive at substantive issues, they once again, as they did for Hindus, center around matters pertaining to gender. I now turn to a number of such issues.

Polygamy. Traditional Hindu law permitted polygamy when the wife could not produce a male child. Since a son was considered essential for the eventual salvation of the father, it was one way of seeking a male child. Adoption was also a possibility, but so was polygamy. The Hindu Marriage Act of 1955 changed that. Although many Hindus objected, the Hindu Marriage Act, in Article 5, lists as the first condition for a Hindu marriage that "neither has a spouse living at the time of the marriage."

Even before the 1955 bill was passed, issues relating to bigamy reached the Bombay High Court. In *The State of Bombay* v. *Narasu Appa Mali*,[30] it was argued that the Bombay Prevention of Hindu Bigamous Marriages Act, 1946, was against the Constitution. It was argued that it was *ultra vires* the Constitution on the grounds that it discriminated between Hindus and Muslims on the grounds only of religion. The court responded that the process of social reform takes place by degree and in that light communities do not have to move at the same pace. There was also a gender issue that surfaced. To the extent that either Hindus or Muslims allow polygamy and not polyandry, they distinguish between men and woman on the grounds only of sex. The court ruled that polygamy was not based on necessity and urged movement on a uniform civil code.

The Madras Hindu (Bigamy and Divorce) Act, 1949, was challenged in *Srinivasa Aiyar* v. *Saraswathi Ammal*.[31] It was judged that the bill did not interfere with religion since one could adopt a son if one did not have one through marriage. The Uttar Pradesh Government Servant Conduct Rules, 1946, ruled that "no government servant who has a wife shall contract another marriage without first obtaining the permission of the Government, notwithstanding that such subsequent marriage is permissible under the personal law for the time being applicable to him." This was challenged in *Ram Prasad* v. *State of U.P.*[32] The petitioner was a Hindu who wanted to remarry in order to have a son. Since he had the option of adoption the court ruled polygamy could not be considered essential to the Hindu religion.

Although the last mentioned case has implications for Muslims, it was a few years later when an issue of Muslim personal law arose on this issue.[33] In *Itwari* v. *Asghari*, the petitioner asked the court to order the restitution of conjugal rights with his first wife. The court denied the request and pointed out that this request puts in doubt the conditions under which the second marriage took place. The burden of proof rests with the husband to show that the taking of a second wife involved no cruelty to the first. The court then made a statement of universal import and included Muslims under general humanitarian standards.

There are no divergent forms of cruelty such as Muslim cruelty, Hindu cruelty, Hindu Cruelty [*sic*] or Christian cruelty but the concept of cruelty is based on universal and humanitarian standards.[34]

In *Shahulameedu* v. *Subaida Beevt*[35] the Kerala High Court held that the wife of a Muslim who had taken a second wife but who still cohabited with him was nevertheless entitled to maintenance under the Code of Criminal Procedure. The court proceeded to state that the Qur'an urged monogamy for Muslims and that polygamy was the exception to the rule. It pointed to Muslim countries that had prohibited polygamy and once again urged movement toward a uniform civil code.

In *B. Chandra Manil Kyamma* v. *B. Sudershan*,[36] a Hindu male, desiring to enter a second marriage over the objection of his first wife, converted to Islam and contracted the second marriage. The court held that the second marriage was invalid and a religious conversion did nothing to validate it. And in the words of Kiran Deshta, "The court emphasized that strictly speaking both Hindu and Muslim Tenets were against the second marriage during the life time of the first wife and, therefore, this marriage is void."[37]

While acknowledging, then, that Islamic law permits polygamy, the courts have moved in the direction of questioning the conditions under which a second wife is taken and the desirability of that practice even for Muslims. To the extent that Muslims still consider this a provision of Islamic law, it is a conflict which impedes progress toward a uniform civil code. Moreover, it is beyond dispute that such issues relating to polygamy are issues of gender.

Divorce. In addressing a Muslim audience, Tahir Mahmood sought to clarify the Muslim understanding of *talaq*. It is commonly held among Indian Muslims that a husband can divorce his wife by the triple *talaq* or triple pronouncement of divorce in one breath. By saying "I divorce you" three times, the wife is divorced. Mahmood seeks to clarify what he considers the true Muslim position. There is only one process of divorce by the husband.

The husband may, if he is convinced that his marriage has irretrievably broken down, quietly pronounce one single talaq. Following this pronouncement of divorce, he has the freedom to revoke it within the period of iddat—and is in fact, greatly encouraged to do so. If he has not done so and the period of iddat expires, the marriage stands dissolved.[38]

After this, if the husband and wife agree, they can reconcile and enter a new marriage contract. This policy keeps the divorce revocable and the marriage bond renewable. This is continued to a second occasion when a husband may feel the relationship strained and once again want to dissolve the marriage bond. There is no time limit between these two events, so that if at any time throughout his life, the husband once again issues a *talaq* that will be considered a second *talaq*. Again, during the *iddat* period the divorce is revocable, and after that the marriage may be contracted a third time if both husband and wife are agreed. But, according to Mahmood, *Shari'at* does not see this as a pattern to be repeated indefinitely. It allows this only twice. If a third *talaq* is uttered, the marriage is dissolved and cannot be restored either during the *iddat* period nor after it is over. If, however, the wife married again and then because of the death of her husband or divorce, she is free again, with mutual consent she may again marry her first husband. This is a brief account of Mahmood's understanding of *talaq*. It is also his view that Muslims should reform their practices of the triple *talaq* accordingly. Such a change would involve reform from within with no help from the government. But if a uniform civil code were to be acted upon in the present historical setting, it is not Mahmood's view of the law that is commonly practiced or believed, but rather that of a triple *talaq* uttered in one breath. So, whatever conflict would arise would not involve the "correct view" of Mahmood but the "incorrect view" that is commonly practiced and believed by the majority of Indian Muslims. Since there is strong criticism of this practice not only from a minority of Muslims from within, but also by many from without the community, this is likely to be divisive, and it is a gender issue.

Mahmood also finds the law on *khul'* is not widely understood by Indian Muslims.[39] The law of *khul'* is analogous to the husband's right to *talaq*. Just as a husband may dissolve a marriage that is irretrievably broken, so may a wife. But that law is not commonly known and where it is, a male-dominated society may compel a wife to continue in the marriage bond. She has the courts to seek enforcement of her decision, and the courts may not even inquire why she has chosen this course of action. But once again, if equality were to be part of a uniform civil code, while this view of Muslim family law might embody it, the law as practiced would not and it is that social setting in which the case for equality will be argued. This too is a gender issue.

Maintenance

Perhaps the most controversial event involving Muslims in recent years, with the possible exception of Ayodhya, is the Shah Bano case and its aftermath. Although this case became public in 1985, its roots go back to 1978 when Shah Bano, a Muslim woman, was divorced from her husband after forty-four years of marriage. As required by Muslim law, he returned Rs 3,000 which had been her marriage settlement (*mahr*) from her family. Rather than accept this settlement, Shah Bano sued her former husband for maintenance under the Code of Criminal Procedure. As a result, the court awarded her Rs 180 per month. Her husband appealed to the Supreme Court, arguing that as a Muslim he had to obey the *Shari'at*, which requires only that he pay her maintenance (*iddat*) for three months. The Court held that under Article 125 of the Code of Criminal Procedure a husband was required to pay maintenance to a wife without means of support.[40] This judgment made the Code of Criminal Procedure applicable to Muslims and also gave it priority over Muslim personal law in this matter. In this judgment, Article 125 of the Code of Criminal Procedure was applicable to all Indians on a secular basis.

One Muslim writer indicated that the agitation following the Shah Bano decision was "the biggest ever launched by Muslims, post-independence."[41] The Muslim community was most incensed by two aspects of the decision. First, the Chief Justice of the Indian Supreme Court disparaged Islamic law and the status of women in Islam, and held that the Court's interpretation was in keeping with the *Shari'at*. In the eyes of many Muslims the Supreme Court had taken upon itself the task of interpreting Islamic law. Many of the clergy contended that it was inappropriate for a secular court to interpret religious law. The struggle against the secularization of family law was thus continued among Muslims. Second, the Chief Justice urged Parliament to move toward a uniform civil code. This seemed to threaten the continued practice of Muslim law in areas of succession, inheritance, marriage, and divorce, all of which are laden with gender issues.

While the Indian government was initially supportive of the Shah Bano judgment, Muslims succeeded in pressuring the government to pass the Muslim Women (Protection of Rights on Divorce) Bill of 1986, exempting Muslim women from Article 125 of the Code of Criminal Procedure, the article under which Shah Bano was previously awarded maintenance. The bill was opposed by women's groups, who saw it as a step back for women, and by militant Hindus who once again saw Muslims being specially treated.

The provisions of the Muslim Women (Protection of Rights on Divorce) Bill, 1986, are important to note since this bill both provides for Muslim women exclusively and at the same time is a bill enacted not by the Muslim community itself but by Parliament. It provides for a reasonable and fair maintenance for the divorced woman by her husband during the period of *iddat*. Where she maintains children born to her she is to be provided maintenance for two years from the birth dates of the children. She is to be provided the sum or *mahr* agreed to be paid to her at the time of her marriage according to Muslim law. And she is to have returned to her all properties or gifts given to her before or at the time of the marriage by relatives or friends or her husband and his relatives and friends. If she is unable to support herself, other provisions are made for her support. As a last resort, if neither the husband nor her family or her heirs are able to provide the support, support should be provided by the State Wakf Board. It seems clear that this legislation makes provisions that go beyond Muslim law as commonly practiced. And these provisions are mandatory upon the former husband and others. Failure to fulfill these requirements can result in fines and/or jail sentences up to one year.

It is apparent that even reform-minded Muslim intellectuals are prepared to criticize Muslim practices when talking within their community, yet resist criticism from those outside the community. This demonstrates a recognition that changes need to be made even when the attempt to impose those changes from the outside are resisted. Of course there are those who might be more pleased if nothing were changed.

Moreover, one must distinguish between Muslim practices that fall short of Muslim law ideally conceived, that is, how Muslim law might be constructed.[42] Tahir Mahmood has written a great deal on Muslim personal law and also on the uniform civil code issue. Gender issues are often at the heart of his discussions. In defending Islamic law against the accusation that it contributes to the degradation of women, he lists twelve things as the minimum that Islamic law provides for women.[43]

(i)   right to upbringing and education on a par with boys in their parents' family,

(ii) full freedom to choose a life partner and negotiate terms of married life,

(iii) an absolutely independent status in the husband's home *without severance of any rights in the parents' family*,

(iv) an unconditional right to receive *mahr* from the husband,

(v)   right to work and earn before and after marriage,

(vi) freedom to walk out of an irretrievably broken marriage and to quickly remarry,

(vii) important rights to post-divorce relief until remarriage,

(viii) right to child custody during marriage and after its dissolution,

(ix) full freedom of remarriage on becoming a widow,

(x)   shares by inheritance in the properties of all relatives in the family of birth and in husband's property after marriage,

(xi)   full ownership of all kinds of property and unrestricted rights over its management and disposal,

(xii)   right to act as qazi or mutawalli and in other public capacities, to attend public prayers in the mosques, to participate in social activities, and so forth.

It is not Mahmood's contention that all of these are being implemented in the Islamic community in India today. It is not even the case that Muslim women and men are aware of all of these provisions in his construction of Islamic law. But, whether Indian Muslims know it or not, Islamic law makes these provisions for women. But it is not this law that is operational in India today. In many instances, what is practiced "on the ground" is decidedly different, and it is these operational practices that have been judged as degrading to women. When speaking to Muslim audiences, Mahmood is quick to point this out to them. But he also wants them to be aware of the possibilities Islamic law holds for them, and wants critics outside the community to be aware of this as well.

From the point of view of this essay, then, four inferences can be drawn from this. The first is that when it comes to the content issues at stake, they cluster around the issue of gender. The second is that to the extent to which one is dealing with Islamic law in any ideal sense, participation in a uniform civil code is more easily handled. To the extent to which the issue is prevailing practices, it is less easily handled. Third, it would seem that this is frequently a rhetorical issue. Incendiary statements from outside a community, directed at any community of which one is not a part, are bound to impede progress. Finally, although the Constitution of India attempted to embody gender equity, and although that is a significant part of the struggle for a uniform civil code, the conflicts that center around gender issues and the social setting in which Indian law is implemented suggest that gender equity has yet to be achieved.

Notes

1. Of the 207 credentialed members of the Constituent Assembly who signed the register on December 10, 1946, only 5 percent were female, *Constituent Assembly Debates*, vol. I, pp. 8–14.

2. Nancy Falk, "*Shakti* Ascending: Hindu Women, Politics, and Religious Leadership During the Nineteenth and Twentieth Centuries," in *Religion in Modern India*, ed. Robert D. Baird, 3rd ed. (New Delhi: Manohar Books, 1995), pp. 298–334.

3. Robert D. Baird, *Essays in the History of Religions* (New York: Peter Lang, 1991), pp. 95ff.

4. Cf. Robert D. Baird, "Expansion and Constriction of Religion: The Paradox of the Indian Secular State," in *Religious Conscience, the State and the Law: Historical Contexts and Contemporary Significance*, ed. John McLaren and Harold Coward (Albany: State University of New York Press, 1999), pp. 189–205.

5. Upendra Baxi, *Towards a Sociology of Indian Law* (New Delhi: Satvahan Publications, 1986), pp. 45ff.

6. B. B. Chatterjee, *Impact of Social Legislation on Social Change* (Calcutta: Minerva Associates, 1971).

7. Baxi, *Towards a Sociology of Indian Law*, pp. 62–63.

8. P. C. Chatterji, *Secular Values for Secular India* (New Delhi: Lola Chatterji, 1984).

9. Robert D. Baird, "Uniform Civil Code and the Secularization of Law," in *Religion in Modern India*, ed. Robert D. Baird (New Delhi: Manohar Books, 1981), pp. 417–445.

10. *Seshammal and Others v. State of Tamil Nadu*, Supreme Court Cases, vol. II, Pt. I, 1972, 11ff.

11. *Bira Kishore Deb v. State of Orissa*, A.I.R. 1964 SC 1501.

12. *Sri Venkataramana Devaru v. State of Mysore*, S.C.J., Vol. XXI, 1958, 390.

13. J. D. M. Derrett, *Hindu Law, Past and Present* (Calcutta: A. Mukherjee, 1957), p. v; also see Donald Eugene Smith, *India as a Secular State* (Princeton, N.J.: Princeton University Press, 1963), pp. 277ff.

14. *Why Hindu Code Is Detestable* (Calcutta and Allahabad: Shastra Dharma Prachar Sabha, n.d.), p. 31.

15. P. B. Gajendragadkar, *The Hindu Code Bill* (Dharwar: Karnataka University, 1951), p. 46.

16. For an analysis of the ultimate values to which Jawaharlal Nehru appealed in his legitimation of his concept of the "secular state" for India, see Robert D. Baird, "Religion and the Legitimation of Nehru's Concept of the Secular State," in Baird, *Essays in the History of Religions*, Toronto Studies in Religion, vol. 11 (New York: Peter Lang Publishing, 1991), pp. 119–139.

17. *Report of the Hindu Law Committee* (New Delhi: Government of India Press, 1955), p. 15.

18. Ibid, p. 19.

19. Ibid., p. 22.

20. Ibid., p. 25.

21. Ibid., p. 26.

22. Ibid., p. 30.

23. Ibid., p. 6.

24. Ibid., p. 26.

25. Ibid., p. 30.

26. Tahir Mahmood, *Uniform Civil Code: Fictions and Facts* (New Delhi: India and Islam Research Council, 1995), pp. 55ff.

27. The bills of 1955–56 that are sometimes called the "Hindu Code Bill" are: The Hindu Marriage Act, 1955; The Hindu Succession Act, 1956; The Hindu Minority and Guardianship Act, 1956; and The Hindu Adoptions and Maintenance Act, 1956.

28. Kiran Deshta, *Uniform Civil Code: In Retrospect and Prospect* (New Delhi: Deep and Deep Publications, 1995), p. 59.

29. Mahmood, *Uniform Civil Code: Fictions and Facts*, p. 152.

30. A.I.R. 1952 Bom. 84.

31. A.I.R. 1952 Mad. 193.

32. A.I.R. 1957 All. 411.

33. *Itwari* v. *Asghari*, A.I.R. 1960 All. 684.

34. Ibid., 687.

35. (1970) K.L.T. 4.

36. (1989) A.P. 1. HLR 183.

37. Deshta, *Uniform Civil Code In Retrospect and Prospect*, p. 81.

38. Mahmood, *Uniform Civil Code: Fictions and Facts*, p. 81.

39. Ibid., p. 84.

40. For a good reference volume of the Code of Criminal Procedure, see R. P. Kataria, ed., *Criminal Major Acts* (Allahabad: Orient Law House, 1991).

41. Asghar Ali Engineer, ed., *The Shah Bano Controversy* (Bombay: Orient Longman Limited, 1987), p. 1.

42. I once made a point that the study of religion proceeds on the levels of "the real" and "the ideal." See Robert D. Baird, *Category Formation and the History of Religions* (The Hague: Mouton & Co., 1971), p. 20. The same can be said of law. Law on the ideal level is what is enacted and what is ideally constructed as the way people ought to live if they lived according to the law (Muslim or otherwise). The real level is what is in fact operative in society as lived. No value judgment is being made here. I am merely observing that what is lived and what is constructed as an ideal by which people ought to live are not always identical.

43. Mahmood, *Uniform Civil Code: Facts and Fictions*, pp. 74–75.

Bibliography

Books and Articles

Baird, Robert D. *Category Formation and the History of Religions.* The Hague: Mouton & Co., 1971.

———. *Essays in the History of Religions.* New York: Peter Lang, 1991.

———. "Expansion and Constriction of Religion: The Paradox of the Indian Secular State." In *Religious Conscience, the State and the Law: Historical Contexts and Contemporary Significance,* ed. John McLaren and Harold Coward. Albany: State University of New York Press, 1999.

———. *Religion in Modern India.* 3rd ed. New Delhi: Manohar Books, 1995.

Baxi, Upendra. *Towards a Sociology of Law.* New Delhi: Satvahan Publications, 1986.

Chatterji, P. C. *Secular Values for Secular India.* New Delhi: Lola Chatterji, 1984.

Derrett, J. D. M. *Hindu Law, Past and Present.* Calcutta: A. Mukherjee, 1957.

———. *The Death of a Marriage Law.* Durham: Carolina Academic Press, 1978.

———. *Religion, Law and the State in India.* London: Faber and Faber, 1968.

Deshta, Kiran. *Uniform Civil Code: In Retrospect and Prospect.* New Delhi: Deep and Deep Publications, 1995.

Dhagamwar, Vasudha. *Towards the Uniform Civil Code.* Bombay: N. M. Tripathi, 1989.

Engineer, Asghar Ali, ed. *The Shah Bano Controversy.* Bombay: Orient Longman, 1987.

Gajendragadkar, P. B. *The Hindu Code Bill.* Dharwar: Karnataka University, 1951.

Khan, Maulana Wahiduddin. *Uniform Civil Code: A Critical Study.* New Delhi: The Islamic Centre, 1996.

Mahmood, Tahir. *Uniform Civil Code: Fictions and Facts.* New Delhi: India and Islam Research Council, 1995.

———. *Personal Laws in Crisis.* New Delhi: Metropolitan, 1986.

———. *Muslim Personal Law: Role of the State in the Subcontinent.* New Delhi: Vikas Publishing House, 1977.

———. *Minorities and State at the Indian Law.* New Delhi: Institute of Objective Studies, 1991.

Parashar, Archana. *Women and Family Law Reform in India.* New Delhi: Sage Publications, 1992.

Raina, Dinanath. *Uniform Civil Code and Gender Justice.* New Delhi: Reliance Publishing House, 1996.

Report of the Hindu Law Committee. New Delhi: Government of India Press, 1955.

Singh, Alka. *Women in Muslim Personal Law*. New Delhi: Rawat Publications, 1992.

Smith, Donald Eugene. *India As a Secular State*. Princeton, N.J.: Princeton University Press, 1963.

Subbamma, Malladi. *Islam and Women*. New Delhi: Sterling Publishers, 1988.

Court Cases

B. Chandra Manil Kyamma v. *B. Sudershan* (1989) A.P. 1. HLR 183.

Bira Kishore Deb v. *State of Orissa* A.I.R. 1964 SC 1501.

Itwari v. *Asghari* A.I.R. All. 684.

Ram Prasad v. *State of U.P.* A.I.R. 1957 All. 411.

Seshammal and Others v. *State of Tamil Nadu*, Supreme Court Cases, Vol. II, part I, 1972.

Shahulameedu v. *Subaida Beevt* (1970) K.L.T. 4.

Srinivasa Aiyar v. *Saraswathi Ammal* A.I.R. 1952 Mad. 193.

Sri Venkataramana Devaru v. *State of Mysore*, S.C.J., Vol. XXI, 1958, 390.

The State of Bombay v. *Narasu Appa Mali* A.I.R. 1952 Bom. 84.

Eight

The Personal and the Political
Indian Women and Inheritance Law

Srimati Basu

The subject of reform of personal laws and the establishment of a uniform civil code in India has been a strident question in recent years. It has been debated by scholars on the grounds of constitutional validity and used by political parties to spike conservative agendas at election time, and has generally functioned as a grand theoretical straw issue with an aura of profound importance. Meanwhile, personal law is being re-formed every day in courtrooms. Some recent examples of paradigm shifts include the 1999 decision granting "natural guardianship" to Hindu mothers, which has transformed the ideologies and strategies of divorce and custody claims (SC Cuts 1999), the contradictory decisions given under the seemingly regressive Muslim Women (Protection of Rights on Divorce) Act (1986) which demonstrate the interaction between jurisprudence and politics (Begam 1989), and the establishment of Family Courts in several Indian cities where clients present personal law issues unmediated by lawyers. Personal law is also being reworked in families and communities through strategies that both call upon and bypass existing laws, playing upon the dynamics of kinship, caste, class, and gender. It is impossible to discuss the future of personal law in India without considering the contemporary workings of law and the eddies of its relationship to the state, and as is always the case with personal law, issues of gender illuminate these binds between religion, politics, and law particularly well.

Gender issues immediately complicate the very definitions of "personal law" versus a "secular code" because they focus the analysis on differential interests: whose rights are represented in either of these alternatives? Who should speak for change on behalf of whom? Religious communities do not have unitary interests when it comes to family law, and women's interests have not been prioritized in the present forms of personal law despite a lot of rhetoric to the contrary. Under each set of personal laws, male privilege is strongly entrenched under the rationale of "tradition" and "scriptural sanction."[1] But these traditions or sanctions are, of course, not self-evident. They reflect the choices of those who claimed to have interpreted religious texts, and they represent the privileges of the interpreters, their selections, exclusions, and silences (Mani 1990; Pathak and Rajan 1989). Hindus, Muslims, and Christians do not "naturally" have access to a set of clearly defined rights; rather, they have been created as legal Hindus, Muslims, and Christians as a result of historical directives. For example, Indian Sikhs and Buddhists are considered legally Hindu despite having very different scriptural sanctions, and Indian Christian laws reflect the laws of particular colonizers in different regions, e.g., the French or Portuguese, rather than a common theological core. Personal laws include numerous non-scriptural components, such as many changes in Hindu law supposedly undertaken for purposes of equity and modernization. As Archana Parashar (1992) has convincingly argued, there were many opportunities to effect comprehensive gender equity that were foiled by legislators on the grounds of preserving patriarchal traditions, or "Indian culture" as they defined it.

Is a uniform civil code the magic alternative? Again, the answer depends on the interests that would be represented in the new uniform civil code. The version championed by the Hindu right, for instance, is based on reforming other personal laws to make them similar to Hindu law, an eminently unsatisfactory situation given the extreme gender inequity within present law (Agnes 1995; Kapur and Cossman 1995). That is, this revised version is aimed at bringing Muslim men's rights "down" to Hindu men's and is not really concerned with equity across genders. Propositions to reform each set of personal laws instead, or suggestions such as that by Kishwar (1995) that personal laws be reformed along with an optional civil code instead might be more equitable alternatives. But here again is the critical question: who will do the negotiating and reforming? How will equity be ensured?

Evaluating the effectiveness of a uniform civil code thus requires an analysis of the workings of law in relation to the state. We need to pay attention to the people who are involved in the encoding of law and the political and economic interests they represent, in terms of gender, caste, class, and religion. This process must be examined at every level: in the actions of administrative officers, police officers, and agencies who execute laws, judges who interpret them, and family realms in which the "personal" is ultimately decoded to shape practices and relationships. "The state" can thus be demystified, and we are able to examine the disparate elements and interests that make up "the state" and analyze the political workings of "personal" law.

In this essay, I place gender center stage in examining the question of personal law, focusing on the ways in which gender-based power and privilege affect Indian men's and women's access to and use of the law. Who is an appropriate legal subject? How is such a subject created within family and personal realms? What are the preferred scripts of masculinity and femininity that allow one to be the optimal legal subject? That is, I analyze how legal rights are decoded and recoded in courtrooms and family settings after they have been "put into law." Within personal law, I concentrate on the topic of inheritance (an area which is able to bring together economic and ideological issues) and on three principal fields in which I see this decoding and recoding occurring: (1) ways in which women are persuaded that claiming their legal inheritance is not seemly; (2) legal maneuvers by families challenging the claims that women have made; and (3) criteria created by judges in adjudicating inheritance claims.

Without going into much detail about the constitution of the colonial and postcolonial gendered subject in India, which is outside the scope of this paper,[2] let me emphasize a couple of important concepts that frame the discourse on women and inheritance. First, it is useful to remember the negotiation between discourses of liberty and modernity vs. alleged "Indian traditions" that marked the debates over colonial and postcolonial lawmaking, a conflict which continues to suffuse contemporary judicial rhetoric (Parashar 1992). Dipesh Chakrabarty contends that the most significant opposition to egalitarian rhetoric was to "two fundamental tenets underlying the idea of 'modernity': the nuclear family based on companionate marriage and the secular, historical construction of time" (1992, 343). That is, women's lives, affected by ideals of joint family roles and ineffable "tradition," were at the center of this debate.

Second, a more specific point pertaining to the history of inheritance law illustrates the above play of discourse. The Hindu Succession Act, passed in 1956, ostensibly improved the situation because it gave widows the right to absolute (as opposed to usufructuary) maintenance and made provision for daughters to be heirs in cases of intestate succession of self-acquired property. The Act was far from being a testimonial to gender equity: it did *not* challenge the greatest privileges such as the Mitakshara coparcenary or the exemptions to equal inheritance for agricultural land (Agarwal 1994). It was based on north Indian Brahmanical patriarchy and marginalized the rights of matrilineal communities for questions of "Hindu" succession. Even within north Indian communities, it eroded the property rights of widows who had customarily been entitled to marital property despite remarriage by making remarriage an event forcing all Hindu widows to forego property (Chowdhry 1994; Agarwal 1994).

Even so, the passage of the Act occasioned widespread anxiety among legislators. "The purity of family life, the great ideal of chastity, and the great ideal of Indian womanhood" were at stake, according to Pandit Thakur Das, a member of the legislative assembly. He contended that property rights for women were an example of "equality run mad" (quoted in Kapur and Cossman 1996, 56). This statement is typical of responses that resist property law reform, which invoke the destruction of the "Indian family" as an inevitable outcome of granting property rights to women. The President, Rajendra Prasad, declared that he would veto the Act unless the notion of the coparcenary was retained (Agnes 1996, 64). Even B. R. Ambedkar, who as Nehru's law minister was the prime champion of post-independence legal reform and who resigned in protest when the Hindu Code Bill did not pass in its original comprehensive form, opposed drastic reform because he felt this could "perturb many families." He fully supported the theoretical idea of daughters being included as heirs in case of intestate succession, but when the Select Committee of the Constituent Assembly suggested that daughters and sons be treated as equal with respect to the quantum of inheritance, he "described this alteration as an effort by his enemies to make the entire reform process appear ridiculous, and thereby cause the entire reform process to be abandoned" (Parashar 1992, 124).

The Hindu Succession Act (1956) stands as a prime signifier for the contemporary position of Indian women with respect to personal law. It includes some changes that give Hindu women greater access, while veiling the significant patriarchal and patrilineal scripts on which the personal law is grounded. Debates about women's inheritance replay the discursive contest between modernity and "Hindu tradition," vaguely and broadly defined in ways usually disadvantageous to women. Ironically, these slight changes cast as far-reaching reforms are also used as ideals against which laws of other communities, e.g., so-called Scheduled Tribes, are judged (Basu 1999a). The bottom line is that at best the Hindu Succession Act (1956) improved the situation for some women, particularly widows, in some communities, thereby emphasizing that women's best economic options lay within marriage. Numerous studies show that the inheritance provision for daughters are rarely availed of, that women generally turn down shares of natal inheritance.[3] A significant issue is also the ways in which the provisions of the Act are re-interpreted by judges according to their own cultural perceptions. In other words, the Hindu Succession Act (1956) demonstrates the ways in which the discourse of modernization and development is deployed with relation to gender, as well as the resilience of patriarchal notions of property and the hegemonic status of a particular construction of Hinduism.

Does the Hindu Succession Act Fail Because Indian Hindu Women Just Don't Want Their Parents' Property?

I want to start by challenging the common notion that inheritance provisions are not availed of because Hindu Indian women are conservative and "tradition"-bound, and docilely accept the resources meted out to them within the family. I urge you instead to think of the broader socioeconomic and cultural matrix involved in making decisions about inheritance, which may show that Indian women are often instead optimizing the choices available to them and prioritizing their options.

To illustrate the complex binds from which women make decisions about property,[4] let me begin with the example of a woman here called Shipra. Having lost her mother as an infant and her father at ten, she had been raised by a paternal uncle and his wife and later lived in her brother's household. Her father had paid for the weddings of her two sisters, and her brother was responsible for her wedding costs. When it came time to divide the eighteen parcels of land owned by her father and uncle, and to get a portion of her mother's inheritance from her maternal uncles, her brother had asked if she would sign over her portion to him by registered deed, promising that he would compensate her with a lot of wedding gifts. In fact, however, she was married off hurriedly to a man visiting briefly from Delhi, and was given only a few articles of clothing as gifts, and no jewelry or household goods at all. Having already signed away her portion, Shipra thus received no property in any form, nor was she able to count on long-term help from her brother after marriage as she had hoped.

What is most significant, perhaps, is that her decision was not merely a calculated economic bargain that did not pan out as she had hoped. Having little access to either education or an independent income, her options were to be dependent either on her brother or on a putative husband, and as a single woman she could not afford to decline the "deal" he offered, whether she was aware of its ephemerality or not.

Shipra's "choice" is similar to that of many women I interviewed, who were asked formally to resign their claims by registering their shares in their brothers' names. The process of families undertaking the registration reveals that ignorance of legal provisions was not the cause of women's disinheritance; rather, innovative avenues such as the registration were regularly used to bypass legal intent. Shipra's sister's case, on the other hand, appeared more atypical in that she, in exchange for her signature, had asked for money from their brother and maternal uncle to help pay for a new residence. It turned out, however, that she took only the minimal amount of Rs 2,000 for a share worth about Rs 100,000, and even this unequal exchange was interpreted in their family history as an instance of a daughter having "extracted" money from her brother and uncles. The extraction of *any* natal family resources was thus a culturally pejorative act for the woman, and the specter of such greed was used to control the behavior of all potential female heirs.

This specter of the greedy and acquisitive woman is one of the most significant symbols that deter women. In combination with ideologies of the necessity of marriage for all women, that is, marriage as women's preferred route to property, and of women's severance from the natal family upon marriage, that is, of women losing all claim upon natal family property when they "transfer" families, it invokes a script of femininity where the woman is to be completely non-desiring, and fulfilled by marriage as an economic and cultural goal in itself. The material conditions of women's lives, such as their relative disadvantage in the labor market and lack of independent access to housing, further ensure compliance.

Patterns of property ownership among the women interviewed illustrated these ideologies and the corollary socioeconomic conditions. Marital property was the most likely route for women to be propertied. In this sample, some of the middle-class women, who had traded gold jewelry in order to purchase their residential homes, had titles in their names, and a large number of the poor women had temporary huts in their residential colonies registered in their names. Neither group had legal ownership or control over their husbands' family property during the husbands' lifetimes. As widows, a few women became de facto owners and managers of family property or received a share of affinal property if they had lived in joint patrilineal households. Perhaps most importantly for this essay, no women with brothers had been given any natal property. A few brotherless women expected to claim their shares without ill feeling, but unmarried women who had brothers did not expect to get equal portions. One other atypical route was for the chain of inheritance to be diverted in favor of women in cases where they

had been eldercaregivers to neighbors or relatives who would not customarily have been their responsibility. In sum: given that women usually acquired property following marriage, more commonly as widows,
or at any rate enjoyed the benefits of their husbands' and affines property in their lifetimes while being largely deprived of natal family property, it may be postulated that in these cases marriedness per se was
meant to be the prime productive resource, the chief means of determining a woman's standard of living. By comparison, women's labor
market resources were of secondary importance in all economic classes.

Tables 8.1 and 8.2 depict the range of responses to accepting family
property. Let me point out a few significant points: First, the difference
between women who feel that daughters *should* get family property in
an ideal situation (Table 8.2.1: 66.7%) and those who would *actually*
claim it (Table 8.1.6: 18.3%), indicating that they held back largely because of difficulty in overcoming entrenched practices rather than because of an inherent belief in women's lesser claims. Second, the pre-
dominance of the rationale about family rifts caused by women who
claimed family property (Table 8.1.1: 41.7%). These fears were not de-
lusions, as later examples will show. Most women who claimed their inheritance shares faced legal battles and severe ostracism from their
families. It is also important to note that this fear was closely tied to an
obverse feeling of pride and empowerment in some cases (Table 8.1.5:
20%), that is, women felt they were contributing to the prosperity of
their natal families by not withdrawing their portions. Given the labor
market situation, where women rarely had enough surplus income to assist their natal families from their wages, and a powerful cultural ethos
that women lost their families of birth at marriage and were completely
assimilated into their affinal families, the idea of continuing support to
the natal family is thus in itself a strong mark of contesting ideological
prescriptions.

Third, rationales such as dowry being equivalent to inheritance, or
eldercare being the province of all sons, were also ideological specters
justifying a patrilineal division of property. For example, dowry could
stand as the equivalent of inheritance only in the thinnest symbolic
sense. In these families, particularly the better-off ones, expenditure for
sons' weddings was often close to that for daughters. Moreover, a substantial portion of daughters' wedding costs went into entertainment or
gifts for the bride's affines, not for a property fund for the woman, and
most women considered personal resources and gold insignificant as
forms of property anyway. As for the hope that brothers' families would
provide lifelong gifts and gifts on ritual occasions if sisters had not
"cashed in" their property claims, few of these women got gifts regu-

Table 8.1. Respondents' Attitudes toward Taking Property
(in Percentages)

	Attitude toward taking natal property*	KE[1] N = 14	KC[2] N =16	SN[3] N = 30	Total N = 60
1	Don't want, it causes rifts with brothers/sisters-in-law; want smaller share to prevent rift.	50	37.5	40	41.7
2	Get dowry/lifelong gifts instead	28.6	25	50	38.3
3	Share husbands' wealth and affines' property instead	50	25	40	38.3
4	Could get property in sonless family	14.3	6.2	36.7	23.3
5	Want natal family's prosperity instead	7.1	37.5	16.7	20
6	Women should take natal property	0	18.8	26.7	18.3
7	Can't get property as per "custom"	0	12.5	26.7	16.7
8	Not enough property for multiple shares	7.1	12.5	23.3	16.7
9	Property goes to eldercaregivers	14.3	25	0	10
10	Should take if woman is poor or in trouble	7.1	18.8	0	6.7
11	Have own wages instead	21.4	0	0	5
12	Other	35.7	18.8	10	18.3
13	Do not know/Unknown	7.1	6.2	0	3.3

*Percentages show frequency of responses in particular categories; since some answers could be multiple, the percentages do not add up to 100.
1. KE = middle middle-class neighborhood.
2. KC = lower middle-class neighborhood.
3. SN = poor squatter colony.

larly, and they were particularly disappointed with the failure of their brothers to provide substantial help for their children's weddings as is the customary expectation. While some women did receive property for

Table 8.2. Respondents' Attitudes toward How Property Should Be
Distributed Ideally (in Percentages)

	Ideal distributions of property*	KE N = 14	KC N =16	SN N = 30	Total N = 60
1	**All children should be equally entitled**	**64.3**	**75**	**63.3**	**66.7**
1a	Equally between all children; to all children in very wealthy families	50	43.8	60	53.3
1b	According to children's needs/ abilities	14.3	37.5	10	20
1c	Parents should give to all children; refusing share is daughter's choice	0	25	3.3	8.3
2	**Should go to sons**	**28.6**	**43.8**	**43.3**	**40**
2a	To sons, while daughters get from affines	21.4	37.5	10	20
2b	To sons, while daughters get dowry	0	18.8	20	21.7
2c	To sons, per "custom"; to sons, to prevent family rifts	7.1	6.3	20	13.3
2d	Daughters should not demand share; can take property if offered by brothers	0	12.5	6.7	6.7
3	**Should go to daughters and sons, but unequally**	**28.6**	**25**	**33.3**	**30**
3a	Small token to daughters only; immovable property only to sons, other shared	28.6	18.8	20	21.7
3b	To daughters, if family sonless	0	6.3	16.7	10
4	**To eldercaregiver**	**7.1**	**25**	**10**	**13.3**

*Percentages show frequency of responses in particular categories; since some answers could be multiple, the percentages do not add up to 100.

undertaking eldercare, this was usually a contentious issue and eldercare was most often a screen for male entitlement; that is, all sons received property in equal shares even when only one of them was responsible for eldercare, and daughters who undertook eldercare received no shares of property in return.

Reform in personal law was thus essentially irrelevant in these cases, and the distribution of wealth and resources by gender was not disturbed at all. Inheritance decisions at the micro-level were not visibly inflected by legal change, and the state and legal apparatus were dim, distant specters. Who, then, gained from the reform? For women, a positive possibility was opened up to the extent that the Act recognized them as (somewhat) equal legal subjects, though it was effectively limited by economic and cultural factors. The state received the benefit of appearing progressive and relevant, being caring toward Hindu women. On the other hand, given that the distribution of material resources did not really change, the law was a cosmetic overlay in no danger of threatening power relations.

We Can Take Them to Court If They Don't Act Like They're Supposed To

In the above cases, the inheritance provisions of the Hindu Succession Act (1956) seemed almost irrelevant. The cultural preference and pressure was for women to follow customary disentitlement to property despite legal provisions to the contrary, and the legal realm was seen to be distant from the "real" workings of families. But when women did not stay within these boundaries and asserted their legal claims, or when it was assumed that they would do so (with similar results, effectively), the matter inevitably was litigated. Even though families in this sample were extremely disinclined toward starting litigation in other contexts, including cases of disputed property where they had distinct possibilities of winning, litigation ensued in *every* family where women asked for property. That is, ignorance of the law could not have been a significant reason why Hindu Succession Act provisions were not used by women, and neither were families averse to favoring formal law over customary law. On the contrary, it was clear from several of these cases that families were well aware of legal provisions as well as ways to circumvent them legally.

An account about Vimla's family provides an example. One of the most common devices for disinheriting daughters is to bypass testamentary succession altogether and leave property directly to sons as premortem gifts, whereby legal challenges from female heirs can be avoided altogether. Yet in the following episode narrated by Vimla, it is impor-

tant to note how this legal device solidifying male inheritance was justified through the specter of female greed, disloyalty, and unpredicta-
bility. Vimla's father-in-law had bought his two elder sons pieces of urban land and apartments in their own names. As for his youngest son,
Vimla's husband, it was assumed that he would inherit the common
residence where his parents had lived with him, a middle-income group
flat in Delhi, as an eldercare reward. Nothing had been said about the
father-in-law buying anything for his daughters. Yet, according to Vimla's account, in a conversation with her husband, her elder brother-in-
law told him:

> Get the flat in your own name now; your father is here now but he
> might be dead soon. Look, between us brothers there is a lot of
> love, but these 'ladies' who are there, they can say this is the house
> that belonged to the father and so they too have a share in this, but
> if father had willed it already then no one could have any com-
> plaints. . . . I can give you a surety about myself, that I will say I
> want this to go to my younger brother, but I cannot say anything
> about my wife; she could make a claim later on.

Both wives and sisters were cast in grasping, mercenary roles here,
in opposition to "pure" and selfless sons, as a way to justify the disentitlement of women. Sisters and sisters-in-law are also usually depicted
as having conflicting material interests with regard to property, and so
it is notable that here women from both sides were seen to have a common overreaching greed.

While legal strategies were used here by male heirs to settle the
situation once and for all, in other cases the law was either ignored or
treated as a tool of intimidation when women did voice a legal claim to
property. The greatest family wrath seemed to come down upon these
women for failing to have been deterred by ideological proscriptions.

Ganga told me about an ongoing family conflict that in a way recre-
ated the horror projected by Vimla's brother-in-law. Ganga's husband
and one of his brothers had looked after an old bachelor paternal uncle,
putting him in a hut next to their own at their squatter colony. Upon
his death it was apparently assumed that her husband and his *four* brothers (not just the ones directly responsible for eldercare, but all the male
heirs, there being no other male cousins) would share the uncle's cash
savings. When the brothers went to the bank and courts for this purpose, however, they were told that because of the uncle dying intestate
the money belonged to all nieces as well as nephews, and the men
needed signed releases from all the female heirs.

As the brothers anticipated, the female cousins signed a document
saying they did not need the money and that it could go to the males.

But their only sister decided that she was entitled to an equal share. From the total pot of Rs 200,000, each of the five brothers offered her a couple thousand from each of their shares, but being employed in political party work and hence relatively wise about financial matters, she saw through their ploy and brought a legal case against them. According to Ganga, their extended family and community felt she should be able to get a share if she wanted it, and that the courts would see that her claim was legitimate if she persisted, but the brothers were so outraged that they would not even let her into their houses, and were determined to use their own considerable political clout to influence the legal outcome.

In this instance, the property being contested was not a direct ancestral inheritance of indivisible rural land to which men might claim privileged access, nor was it a precise "payment" for eldercare because only two of the five male recipients were the caregivers. The sister had been deserted by her husband and had a small business besides doing political party work, so it was not as if she were enjoying property from her affinal family. The rage against her was simply because in her persistence she had rudely violated the gendered boundaries of property entitlements. As in the previous case, brotherly solidarity was viewed by the men as benevolent, whereas the sister was believed to have demonstrated treachery by revealing the embarrassing conspiracy of their efforts to keep the money.

In these and other cases, including the bargain to Shipra's sister described earlier, the "compromises" offered to women were notable. They were usually incredibly paltry sums compared to the actual inheritance, indicating that the Hindu Succession Act (1956) had not altered the connotations of "rightful" heirs to family property and that female heirs were still being treated as an absent or violently transgressive cultural category. And yet, in contrast to the familial and cultural realm, the Hindu Succession Act (1956) *had* changed matters in the realm of formal law. Ironically, women who took property claims to court among these families all won, an indication of the futility of litigating cases claiming women had no rights to the property and indicating that the law did provide minimal protection.

The Courts Constitute and Reflect
Cultural Systems

This process of both admitting and limiting women's rights to inheritance (as a consequence of and in connection with reformed succession law) is also well exemplified in the attitudes of courtroom judges. On the one hand, the aforementioned experiences of women who litigated their claims and won is borne out by my survey of appellate cases on succession reported in the *All India Reporter* journal between 1988 and 1991. Of a total of 159 succession and inheritance cases, of which 119 or 74.8 percent were considered to have significance for issues of gender, women won in 66.4 percent of the cases and lost in 29.4 percent.[5] There have been several recent instances of judges and magistrates altering women's legal entitlements and hence by extension the signifiers of femininity, for example in making both daughters and sons successors to railway quarters, deeming women to be heirs to coparcenary property in some cases, and forbidding the exclusion of children born out of wedlock from parents' property (Theophilus 1996; Thukral 1992). On the other hand, the very authors who laud these judgments point to the many remaining exclusions. The terms on which women won and lost cases are significant, showing the persistence of cultural discourses about property despite the attempt to exorcize them from formal law. These legal judgments provide rich texts for illustrating the ways in which gender is constructed, and who and what the Indian woman is supposed to be.

In many cases, judges depicted themselves as being sympathetic to women raising property concerns in court. Notably, however, such women were interpreted as morally righteous, unretaliating, simple, or helpless, i.e., constructed as deserving, "feminine" candidates of patronage. Thus, in *Joti Dadu Navale vs. Monikabai Kashinath Mohite*[6] the judge openly rebuked a brother for trying to oust his sister from their parents' property:

> The defendant has not succeeded in painting a very glorious picture of himself before the Court. On his own showing, he is a grabber. He has no regard for the rights of his own sister; that she wants only a quarter share but he was not inclined to give even that pittance.

The moralistic tone here clearly spilled beyond legal boundaries. By referring to the potential illegality and manipulative intent of the brother's adoption as an adult, his sister's plea for less than her fair share, and his attempt to carry out a legal ouster to deprive her entirely, the judge portrayed the defendant as someone grasping the wealth of his adoptive family all for himself. By not having demonstrated any token attempts to support the sister with her wedding expenses or otherwise, the defendant had done nothing to show that he had balanced his privilege of a greater share of inheritance (as a male heir) with the corresponding symbolic responsibility (as a man) of taking care of those who inherited less, and thus had no favorable ideological excuse that the judge could use to justify his legal overreaching. Similarly, some widows were depicted as deserving the Court's extra protection because of their age or their lack of legal knowledge, while their opponents' attempts to maneuver them out of their property was treated harshly. For example, In *A.Venkappa Bhatta vs. Gangamma*,[7] the widow who sought a share from the brothers-in-law controlling joint family wealth was described as

> an old lady in late sixties and literate, not well versed in the ways of the world . . . leading the sheltered life of a widow in an orthodox family. . . . very much under the influence of the first defendant, *kartha*[8] of the family and brother of her late husband. She had no sons or support to look to.

Again, the Court assumed the favored garb of protector of the most vulnerable. It is no coincidence that the lack of sons was added to her sources of weakness (she had two daughters), because the judge assumed that sons are invariably responsible for the financial and social support of parents. A similar role for daughters, who were presumably patrilocally[9] married and retained no interest in property, was not even brought up, and a conclusion that the mother had "no support" was drawn.

Women's perceived helplessness and weakness could thus be a strong ground for judicial support for them. That is, in such decisions women got judicial approval for successfully matching a favorable image of "woman," representing an ineffable "Indianness" that could be comfortably championed through law. This ideal of passivity could be deliberately invoked, such as in *Parnam Balaji vs. Bathina Venkataramayya*,[10] where a sale made several years previously by a woman whose husband had appointed her as her sons' guardian was claimed as invalid by the family, *including the woman*. They alleged that she had no right to sell because under prevailing Hindu law women did not have the right to be appointed as legal guardians who could make financial decisions. The judge did not invalidate the sale, finding that the woman had acted under the implicit authority of her husband, the official *kartha*, but explored the profound legal questions of whether women could be guardians of their children, surrogate *karthas* of the family with the husbands' permission, and even whether they were "adult members of the family" (as *karthas* needed to be) under Hindu law. In finding that women could not legally occupy those roles, the fundamental alienation and secondariness of women within "reformed" Hindu law were underlined. While the woman in this case could not win by calling upon her innate legal paralysis within contemporary law, the judgment made it clear that it was the firmness of her surrogate contract that was the determining factor, and that she did not in fact have rights to adult status or guardianship within the Hindu joint family.

Decisions dealing with property distributed on the basis of eldercare received more mixed reactions from judges, with support swinging between the validation of strong inequities in Hindu property law on the one hand and an understanding of inheritance as a reward for caregiving on the other. In *Sushila Bala Saha vs. Saraswati Mondal*,[11] the judge upheld the validity of a will where a mother left her property to one daughter (of two daughters and a son). It was decided that the distribution was not unnatural as alleged because the daughter had resided with the mother and had "looked after her comforts," whereas the son had not only failed in his "bounded [*sic*] duty" to maintain his mother but had also stolen from her, tried to defraud her, and forced her to leave her home in fear of her life. The judge clearly supported eldercare as a possible basis of property division rather than gendered rights. Yet even here, the trace of entitlement patterns differentiated by gender was seen in the reference to the *son's* duties to maintain the parent and thereby deserve a share of property, although the reward in this case was deflected because of his neglect and criminality.

In other cases, such as *Paramma vs. Chikarangappa*,[12] male entitlements to property were blatantly protected. Here, the father made a gift of one acre of land to the daughter he was living with (he had two daughters), calling the sons "lazy and vagabond." Because this land was part of the joint family estate and the daughter did not have a direct share in it, one of the few ways he could give it to her was by claiming that it was a "gift for pious purposes." The sons claimed that the gifted land was the most productive portion of the joint family estate of six or seven acres and that their father was therefore depriving them of their means of livelihood, pointing also to his obvious contempt for them and throwing in allegations about his having had a concubine. The court focused on the jointness of property and held that the gift was too large and was thus unjustifiable.

This case is a vivid example of the persistent obstacles to women's getting family property despite their attempts to overcome gender roles that rationalize their disentitlement. Whether or not women maintained ties with the natal family and assumed responsibilities like eldercare that were customarily undertaken by sons partly as a justification for receiving property, the persistence of the *legal* notion of the joint family to which only males have property rights by birth prevented the parent from rewarding daughters for help or from changing the gendered nature of inheritance despite the sons' ill treatment. The Court's support of the idea that only sons were permitted to derive a livelihood from "joint family property" and hence that daughters should only draw on individual or affinal resources, while reflective of the letter of the law, showed the paralysis of the judiciary in the inability to apportion property according to paths of affection or reward, and bowed to the patrilineal model of generational resource distribution that excluded women from sharing their natal families' wealth.

On the one hand, judges were obviously enamored of "progressive" changes made in Indian law as a result of post-colonial legislation, which mirrored a modern image of their adjudication. Several cases dealing with Section 14 of the Hindu Succession Act (1956) elicited profuse praise from judges about the "ameliorative social reform" (e.g., *Kamini Bewa vs. Srimati Dei*[13]). Yet at other times, the judiciary put the weight of its authority behind extra-legal ideologies about property and family roles that appear to run counter to the spirit of such legislation, making legal reform appear merely cosmetic. In the cases *Ajit Kumar Maulik vs. Mukunda Lal Maulik, Bhagwan Kaur vs. Chetan Singh*, and *Dharam Singh vs. Aso*,[14] the disinheritance of daughters was seen as a mark of "natural" dispensation of property, as evidence of mental stability because of adherence to custom. The marriage of daughters was regarded even by the judges as an event bringing about a disentitlement to property and being equivalent to sons having self-supporting incomes. In *Khusbir Singh v. The State*,[15] the Court claimed that a man's will made out to the son and excluding a daughter of a second marriage was quite rational because he "may well have wanted to solemnize his daughter's marriage during his lifetime and that may have led him to disinherit her," and quoted a previous judgment saying that "the two currents of natural affection and settlement of properties can flow in distinct channels, and that the change in the course of one need not necessarily have any effect on the direction of the other." The Court thus lent weight to the notion that dowry or marriage expenses can be regarded as equivalent to property shares, and fed the assumption that giving dowry was a legitimate ground for disinheritance, even though the son here got a house and a business and the daughter could at best have gotten some money in the bank, a far smaller share, as a dowry. The further justification of "channels of affection" provided gratuitous support for ideologies of women's disentitlement from property, implying that property distribution must follow pre-determined cultural routes, changes in law notwithstanding, and could not be affected by emotions or needs.

Especially notable in these cases is the ease with which customary social practices predating the laws came to be viewed as "natural behavior" motivating the dispensation of property, such as the idea that daughters with sons should be viewed preferentially because male heirs "kept" property within the "family." Often, blatant forms of gender discrimination were endorsed by judicial authority as immutable "facts" about Hindu practices, while the equality lauded in post-colonial laws simply faded away in that context. As Kapur and Cossman point out, legal judgments actively contribute to women's economic subordination: "[w]omen are not simply assumed to be economically dependent, but rather, the assumptions that inform the law continue to constitute women as economically dependent" (1996, 136). Thus, the preservation of ineffable "Indian" traditions validates the distribution of material resources.

With respect to the Hindu Succession Act (1956), the concepts most in need of change are the Mitakshara coparcenary, the notion of the Hindu Undivided Family and its male *kartha,* and exemptions applicable to agricultural land, which all evoke nebulous "traditional" family forms rather than evaluating how land, residence, work, and wealth are in fact distributed. Even though legal advances are likely to be undone in families and in courtrooms, there is symbolic and strategic significance in negotiating a baseline of legal equity. It seems important to maintain legal literacy as an important goal, even though, as noted before, ignorance of legal provisions is clearly not the core or even a large part of the problem. The ideal is, rather, to improve and transform what legal literacy means, e.g., working to question ideas that act as ideological screens, or having better conversations about what taking advantage of the available law might realistically mean. On the topic of inheritance, in particular, it seems important not to abandon the notion that women should be equal sharers (and not dependent grantees) of family resources, keeping in mind the research (e.g., Agarwal 1994) showing the economic and ideological benefits of women as property owners both in India and worldwide.

Feminist scholars and organizations have attested to the difficulties of taking sides on the issue of "personal law" versus the "uniform civil code," given the difficulties of accomplishing radical change at either the legal or social level. Some have advocated unequivocally for a uniform civil code. Regarding allegations that supporting a uniform civil code furthers the Hindu conservative agenda, Indira Jaisingh argues for the need to foreground women's interests and to point out how Hindu men have benefited most from multiple personal laws (1995, 28). Others have suggested extensive reforms within personal law, such as Madhu Kishwar's proposal (1995) to have an optional uniform civil code that would give women a default set of laws if their communities did not adequately reform legal inequities. As Agnes points out, the issue is represented as being politically polarized, constituted in terms of "binaries." It is critical, she suggests, to keep women's economic interests firmly in mind in either case, to "explore alternate measures which could safeguard women's rights without evoking the controversy of the uniform code" (1996, 62).

These feminist debates echo a broader pattern of polarization. All too often, "personal law" is discussed as if it were an entity inherently opposed to the "uniform civil code," as if everyone should line up and be counted on one side or the other. In this essay, I wanted to lay out and personalize the cultural workings of "personal law" as a way to complicate this opposition, to indicate that the problem lies not merely in the non-existence or even non-implementation of laws but in the cultural configurations of gender and law and their relationship to the state. As Linzi Manicom contends in an essay theorizing the workings of gender in the South African state, "[i]t is not just a matter of adding in women as a constituency or objective of state policy, of looking at the differential impacts and implications of state practices for men and women. Posing the relationship in this externalized way exempts both categories of 'state' and 'women' from interrogation in terms of one another; it disguises their mutual constitution in the historical process" (1992, 445). In this case, the motives attached to legal reform (building a secular state or punishing uppity religious minorities, being modern enough to protect women or protecting powerful landowner interests) are woven with the meanings of the Indian nation and its complex interests.

Such a conclusion can lead to paralyzing pessimism, but also possibly to attempts to advocate reforms for women by negotiating with the complex interests of the state. Kapur and Cossman contend that feminist engagements with law may be viewed as a "discursive struggle, where feminists seek to displace ideas of women's roles and identities" (1996, 15). That is, the legal realm should be viewed as a site of contest and struggle. Whether or not the meanings get transformed in subsequent cultural encounters, it is important to recognize and validate principles of equity through law. Rekha Pappu emphasizes the need for feminists to address not just patriarchal relations within religious communities but also patriarchal relations fostered by the state in negotiating political power and global capitalism. She places the focus for action on "adjudicatory processes" rather than just legal complaints; that is, on including the work of theorists, activists, and lawyers as part of a process which "effectively draws on, as well as shapes, feminist endeavors and politics outside the courtroom" (1997, 1051). Feminist interventions can thus lay out the legal nexus and the web of connections between law and state, foreground gender implications of proposed and existing laws, and refuse to answer the question of personal law in binary terms.

Notes

1. Parashar (1992) provides a detailed discussion of the Parliamentary debates on the Family Code where this opposition was frequently invoked.
2. See Chatterjee 1990; Nair 1996; Parashar 1992; and Kumar 1993 for extensive discussions of the subject.
3. Agarwal 1994; Basu 1999b; Magu 1996; Sethi and Sibia 1987.
4. The following examples are drawn from my fieldwork in Delhi between 1991 and 1993. I sought interviews with both middle-class and poor urban women, half being women from two apartment complexes in middle-middle- to low-middle-income neighborhoods, and the other half women from a squatter colony of largely temporary huts. I conducted a total of sixty interviews.
5. In 4.2 percent of the cases, women both gained and lost something.
6. AIR 1988 Bombay 348.
7. AIR 1988 Kerala 133.
8. *Karta/Kartha:* the titular head, usually senior male member of the Hindu joint family, and manager of the coparcenary property with discretion to sell or acquire property in the family's best interest (Diwan 1991, 339–42). Women cannot be karthas "in accordance with the texts of Hindu law" (Diwan 1991, 340), a vivid example of a contemporary question of equality closed by reference to alleged ancient authority.
9. Patrilocal refers to cultural systems in which married couples customarily reside with the groom's family following marriage.
10. AIR 1988 Andhra Pradesh 250.
11. AIR 1991 Calcutta 166.
12. AIR 1989 Karnataka 63.
13. AIR 1990 Orissa 155.
14. AIR 1988 Calcutta 196; AIR 1988 Punjab & Haryana 198; AIR 1990 Supreme Court 1888.
15. AIR 1990 Delhi 59.

Bibliography

Agarwal, Bina. 1994. *A Field of One's Own: Gender and Land Rights in South Asia*. Cambridge: Cambridge University Press.
Agnes, Flavia. 1996. "The Politics of Women's Rights." *Seminar* 441: 62–66.

———. 1995. "Redefining the Agenda of the Women's Movement within a Secular Framework." In *Women and the Hindu Right,* ed. Tanika Sarkar and Urvashi Butalia, 136–57. New Delhi: Kali.

Basu, Srimati. 1999a. "Cutting to Size: Property and Gendered Identity In the Indian Higher Courts." In *Signposts: Gender in Post-Independence India,* ed. Rajeswari Sunder Rajan. New Delhi: Kali.

———. 1999b. *She Comes to Take Her Rights: Indian Women, Property and Propriety.* Albany, N.Y.: SUNY Press.

Begam, Sherafennisa. 1989. "Maintenance and Muslim Women: Religious Orthodoxy v. Judicial Activism." *Cochin University Law Review* 13: 279–308.

Chakrabarty, Dipesh. 1992. "Provincializing Europe: Postcoloniality and the Critique of History." *Cultural Studies* 6, no. 3: 337–57.

Chatterjee, Partha. 1990. "The Nationalist Resolution of the Women's Question." In *Recasting Women: Essays In Indian Colonial History,* ed. Kumkum Sangari and Sudesh Vaid, 233–53. New Brunswick, N.J.: Rutgers University Press.

Chen, Marty, and Jean Dreze. 1992. "Widows and Health in Rural North India." *Economic and Political Weekly* 27: WS 81–93.

Chhachi, Amrita. 1991. "Forced Identities: The State, Communalism, Fundamentalism and Women in India." In *Women, Islam and the State,* ed. Deniz Kandiyoti, 144–75. Philadelphia: Temple University Press.

Chowdhry, Prem. 1994. *The Veiled Women: Shifting Gender Equations in Rural Haryana 1880–1990.* Delhi: Oxford University Press.

Committee on the Status of Women in India. 1975. *Towards Equality: Report of the Committee on the Status of Women in India.* New Delhi: Govt. of India, Ministry of Education and Social Welfare, Department of Social Welfare.

Dhagamwar, Vasudha. 1989. *Towards The Uniform Civil Code.* Delhi: Indian Law Institute.

Dietrich, Gabriele. 1986. "Women's Movement and Religion." *Economic and Political Weekly* 21: 157–160.

Diwan, Paras. 1991. *Family Law.* Allahabad: Allahabad Law Agency.

Galanter, Marc. 1989. *Law and Society in Modern India.* Delhi: Oxford University Press.

Gulati, Mitu, and Leela Gulati. 1993. "Remnants of Matriliny: Widows of Two Kerala Villages." *Manushi* 76: 32–34.

Jaisingh, Indira. 1995. "Towards an Egalitarian Civil Code." *Lawyers Collective* 10, no. 6: 28–29.

Kapur, Ratna, and Brenda Cossman. 1996. *Subversive Sites: Feminist Engagements with Law in India.* New Delhi: Sage.

———. 1995. "Communalising Gender, Engendering Community: Women, Legal Discourse and the Saffron 'genda'." In *Women and the Hindu Right,* ed. Tanika Sarkar and Urvashi Butalia, 82–120. New Delhi: Kali.

Kishwar, Madhu. 1995. "Stimulating Reform, Not Forcing It: Uniform Civil Code versus Optional Civil Code." *Manushi* 89 (July): 5–10, 10–14.

Kumar, Radha. 1993. *The History of Doing: An Illustrated Account of Movements for Women's Rights and Feminism in India 1800–1990.* London: Verso.

Magu, Poonam. 1996. "The Hindu Succession Act—Has It Really Helped Women?" *Legal News and Views* 10, no. 8: 1–3.

Mani, Lata. 1990a. "Contentious Traditions: The Debate on Sati in Colonial India." In *Recasting Women: Essays In Indian Colonial History*, ed. Kumkum Sangari and Sudesh Vaid, 88–126. New Brunswick, N.J.: Rutgers University Press.

Manicom, Linzi. 1992. "Ruling Relations: Rethinking State and Gender in South African History." *Journal of African History* 33: 441–65.

Nair, Janaki. 1996. *Women and Law in Colonial India*. New Delhi: Kali.

Pappu, Rekha. 1997. "Rethinking Legal Justice for Women." *Economic and Political Weekly* 32: 1048–1052.

Parashar, Archana. 1992. *Women and Family Law Reform In India: Uniform Civil Code and Gender Equality*. New Delhi: Sage.

Patel, Vibhuti. 1989. "National Conference on Women, Religion and Family Laws in India." *Indian Journal of Social Work* 50, no. 1: 125.

Pathak, Zakia, and Rajeswari Sunder Rajan. 1989. "Shahbano." *Signs* 14: 558–82.

Rosen, Lawrence. 1978. "Law and Social Change in the New Nations." *Comparative Studies in Society and History* 20, no. 1: 3–28.

Sarkar, Lotika. 1976. "Jawaharlal Nehru and the Hindu Code Bill." In *Indian Women: From Purdah To Modernity*, 87–98. New Delhi: Vikas.

Sarkar, Tanika. 1993. "Rhetoric against Age of Consent: Resisting Colonial Reason and Death of a Child-Wife." *Economic and Political Weekly* 28: 1867–78.

Sethi, Raj Mohini, and Kiran Sibia. 1987. "Women and Hindu Personal Laws: A Sociolegal Analysis." *Journal of Sociological Studies* 6: 101–13.

Sharma, Ursula. 1980. *Women, Work and Property in Northwest India*. London: Tavistock.

Singh, Indu Prakash. 1989. *Women, Law and Social Change in India*. New Delhi: Radiant.

Som, Reba. 1994. "Jawaharlal Nehru and the Nehru Code: A Victory of Symbol over Substance?" *Modern Asian Studies* 28: 165–94.

Spivak, Gayatri Chakravorty. 1988. "Can the Subaltern Speak?" In *Marxism and the Interpretation of Culture*, ed. Cary Nelson and Lawrence Grossberg, 271–316. Urbana: University of Illinois Press.

"Supreme Court Cuts the Guardian Knot, Gives Mother Her Due." 1999. *Times of India*, 19 February.

Theophilus, Harrison John. 1996. "Of Women and Legislation." *Deccan Herald*, 17 November.

Thukral, Gobind. 1992. "Judgment Leaves Women Landless." *Hindustan Times*, 4 November.

Uberoi, Patricia. 1996. "Hindu Marriage Law and the Judicial Construction of Sexuality." In *Feminist Terrains in Legal Domains*, ed. Ratna Kapur, 184–209. New Delhi: Kali.

Nine

Observations on the Historical Destruction of Separate Legal Regimes

Kunal M. Parker

The established historiography of Anglo-Indian law places the origin of the "personal laws" in Warren Hastings's Plan of 1772, according to which the early colonial state promised the natives of the newly conquered provinces of Bengal, Bihar, and Orissa that, with respect to "inheritance, marriage, caste, and other religious usages, or institutions, the laws of the Koran with respect to the Mahometans, and those of the Shaster with respect to the Gentoos, shall be invariably adhered to. . . ."[1] Legal historians have long speculated on the origin of this list of topics ("inheritance, marriage, caste, and other religious usages"), with J. Duncan M. Derrett suggesting that Hastings was influenced in creating this list of topics by the distinction between secular and ecclesiastical jurisdiction in England.[2] Although the "personal law" was itself an entirely colonial creation, the promise that the colonial state was simply engaged in an act of "preservation" was ritually invoked in legislation throughout the colonial period.[3]

I want to begin this essay by articulating a relationship between (i) the sphere of the "personal," which the colonial state committed itself to preserving, and (ii) the sphere of the "impersonal," which the colonial state claimed more or less overtly for itself, a sphere bound up with sedimented understandings of sovereignty. If we take the sphere of the "impersonal" to encompass everything that was *not* "inheritance, marriage, caste, and other religious usages or institutions," we obtain a sense of its magnitude. If one is to employ the vocabulary of the familiar Anglo-American division between public and private law, the sphere of the "impersonal" encompassed *both* public and private law, the realms of crime on the one hand, and contract, property, and tort on the other hand. The choice of the admittedly awkward phrase "impersonal" here is deliberate; it is intended to undercut the neutrality of the more common term "general law," which is ordinarily opposed to "personal law," in order to subvert the understanding that the "personal law" is somehow bound up with issues involving identity, while the "general law" is somehow not.

Throughout the nineteenth century, there were numerous discrete points of tension between the realm of the "personal law" and the realm of the "impersonal law." This is not in the least surprising in light of the fact that the legal subjectivities instantiated within the "personal law"—the subjects of marriage, inheritance, and so on—were represented as radically different from the legal subjectivities instantiated within the "impersonal law"—the subjects of property, contract, and so on. In one sense, one can interpret these points of tension as being immanent in the colonial project itself; in justifying itself to its various constituencies, the colonial state was committed in equal measure to "preserving" certain kinds of legal subjectivities and to generating certain other kinds of legal subjectivities.

How is one to understand, however, the way in which the discrete points of tension between the "personal law" and the "impersonal law" were resolved? Of course, instead of collapsing these discrete points of tension into a species of Whiggish narrative, it is important to historicize them with the aim of recuperating the different legal subjectivities that their resolution summoned forth at specific points in time. There would be no insensitivity to historical specificity, however, to suggest that the resolution of tensions between the "personal law" and the "impersonal law" was invariably patterned in ways that were gendered.

This essay argues that the male legal subjectivity was inevitably permitted to develop a hybrid quality, straddling the realms of the "personal law" and the "impersonal law," whereas the female legal subjectivity was inevitably denied a hybrid quality, and forcibly located within the realm of the "personal law." It then considers some of the implications of the creation of these gendered legal subjectivities in terms of the distinction between "law" and "politics" in the context of debates surrounding the reform of the "personal laws."

I will offer two examples to illustrate the construction of a hybrid male legal subjectivity, both drawn from the work of contemporary historians. First, Radhika Singha's work on the creation of a justice system in early colonial Bengal and north India explores the construction of a male criminal legal subjectivity. Under the Nawab's government, the

state did not assert an exclusive claim over taking the lives of its subjects. When an individual took the life of another, therefore, his liability
was principally toward the family of the deceased. Under this system,
the killing of women by male family members—fathers, brothers, husbands, and sons—for irregular sexual behavior, sanctioned by culturally
encoded Hindu and Muslim legal precepts, was considered an offense
against nobody in particular. By contrast, the company asserted an exclusive claim over taking the lives of its subjects. How then was it to
respond when British officials were informed, as they often were, that
men had the unfettered right to chastise, maim, or kill their female relatives for "immorality"? At stake was the company's reputation for "upholding morality." "People of severity complain," wrote Buchanan-
Hamilton, "that since the English government, there is more laxity
among women than formerly, the husbands being afraid of making severe examples in case of frailty, as were formerly usual; for with whatever was done the Nawab's government did not interfere." Singha outlines how the company dealt with the conflict between the new claims
of the state on the one hand, and the concern with accommodating patriarchal codes on the other hand. While British judges were busily con-
juring up the new legal subjectivity of the criminal, focusing on "criminal intent" to identify the severity of a crime "against the public," they
also demonstrated sympathy for men who killed deviant female relatives:

> [British judges] would accept adultery, or the breach of the sexual
> code [by] a near female relation as a circumstance productive of
> "sudden irritation" or "impulse" as distinct from one performed
> with premeditated intent. But there were cases in which it was
> clear that the killing had been planned with some deliberation, or
> that there had been a long knowledge of the "illicit" relationship.
> Here too the background of sexual impropriety was often accepted
> by British judges as a "mitigating factor." Implicitly therefore,
> if not explicitly, the sentences formulated by British judges ex-
> pressed a sympathy for the idea that the violation of male honour
> demanded retribution. In these early trials the distinction between
> the idea of a "lawful" homicide and that for which there were
> "mitigating circumstances" was very blurred indeed.

What Singha is describing is the creation of a male criminal legal subjectivity, associated with legal markers of subjectivity such as "intent,"
"premeditation," "sudden irritation," "impulse," "mitigating circumstances," and so on, that inhabits the sphere of "impersonal" criminal

law, while at the same time inhabiting the sphere of a patriarchal "personal law."[4]

Second, David Washbrook describes the profound tension, occurring in different ways throughout the nineteenth century, between the "personal laws" and the "impersonal laws" of property, contract, and so on. If the "impersonal laws" sought "to free the [male] individual in a world of amoral market relations," the "personal laws" sought to entrench "ascriptive (caste, religious and familial) status as the basis of individual right."[5] In various ways, therefore, the "personal laws" interfered with the (male) individual's abilities to possess, acquire, use, and accumulate property, especially land, through the multiple, complex, and stultifying claims of the Hindu joint family. For the emergent middle classes that occupied the professional spaces created by colonial rule, the shadow of the "personal laws" could prove exceedingly burdensome. Washbrook writes:

> As the law evolved in the first half of the nineteenth century, it tended to favour the principle of community trust at least as much as that of the private property right. In reflection of the contradiction, the courts recognised two different species of property in which owners had different kinds of right: "individual" property which could be possessed and used freely and "ancestral" property which was subject to encumbrance and the claims of the family. However, the balance of the law was inclined to favour the latter at the expense of the former. It was held that if an individual received any substantial help in his business activities from members of his joint-family, then all his business profits were joint-family property and fell on the ancestral side of the line. In South India at least, this was carried so far that if a lawyer, civil servant or other member of the "learned" professions had received support from his family during his education, then his earnings throughout his career belonged to them rather than himself.[6]

The extraordinary difficulties felt by members of the emergent middle classes because of the Anglo-Hindu doctrine of the "gains of learning," to which Washbrook is referring, were eventually resolved to free the individual from the claims of community. Thus a male legal subjectivity, capable of owning, accumulating, and disposing of property, emerged out of the conflict between the "personal" and "impersonal" laws. Albeit in very different ways, both of these examples point to the construction of hybrid male legal subjectivities that straddled the boundaries between the sphere of the "personal" and the sphere of the "im-

personal." This is the case regardless of whether those spheres reinforced each other (as in the example drawn from Singha) or were in
conflict with each other (as in the example drawn from Washbrook).

The history of the construction of female legal subjectivity in nineteenth-century India is entirely different. If the male legal subjectivity
straddled the spheres of the "personal" and the "impersonal" laws, and
was permitted to develop a hybrid quality, the female legal subjectivity
was resolutely situated within, indeed often firmly forced into, the
realm of the "personal laws." In fact, it would not be at all an exaggera-
tion to claim that the female legal subjectivity in nineteenth-century
India has little sanctioned existence outside of the sphere of the "personal laws" generally, and of the sphere of marriage more specifically.
This is evident from an examination of social reform movements directed at transforming the Anglo-Hindu law itself, as well as the dissemination of Anglo-Hindu legal norms to communities with claims to
be governed by legal regimes at odds with the Anglo-Hindu law. I will
mention the former very briefly, and spend a little more time dealing
with the latter.

The recent historiography of social reform relating to Hindu women
in colonial India treats social reform as a series of colossal politico-legal
debates scattered across the nineteenth century—*sati*, widow remarriage, the Rakhmabai case, the age of consent controversy, and so on—
all of which attempted to reform the Anglo-Hindu law of marriage with
a view to producing a specific kind of legal space for women in marriage. (The term "Anglo-Hindu" is critical here because, as Sudhir
Chandra points out, certain legally sanctioned marital rights such as the
right of a husband to compel the restitution of a wife, which was the
source of controversy in the Rakhmabai case, were in fact patriarchal
English *imports* into the Anglo-Hindu law that appeared to have no
sanction in Hindu legal texts.[7]) Historians from Lata Mani to Tanika
Sarkar have shown that these debates, albeit directed toward "improving" the status of women, in fact occluded female subjectivity more or
less entirely, so that the debate is framed by (Indian or British) male
modernizers on the one hand, and (Indian) male traditionalists on the
other, neither of whom envisaged a role for women outside marriage.[8]
What distinguishes these debates is their highly public character, the
fact that they consisted of frontal assaults on the Anglo-Hindu law
itself.

What is arguably more serious, and undoubtedly less well-known, is
the story of the judicial dissemination of Anglo-Hindu legal norms—
commonly represented as "reform"—to a range of groups who claimed
to be governed by legal regimes at variance with the Anglo-Hindu law.

Historians of social reform—content to restrict themselves to exploring the pathologies of the major debates on *sati,* widow remarriage, the Rakhmabai case, the age of consent controversy, and so on—have ignored the judicial "reformist" dissemination of Anglo-Hindu norms that occurred incrementally within the technical vocabularies of the law. This disregard is hardly new. Anglo-Indian judges themselves recognized that their "reformist" activity was shielded from public scrutiny when they boasted that "judicial decisions have *silently* promoted the cause of female emancipation and progress."[9] However, the dissemination of Anglo-Hindu legal norms had the effect of dislodging alternative legal regimes for women, with the result that women in such groups were forced into the legal subjectivity imagined for Hindu women, which, as I have suggested, had little existence outside of marriage. I will discuss three examples of this dissemination of Anglo-Hindu norms that had the effect of situating women within marriage, each of which operated through a different legal modality.

First, G. Arunima's recent work on the transformation of the matrilineal *tarvad* (joint family) in Malabar Nayar communities over the course of the nineteenth century illustrates the colonial judiciary's seemingly willful misinterpretation of custom to effect (i) the slow erosion of the property rights of women within the *tarvad* and (ii) the simultaneous concentration of property rights within the oldest male member of the *tarvad*.[10] Arunima shows in painstaking detail how colonial courts, in the guise of upholding the "true" customs of Malabar Nayars, systematically disenfranchised women in the *tarvad* by ruling that there was "insufficient proof [within the body of Malabar customary law] to determine the authority of a female over a male," by vesting control of the *tarvad* property in the oldest male member thereof, and by drawing a distinction between "family property" and "self-acquisitions" to the eventual detriment of women. Arunima writes:

> [T]hroughout this period tarvads and individual members within them continued to amass landed property, either as part of "family property," or as their self-acquisition. The difference between the two, in this period, lay in the fact that increasingly "family property" constituted the bulk of the purchases, whereas "self-acquisitions" would comprise a few of the investments made by the karnavan [the male head of the *tarvad*] or a younger member. Here too, the difference lay in that while the karnavan could use "family funds" to make "self-acquisitions," others would have to use separate sources of wealth. This invariably meant that a gendered difference emerged amongst the younger kin regarding the right to

"self-acquisitions." Only younger men could have access to "self-acquisitions" as they were the ones with alternative sources of wealth, usually from professional employment. Women of the large tarvads scarcely received any public education in this period, and definitely did not seem to have any professional employment. This made it difficult for them to acquire their "own" property.[11]

Legally denied the possibility of heading the *tarvad* (with the concomitant right to dispose of family property), the legal subjectivity of Malabar Nayar women came over the course of the nineteenth century to approach that of women within the patriarchal Anglo-Hindu law.

Second, the textual Anglo-Hindu law "attacked" custom explicitly where custom had the effect of conferring upon women legal subjectivities in excess of, or at variance with, female legal subjectivity within the Anglo-Hindu law. Two examples are sufficient here, both of which I draw from Sripati Roy's *Customs and Customary Law in British India,* published in 1910. First, in the mid-nineteenth century, among the Talapda kole caste in the Bombay Presidency, custom provided that a woman was permitted to leave the husband to whom she had been married and contract a second marriage (known as *natra*) with another man, entirely without her husband's consent. In a case in which he was charged with adultery, the second "husband" pleaded caste custom in his defense. When the Sessions Judge consulted caste elders, they informed him that, according to caste custom, "a woman can leave her first husband and contract a second marriage with another man," "permission of the caste [was] not necessary as a preliminary to such a contract of second marriage," and "if [the woman] restores to [her first husband] any property she might have acquired by her first marriage, she does not lose her position in the caste."[12] When the case was appealed to the Bombay High Court in 1864, the Bombay High Court sustained the adultery conviction and struck down the custom; in its view, even if the custom were proved to exist, it was invalid as "being entirely opposed to the spirit of the Hindu law."[13] Sripati Roy's commentary on this case, written in 1910, is worth reproducing:

> Apart from law, such custom is certainly reprehensible on social as well as moral grounds. If it is allowed, then the doctrine of polyandry, which is abhorrent to nearly every religious system, will be admitted to prevail among the Hindus. The Talapda caste, though occuping [*sic*] an inferior position in the gradation of castes, are certainly Hindus. The matrimonial bond will have no force at all if it is held that a wife would be at liberty at any moment to leave her husband and without any formalities whatsoever.[14]

Second, in 1901, in the case of *Mohini Debi v. Rai Basanta Kumar Singha,* the Calcutta High Court confronted the question of whether a Hindu wife could refuse to go and live with her husband at his own house on the basis of an agreement whereby the husband had bound himself to live permanently and unconditionally in the house of his mother-in-law. The wife in the case set up a further defense that it was against the custom of her family for the daughter of a Rajah to go and live in the house of her husband. The custom appears not to have been proved to the satisfaction of the Calcutta High Court. Roy reports the resolution of this case as follows:

> Their Lordships decided the question on the basis of the Hindu law and usage and after very carefully considering the various texts on the legal aspects of a Hindu marriage on the conjugal relation and the duties of the married parties and on the marital rights of a Hindu husband, held that such agreement was unquestionably opposed to public policy as "it permanently controls the right of the husband as conferred upon him by the Hindu law, as soon as the marriage is effected."[15]

Finally, during the second half of the nineteenth century, Anglo-Indian law effectively destroyed communities of temple dancing women in southern and western India by criminalizing them under Section 372 of the Indian Penal Code for "sell[ing], let[ting] to hire, or otherwise dispos[ing] of any minor under the age of sixteen years with intent that such minor shall be employed for the purpose of prostitution or for any unlawful and immoral purpose. . . ."[16] Although this might be seen as the construction of a criminal legal subjectivity for women, the contours of the "crime" for which temple dancing women were convicted suggest its intimate relationship with Anglo-Hindu norms of marriage. Temple dancing girls constituted corps of unmarried temple servants who had been dedicated to temple deities as young girls through rites resembling Hindu marriage ceremonies. In the late 1860s, when colonial courts in the Bombay and Madras Presidencies began convicting temple dancing girls for dedicating young girls to temple idols, they focused upon the dedication ceremony as evidence of the "crime" of "prostituting" young girls. In the first such conviction in Bombay, the accused, Jailí Bhávin, was convicted of performing the *shej* ceremony on a child. The ceremony was described as follows:

> A *khangira*, or knife, is put on the ground before the idol, and the girl who is to undergo the ceremony puts a garland on the knife, her mother then puts rice on the girl's forehead, and the

officiating priest then weds the girl to a knife, just as if he were to unite her to a boy in marriage, by reciting the *mantrás,* while a curtain is held between the girl and the knife. The girl becomes a Bhávin, and dedicated to the service of the temple, and cannot marry again, and subsists generally by prostitution after attaining majority.[17]

What is important here is that "prostitution" was defined principally as sexual activity outside marriage, a definition of the word derived from Anglo-Hindu law that had been deployed against Hindu women during the nineteenth century to divest them of property, expel them from caste, and so on. When Anglo-Indian courts convicted temple dancing girls of "prostituting" young girls, therefore, they did so because temple dancing girls were seen, through the performance of a dedication ceremony modeled on Hindu marriage ceremonies, as depriving young girls of the opportunity to contract a "real" marriage and, therefore, as opening up for young girls a life in which sexual activity could take place outside of marriage. Because "prostitution" was defined residually in opposition to marriage, the arguments raised by temple dancing girls that they did not practice "prostitution," understood as mere transactional sexual activity, were entirely unavailing. Anglo-Indian courts occasionally heard arguments by temple dancing girls that they did not participate in the urban sex trade or that they could not be considered "prostitutes" because they were "kept by the same man for a year or more. . . ."[18] Such arguments were uniformly rejected. A Bombay High Court ruling on this question from 1899 suggests why:

> The distinction sought to be made between prostitution and concubinage is . . . without any basis. [T]he life most likely to be led by the girl in consequence of the dedication would be an immoral life, being of the same kind as that of the *Bhavins* . . . or *Basvis* . . . , among whom married life was impossible, and prostitution the usual means of livelihood.[19]

Each of the examples discussed above shows how the female legal subjectivity was forcibly located within the general sphere of the "personal laws," and in particular organized around marriage.

The argument so far may be summarized as follows. Beginning with the colonial division of the legal universe into the spheres of the "personal" and "impersonal," I have attempted to show how the colonial production of legal subjectivities was gendered, so that the sanctioned hybrid male legal subjectivity straddled both spheres, whereas the sanctioned female legal subjectivity was resolutely located within the sphere of the "personal" laws. There were two ways in which the female legal subjectivity was situated within the sphere of the "personal" laws. The first, which has received considerable attention from contemporary historians, consisted of reform movements directed at the Anglo-Hindu law itself—*sati*, widow remarriage, the Rakhmabai case, the age of consent controversy, and so on—which sought to substitute a "traditional" patriarchy with a "new" or "enlightened" one. The second, which has received less attention from contemporary historians, consisted of judicial "reformist" activity that took the form of dislodging alternative legal regimes—in the name of interpreting "custom," the Anglo-Hindu law, or the Indian Penal Code—in order to disseminate Anglo-Hindu legal norms in respect of the legal subjectivity of women. Here, relatively "non-patriarchal" regimes were extirpated by the Anglo-Indian judiciary and the "new" or "enlightened" Anglo-Hindu patriarchal regimes installed in their place.

In order to forge a connection between these developments and the problem of the personal laws in contemporary India, it is worth embarking upon a somewhat lengthy digression into the historiography of Indian nationalism and the "woman question." I draw here upon the work of Partha Chatterjee, who has written very extensively, and certainly most influentially, about these questions.[20] Chatterjee poses the question of why the "woman question" that so deeply occupied social reformers throughout the nineteenth century—*sati*, widow remarriage, the Rakhmabai case, the age of consent controversy—disappeared from public debate toward the end of the nineteenth century. Rejecting the responses of liberal historians (who interpret that disappearance as the occlusion of women's issues by the rise of an atavistic nationalism), Chatterjee argues instead that Indian/Hindu nationalism located the "woman question" within "an inner domain of sovereignty, far removed from the arena of political contest with the colonial state, [where] [t]his inner domain of national culture was constituted in the light of the discovery of 'tradition.'"[21] This took place through a new coding of the familiar distinction between the "world" and the "home." I quote at length a very familiar passage from Chatterjee's work:

The material/spiritual dichotomy, to which the terms *world* and *home* corresponded, had acquired . . . a very special significance in the nationalist mind. The world was where the European power had challenged the non-European peoples and, by virtue of its superior material culture, had subjugated them. But, the nationalists asserted, it had failed to colonize the inner, essential identity of the East, which lay in its distinctive, and superior, spiritual culture. Here the East was undominated, sovereign master of its own fate. For a colonized people, the world was a distressing constraint, forced upon it by the fact of its material weakness. It was a place of oppression and daily humiliation, a place where the norms of the colonizer had perforce to be accepted. It was also the place, as nationalists were soon to argue, where the battle would be waged for national independence. The subjugated must learn the modern sciences and arts of the material world from the West in order to match their strengths and ultimately overthrow the colonizer. But in the entire phase of the national struggle, the crucial need was to protect, preserve, and strengthen the national culture, its spiritual essence. No encroachments by the colonizer must be allowed in that inner sanctum. In the world, imitation of and adaptation to Western norms was a necessity; at home, they were tantamount to annihilation of one's very identity.[22]

As might be expected the "inner" is coded as female, the "outer" as male, so that (i) men are soiled by their necessary negotiation with the "outer" imposed by colonialism and (ii) women represent the "inner," coming thereby to play a very special role in symbolizing, preserving, and perpetuating the nation. In this regard, Chatterjee points out that a "new" or "enlightened" patriarchy comes to define this woman representing the inner "autonomous" domain:

The new woman defined in this way was subjected to a *new* patriarchy. In fact, the social order connecting the home and the world in which nationalists placed the new woman was contrasted not only with that of modern Western society; it was explicitly distinguished from the patriarchy of indigenous tradition, the same tradition that had been put on the dock by colonial interrogators. Sure enough, nationalism adopted several elements from tradition as marks of its native cultural identity, but this was now a "classicized" tradition—reformed, reconstructed, fortified against charges of barbarism and irrationality.

The new patriarchy was also sharply distinguished from the immediate social and cultural condition in which the majority of the people lived, for the "new" woman was quite the reverse of the "common" woman, who was coarse, vulgar, loud, quarrelsome, devoid of superior moral sense, sexually promiscuous, subjected to brutal physical oppression by males. . . . It was precisely this degenerate condition of women that nationalism claimed it would reform. . . . [23]

Chatterjee explains both (i) the disappearance of the "woman question" from late-nineteenth-century public discourse and (ii) the passage of the Hindu Code in the post-independence period in terms of this nationalist arrogation of claims over Indian Hindu women, who were made to inhabit the space of the sovereign, untainted "tradition" that would be removed from negotiation with the colonial state on the one hand, and imposed upon all kinds of women in the post-independence period on the other hand.

My object in citing Chatterjee's work so extensively is that it shows productive connections between late-nineteenth-century nationalist discourse and the colonial construction of gendered legal subjectivities. These are connections that Chatterjee never explores, but with which (I assume) he would not disagree. If men within nationalist discourse were soiled by their necessary negotiation of the constraints put in place by the colonial state in the external world, the colonial male legal subjectivity, as described here, straddled the spheres of the "personal" and "impersonal" laws. If women within nationalist discourse were constructed as "pure" markers of the nation, the colonial female legal subjectivity, as described here, was firmly and often forcibly situated within the "personal" laws and imagined in terms of (typically reconstructed) Anglo-Hindu norms of marriage. But this is not a matter of the isomorphic instantiation within *both* nationalist discourse and colonial law of the gendered distinction between the home and the world. The point is rather that nationalist discourse imagines a kind of female legal subjectivity that *is actively brought into being by colonial law through the destruction of a variety of separate legal regimes.* This connection between nationalist discourse and colonial legal subjectivities can be discerned in the legal texts of the early twentieth century. I quote two related passages from Sir Gooroodass Banerjee's *The Hindu Law of Marriage and Stridhana.* Banerjee states that "Indian life presents almost every possible form of the conjugal relation, from the grossest polyandry verging on promiscuity, to the purest and most rational form of monogamy."[24] For him, the task of the judge is to promote the latter at the expense of the former, given the importance of marriage. He states: "The strong moral sentiment with which [marriage] is associated in the minds of men in civilized society, and the firm conviction they have of its necessity, for the preservation and well-being of the race, have led most people to think that marriage is a natural relation. . . ."[25] I will not quote, but the reader can readily imagine, what Sir Gooroodass has to say about temple dancing girls.

How then is one to explain the coexistence of (i) the disappearance of frontal assaults upon the Anglo-Hindu law—*sati,* widow remarriage, the Rakhmabai case, the age of consent controversy, and so on—from the arena of colonial public debate and (ii) the judicial "reformist" on-slaught against various subaltern women—dancing girls are an excellent example—who continued forcibly to be drawn within the fold of the Anglo-Hindu law, transformed into "new women," as it were, into the 1920s, 1930s, and 1940s? One explanation has to do with the familiar distinction between "politics" and "law."[26]

Within Anglo-American legal history, for example, the distinction between "politics" and law" has been explored productively in the context of capital-labor relations in the nineteenth century to explain how explicitly "political" questions relating to the claims of labor were re-moved from the arena of "politics," transformed into "legal" questions and displaced into the arena of "law," where they could be contained within the intricacies of legal doctrine.[27] This distinction might be made in the context of reformist activity related to women in colonial India. Certain kinds of highly public "reformist" activity surrounding women clearly occupied the realm of "politics," but were eventually relegated to "reformist" law, and therefore disappeared as nationalist discourse removed the "woman question" from the realm of the contest with the colonial state. Other kinds of surreptitious judicial "reformist" activity surrounding women clearly occupied the realm of "law," and therefore continued to flourish even as nationalist discourse claimed In-dian Hindu women for itself. The fact that nationalist discourse never attempted to save the latter women from the colonial state, even as it erased such women—as well as its debts to colonial law—from national history is telling insofar as it exposes the way in which the realms of "politics" and "law" are constructed in the context of "negotiated inde-pendence."

Purely with a view to spurring further exploration of the issue, I will end by attempting to forge a link between the history of the destruction of separate legal regimes governing women during the colonial period with the structure of the post-independence debate about the "personal laws" and uniform civil code that forms the subject of this collection of essays. Although the issue of the "personal laws" cannot be *reduced* to one of gender, it cannot be denied that gender is an extremely important aspect of the "personal laws" debate. It is only to this aspect that I refer. Partha Chatterjee is undoubtedly correct when he suggests that Indian Muslims construct their relationship toward the Indian state exactly as Indian Hindu nationalists constructed their relationship toward the co-lonial state, by removing the "woman question" from the arena of nego-tiation with the state into an inner domain of sovereignty, identity, and culture. In accordance with this analysis, Indian Muslim women come to inhabit the sphere of the "personal law," while Indian Muslim men straddle the spheres of the "personal" and "impersonal laws." The complicity of the Indian state in this situation cannot be gainsaid. Just as in the case of the nationalists' relationship with the colonial state, however, the question of the relationship between "politics" and "law" in the context of this minority "nationalism" remains to be explored. What are the kinds of Muslim gendered legal subjectivities at stake in the battle surrounding the personal law? Which are assigned the status of "politics" (and removed from the arena of negotiation with the state) and which the status of "law" (and abandoned to various kinds of judicial "reformist" activity)? Who pays what price for being claimed by minority "nationalism"? While one must be careful to avoid falling into the trap of supporting a position adopted by the Hindu right, perhaps one might begin to explore the extent to which the construction of the Muslim gendered legal subjectivity in contemporary India has provided justification for the emergence of an Indian Muslim minority politics in contemporary India.

Notes

1. Quoted in John H. Mansfield, "The Personal Laws or a Uniform Civil Code?" in Robert D. Baird, ed., *Religion and Law in Independent India* (New Delhi, 1993), p. 145.

2. Ibid., p. 146.

3. Of course, I am only suggesting that the idea of "personal law," rather than the substance thereof, was a colonial creation. It hardly seems worth mentioning at this late date that the substance of the personal laws was also thoroughly transformed through centuries of interpretation by the Anglo-Indian judiciary.

4. This entire discussion is drawn from Radhika Singha, "Civil Authority and Due Process: Colonial Criminal Justice in the Banaras Zamindari, 1781–95," in Michael R. Anderson and Sumit Guha, eds., *Changing Concepts of Rights and Justice in South Asia* (1998), pp. 51–52.

5. D. A. Washbrook, "Law, State and Agrarian Society in Colonial India," *Modern Asian Studies* 15 (1981): 649, 654.

6. Ibid., p. 657.

7. Sudhir Chandra, "Whose Laws? Notes on a Legitimizing Myth of the Colonial Indian State," *Studies in History* 8 (1992): 187.

8. Lata Mani, "Contentious Traditions: The Debate on Sati in Colonial India," in Kumkum Sangari and Sudesh Vaid, eds., *Recasting Women: Essays*

Kunal M. Parker

198

in Colonial History (1989) 88–126; Tanika Sarkar, "Rhetoric against the Age of Consent: Resisting Colonial Reason and Death of a Child-Wife," *Economic and Political Weekly* 28 (1993): 1869.

9. Statement attributed to Justice West of the Bombay High Court in *Indu Prakash*, 14 March 1887, quoted in Chandra, "Whose Laws?" 187, 210.

10. G. Arunima, "A Vindication of the Rights of Women: Families and Legal Change in Nineteenth-Century Malabar," in Anderson and Guha, *Changing Concepts*, p. 114.

11. Ibid., p. 124.

12. Sripati Roy, *Customs and Customary Law in British India* (1910), p. 557.

13. *Regina v. Karsan Goja*, 2 Bom. H.C.R. 124 (1864).

14. Roy, *Customs and Customary Law*, p. 557.

15. Ibid, at 562–63.

16. This discussion is drawn from Kunal M. Parker, "'A Corporation of Superior Prostitutes': Anglo-Indian Legal Conceptions of Temple Dancing Girls, 1800–1914," *Modern Asian Studies* 32 (1998): 559.

17. Ibid., p. 615.

18. Ibid., p. 614.

19. *Queen-Empress v. Baku*, 24 Bom. 287, 293 (1899).

20. I draw particularly upon the chapter entitled "The Nation and Its Women" in Partha Chatterjee, *The Nation and Its Fragments: Colonial and Postcolonial Histories* (1994).

21. Ibid., p. 117.

22. Ibid., p. 121.

23. Ibid., p. 127.

24. Sir Gooroodass Banerjee, *The Hindu Law of Marriage and Stridhana* (1913) 31 (1984).

25. Ibid., p. 21.

26. I am grateful to Vyjayanthi Rao for this observation.

27. Numerous scholars could be cited here. For a clear exposition of this issue, see generally Robert J. Steinfeld, "Property and Suffrage in the Early American Republic," *Stanford Law Review* 41 (1989): 335.

Bibliography

Arunima, G. "A Vindication of the Rights of Women: Families and Legal Change in Nineteenth-Century Malabar." In Michael R. Anderson and Sumit Guha, eds., *Changing Concepts of Rights and Justice in South Asia* (1998).

Banerjee, Sir Gooroodass. *The Hindu Law of Marriage and Stridhana* (1913) 31 (1984).

Chandra, Sudhir. "Whose Laws? Notes on a Legitimizing Myth of the Colonial Indian State." *Studies in History* 8 (1992): 187.

Chatterjee, Partha. *The Nation and Its Fragments: Colonial and Postcolonial Histories.* 1994.

Mani, Lata. "Contentious Traditions: The Debate on Sati in Colonial India." In Kumkum Sangari and Sudesh Vaid, eds., *Recasting Women: Essays in Colonial History* (1989).

Mansfield, John H. "The Personal Laws or a Uniform Civil Code?" In Robert D. Baird, ed., *Religion and Law in Independent India* (New Delhi, 1993).

Parker, Kunal M. "'A Corporation of Superior Prostitutes': Anglo-Indian Legal Conceptions of Temple Dancing Girls, 1800–1914." *Modern Asian Studies* 32 (1998): 559.

Roy, Sripati. *Customs and Customary Law in British India.* 1910.

Sarkar, Tanika. "Rhetoric against the Age of Consent: Resisting Colonial Reason and Death of a Child-Wife." *Economic and Political Weekly* 28 (1993): 1869.

Singha, Radhika. "Civil Authority and Due Process: Colonial Criminal Justice in the Banaras Zamindari, 1781–95." In Michael R. Anderson and Sumit Guha, eds., *Changing Concepts of Rights and Justice in South Asia* (1998).

Steinfeld, Robert J. "Property and Suffrage in the Early American Republic." *Stanford Law Review* 41 (1989): 335.

Washbrook, D. A. "Law, State and Agrarian Society in Colonial India." *Modern Asian Studies* 15 (1981): 649, 654.

Ten

Who Was Roop Kanwar?
Sati, Law, Religion, and
Postcolonial Feminism

Paul B. Courtright and Namita Goswami

Who was Roop Kanwar? Who was she to whom? There is much that is unknown about her, and there is much that she has become to many since her death on her husband's funeral pyre on September 4, 1987. She has become at one and the same time a goddess, a wife, a woman, and a victim. This essay will explore some of the interpretations that have been offered about the death of Roop Kanwar since that fateful event. First, we will review the events of the case in its early stages. We will then explore the various levels of meaning of her death in terms of its significance as a religious event in its local cultural context and in terms of its significance in some contemporary, postcolonial feminist studies.[1] Since we as authors come from different cultural backgrounds, generations, and periods, we will conclude our discussion with what we call simply "personal narratives" in an effort to set forth our own individual reactions to Roop Kanwar's death.

Background

There is little dispute about the following facts and sequence of events regarding Roop Kanwar's life and death in the village of Deorala (near Jaipur) in the State of Rajasthan. Roop Kanwar's marriage to Maal Singh, son of Sumer Singh, took place on January 17, 1987. Her family had originally been from Ranchi, in Madhya Pradesh, but had moved to Jaipur where her father, Pal Singh Rathore, owned a transport agency. She was the youngest of six children, four boys and two girls. Various newspaper and magazine accounts reported that during the seven

200

months that she had been married, she had only spent about a month in Deorala. She had been educated up to the tenth grade or "standard," and her family claims she had been a very pious girl, a devotee of the Goddess Rani Sati, and visited her temple in Ranchi every day. She recited verses for up to four hours at a time. Maal Singh, a science graduate, had been seeking a clerical job at the time. Maal Singh's father and Roop Kanwar's father-in-law, Sumer Singh, taught Hindi at the local government school. The family lived in a comfortable home according to the standards of life in Deorala.

On September 3, while having dinner with his father, Maal Singh complained of stomach pains. Accompanied by Roop Kanwar, Maal Singh was taken to the local district hospital where Dr. Magan Singh treated him. Later that evening Roop Kanwar returned to Deorala. In the early hours of the next day, to the shock of everyone, Maal Singh suddenly died. The official cause of death was listed as gastroenteritis. His body was returned to Deorala by 6 A.M. on the morning of September 4.

At this point in the narrative, our compilation of the press reports, in both Hindi and English language sources, presents a more uncertain and contradictory picture. Some reports stated that when Roop Kanwar heard of her husband's death, she told her father that she wanted to become a *sati*. Others stated that family members had taunted Roop Kanwar after Maal Singh's death and blamed her for bringing misfortune to the family.

Some accounts alleged that Roop Kanwar accompanied the funeral procession with the body of her husband and that she sat on the pyre with her husband's head on her lap prior to its being lit. Still others alleged that she ascended the pyre after Pushpender Singh, Maal Singh's fifteen-year-old brother, ignited the pyre.

There are even conflicting reports as to the actual time and circumstances of the immolation. Certain reports indicated that five hundred people witnessed the event. Perhaps in response to police questioning, other eyewitnesses stated that the number had actually been about twelve. Some claimed that the funeral pyre was lit at 1:30 P.M., with four thousand to five thousand people present, while others maintained that her body was lit between 10:30 and 11:30 A.M., with the ceremony ending by 12:30 or 1 P.M.

Word of the event first reached Ajitgarh police station, about 4–6 km away, at 2:20 P.M., and the police arrived in Deorala by 2:30 P.M. By the time the police arrived, all ceremonies had been concluded, and the police claimed that because of the large number of people, they decided to leave the site and return with adequate reinforcement. The Deorala village *patwari* (part-time police officer), Sawant Singh, had informed the authorities at Ajitgarh, although there is doubt about whether he was present at the incident. Police arrived with reinforcements by 5 P.M., claiming that the delay had been caused by vehicle trouble. A case was registered under Section 306, abetment to suicide, of the Indian Penal Code (I.P.C.), and the police claimed they also attempted to make a case for murder under Section 302.

On September 5, the collector of Sikar District, M. K Sahai, arrived to "verify facts." He determined that action would be taken after September 16, so as not to disrupt post-cremation funeral rites and offend the religious sentiments of the family and the community. On September 9, Roop Kanwar's brother-in-law, Pushpendra Singh, who had lit the funeral pyre, was arrested. He was released on bail on September 14.

On the same day in Jaipur, thirteen women's voluntary and social organizations demonstrated outside the Secretariat building. Chief Minister Harideo Joshi declined to meet with representatives of the women's groups. The protesters filed a writ in the Rajasthan High Court to block the performance of the *chunri mahotsav*, or concluding death ritual according to Rajput practices, to be held on September 16. On September 15, Chief Minister Harideo Joshi condemned the *sati* incident as "unlawful" and "improper" and promised "stern action" against the guilty. In response to the writ filed by the various women's groups in Jaipur, the Rajasthan High Court ordered the state government to ensure that no public function be held which "may have the effect of glorification of the institution of *sati*."

The High Court ordered that state roadways in and out of Deorala be closed. Nevertheless, buses, jeeps, tractors, and camel carts entered Deorala village until 4 A.M. the morning before the *chunri mahotsav*, when the district authorities had finally stopped all vehicles at Ajitgarh. Still, many visitors, the majority of whom were women, walked the distance to reach the site of the cremation/immolation, the "*sati sthal*." The collector, the superintendent of police, and the deputy superintendent of police for the district were not present, but there were reportedly between 200,000 and 400,000 people gathered at the site. Because the Rajput cremation ground in Deorala is not an open space on all sides, the size of the crowd was difficult to measure accurately.

On September 16, the *chunri mahotsav* took place as planned despite the High Court's directive regarding the "glorification" of *sati*. Prominent Rajput leaders, including Kalyan Singh Kalvi, president of the state unit of the Janata party; Rajindra Singh Rathore, state chief of the Yuva Janata (the youth wing of the Janata party); and Deependra Singh

Shaktawat, joint secretary of the Pradesh Congress Committee, attended the ceremony and offered prayers and made donations. Women outnumbered men at the *mahotsav*. The makeshift police station was moved to Ajitgarh, the closest town to Deorala. About a thousand Rajput men from the *Sati Dharma Raksha Samiti* guarded the funeral site. The final ceremony had originally been planned for 10 A.M. but was advanced by two hours. By the time the authorities arrived, the rite was concluded.

On September 17, Rajasthan Home Minister Mr. Gulab Singh Shekhawat declared that "all culprits are to be arrested in the next twenty-four hours."

On September 19, a front-page news article on the incident at Deorala appeared in the *New York Times*, entitled "India Widow's Death at Pyre Creates a Shrine," under the name of Delhi bureau chief Steven R. Weisman. The article, later syndicated in other newspapers in the United States along with similar articles in other major newspapers around the world, contributed to a media frenzy both within India and abroad. The village of Deorala became known throughout the world. Sumer Singh and three other relatives were arrested. Bapu Lal Sharma, a local religious leader, and Bansi Dhar, a local barber, were also arrested.

On September 21, the National Federation of Indian Women protested outside the residence of the Union Home Minister Mr. Buta Singh in New Delhi. They demanded the resignation of the Rajasthan chief minister and the state home minister as well as steps to prevent construction of a temple at the *sati sthal,* the site of Roop Kanwar's immolation. They also wanted (a) a ban on all organizations propagating the practice, (b) effective utilization of the mass media to mobilize popular opinion against the practice, (c) more funds for widow rehabilitation, and (d) stern action against those members of the Congress Party who were supporting the atrocity. The women's wing of the Central Reserve Police Force used violent means to restrain the demonstrators.

On September 23, Home Minister Buta Singh declared the *sati* incident to be reminiscent of the "dark ages." The next day, the Rajasthan cabinet amended the Rajasthan Religious Places and Buildings Act, 1954, adding a new subsection banning the construction of *sati* temples and buildings glorifying *sati*, the collection of money for such temples, and the holding of fairs (*melas*) where *sati* had been committed. On September 26, widows marched in protest in New Delhi against *sati* and the government's failure to implement social welfare schemes for widows. They also criticized Prime Minister Rajiv Gandhi for his silence on the issue. On September 28, Rajiv Gandhi declared *sati* to be a "national shame." In an open letter to Rajasthan Chief Minister Harideo Joshi, Gandhi urged prompt and severe action against all culprits, the prohibition of any shrine or construction to commemorate the incident, and a speedy investigation and prosecution of the case.

On October 1, the Prevention of Sati Ordinance was passed in the Rajasthan Assembly. It defined *sati* as "the practice of burning or burying alive any widow along with the body of her husband or with any article or object, irrespective of whether such burning is voluntary on the part of the widow." The ordinance provided stringent punishment for abetment and glorification of *sati*. Special courts were to be set up for trial of offenses under this measure. The term "glorification" included observing ceremonies, staging processions, and collecting funds for construction of temples to perpetuate the memory of a woman who has committed the act. Abetment to *sati* included inducing the widow to get burned or attempting to convince a widow that the act would bring some spiritual benefit to her, her husband, or her family. The force of the law shifted the onus of proving innocence to the accused.

The passing of this ordinance created a strong response from some leaders in the Rajput community as well as among many feminists and activists. Rajput community leaders denounced what they regarded as government interference in their customs and traditions. Feminists criticized the need for a new law, stating that there were already specific provisions in existence within the Indian Penal Code to prevent such an event, and that the laws already in place needed to be vigorously enforced. The problem, according to the feminists, resided with the inability of state authorities to implement these laws. In addition, under particular provisions of the ordinance, a woman attempting to commit *sati* is punishable by fine and imprisonment. The Rajasthan High Court declared that the ordinance would not retroactively apply to those held in the Roop Kanwar case.

Prohibitory orders under Section 144 of the Code of Criminal Procedure were implemented in Deorala preventing the assembly of five or more persons, holding meetings, taking out processions, using megaphones, or carrying weapons in the village from October 1st to the 31st.

On October 8, the *Sati Dharma Raksha Samiti*, an informal group of Rajput activists, held a rally in Jaipur to protest against government "hurdles" in observing the last rites of Roop Kanwar's *sati* and the alleged police harassment of innocent persons. Approximately 70,000 Rajasthanis, mostly Rajputs, protested in Jaipur's Ramlila grounds (an area set aside for re-enactment of the story of Rama) and celebrated Roop Kanwar as a *devi*, an incarnation of the goddess. Within a month after Roop Kanwar's death, the controversy had become fully formed: archaic and inhuman practice vs. defense of community values. In a more abstract sense it emerged as modernity vs. tradition, secular state vs. Hindu *dharma*. In this process, Roop Kanwar as a person disappeared into the mythic categories of goddess and victim.

In the months and years since the intense sequence of events in Deorala and beyond, many books and scholarly articles have been written and many academic conferences and debates have taken place about the meanings of Roop Kanwar's *sati*. In the remainder of this essay, we return to our original question: Who was Roop Kanwar? Through the lenses of religious studies and feminism, we attempt to re-engage her humanity. We recognize the limitations of our enterprise. We are drawn into this quest knowing that she remains a mystery.

Roop Kanwar and the Satimata Tradition
in Eastern Rajasthan

An examination of the religious dimensions of Roop Kanwar's *sati* requires a careful look at the regional and local religious practices and family traditions of the community to which she belonged. Roop Kanwar was described as a quiet, pious young woman who was devoted to Rani Sati Mata, a fifteenth-century Rajput noblewoman who became a *sati* on the death of her husband and came to be venerated by both Rajputs and Marwari merchant communities in the Shekhawat region of eastern Rajasthan.

Over the past two centuries most of the Marwari families have left the Shekhawat region and moved to major urban and commercial cities, especially Calcutta and Mumbai, though many continue to maintain estates (or *havelis*) in the Shekhawat region, some of which have been transformed into tourist attractions. Centered in Jhunjhunu, a few hours' drive north of Deorala, the temple to Rani Sati Mata has prospered along with the extraordinary accumulation of wealth by the Marwari community over the last two centuries. In this network of communities, Rani Sati Mata is venerated as a lineage deity and protectoress (*kuldevi*), and her blessings are sought for protection against various kinds of chaos—financial, medical, spiritual, and social. Daughter temples to the complex at Jhunjhunu have been built in all the major cities where Marwari families and charitable trust organizations have become established, with the wealthiest and most active community being located in Calcutta.

Although the Rani Sati temple in Jhunjhunu is the largest and best known, a number of *satis* have become established over the past fifty years in towns and villages in eastern Rajasthan as incarnations of the goddess in temples of various size and affluence. These temples generally follow the Rajput and Sanskritized model of Jhunjhunu, but are also often managed by members of particular castes. They have become places of local veneration and sponsor annual fairs where devotees come for ceremonial and social purposes. Indeed, most of the major caste groups in eastern Rajasthan have their own *satimata* (literally "*sati*-mother" or, in other words, Sati mother-goddess).

Beyond the institutional religious level, it is important to note the role of the *kuldevi* in Rajasthani and particularly Rajput tradition. The *kuldevi* is the goddess, a form of Durga, who protects the families of various lineages. Just as in ancient mythology when the goddess Sati, the wife of Shiva, had entered the fire when her father Daksha excluded Shiva from his sacrifice, thus condemning him to a kind of social death of exclusion, and was then reborn as Parvati, so the *kuldevi* in many families had also been a *sati* in the life previous to her deification. She wields her protective powers in response to the veneration she receives from her devotees, and it is the work of women to maintain the cycles of ritual activity on behalf of their husbands. Hence, through the exercise of ritual action, wives are understood to be instrumental in their husband's well-being.

Over the past century, the status of the Rajput community has substantially weakened. Through a series of negotiations, the British Raj successfully exercised authority over Rajput states, while the monarchs of formerly autonomous Rajput states retained their titles and regal lifestyles even as their political powers waned. Part of the compromise that formed the nation of India in 1948 was that Rajput kings would retain compensation from the central government in return for joining the new country and forming the state of Rajasthan. From the 1950s to the 1970s, a series of land reforms was instituted that further undercut the Rajput dominance and redistributed increasing economic power to other communities. In the 1970s, after the central government abolished the privy purse arrangement enjoyed by the Rajput monarchs, the full decline of Rajput hegemony in the region was completed. But while the real economic and political power of Rajputs as a community has weakened, its nostalgia for its glory days of heroic combat and chivalry have become a constant thread in its culture. Nostalgia is aggressively marketed through its tourism industry, from the Palace on Wheels, a series of former Rajput maharajas' personal railroad cars, to the performance of the heroic epic of Pabuji in luxury hotel courtyards for the tourists, and to the use of the maharaja as the logo for the national airline, Air India.

Many Rajputs resent the decline in their status and blame the central government for cheating them out of their lands, resources, and positions of leadership to which they were traditionally entitled. From their perspective, the media representations of Rajputs as backward, intensely patriarchal, and rustic have become injurious to their sense of honor and tradition. Many view the cosmopolitanism of the cities, especially Delhi, as an expression of the disintegration and loss of a distinctively Indian identity. Furthermore, the rising power and visibility of women's organizations and their critiques of patriarchy and advocacy of new and more autonomous opportunities for women represent threats to the Rajputs' traditional ways of life. Many Rajputs point to what they see as the blatant hypocrisy of a state which markets their exotic and romantic traditions in pursuit of tourist dollars while disdaining them as rustics who have not adapted well to new conditions of a modern democratic and secular society.

With this background in mind, it is hardly surprising that many Rajputs resented the media feeding frenzy for both international and domestic consumption in which Rajput traditions and values were depicted as medieval, retrograde, and violent. These representations sparked an intense defensive reaction toward the veneration of *sati* as part of its heroic tradition, and the authorities' attempts to block or regulate its meanings in negative directions were seen as an infringement on the Rajputs' integrity as citizens whose religious practices are supposed to be protected and respected by the state. This sentiment fed the broader process of enhancing the appeal of Hindu nationalism, or *Hindutva*.

Roop Kanwar, *Sati*, and Its Discontents: Postcolonial Feminist Debates

The 1987 *sati* of Roop Kanwar was followed by widespread condemnation by the government, women's groups, and academics. The government expressed its shame and reiterated its commitment to progress and modernization to counter backwardness and atavistic religious or cultural beliefs. Feminist scholars and activists such as Madhu Kishwar, Kumkum Sangari, and Rajeswari Sunder Rajan pointed out the state's dereliction in preventing the *sati* and its subsequent glorification by Rajputs and government authorities. By designating Roop Kanwar a goddess and by constructing *sati* as a phenomenon intrinsic to Hindu culture, Indianness, and Rajput identity, various right-wing factions were able to divert attention away from critical feminist and national issues such as increasing female infanticide, low literacy rates, legal and property rights, and the role of the secularist state in enforcing justice. Moreover, rather than attributing the *sati* to backwardness and illiteracy, much as the British had attributed *sati* to India's lack of modernity, feminists pointed out the economic and caste-based interests that were served by the immolation in the literate and relatively "modern" community of Deorala.[2]

Colonial and postcolonial discourses of *sati*, such as tradition vs. modernity, ritual vs. crime, victim vs. goddess, particularly in terms of their resurgence after the 1987 *sati* of Roop Kanwar, attempt to define and contain the practice. This form of containment is crucial for developing and instituting state policies and programs of action. Roop Kanwar's *sati*, however, constitutes a critical moment in post-independence India. Born in Ranchi and raised primarily in Jaipur, she was an urban and educated young girl who could not be accommodated as a passive and pious village woman fulfilling her duty as a Hindu wife. Her wedding photograph shows a strikingly pretty young woman, smiling and staring directly into the camera. Her eyes and face are not lowered as is customary for shy, demure, and newly wed women. Instead, she comes across as vivacious and dynamic.

Roop Kanwar's immolation has become a critical lens for analyzing gender in postcolonial India because of the contradictions in the various narratives that the *sati* has elicited. Her *sati* has been variously constructed as religious phenomenon, indigenous practice, emblem of culture, sign of backwardness, and feminist nightmare. Her *sati* became a site upon which her Rajput community sought to counter secularist state interference. *Sati* came to be defined as a "tradition" and practice central and intrinsic to Rajput self-identity. Under the ground rules of the modern secular state in India, the government does not interfere in a community's religious practices. Roop Kanwar also became the symbol for Hindu nationalists and traditionalists to imagine a nation formed through rigid caste, gender, class, religious, and national (Western vs. non-Western) demarcations; for the state to proclaim its commitment to secularism and progress by passing the Anti-*Sati* Prevention Ordinance (October 1987) without implementing measures for actual enforcement; and for feminists to demonstrate her victim status while also focusing the horror and outrage of a nation on the plight of Indian women. In both colonial and postcolonial contexts, these discourses became representative of the general status of women in India. In other words, Roop Kanwar became an icon of both nostalgia and negation. She was both not enough and too much an expression of female presence.

The immolation also constitutes a rupture in the self-understanding of the state. As Rajeswari Sunder Rajan points out, "While women belong to their communities through affiliations and participatory membership they are also reduced through functionalism and symbolic status. State judgements propagate paternalistic attitudes of protection, moral dicta, benevolence, and finally control of women."[3] The project of postcolonial feminism, whether in India or abroad, has been to illustrate how to understand the status, meaning, and content of "Hindu tradition" while also fighting charges of "Westernization" and "inauthenticity." From this perspective, more often than not, colonization, nationalist movements for independence, and postcolonial anxieties about nation and culture turn out to be narratives of betrayal for women. In other words, as Lata Mani has argued, discourses of colonialism, nationalism, progress, and modernity that are putatively about women, or are meant to alleviate the condition of women, are the means for furthering other agendas of power and dominance, be they by colonizers, state authorities, or indigenous patriarchies. Women remain objects rather than subjects in their own lives.[4]

Iconographic, literary, religious, political, and cultural representations of Roop Kanwar function in the larger context of the debate on *sati*. These include: the status, meaning, and content of "Hindu tradition" as it has been evoked within colonial discourse and as it functions within contemporary debates; the representation of *sati* in both colonial literature including travel narratives, eyewitness accounts, and court and legislative documents; accounts of Roop Kanwar's *sati* in leading Indian national newspapers, local vernacular newspapers, popular display, local religious iconography, devotional ballads, and popular film songs; and feminist research, investigative, interpretive, and journalistic accounts. These materials provide a means for investigating the political battles being waged by various factions such as traditionalists, neo-traditionalists, nationalists, and reformists in the context of the increasing impetus placed on "modernization" and economic "development."

Rajeswari Sunder Rajan, Madhu Kishwar, and Vasudha Dhagamwar have also carefully scrutinized the language of the Prevention of Sati Ordinance. Madhu Kishwar emphasizes that both murder and suicide are punishable offenses under the Indian Penal Code. A new law was not necessary in order to prevent or handle Roop Kanwar's death. In fact, by forming a special law, the government recognized and conceded that *sati* "constitutes a special category distinct from murder or suicide."[5] Rajeswari Sunder Rajan has analyzed the contradictions at the heart of the Commission of Sati (Prevention) Act, which seeks to address both its occurrence and subsequent glorification. The provisions against abetment and glorification contain an ambivalence regarding the status of the woman's will, that is, her actions are represented as either voluntary or involuntary. "Where a sati has been foiled, the woman will be tried for 'the offence of attempt to commit sati'. Here her motivation is considered ascertainable and hence assessable by the same criteria as suicides." These include state of mind, circumstances of the event, occurrence of the event, intoxication, or "other factors impeding the exercise of her free will." Where her *sati* has been completed, those involved will be charged for "abetment," not murder.[6]

Vasudha Dhagamwar conducts a thorough investigation of the actual wordings and provisions of *sati* legislation and the Indian Penal Code, from 1812 when the British government first formulated its policy on the practice until the 1987 Commission of Sati (Prevention) Act. She questions whether enjoinment by a religious text of any particular practice is a sufficient basis for its occurrence or encouragement. "Both the 1987 Acts particularly mention that the offence is 'irrespective' of whether the Act is 'voluntary . . . or otherwise'. . . . The two Sections 3 of the 1987 Acts differ only in the quantum of punishment. Note, both these sections punish the woman who is rescued. . . . True: S.3 and 4 do not distinguish between voluntary and involuntary *sati*. But in effect they treat all *sati*s as voluntary. That is why the woman is punished and that is why those who kill her are punished for abetment, and not for murder. This problem arises for semantic reasons. Had the law used the words 'burning or burying a woman' the woman could not have been perceived as anything but the victim. The only grammatical construction with *sati* that is possible is 'she committed *sati*'. This then leads to the fiction that she is the actor or principal offender; the others only abet her."[7]

Feminist scholars such as Lata Mani, Uma Narayan, Rajeswari Sunder Rajan, Kumkum Sangari, Radha Kumar, Urvashi Butalia, Tanika Sarkar, and Gayatri Spivak have resisted the easy interpretation that reduces Indian women to either abject victims or unworldly heroines. They argue against the emblematic status granted to *sati* in both international and national contexts, as it reinforces traditional stereotypes of Indian women as backward, illiterate, and victims of static traditional structures or as hyper-spiritual heroic exemplars of eternal *dharma*. Because the state has also been the cause and instigator of many gross injustices against Indian women, they question the role of the state as guarantor of the rights of women. They contend also with the increasing participation of women in the Hindu right. Rather than attributing such participation to false consciousness, they attempt to understand the community and agency that religion does in fact seem to provide. *Sati*, moreover, cannot be understood as a singular, unchanging phenomenon. Rather, it must be articulated in terms of specific cultural, historical, and socioeconomic factors that form varied and contingent configurations.[8] Whoever people think Roop Kanwar is—local manifestation of the eternal Durga at one end of a continuum to abused and murdered victim of the rages of patriarchy at the other—she is a historically contingent, embodied female human being who is now dead and gone. We can only imagine what she might make of these various constructions of her.

Taking Spivak's poignant and controversial statement that the "subaltern cannot speak," we shift registers from co-authorship to speak in our own individual voices.

Two Narratives: Goswami

Spivak rhetorically captures the foreclosure that occurs when Indian women are defined as either helpless victims or as super-strong heroines. They either have no control over their own lives or they naturally endure, even to the point of feeling no pain when burning alive on a funeral pyre.[9] Feminists such as Spivak, in formulating an ethics and a politics, emphasize that ". . . finding the subaltern is not so hard, but actually entering into a responsibility structure with the subaltern, with responses flowing both ways: learning to learn without this quick-fix frenzy of doing good with an implicit assumption of cultural supremacy which is legitimized by an unexamined romanticization, that's the hard part"[10]

She undertakes an investigation of "object formation and subject constitution . . . either . . . the subaltern's protection as object from her own kind or her achievement as a voice assimilable to the project of imperialism."[11] The subaltern cannot speak, not because she doesn't speak or hasn't spoken, but because she does not have a subject position which can render her voice intelligible. As Spivak points out, she becomes either an object of rescue for colonizers and benevolent indigenous patriarchies ("white men are saving brown women from brown men") or a self-determining and thereby transparent subject ("the women wanted to die").[12] In other words, what other scripts are available for Indian women and how does one go about recuperating them responsibly?

As one woman of Indian descent working in American academia attempting to make sense out of Roop Kanwar, it is useful to describe the intellectual territory I find myself in. In this analysis, I attempt to write about the process of entering into a "responsibility structure" with Roop Kanwar. Roop Kanwar is the subaltern because she has no position from which she can speak. This is not simply because she is dead. Her voice is unavailable to us because our attempts to understand her death are limited and, in many ways, over-determined or pre-determined by the scripts we have available to us, the scripts that in fact make sense to us, regardless of the particular agendas we may bring to the issue of *sati*. This particular death cannot be understood in isolation from the dominant and normative history of *sati* that functioned and was created as part of the colonial project. Yet, is there a way in which Roop Kanwar can rise beyond her symbolic status or is there a way for us to do scholarship that will not reduce her to symbolic status?

While Spivak's extensive critique of Foucault, Deleuze, and Derrida requires careful scrutiny, I am more interested in the pragmatics of good scholarship, in essence, an ethics or what Spivak terms "plot[ting] a history."[13] If the Western subject is no longer homogenous but is in fact fragmented, contradictory, and heterogeneous, how can one think of the subaltern as authentic, unified, and non-heterogeneous? Have we missed something in trying to give those whom we presume to speak of or speak for a completely coherent identity, victim or heroine? Given that any attempt to narrate or seek closure involves violence and that there is no unproblematic position from which one can speak, how does one write about Roop Kanwar?

Coming to terms with and elucidating my own position compels an analysis of writing as a woman and as a feminist of Indian origin within U.S. academia. This is not to suggest what Chandra Mohanty terms an "osmosis thesis" whereby feminist politics or ethics somehow naturally emerge from being Indian or from being female or, for that matter, from being located and privileged within particular first-world academic structures.[14]

Sati and the concomitant debates of the status of women in Indian tradition and culture have become a litmus test of sorts for feminists of Indian origin within U.S. academic structures in various disciplinary frameworks. While the resentment that accrues from having to defend one's "culture" wholesale or not at all, albeit from the dubious position of "Westernization," merits attention, I focus on what I perceive to be a more critical issue. Leaving the hornet's nest of "identity" behind, I attempt to speak of the disjuncture between the compulsion to narrate and, simultaneously, remaining narratively paralyzed. Something about *sati* seems to demand a response. How can one remain an ethical scholar, fair and open-minded, and yet not be horrified when a nineteen-year-old girl is burned alive? Or am I longing for an objectivity that in my heart I know to be impossible?

Although I oppose the practice of *sati*, I hold this in abeyance as a means of resisting the impulse to make Roop Kanwar speak my politics. Nor do I believe that being an Indian woman grants me privileged access to her particular experiences. Instead, I trace my attempts to imagine her, whether through scholarly writings about her or through visiting her home and the site of her immolation.

On July 1, 1999, I visited Deorala with my mother and father and a Rajput acquaintance, a manager at a hotel chain with locations throughout Rajasthan. He seemed to be a kind and gentle man. His stocky appearance and trademark Rajput moustache gave him a somewhat distinguished aura. We met him through family friends in Jaipur and he graciously offered to accompany us to Deorala, since he knew the region well. The roads are treacherous during the monsoons and the drive, normally two hours, took longer than expected. We were also avoiding bus-, car-, and vanloads of *Jat* youth shouting slogans on their way to a *Jat* reservation rally in Jaipur. Claiming minority status, they demanded reservations in all state-owned schools and offices. There was not a single woman among them. Our acquaintance made a number of derogatory comments about the *Jat* community in Rajasthan, contrasting their "habits" and "beliefs" with those of his own community. He accepted the muted and rather vague description of my interest in Roop Kanwar that I had given him, perhaps because he had received adequate reassurances from my father as well as our mutual friend that I did not represent the foreign press or feminists, nor was I the Delhi-bred city girl. The presence of my parents, my fluent Hindi, and my clothes assured him that despite being a student in the United States, I had retained my Indianness and sense of respect for my culture.

En route, he emphasized that the Rajput community had received a lot of bad press after the Roop Kanwar incident. Various factions, particularly the Indian media, had used the *sati* to prevent Rajput leaders from making gains in politics. He stated point blank, "In this age no one can force any girl to do something like this. And she was educated." Not only had she been schooled, he insisted, but her education had been in English. He acknowledged that coercion did exist in prior times, and the question of individual choice did not exist then. But he countered that people from other communities, by giving *sati* a political taint, were taking advantage of the situation.

Roop Kanwar, he continued, in fact dressed herself as a bride, sat on the pyre, and laid her husband's head on her lap. Her becoming a *sati* proves her happiness in her marriage. Without *sat* ("truth") she could not have even sat upon the pyre. She even asked her brother-in-law to light the pyre. She may have brought a lot of dowry but there had been no demands on their part. There had also been no financial gain for the family after the *sati*. Since her marriage had taken place in a middle-class family, she could not have incurred a lot of hardship in her home.

My mother commented that Roop Kanwar had not been pregnant at the time of her death nor had she become pregnant shortly after her marriage, as is most often the case. She wondered whether this could be a reason for her possibly having been unhappy with her husband. Our companion did not know how to answer that question. It is not unusual, however, to not inform the natal family immediately when death has occurred. It is customary, moreover, for them to visit two or three days after the death. He pointed out that people from the *Jat* community also visited the site and had participated in the *chunri mahotsav* (the ritual that takes place marking the thirteenth day after the death) even though they did not believe in the practice. Even Brahmin girls have become *sati*s.

He also told me about a woman who had lost her husband in the ongoing Kargil crisis with Pakistan. She wanted to become a *sati* but the body of her husband could not be found. She had not eaten anything since hearing of her husband's death. Even Bhairav Singh, the chief minister, had gone to receive her *darshan* (to be in her presence in order to receive her blessing). Veneration of self-sacrificing saintly women is widespread in Rajasthan.

He stated that Rajputs see widows as ill omens. I listened incredulously as he stated that the conditions of women that feminists tend to describe do not actually exist. There are three primary stratifications of women in Rajput society. At the highest are the royal families who have no limitations on their actions. The middle classes are changing through education, though until recently women could not even leave the house to buy vegetables. Among the lower classes, women face a lot of difficulties. Daughters-in-law are treated like servants and not daughters. Widows also are mistreated. The *Jat* community, however, relies primarily upon agriculture. Women bear the brunt of labor, having to work in the fields and at home. He remarked resolutely that when the *Jat*s come to power they will commit so many atrocities that we will forget the Mughals and the British. He also recommended that I read the four-volume work by Colonel Todd on Rajput glory and history.

Along the way, we stopped for some tea and he proceeded to ask men by the side of the road whether Roop Kanwar's *sati* had been voluntary. This would turn out to be the general trend of the day. Most emphatically stated that she had voluntarily ascended the pyre. *Sati* should occur, in fact could only occur, when the presence of *sat* has been established. The response contained a paradox. If *sat* were the present and determining factor, then what becomes of choice and will? If the presence of *sat* implies a possession without individual choice, then *sati* is simply a transformation. If, however, being possessed by *sat* indicates a willful decision, then *sati* is an action, a matter of individual choice. On the one hand, the people we spoke to wanted to retain Roop Kanwar's own volition. On the other hand, they sought to preserve the miraculous and divine aspect of *sat* which can transform a worthy and pious woman into a goddess who does not feel any pain.

My mother and I met two women walking down the road carrying sieves. They were from *Jat* farming families. One looked older, about fifty or so, while it was hard to tell the age of the younger woman. I noticed that unlike most of the women we had encountered, they did not cover their faces when walking past the men by the road. My mother asked them about Roop Kanwar, and I realized at that point that I had not really been talking, except with our companion. I sensed the hesitation among the people we encountered to talk to me directly. They either answered my parents or our acquaintance. Perhaps as an unmarried young woman with no children I did not have an explicit social identity to frame social interaction, particularly with men. I also did not understand the language they were speaking. Even though they understood Hindi, they responded in Marwari. My mother, however, who has a way with languages, understood what they were saying.

The women were talkative, spirited, and humorous. They were convinced that the *sati* had been a forced one. In fact, the whole practice did not make sense because a man does not ascend the pyre when his wife dies. The older woman had recently become a widow. She laughed at the thought of following her husband, saying that living with him had been enough *tapasya* (penance). She felt like she had accumulated enough karmic points for that alone without having to follow her husband around after he died. Now that she was alone, she was actually enjoying life and didn't have much to complain about.

They told us about a woman in Triveni, a town nearby, whose *sati* had been foiled by policemen and her *sat* had left her. Apparently, she had kicked some cow dung and it turned into a coconut. Her husband's pyre had also lit itself. People from all over Rajasthan were going to seek her *darshan*. Ultimately, they asked, what did they know of such things? They were just women working in the fields. They recommended that we visit Triveni.

We reached Deorala, a muddy, quiet, and dreary village. My mother remarked that she could not understand why Roop Kanwar's parents had married off their educated, city-bred daughter into such a place. She could not have been happy here. My father parked the car and children immediately surrounded it while people came out of their houses to look at us. The *sati sthal* (site of the *sati*) is located at the back of the village in the cremation ground. Two men were guarding the site and refused my request to take pictures. They said that they would lose their jobs. I could, however, go beyond the boundary of the cremation ground. The place had a haunted look.

We approached Roop Kanwar's home. It is a brightly colored structure, bigger and better-maintained than most of the other houses in the village. Peacocks were running around although most people were indoors and came out only when they saw us approaching. As we entered the front room, where the body had been placed and where Roop Kanwar allegedly dressed herself in her bridal finery, a throng of young men gathered at the window to listen in on our conversation.

Sumer Singh (Roop Kanwar's father-in-law) greeted us cordially. He had just finished his *puja* and was rolling up his mat. He looked old, frail, and tired, dressed in a simple shirt and *lungi*. He asked us to sit down on the one sofa in the room. My mother later pointed out that the sofa must have been a part of Roop Kanwar's dowry. It was of the same kind that she herself had brought to my father's home when they got married.

My conversation with Sumer Singh took place in Hindi. I thanked him for agreeing to meet with me, as I knew that the press and other factions investigating the event had hounded him. He said that I have a wish or hope and that it is his duty to attempt to fulfill it. I asked him to relate the events that led to the *sati*. Sumer Singh proceeded to tell me that his son had never been sick a day in his life. A few days before the *sati*, however, he had an accident of sorts when he fell down from a tree. He felt all right for a day or so, but on the evening of September 3rd he complained of pains in his side while they were eating dinner. They took him to the local dispensary but when they couldn't help him they asked a friend to drive them to Sikar hospital. He himself had returned home that night with Roop Kanwar and the doctor, Magan Singh.

Magan Singh had run away after the *sati* because he had been suspected of drugging Roop Kanwar. It had also been alleged that he had been having an affair with Roop Kanwar. Certain press reports had also accused Sumer Singh and Magan Singh of plotting the whole thing once it had become clear that Maal Singh would not survive. Although Magan Singh had been arrested, along with the priest who presided over Maal Singh's funeral rites and hence also the *sati*, he was released shortly thereafter because of lack of evidence. I did not, however, ask Sumer Singh about all these conflicting reports and rumors.

When they received word of Maal Singh's death on the morning of September 4th, they immediately brought the body back home. Roop Kanwar observed the body calmly and told him about her decision to become a *sati*. Family members attempted to dissuade her, but she gave specific instructions about what had to be done. Her dowry was to be given to her sister-in-law when she got married. Sumer Singh, apparently, had even wanted to find another suitable husband for her, but he could not have slapped her or forced her to not ascend the pyre, and he had been astounded that certain women had even suggested such a thing. She locked herself in her room and dressed herself in her wedding clothes. I asked him whether she had left *mehndi* (henna designs on the palm) marks on the wall of their home as is customary before a *sati*. He said there had been no time for such elaborate preparations.

She accompanied the funeral procession to the cremation grounds and sat on the pyre with her husband's head on her lap. Sumer Singh himself had been so traumatized and distressed that he became unconscious and was taken to Sikar hospital. His fifteen-year-old son lit the pyre as per Roop Kanwar's instructions. By the time he returned home, the ceremony had been completed.

Most people do not realize that they have lost two young members of their family. His son had wanted to pursue a science degree and had just taken his exams. His daughter-in-law had been a loving girl who had two aunts living in this same village. She had had an affectionate relationship with him, calling him "papa." She would ask her brother-in-law and sister-in-law to call her immediately whenever he came home if she had gone out to visit her aunts or anyone else in the village, so that she could prepare his favorite meal. She had been happy in that home.

He had no idea about the huge funds that the media claimed had been collected after the event, and he had not received any benefits. Instead, the government has even taken away his pension, which to this day he has not received. He was arrested and questioned exhaustively without so much as receiving a glass of water. He spent that night in jail hungry. His younger son was also arrested. This has taken quite a toll on his wife, who has become sick and bedridden. She stays indoors away from people, especially visitors. His younger son, the one who lit the pyre, is now married. This, according to him, provides ample proof that no foul play occurred. What family in these days would marry their daughter into such a home?

Then, surprisingly, he asked me if I was Indian. We had been speaking in Hindi all along and my parents were present throughout the conversation. He said that he had been doing some reading on the history of *sati*. A friend of his had sent him a copy of V. N. Datta's book on the subject.[15] I asked him how he looked back on the event. He turned to look at the shrine on the left side of the room. It had Roop Kanwar's wedding picture in it as well as the cheap photo collages of the *sati*. Both had been reprinted and sold extensively. He didn't quite answer the question but pointed to all that his family had suffered during its aftermath.

As I left the front room, a group of children gathered in the inner courtyard with one of the young men who sat at the window listening to our conversation. They asked me to take pictures of them, which I gladly did. They seemed to enjoy it greatly. The inner courtyard leads into a smaller courtyard and a back room. I glanced in the room to see if I might get a glimpse of Maal Singh's mother. A young and very pretty girl was standing there, smiling broadly with a playful look on her face. One of the men pointed out that she was Pushpendra Singh's wife, the new daughter-in-law in the family. She stayed behind the doors of the courtyard watching the children pose for me, and she refused to come out or let me take her picture. Whenever I approached her, she covered her face with her *chunri*. She was wearing the traditional bangles that are a part of Rajput wedding ceremonies. These bangles are never to be taken off, as to do so would cause harm to come to one's husband. Many journalistic and feminist reports (both from 1987 and contemporary accounts) point to the problem of girls being married off extremely early in Rajasthan, sometimes as soon as they reach puberty. Many justify this practice by claiming that the girl does not live with her husband until she reaches a mature age, which is about fifteen or sixteen. I knew all this, yet it shocked me to see how young she seemed. I also realized that my attempts to take her picture indicated my willingness to objectify her, to capture her, perhaps so as to prove that she was indeed a victim deserving rescue. I did not know anything about her and had not even spoken to her. I left wondering what would it have been like for her to be a daughter-in-law in this home with Roop Kanwar.

We went in search of Roop Kanwar's aunts but were only able to talk to one of the neighbors. Every time Roop Kanwar's name came up she would intersperse her sentences with *Sati Mata Ki Jai* (Victory to the Sati Mother) and then proceed talking. The woman we spoke to conversed mainly with my mother in the inner courtyard of her home while the men waited outside.

The neighbor said that on the fateful day she heard a commotion and saw Roop Kanwar running around the village screaming that she wanted to become a *sati*. She then accompanied the funeral procession to the cremation ground. This directly contradicted Sumer Singh's description of her as calm and collected. She also said that Sumer Singh had indeed been there because he was the one who was placing wood on the funeral pyre. He also put her back on the burning pyre when she fell off, half-conscious. Certain newspaper reports also claimed that Sumer Singh abetted the *sati*. She witnessed this from the rooftop of one of the homes surrounding the cremation site. Thousands of people gathered at the cremation ground. Her son, who could not have been more than ten or twelve at the time, said that Roop Kanwar seemed very tranquil, her body and her clothes burning in sections. When my mother pointed out that his account contradicted his mother's, he said that she may have been frantic before the *sati* but on the pyre itself she was serene and glowing. In fact, the light of *sat* emanated from her body. They ran out of wood so people had to bring *ghee* (purified butter) from their homes because the bodies were not fully burned.

We walked back to the car and I went past the *sati sthal* again. I had approached it earlier, trying to imagine the pyre burning, the enormous crowds, and the carnival atmosphere. The place had an uncanny and haunted look. My mother described to me how she felt ill at ease in Roop Kanwar's home and at the site. I could not feel anything. I had distanced myself from the actual material reality of a young girl, the age of some of my students, who burned alive. I did not know her. I felt completely alien from her world and I resented that alienation. Yet I also felt familiar with her world. I resented that familiarity as well.

I knew before I left the United States that I would not come any closer to the truth of what actually happened on that day. I went to Deorala realizing that even if I learned the truth, it would not have gotten to how I ultimately argue her moral authority. Roop Kanwar's moral authority does not come from our knowing her. Nor does it come from designating her as a victim or as a willing participant in her own subjugation. Instead, it comes from recuperating her humanity without the reassurance that she was indeed a good person or a pure victim. This entails reclaiming her personhood without knowing who she was and who she could have been. She will always be greater than the sum of her various parts. Respect for this ambivalence, and ultimately respect for her, requires acknowledging that knowledge must always fall short of its subject of inquiry.

Who was Roop Kanwar? And why Roop Kanwar? While the former question involves recuperating her character, her agency, her history, and her will, the latter demands that we focus our attention and our gaze upon ourselves. As Rajeswari Sunder Rajan points out, "For defenders of sati today all satis are voluntary, and for its opponents all of them are coerced. But when the individual woman's subjectivity is read in terms of intention, intentionality can only be a matter of conjecture and, finally, ideological conviction."[16] But scholarship, good scholarship that is, demands a different kind of responsibility. In terms of Roop Kanwar, every representation must at some level be a violation. Though we must describe, we cannot help but distort, for revelation is also simultaneously a concealment. Given our access to the means of production of knowledge and the mechanisms of its dispersal, how would we know that we are doing justice to her? Even though we can never know Roop Kanwar, we must form some kind of imaginative relation to who we think she is. And, moreover, we must assess what components of her identity we ask her to contain. Imaginative, however, does not imply that the horror of her experience is less real or that we can obscure or elide material and historical realities of the status of women in contemporary India. Given that particular images of Indian women are over-determined, what would it mean to subvert that history, to confront a situation not just as a relic of the past but as a reality continually signified in academic, political, and everyday discourse? Could my own desire to know her be part of the voyeuristic gaze that turned her into an unworldly heroine or spectacle, or could I, through good scholarship and self-conscious awareness of my own privileged positioning, shape it into a witnessing, the actual process of bringing those experiences to the forefront of what informs my politics and my profession? Roop Kanwar experienced a hyper-visibility that was in fact a profound invisibility. Her experience as an Indian woman was extraordinary. Yet, in terms of the everyday reality of many Indian women, her life was sadly ordinary. How does Roop Kanwar's death seem to carry the promise of a certain awakening, not in terms of who she was or what she may have wanted for herself, but for ourselves?

Paradoxically, gazing at the photograph of Roop Kanwar led me to the experience of gazing into a mirror. My father was stationed in Poland at the time of Roop Kanwar's death. He briefly mentioned the constant presence of journalists and representatives of women's organizations at the Indian embassy in Warsaw. I was fifteen at the time and living in Guwahati, Assam, in eastern India. In thinking back, I realize that his response had been a muted one, constrained perhaps by having to "defend" Indian "culture" and "tradition" while pointing to the widespread condemnation of the incident by the government, women's groups, and indigenous academics. Roop Kanwar was only four years older than I was, yet our worlds could not have been more different. As the daughter of a diplomat, I grew up in various parts of the world, attending both Indian and American schools. I knew I would not marry early. I would build a career and hopefully come to the United States to further my education. My parents, although practicing Hindus, encouraged belief in a supreme being regardless of the shape that it took. In addition to Ganesha and Laxmi, Mary and Jesus also had a place in our home. I could not understand the religious fervor, which, according to newspaper reports, had caused the event and its aftermath. I did not, however, attribute these ideas to "Westernization." Through my travels and experiences in countries as diverse as Canada, Libya, Greece, Venezuela, Italy, England, Lebanon, Poland, France, Portugal, Saudi Arabia, Spain, etc., I learned that explanations for cultural practices, notions of identity, and ideas about femininity are shifting and contested things. When one inhabits or comes to occupy a particular space of embattlement, where people have a stake in defending themselves and in representing themselves, these categories can become reified.

Twelve years later, as I revisit Roop Kanwar, I do not find myself in the same predicament as my father had been in. Like many feminists before me, both here in the United States and in India, I resist the dilemma of picking loyalties that rely on a false duality between Indian and feminist. While feminists from a variety of disciplines and perspectives have critiqued this notion of divided allegiance, the task I set before me requires exploration of the gap between our ideas and frameworks of analysis and how they are actually felt. What do I owe Roop Kanwar, and why? As a woman? As a feminist scholar? As an Indian? As a human being? I believe that questions of cultural embattlement, racism, sexism, homophobia, imperialism, neo-colonialism, among others, ultimately rest upon acknowledging and fighting for a notion of personhood that recognizes ambivalence. What would it mean to think of ourselves and of others as incomplete, changing, contradictory, fearful, strong, and strange? That despite the horror of a nineteen-year-old girl who burned alive, can we resist the impulse to foreclose judgment on anyone who might have a stake in this issue? What would that actually feel like?

After ten years of academic work in feminism, philosophy, postcolonial theory, and cultural criticism in the United States, I do not mean to suggest that questions of justice and culpability are not critical or that they should simply be ignored for the sake of postponing narrative closure. Roop Kanwar as a *devi*, victim of patriarchy and its religions, feminism's icon of the subaltern, representative of the status of women in India, daughter, wife, teenager, must accompany acknowledgement that we will never know who she was and what she could have been. This ambivalence, as a complicated person with a variety of factors shaping her character and her choices, rather than one thing or another, grants her moral authority. Change takes time and I believe the going might be easier if we choose to see our enemies and our friends, those whom we write about or work for from our various locations, and those who seek to represent themselves, as the same complicated, perspectival, and fallible beings as we see ourselves.

Paul Courtright's Narrative

My own interpretive pilgrimage to the site of Roop Kanwar's *sati* has required many pauses along the way of attempting to "make sense" of her death. The cultural and geographical distance that separates the American university from Deorala is, of course, enormous. Even though my earlier research on Hinduism has taken me to India many times, there is no question that I am an "outsider," standing at the periphery of much of the intensity of the debates that Goswami summarizes above. Finding a voice and point of view that can make a constructive contribution to making sense out of Roop Kanwar's death has been my principal challenge. For me the shore from which I depart to reach Deorala and its meanings is that of the academic study of religion.

Embedded in the field of the academic study of religion is an intellectual commitment to take seriously religious constructions of experience and action, to consider the distinctive points of view and display that lead us to call something "religious." In most cases this is not particularly problematic. Religion is about deities, shrines, ritual specialists, icons, prayers, songs, and so forth. The academic study of religion resists premature closure on the value of such phenomena and practices, preferring to linger over the thick details of what is being studied in terms of its own frames of reference. Indeed, the academic study of religion tends to resist what are sometimes termed "reductionist" translations of religious symbols and actions into political and economic power relations in ways that cause what has presented itself as religious to disappear into something else.

In the case of Roop Kanwar, as Goswami has shown, what was presented in Deorala as religious Roop Kanwar's *sati*, and her agency as one who somehow took control of the deluge of events that led to her immolation, have been interpreted in various ways by modernist and postcolonialist feminist voices as a concealment of what was "really" happening. That is, the symbolism of the *satimata*, her blessings, her divine self-disclosure, the spectacle that drew the tens of thousands of people from surrounding towns and villages, was a deception. What was really taking place was an attempt to conceal a murder and then profit from its commodification and marketing. Furthermore, it was an attempt, conscious or not, to reinforce the values of patriarchal hegemony. What was originally presented as religious became translated into a collective expression of false consciousness and deceit.

At this point in the interpretive process I find myself in a sort of double space. On the one hand, I appreciate the coherence and force of the perspective that sees Roop Kanwar as a victim of an elaborate system of symbols, practices, and narratives that restricts the place of women even as it elevates her to the status of a goddess. Yet, as one engaged in the study of religion, I need to press the question, "what's religious here?" Many of the people who came to Deorala in the days and weeks after Roop Kanwar's death came for her *darshan,* some kind of personal and visual contact with the place on the earth where Roop Kanwar had once stood. What are we to make of their responses? Do we dismiss them as "superstitious," somehow inhabiting a less adequate form of knowing reality than the perspectives that would see the religious as a mystification of a political and economic reality that is apparent to those who are modern or secular in their ways of knowing? And what *authorizes* such a self-perception? Hence, the part of me that is also modern and informed by various theoretical perspectives of social processes leads me in the direction of rejecting the religious claims that have been made for *sati* in general and Roop Kanwar in particular. At the same time the part of me that feels obliged to take religion seriously on its own terms leads me to say "wait a minute."

Those people who came to Deorala for Roop Kanwar's *darshan,* and the other *sati* shrines and temples across India, are also part of the human community. For them the categories of *sat, shakti,* and *mata* have status in their experience, as those of self, agency, and patriarchy do in my experience. I find a perplexing irony in my location as an "outsider" who feels drawn to imagining what goes on in the experience of those who look to the *satimata* as one who has agency of her own to intervene on their behalf as they attempt to navigate the vicissitudes of life's uncertainties. Who has the authority to say they are wrong?

This doubleness of standpoint carries with it its own forms of vertigo, and it reminds me of the ways in which I cannot sit comfortably in either the standpoint of the devotee or the critic. Both frames of reference are grounded in their respective epistemologies and politics. Perhaps what the outside interpreter might contribute to a process of sense-making is the perception that religion resides in the interstices of social, political, and economic dimensions of the situation. It has no autonomous reality apart from them. The categories of *sat, shakti,* and *mata* do not appear in the world independently of the voices and practices of those who use them.

My own brief visit to Deorala, on an occasion separate from Goswami's, also felt like a pilgrimage to a haunted place. I went with a young Rajput friend whose caste affiliation enabled me to visit Sumer Singh's home, though he was not there. I stood in the room where Roop Kanwar and Maal Singh had lived briefly together and from which the fateful events of September 4, 1987, had been launched. On the wall were photographs of the young married couple from the wedding and the lithograph of her in the midst of the fire that was reproduced in the newspapers and which had become an icon during the controversy that followed. On another wall was Maal Singh's college diploma. In a niche on the wall was a sort of shrine to Roop Kanwar, with a iconic depiction of her in the midst of the fire yet not being consumed, in the same tradition of representation I had seen at larger and smaller shrines in other areas of Sikar and Jhunjhunu districts. Later we went to the cremation ground. The feeling of absence in this space was palpably present. My companion was anxious to leave. The ritual space that had been a locale of such feverish ritual activity and media coverage twelve years before looked all the more abandoned and haunted.

The ban on the glorification of *sati* has prevented a shrine from being built on the site, and a police presence continues to be maintained at the site after nearly twelve years. There was a sense of both forgetting and remembering at that place. There was the India that wanted to forget that Roop Kanwar ever happened, bursting in like a ghost from a precolonial past; and there was an India that wanted to remember the heroic days when, as one Rajput retired military officer once told me, "Yes, in those days of Rajput kings, before British times, before independence, those women who became *satis*, they knew how to die like men." The longing for heroic presence in a post-heroic age, the longing for orders of gender separation and specificity in a post-gendered age, and the longing for an unambivalent sense of what it means to be Indian in an age of multi-national Indianness, those longings hung over the abandoned but guarded cremation ground in that out-of-the-way but immortalized place called Deorala.

Notes

1. While the term "postcolonial" is itself a contested one, we refer predominantly but not exclusively to feminists emerging from within the Indian subcontinent and from feminists of Indian origin within the U.S. academy. It is not meant to be representative or reductive of the many diasporic and national identities that fall under the rubric of "postcolonial."

2. See Rajeswari Sunder Rajan, *Signposts: Gender Issues in Post-Independence India* (New Delhi: Kali for Women, 1999).

3. Sunder Rajan, *Signposts*, 5.

4. Lata Mani, *Contentious Traditions: The Debate on Sati in Colonial India* (Los Angeles: University of California, 1998), 1–9, 152; idem, "Multiple Mediations: Feminist Scholarship in the Age of Multinational Reception," *Feminist Review*, no. 35 (Summer 1990): 35.

5. Madhu Kishwar, "The Burning of Roop Kanwar," *Manushi: A Journal about Women and Society*, no. 42–43 (1987): 20–24.

6. Rajeswari Sunder Rajan, *Real and Imagined Women: Gender, Culture, and Postcolonialism* (London: Routledge, 1993), 24.

7. Vasudha Dhagamwar, "Saint, Victim, or Criminal?," *Seminar* 342 (February 1988): 38.

8. See Mani, *Contentious Traditions;* Radha Kumar, *The History of Doing: An Illustrated Account of Movements for Women's Rights and Feminism in India 1800–1990* (London: Verso, 1993); Tanika Sarkar and Urvashi Butalia, eds., *Women and the Hindu Right: A Collection of Essays* (New Delhi: Kali for Women, 1995); Sunder Rajan, *Real and Imagined Women;* Kishwar, "The Burning of Roop Kanwar"; Gayatri Spivak, "Can the Subaltern Speak?" in Cary Nelson and Lawrence Grossberg, eds., *Marxism and the Interpretation of Culture* (Urbana: University of Illinois Press, 1988); Kumkum Sangari and Sudesh Vaid, eds., *Recasting Women: Essays in Indian Colonial History* (New Delhi: Kali for Women, 1989); Uma Narayan, *Dislocating Cultures: Identities, Traditions, and Third World Feminism* (New York: Routledge, 1997).

9. See Sunder Rajan, *Real and Imagined Women.*

10. Gayatri Spivak, *The Spivak Reader: Selected Works of Gayatri Chakravorty Spivak*, ed. Donna Landry and Gerald Maclean (New York: Routledge, 1996), 293.

11. Spivak, "Can the Subaltern Speak?" 299–306.

12. Ibid., 297.

13. Ibid., 297.

14. Chandra Mohanty, "Feminist Encounters: Locating the Politics of Experience," in *Destabilizing Theory: Contemporary Feminist Debates*, ed. Michèle Barrett and Anne Phillips (Stanford: Stanford University Press, 1992), 77.

15. V. N. Datta, *Sati: A Historical, Social, and Philosophical Enquiry into the Hindu Rite of Widow-Burning* (Riverdale: Riverdale Co., 1988).

16. Sunder Rajan, *Real and Imagined Women*, 18.

Eleven

"Where Will She Go? What Will She Do?"

Paternalism toward Women in
the Administration of Muslim Personal
Law in Contemporary India

Sylvia Vatuk

I argue in this essay that in India a "paternalistic" approach toward women and their needs permeates the legal process, in particular the manner in which the personal law is in practice administered in the courts. I draw for this insight upon seven months of anthropological fieldwork in the city of Chennai, where I examined the impact of Muslim personal law (MPL) on women. For much of this time I was observing, conducting interviews, and examining case files in the Chennai Family Court. Of course, these paternalistic attitudes affect all women who have occasion to become involved with the family court system, regardless of their religion. But because Muslim women were the specific focus of my research, I will focus here on their experience, as a particular case of a more widespread phenomenon.

The broad theoretical context for my research lies in current discussions in the legal-anthropological literature about issues of power and resistance in the relationship of individuals to the law. Students of law and society increasingly view the law not as a set of rules that mold human behavior, but as a resource, utilized by active agents to negotiate the conditions of their lives, pursue personal goals, and resist hegemonic definitions of selfhood (cf. Lazarus-Black and Hirsch, eds., 1994). By observing what actually goes on when women seek help from the state in resolving family disputes and examining it within its broader social and cultural context, these scholars have suggested that women are frequently able to use legal proceedings to "resist" male domination and generally pursue personal ends that may be quite extraneous to the official purposes for which these judicial institutions were designed (Hirsch 1998).[1] With these ideas as a point of departure, my own study was intended to explore Indian Muslim women's use of religious and civil courts, asking whether and how MPL, as administered in practice in India, impacts women in their efforts to accommodate and/or overcome the constraints and disabilities to which they are subject in a heavily male-dominated social milieu.

Despite all the rhetoric in India about gender bias in MPL and the frequent calls for its reform, we have almost no hard data on how Indian Muslim women are actually affected in practice by this code of law. A great deal of scholarly and activist effort has been devoted in recent years to describing the ways in which Muslim women suffer as a consequence of the freedom given to Muslim men to divorce at will and marry multiple wives. But the literature on this subject is largely anecdotal and highly polemical. In part this is because statistics that might shed some quantitative light on these matters are difficult or impossible to come by. India has no system of compulsory registration of marriage or divorce. Most Muslim marriages and a significant proportion of unilateral divorces (*talaq*) and divorces by mutual agreement (*khul'* and *mubarat*) are recorded by the clerics who conduct them. But the data on marriage is not recorded in a way that is amenable to quantitative analyses of polygyny. Estimates of the prevalence of unilateral and other forms of divorce would be feasible. However, as these records are not public documents, they are not easily accessible and to date have not been extensively used by scholars.[2]

In this research, one of my purposes was to partially remedy, from a qualitative rather than a quantitative perspective, the present lack of empirical information about how the existing system of personal law in India affects the lives of Muslim women. A second purpose was to contribute, from a comparative perspective, to the theoretical debates I have outlined above concerning issues of state power, the law, and women's resistance. My preliminary findings point to an ongoing tension between what I have called the "paternalism" that pervades the administration of family law generally in India and women's attempts—still very rare and usually only partially successful—to exert some control over their own destiny by making use of what the law purports to offer them in this regard. What these efforts often amount to is resisting, whether actively or through refusal to cooperate, the judicial system's attempts to exert paternal control over their life choices.

I employ here the important distinction, familiar to students of law and society, between the law as written and the law as practiced, between what the law *says* and what it actually *does*, when real women with concrete problems seek relief from the courts. Even where the law itself is free of obvious gender bias or is explicitly designed to confer some special benefit on women, they may have difficulty successfully availing themselves of its provisions. In the Indian context there are many reasons for this, one of the more important ones being the attitudes of those who are responsible for dispensing justice. They harbor assumptions about what women are like and what roles they ought to perform—or are even capable of performing—within their families and in society at large. These assumptions predispose them to take a paternalistic approach toward the needs of the women who come before them, whether as plaintiffs or respondents, in matrimonial and other related kinds of legal suits.

By "paternalism" I mean an attitude based on a view of women as inherently weak and vulnerable and consequently in need of lifelong material and symbolic support and protection from the men in their lives: fathers and brothers before marriage, husbands thereafter, and sons or other close male relatives in the latter's absence. Those responsible for administering the personal laws tend to believe, as do most Indians, especially of the upper and middle classes, that the proper place for an adult woman is within a marital relationship. They are inclined to consider it preferable, whatever the quality of that relationship, for her to remain under the conjugal roof rather than return to her natal home or strike out on her own. Their position is premised in part on the notion that a woman is by definition economically dependent on the earnings of a man. If she leaves her husband, some other man will have to take over this responsibility. For her to earn her own living is almost inconceivable.[3] The presumed social and sexual vulnerability of a woman without a male protector also plays a role in the paternalistic approach taken by those who administer the family law. Here the issue is one of preserving her status as a "respectable" woman. Even if she succeeds in remaining chaste, it is assumed that those around her will never cease to suspect otherwise. Fears related to the stigma of divorce combine with fears of its material consequences to produce the rhetorical questions that I heard repeatedly during the course of my research: "Where will she go, what will she do, if she and her husband cannot be reconciled?"

In order to "save" women by "saving" their marriages, lawyers, court-appointed social workers, and judges alike make ample use of delays, attempts at mediation, and pressures to reach a compromise. Bureaucratic delays are not deliberately designed to thwart women's access to justice, but are built into the Indian judicial system (cf. Moog 1997).

Family Courts in India

Family courts operate today in the major cities of most states of the Indian Union, pursuant to central legislation passed in September 1984 as the Family Courts Act (FCA) (see Tiwari and Zaidi 1997).[4] These courts have civil jurisdiction over all matrimonial suits, regardless of the religion of the parties, and are also empowered to decide cases registered under Chapter IX, Section 125 of the Code of Criminal Procedure (CCrP), which covers orders of maintenance for destitute wives and children.[5] The Chennai Family Court was established in 1988. Initially one judge handled its entire caseload, but this number was later increased to three. Currently the principal judge is a man and the two additional judges are female.[6]

The original impetus for the establishment of family courts came from women's activist organizations that were critical of, among other things, the adversarial nature of matrimonial proceedings in the existing civil courts, procedural complexities, and long delays in resolving cases (Committee on the Status of Women in India 1974). They saw all these features of the existing system as particularly disadvantageous for women, who tend to be less well-informed about the law than men and to have fewer financial resources with which to fight a legal case. As eventually enacted, the FCA cites as its main purpose, "to promote conciliation in and secure speedy settlement of disputes relating to marriage and family affairs." To the former end, provision is made for family counselors to guide disputing parties toward amicable settlements. Clarification as to the kind of settlement envisioned is found in the section concerning the selection of family court judges. There it is laid down that they should be "persons committed to the need to protect and preserve the institution of marriage."

Under the FCA, advocates are not permitted to represent clients in court, except under special circumstances and with the express permission of the judge. This clause was intended to enable greater access to the courts by the poor as well as to create a more informal atmosphere where litigants would be free to state their own cases, not in legalistic language but in their own words. In practice, however, it is almost impossible to navigate the court system without an advocate and few are so foolhardy as to attempt it. Any litigant who does come to court alone is quickly propositioned by a tout or by an enterprising advocate who operates a makeshift and continually moving office within the space of the family court itself. Advocates draft all petitions (in English), advise their clients, and accompany them to court. But it is still necessary for the parties to a suit to appear in person for each hearing, usually scheduled at one-month intervals. For many, especially for poor women, this is a great hardship. In part because of this requirement, a high percentage of cases are eventually "dismissed for default of plaintiff," that is, because the plaintiff has failed to appear for three consecutive hearings.

In this and many other ways, the family courts have not lived up to the hopes of those who originally fought for their establishment (Agnes 1991, 1994; Nagasila 1991, 1992; Ramaseshan 1989). The persistence of the problem of long court delays, one of the original rationales for setting up specialized family courts, is one focus of criticism. I am aware of no published studies that provide comparative statistics on how long it takes for cases to be resolved under the new system, though there is impressionistic evidence that matrimonial cases are indeed being processed faster than before. But this does not mean that anyone filing suit in family court can expect a swift decision. Between 1988 and 1997 cases took anywhere from two months to seven years to be resolved; the median time was approximately two years.

Legal scholars and feminist activists are especially critical of the Act's avowed emphasis on preserving the family, pointing out the incompatibility of this goal with that of ensuring women's well-being. In the words of a social worker attached to a private welfare organization in Chennai,

> The bias [in the family courts] is in favour of holding the status quo of the marriage. In this, it is always the woman who is pressurized into adjusting or submitting, particularly as in most cases she is less educated, less articulate and less assertive. (YMCA 1990)

The same theme is echoed by O. Chinnappa Reddy, a former Justice of the Supreme Court of India:

> The Act is supposed to remove the gender bias and to put disadvantaged women in a position of advantage . . . [T]he historically disadvantaged position occupied by women has been sought to be removed . . . not by restricting the dissolution or disruption of the marriage but by the enactment of laws, giving the right of divorce and the right to maintenance to woman. . . . The commitment [of the Act] should be not to protect and preserve the institution of marriage but to endeavour to secure to women a life with dignity and honour. (National Commission for Women, New Delhi 1994:9)

Counseling in the Family Court

Couples engaged in matrimonial litigation or maintenance suits are required to undergo counseling (routinely referred to in case files as "reconciliation") before their case goes before the judge. In Chennai, most of those engaged as counselors have no professional training for the task. They are not paid a salary, but receive only a nominal *per diem* stipend that barely covers their transportation costs. Those who volunteer to serve the usual three-month term are well-meaning, socially conscious, upper-middle-class, Hindu or Christian, Western-educated men and women, often retirees, who see their work as a way of contributing to the welfare of those less fortunate than themselves. They sympathize with the women they encounter in court and are often quite insightful about the complexity of the situations in which the latter find themselves. But, imbued as they are with the kind of paternalistic attitudes I have referred to, and operating within a system whose goal is to preserve the institution of marriage, they cannot but commit themselves to getting couples back together. With this end in view, they insist that couples return again and again to the court for more "reconciliation" sessions. Only when they realize that there is no hope of saving the marriage do they turn to brokering some kind of compromise settlement.

Where, as in India, power asymmetries between husband and wife are marked and where the burden of adjustment within most marriages falls primarily on the wife, "compromise" is a gender-linked concept. It is the role of the wife to meet her husband's needs and demands, to comply with his wishes, and bear stoically all manner of personal hardships. Thus, in the process of working out "mutually agreeable" settlements in the family court context, husbands tend to be given considerably more leeway than strict gender equity would dictate. Wives are often pressured, even browbeaten, by counselors into settling for outcomes that may be grossly unfair and contrary to their best interests. Thus, divorce settlements regularly have the wife giving up all financial claims on the husband, including the *mahr* amount to which she is entitled, often in return for custody of a young child in whom the husband has never shown any interest and would not in any case have a claim on for many years in the future. Where maintenance is the issue, once reconciliation attempts have been abandoned, counselors, lawyers, and judges all concentrate on trying to persuade the husband to offer to pay some amount of support for his wife and children. They rationalize this approach by pointing out that there is little value in issuing an order that realistically cannot be enforced, unless the man is a government employee and therefore subject to salary attachment. If he can be prodded into making a commitment to pay a modest amount, it is more likely that the money will actually be forthcoming.

In the context of family court negotiations, women are regularly encouraged to drop criminal charges they may have filed against their husbands, to withdraw or reduce property, maintenance, or custody demands, and even to resume living with men who may have subjected them to long-standing abuse in the past. A legal discourse of "rights" is thus transformed into a discourse of "welfare," whose defining terms are set, not by the woman herself, but by her counselor, her advocate, the judge, and, in the last analysis, by the realities imposed by the society within which she lives.

Muslim Personal Law in India

As in many other formerly colonized states in Asia, Africa, and the Caribbean, the Indian legal system is "pluralistic." It is pluralistic in the sense that there are distinct codes of personal law for adherents of each of the major religious faiths. Furthermore, a state-sponsored system of codified law and civil and criminal courts coexists with a whole range of other less formal and unofficial (though sometimes their decisions are officially recognized) community or religious dispute-settlement bodies. For Muslims, these include *qazis'* offices, *Shari'at* courts, caste, *qaum*, or sect *pancayats*, and *jamat* committees or councils of elders associated with local mosques.[7] Men and women who are experiencing family difficulties normally approach such bodies before, or instead of, turning to the civil courts. The family court is a place of last resort; only a minuscule percentage of those who experience marital difficulties ever use it. Most still prefer to resolve family disputes by more familiar, informal, local means.[8] Both these formal and informal aspects of legal pluralism are a legacy of British colonial rule, inspired in part by pre-colonial Muslim practice, whereby non-Muslim subjects were permitted to govern themselves in matters related to the family and caste (Cohn 1989; Nair 1996).

MPL in India today is still largely uncodified. The statutes most relevant to the work of the family court are the Dissolution of Muslim Marriages Act (DMMA)—under which a Muslim woman may file for divorce—and the 1986 Muslim Women's (Protection of Rights on Divorce) Act (MWA)—whose best-known provision, notwithstanding its

Table 11.1. Muslim Cases as a Percentage of
Total Cases Filed in 1996

	OP*		OS**		MC***		Total
	Number	%	Number	%	Number	%	
All Cases	1367	74%	47	2%	441	24%	1855
Muslim Cases	10	19%	18	34%	25	47%	53
% Muslim		0.73%		38.3%		5.67%	2.86%

* Original Petitions
** Ordinary Suits
*** Maintenance Cases

misleading title, denies a destitute, divorced Muslim woman the right to sue her ex-husband for maintenance under the relevant Indian criminal code (see below).[9] For matters not falling under the purview of either of these Acts, family court judges have available to them a number of "authoritative" English-language texts on Muslim personal law (e.g. Hidayatullah 1990). Most of those currently in use are of fairly recent vintage. They are authored by English-educated Indian legal scholars drawing upon classical Arabic *Shari'at* texts (often in translation) and Indo-Persian commentaries thereon, supplemented by the large body of case law that has been produced by the British-Indian and post-independence courts over the course of the last two centuries.

Muslims in the Chennai Family Court

In their daily practice, however, judges rarely need concern themselves with the intricacies of MPL. Firstly, in Chennai at least, they rarely encounter a Muslim case. Muslim litigants are represented at a much lower rate in proportion to their population than are people of other religions. The city of Chennai had in 1991 almost four million people, of whom 8.7 percent were Muslim. But in no year during the period 1988–1997 did more than 4 percent of the cases registered in family court involve Muslims.[10] Secondly, a substantial portion of the suits filed by Muslims in these courts—in Chennai approximately half—do not involve issues of MPL at all (Table 11.1). Most numerous among them are suits filed under Chapter IX, Section 125 of the Code of Criminal Procedure (CCrP), by destitute women seeking awards of maintenance (up to a maximum of Rs 500 per month) against husbands from whom they are living separately. Section 125 provides relief to women of any religion who have no other means of support (Muzumdar 1989; Verma 1988).[11] Because, however, the MWA denies its use to Muslim women who are *divorced*, only those Muslim women who are still married can obtain maintenance for themselves under the CCrP. A divorcée may, however, ask the court to order her former husband to pay her in order to maintain their children.[12]

The second most common type of case to be filed by Muslims in the Chennai Family Court is for "restitution of conjugal rights" (RCR). This legal remedy is available in India to persons of any religion. Its purpose is to compel a spouse who has left the matrimonial home to return to it and, in the formulaic phrase repeatedly encountered in court documents, "restore to the petitioner the comforts and bliss of married life." Theoretically a person of either sex can file for restitution. In court records I found numerous instances of Hindu and Christian women making use of this law, but every petitioner in the sixty-three restitution suits filed by Muslims in the ten-year period of the Chennai court's existence was male (Table 11.2).[13]

Suits for RCR seem often motivated by a desire to harass or threaten a wife, or to retaliate against her for making a police report or filing for divorce or maintenance. This is consistent with the fact that the proportion of RCR cases dismissed as "withdrawn," "not pressed," or "for default of plaintiff" is higher than for any other kind of case, almost 85 percent. Those cases that are pursued to judgment almost invariably succeed. However, there are no mechanisms to enforce restitution orders. In some cases the mere filing of such a suit may be enough to induce a wife to return to her marital home. But if she is determined not to return, there is little that a judge—or a husband—can do to make her. One serious consequence, however, of an order for RCR is that it makes a wife ineligible to claim the right of maintenance.

The number of divorce suits filed by women under the DMMA are, in Chennai at least, only slightly lower than the number of RCR suits—fifty-seven in the years 1988–1997 (Table II). This Act allows a Muslim woman to obtain a divorce from an unwilling husband, or from one whose whereabouts are unknown, on grounds that include his cruelty, desertion, failure to maintain or to perform his marital obligations, impotence, insanity, leprosy or "virulent venereal disease," or being imprisoned for a period of seven or more years. It was passed in 1939 in response to pressure from the Muslim religious establishment, then concerned about a growing trend whereby Muslim women, desperate to extricate themselves from abusive or otherwise intolerable marital unions, had resorted to renouncing Islam and converting to Christianity

Table 11.2. OS Cases, Muslim 1988 to 1997

Year	Muslim Cases	DMMA	RCR	Other*
1988	6	3	3	0
1989	18	4	6	8
1990	14	5	6	3
1991	18	2	4	12
1992	21	6	6	9
1993	18	5	8	5
1994	27	12	11	4
1995	17	6	9	2
1996	18	9	7	2
1997	10	5	3	2
	167	57	63	47

* "Other" includes suits for declaration of the validity of a marriage or divorce or of the marital status of one of the parties. Also suits for child custody, maintenance above Rs 500/month, injunctive relief, return of property, and three cases of Muslim men filing for divorce under the mistaken impression that they can or are required to do so under DMMA.

or Hinduism. Under MPL at that time, such an act of "apostasy" automatically voided their marriages. Faced by the unpleasant prospect of Muslim women abandoning the faith in droves, a group of clerics proposed legislation that would offer another way out to such women and, at the same time, make it no longer possible for a woman to invalidate her marriage through apostasy.[14]

Half the divorce suits registered in the Chennai Family Court were dismissed, either because the woman withdrew the suit or because she simply neglected to pursue it. In some cases the record shows that the husband had pronounced *talaq* or the couple had come to an agreement for *khul'* while the case was still in litigation, making the matter moot. Most of those whose suits were not dismissed for one of these reasons succeeded in obtaining a divorce decree. Rarely, if ever, was a divorce suit dismissed by the judge for lack of evidence or for failure to prove the grounds cited. But almost invariably—unless the husband failed to contest the suit or his whereabouts were unknown—a "compromise," usually drafted in the form of a so-called "joint endorsement," accompanied the judgment.

Muslim men do not come to court for a divorce, since under MPL they may divorce unilaterally by merely pronouncing the word *talaq* ("divorce") three times on three successive occasions, or all at once. The wife need not even be present. A man is legally required at this time to pay his wife her *mahr* ("dower"), in whatever amount he promised at the time of their marriage,[15] and provide money for her maintenance for a period of three months thereafter (*iddat*). There exists no enforcement mechanism for these financial obligations, however, and there is considerable evidence that they are honored more in the breach than in the observance.[16]

It is also possible for a Muslim woman to initiate an extra-judicial divorce. However, she cannot do so unilaterally. In order to obtain this kind of divorce (*khul'*), her husband must consent to release her from the marriage. In exchange, she must pay him a financial consideration. Typically this means relinquishing her claim to any outstanding *mahr* and to maintenance during the *iddat* period. If she has already received her *mahr*, she must repay it. Occasionally a man will bargain for some additional payment as well. If a woman cannot get her husband to agree to *khul'*, some schools of Islamic law provide that, if she is suffering great hardship, an Islamic judge (*qazi*) may be approached for a divorce decree (*faskh*). Even today there are *qazis* in India who will accommodate a woman in this way, but most seem to regard it as beyond the scope of their authority, in line with their understanding of *Shari'at*.[17]

Muslim Women and Marital Conflict

For the purpose of the following discussion I have analyzed in detail the files in a sample of twenty randomly chosen Muslim cases from the year 1992. The documents consist, for the most part, of petitions and counter-petitions by the parties involved. Since there is no way to establish the truth of any of the narratives, I am using them principally for what they reveal about general patterns of marital conflict and relief-seeking patterns among Muslims in this part of India. The women involved in these cases married at ages ranging from twelve to forty-nine—for some in the higher end of this range, the marriage may not have been their first. The husbands are typically five to ten years older than their wives. Even though the minimum age at marriage for girls is eighteen years (as per the 1978 Child Marriage Restraint Act), almost a third of these women claim to have been younger than this when they married. Twenty percent were under sixteen years of age. Most of the marriages were arranged by the respective parents; few couples had the opportunity to become acquainted with one another before the ceremony. There were a small number of "love marriages," mostly involving

Muslim men married (under MPL) to Hindu or Christian women converted to Islam. One love marriage of this kind took place in a Hindu temple, another under the Special Marriage Act (SMA). The latter men, though Muslim by birth, are not entitled to pronounce *talaq*, but must file for divorce under the statutes that apply to the type of marriage they contracted.[18]

Despite a long-standing preference among south Indian Muslims for arranging marriages within a close circle of kin (Mines 1976; Khan 1994; Fanselow 1986; Vatuk 1990), very few court petitions give any indication that the spouses were related prior to the marriage. It is impossible to know whether silence on this matter indicates that no such relationship existed or that the information was not considered relevant to the narrative at hand. I am inclined, however, to accept the former interpretation. If I am right, the data suggest that couples who are close relatives are less likely than those who married as strangers to have the kinds of problems that bring couples into family court. Furthermore, if they do have marital difficulties, they are less likely to resort to the law as a way of solving them.

Almost without exception, the women in this sample were living apart from their husbands and often had been for many years. Most were married for a short time before the separation occurred, but several years had usually elapsed between that time and the time of the court filing. Almost every woman had at least one child and was living—usually with that child—in the household of her own parents or that of an adult sibling. If she was living with another man, this fact was, of course, unlikely to appear in any petition filed by her. Occasionally such an allegation was made by a husband in a plea for RCR or in a counter to a divorce or maintenance petition filed by his wife.

Women's petitions often referred to "dowry" gifts: cash, jewelry, and other material goods given by their parents to their husband and his parents at the time of the wedding.[19] After the wedding the wife almost always joined the household of her husband and his parents and siblings, thus beginning married life in an extended family household. Very few couples set up housekeeping on their own immediately after the wedding or moved in with the wife's parents.

The specific nature and source of the marital tensions that eventually led to the filing of a suit in court naturally vary from case to case, but certain patterns recur. Complaints about in-laws, especially mothers- and sisters-in-law, are common. The latter are reported to have insisted that the new bride take on the lion's share of the housework, prevented her from spending time alone with her husband, and forbade her to visit her natal family on holidays or in times of illness. They criticized her for the way she performed her household tasks, accused her of laziness or slovenliness, of showing insufficient respect and deference to them and to her husband, or of behaving in a seductive manner toward other men. They harassed her with recriminations about the quantity or quality of the dowry items they received and subjected her to demands that she extract additional money and goods from her parents. Verbal harassment escalated sooner or later to physical abuse and eventually to the woman either being forcibly ejected from the house or leaving on her own initiative, usually with the help of members of her natal family.

A common theme is the husband's "suspicion" of his wife, sometimes culminating in accusations of adultery. More than one woman reported having been regularly beaten and/or locked in the house every time her husband went out, so that she would be unable to seek out male companionship in his absence.[20] One educated working woman told of visits by her husband to her place of employment, where he spied on her and subjected her to public rebukes. In his response he claimed his actions were justified by her refusal to quit her job, as he had demanded.

A high percentage of the women also complained that their husband had been unfaithful, usually with a neighbor, co-worker, or close relative. Others complained of his contracting another marriage and then either bringing the second wife to live in the same house or setting her up in a separate household that drew assets needed by the first wife and her children. Neither of these arrangements was considered to be tolerable. In one case a second wife petitioned the court with a complaint that when she married, her husband failed to reveal that he already had a wife. He made her live in the home together with his first wife and do all the housework, while he neglected her needs, providing inadequate amounts of food and clothing. Other common allegations against the husband included alcoholism, drug abuse, and gambling. In two cases, a mother-in-law was accused of performing black magic, the first in order to cause her daughter-in-law to abort, the other to make her sexually repellent to her husband.

There is evidence in some of the petitions that men are not always eager to take advantage of their freedom to pronounce unilateral divorce, even when they have no desire to remain married. For example, in one petition the wife complained that her husband refused to pronounce *talaq*, demanding instead that she go to the religious authorities to ask for *khul'*. She refused to do this, not wanting to put herself on record as the initiating party for the divorce, as she knew that if she did so she would "get a bad name." She was also unwilling to give up all financial claims on her husband as she would have to do if they divorced by means of *khul'*. Her husband eventually did pronounce *talaq*, doing so in the courtroom of the first additional judge on the day he was summoned to answer his wife's suit for maintenance! Like many other Muslim men, he was aware of those provisions of the MWA that enable a man to avoid financial responsibility for a divorced wife.

Before approaching the civil authorities, most couples made repeated attempts, often extending over a period of several years, to find a solution to their marital problems. They had sought the advice of family members, more distant kinsmen, neighbors, friends, and work associates. Later many turned to the local mosque committee or to a local cleric for help. Typically these consultations ended in the drafting of a joint agreement, whereby both parties promised to improve their behavior in the future. But such agreements seldom held for long. Eventually some of the women went so far as to file criminal charges against their husbands and/or parents-in-law for domestic abuse or dowry harassment. Those women who went to the police or ended up in court almost always received considerable financial, practical, and moral support from their natal families—parents and brothers in particular. Without it, few women, regardless of their economic stratum or level of education, could take legal action against their husband. Those who do are clearly atypical, since it is unusual for Indian parents—whatever their religion and no matter how fond of their daughter they may be—to actively take her side when she is having marital problems. They tend to be reluctant to take such a daughter back into their home once they have given her in marriage, often at very great expense. Thus they pressure her, or even compel her, to remain with her husband. In this they are motivated both by a fear of incurring social disgrace and by their inability or unwillingness to assume the financial burden of supporting her for the rest of her life. Even if they can afford to do the latter and are not unduly fazed by the prospect of having to defend their action to outsiders, they may still have doubts about whether the best solution is for her to live out her life as a divorcée, a veritable social outcast.

When I raised the issue of the stigma of divorce with Hindu legal practitioners, some expressed the view that a Muslim woman has an easier time in this situation than a Hindu, because Muslim parents are less likely to insist that their daughter remain with an abusive husband. They believed the stigma of divorce to be minimal among Muslims and pointed also to the possibility of remarriage. They felt that among Hindus, on the other hand, a second marriage for a divorced woman is still almost out of the question.[21] Muslim interviewees tended to begin by crediting their religion with being more realistic and humane than Hinduism, in allowing easy divorce for couples who find it impossible to live harmoniously together, and in permitting—even encouraging—remarriage for both partners. But when pressed, they also cited the stigma of divorce as a serious problem for women locked in unhappy marriages and seeking a way out. They also acknowledged that, whatever the Qur'an may say, in practice it is difficult in India to find a man willing to marry a divorced woman, especially if she is no longer very young or is the mother of children.

It is quite clear that, when one begins to examine the actual practice of MPL in India, one is faced with a far more complex situation than appears on the surface. At this point I am not far enough along in my analysis to make any definitive generalizations about the impact of this code on Indian Muslim women. However, I can make some preliminary observations and point to certain issues that need further study.

First, it seems clear that in practice, the family courts play a very limited role in the administration of MPL. Very few Muslim matrimonial disputes ever reach the courts: they are nearly always dealt with informally at the family and community level and with the help of various kinds of religious bodies, functionaries, and private religio-legal experts. Of course, the same is true for other religious communities, but Muslims make even less use of the family courts than others. Two important reasons for this are the availability for Muslims of extra-judicial divorce and the ineligibility of divorced Muslim females for maintenance under Section 125 of the CrCP. However, my study in Chennai suggests that even in situations where they have the same opportunity to obtain relief under the law, Muslims are less likely to do so than Hindus or Christians.

Second, when Muslims do come into the family court, they are most likely to come to file under a law that is not part of MPL—for example, to ask for maintenance or child support under CCrP or to file for RCR. Very little use is made of the two chief MPL statutes, the DMMA and MWA.

Third, neither the situations that bring Muslim, Hindu, and Christian women into court, nor the way their problems are dealt with by the judicial authorities and other court staff, nor the outcomes of their time in court, are very different, notwithstanding the well-known differences in the three personal law codes. Although my study was not designed to compare the family court experiences of Muslims with those of Hindus and Christians, this conclusion is drawn from a count of all cases, by type, filed in the Chennai Family Court over a one-year period and the reading of a random sample of those cases. A careful comparative study of this question would be a valuable contribution to our understanding of the way the Indian personal law system works and to what extent—in practice—one code has any clear advantages (for women) over the others.

Unilateral, extra-judicial divorce and polygyny are the provisions of MPL that have attracted the most negative attention and are the chief foci of criticism by proponents of a uniform civil code of personal law (UCC). My research was not designed to determine the prevalence of these practices, but rather to put them into some kind of context. My evidence suggests that even though the possibility of being unilaterally divorced doubtless weighs heavily upon the wife in any troubled marital relationship and accentuates the need for her to be submissive and placating at any cost if she wishes to remain married, most *talaq*s are probably not pronounced "on a whim," as the popular stereotype would lead one to believe. Interviews and court petitions reveal that a great deal of calculation—and frequently negotiation with the wife—goes into the decision to pronounce a divorce. If there is some clear advantage to divorcing the wife, rather than just living separately from her, then it is likely that a man will divorce her. Evading a maintenance suit (as per the MWA) provides just such a motivation, as my data clearly indicate. But otherwise, many men don't bother with this formality. In this they do not differ from their Hindu and Christian fellow countrymen, for whom the inclination to simply desert the wife (or kick her out of the marital home), rather than divorce her, is even more compelling, since the latter can only be accomplished after a lengthy and expensive court procedure.[22] One reason why Muslim men are sometimes reluctant to take advantage of that provision of MPL that allows extra-judicial divorce is the social opprobrium it attracts. Among other things, a man who has pronounced *talaq* may have difficulty finding another wife. This is probably one of the main reasons why men often try to induce their wives to ask for *khul'*. Financial considerations may also weigh more or less heavily in their calculations, depending upon the amount of *mahr* that had been promised and the likelihood that they can avoid paying it.

If the allegations contained in women's court petitions are to be relied upon, extra-marital liaisons are very common among Muslim men, as they are among Hindus and Christians. Polygynous marriages are less often reported. Even though polygyny is an accepted practice in Islam, and the simple fact that a man has taken a second wife is not regarded as a legitimate reason for the first wife to feel aggrieved, my data suggest that it frequently causes extreme marital discord, because the man almost inevitably shows favoritism toward one or the other wife or is perceived by one or the other to be doing so. And notwithstanding a Muslim man's right under MPL to marry up to four wives at a time, the courts are in practice sympathetic to Muslim women who complain about their husbands' second marriage in a divorce or maintenance petition. Thus "cruelty" under the DMMA may be interpreted to include a man's forcing his first wife to live under the same roof as the second.

Insofar as the actual administration of MPL by the family (and other civil) courts in India is concerned, I have identified, in the approach taken by the judicial authorities to the women who come before them, a pervasive paternalism based upon unexamined assumptions about woman's "nature" and her proper "place" in society. Most important of these is the notion that the institution of marriage provides the only secure guarantee of a woman's well-being. Ideas like this are, of course, widely shared by people of all religions. They are not only consistent with but also help to perpetuate those economic and social structural realities of women's lives that force them into overall dependency on the men in their lives. The paternalistic attitudes toward women that this ideology generates ensure that even if a woman who is having marital difficulties can overcome the many barriers that hinder her access to the civil court system, her chances of actually obtaining there what the law theoretically has to offer her are relatively small.

The issue of women's "resistance" in the context of legal proceedings in the family courts is difficult to sort out. I have ample evidence that the women with whom I spoke are impatient with the way counseling is carried out in the courts, that they resent the time and money spent coming to court month after month, sitting for hours, on the floor, without water or toilet facilities, while they wait, often only in order to hear that they should come back again next month. They often distrust the intentions of the police, lawyers, judges, and other staff of the family court who hold such power over their lives. As they wait, they exchange with one another stories that help to reinforce their conviction that nothing positive will come of their efforts to obtain justice. And they exchange advice about how to deal with what is happening to them. In the sense that these women are aware of what they are up against, but have decided to try to use the law to ameliorate their situation anyway, they cannot be regarded as the passive victims of a patriarchal order, as they are so often assumed to be. But on the other hand, however much "agency" they may exert in the process of dealing with the law, the realities of their situation are such that they can only hope for limited success.

Notes

This paper was written while I was a Faculty Fellow of the Institute for the Humanities at the University of Illinois at Chicago. My research in India was supported by a Fulbright-Hays Senior Research Fellowship and a sabbatical leave from the University of Illinois at Chicago. In Chennai I was affiliated with the Madras Institute of Development Studies. For their cheerful assistance I am extremely grateful to my research assistant, Ms. R. Saraswathy, and to the employees of the record room at the Chennai Family Court, who patiently retrieved from their massive collection of materials the individual files that we required. I thank the then Chief Justice of the Chennai High Court for facilitating my research in the Family Court and the then Acting Principal Judge of that court for arranging for me to consult the relevant files under her jurisdiction.

1. The employment of such strategies is not, of course, restricted to female litigants. For India, see Cohn's (1965) and Moog's (1997) discussions of the way courts are used for purposes other than those for which they were intended.

2. In order to get an idea of what these records contain, I was kindly permitted by a *qazi* in another Indian city to copy his divorce register for the year 1992. In a jurisdiction in which approximately 4,000 marriages are contracted each year, the register contained details on 450 divorces. Slightly more than half of these were of the *khul'* type; in almost all these cases the woman was recorded as having given up her *mahr*. In cases of *talaq*, it was usually noted that the *mahr* due the wife had been deposited with the *qazi* and later paid out to her.

   To put these figures into perspective, it must be stressed that there is no requirement that a divorce be pronounced in the presence of or registered with any religious or civil authority. The chief reason for registering a *talaq* is for a man to obtain an "official" paper, documenting the dissolution of the marriage. Since a woman cannot simply "pronounce" *khul'*, it is usual for her to go to a *qazi* or other cleric for help in negotiating with her husband and drawing up the necessary contract. For this reason, it is probable that a higher percentage of *khul'* divorces than *talaq*s end up being recorded.

3. The validity of the assumption that most married women in urban India depend on their husbands' earnings for support is probably borne out by statistics, although levels of labor force participation by women, especially among the poor, are certainly much higher than the proponents of this view realize. In my sample of Muslim women drawn from court files in Chennai, there were only a handful who had ever worked outside the home, though some may have engaged in home-based income-producing labor (such as making specialty food items, garments, handrolled *bidis*, and the like).

4. By 1994 there were fifty such courts in operation (National Commission for Women 1994: 19); there may be more today.

5. In places where no family court exists, matrimonial cases and applications for maintenance under the Code of Criminal Procedure are handled, as in the past, by the regular civil courts.

6. The Act specifies that preference in the appointment of judges is to be given to women, presumably under the assumption that they would deal more fairly and sympathetically with female litigants. Neither of the female judges in the Chennai Family Court is married. The gender and marital status of these judges was noted more than once by lawyers and litigants to whom I spoke in Chennai. There was no unanimity, however, about their relevance to the way matrimonial disputes were dealt with in the courtroom.

7. See Moore 1998 for a rich ethnographic account of one rural Muslim woman's experience with such a body in the context of a matrimonial dispute.

8. Moog (1997: 60–63) maintains that in India, the notion of the court as a place of last resort is by no means restricted to those who are having marital difficulties. This attitude toward the courts is widespread among the populace, stereotypes about India as an excessively litigious society notwithstanding. He provides compelling comparative data from the U.S. to support his contention.

9. The passage of this law followed the award by the Supreme Court of India, on appeal, of a decree of maintenance under Section 125 of the CCrP against the former husband of an elderly Muslim woman named Shah Bano. There is by now a huge body of literature on this case, on the debates that it unleashed, on the events that led up to the passage of the MWA, and on the implications of this change in the law for Muslim women. Engineer (1987) has collected many of the relevant documents as well as contemporary news items and public statements about the case. Some useful analyses include those by Kishwar 1986; Kozlowski 1989; Pathak and Sundar Rajan 1989.

10. For example, in 1996 less than 3 percent of the 1,855 original suits filed involved Muslim litigants (see Table 11.1). I am limiting my count here to cases filed under the three main headings of "Ordinary Suits" (OS) "Original Petitions" (OP) and "Maintenance Cases" (MC). Other types of cases registered in the Chennai Family Court include suits for orders of execution, interim orders, injunctions, etc. These, however, are always secondary to an earlier suit of the OS, OP, or MC type, and so have not been included in my calculations.

11. Critical perspectives on the operation of the law as regards awards of maintenance in the contemporary context in India are offered by Agnes 1992a, 1992b, and Kishwar 1993.

12. There has been some controversy over whether the jurisdiction of family

courts as specified in the FCA is properly interpreted to include jurisdiction over maintenance suits filed under the MWA against a woman's natal relatives or, in their absence, the local Waqf Board (see Agnes 1994). In my perusal of the Chennai Family Court files for the years 1988–1997, I found two such cases, neither of which resulted in a judgment. I do not know whether this represents the totality of suits filed under the MWA in Chennai during this period. It is conceivable that other civil courts of the city also entertained similar suits during these years.

13. For a historical perspective on this legal remedy in Indian law, see Chandra 1998.

14. For further details and discussion of the events leading up to the passage of the DMMA, see Masud 1996; Minault 1997; Lateef 1990.

15. The payment (or promise of payment) of *mahr* is one of the conditions for a legal Muslim marriage.

16. For example, in a study of 100 divorced women in Bombay, Merchant (1992: 111) found that 60 percent had not received their *mahr* after divorce. Note that she does not distinguish those who were divorced by *talaq* from those who obtained *khul'* (see below) or a civil divorce under DMMA. Nor does she provide information concerning maintenance for the *iddat* period for the women in her sample.

   Mahr amounts reported in Chennai Family Court petitions tended to be minimal in any event, almost regardless of the economic standing of the husband. The conventional figure of Rs 568 was cited in the vast majority of cases, and rarely was it above Rs 1,500.

17. MPL also recognizes other forms of divorce, including one by mutual agreement, *mubarat*, but these seem to be little known or resorted to, at least in the parts of India where I have investigated the matter.

18. Technically, insofar as matrimonial causes are concerned, MPL applies to persons married under Muslim law, that is in a Muslim ceremony, the central features of which are the signing of a *nikah* contract and the payment (or promise of payment) of *mahr* ("dower") by the man to his bride. Thus someone married under the Special Marriage Act (SMA), even if he or she was born of Muslim parents, would be governed, in the event of a divorce suit, by the provisions of that Act. Conversely, a Hindu woman who contracts a *nikah* with a Muslim man must file for divorce under the DMMA, rather than under the Hindu Marriage Act.

19. Although the practice of giving "dowry" is not sanctioned by Islam, it has been spreading rapidly within the community in recent decades and is often cited by Muslims as a serious and growing social problem.

20. A recent study of women who had registered criminal cases for domestic abuse in the main All-Woman Police Station in Chennai likewise cites the husband's "suspicion" of his wife as a major precipitant of marital discord (Natarajan 1997, 1999).

21. These observations can be interpreted from one angle as a self-critique of

excessive Hindu orthodoxy, but from another angle they are clearly part of a more general discourse about the relative "immorality" of the Muslim woman in comparison to her Hindu sisters.

22. The procedure is especially onerous for Christian men, who must prove adultery. Christian women wanting a divorce must prove adultery *combined with* desertion or cruelty.

References Cited

Agnes, Flavia
  1991 [See Flavia]
  1992a *Give Us This Day Our Daily Bread: Procedures and Case Law on Maintenance.* Gender Justice Series, Book II. Mumbai: Majlis.
  1992b "Maintenance for Women: Rhetoric of Equality." *Economic and Political Weekly* 27: 2233–2235.
  1994 "Family Courts and Minority Rights." *The Lawyers* 9, no. 5: 27–29.
Chandra, Sudhir
  1998 *Enslaved Daughters: Colonialism, Law, and Women's Rights.* Delhi: Oxford University Press.
Cohn, Bernard S.
  1965 "Anthropological Notes on Disputes and Law in India." *American Anthropologist* 67/6/2: 82–122.
  1989 "Law and the Colonial State in India." In *History and Power in the Study of Law,* ed. J. Starr and J. F. Collier, pp. 131–152. Ithaca: Cornell University Press.
Committee on the Status of Women in India
  1974 *Towards Equality.* New Delhi: Government of India, Department of Social Welfare.
Engineer, Ali Asghar, ed.
  1987 *The Shah Bano Controversy.* Bombay: Sangam Books.
Fanselow, F. S.
  1986 "Trade, Kinship and Islamisation: A Comparative Study of the Social and Economic Organisation of Muslim and Hindu Traders in Tirunelveli District, South India." Ph.D. dissertation, Social Anthropology, London School of Economics.
Flavia [Agnes]
  1991 "A Toothless Tiger: A Critique of the Family Courts." *Manushi* 66: 9–16.
Hidayatullah, M., and Arshad Hidayatullah
  1990 *Mulla's Principles of Mahomedan Law.* 19th ed. Mumbai: N. M. Tripathi.
Hirsch, Susan F.
  1998 *Pronouncing and Persevering: Gender and the Discourses of Disputing in an African Islamic Court.* Chicago: University of Chicago Press.

Khan, C. G. Hussain
  1994   *Marriage and Kinship among Muslims in South India.* Jaipur: Rawat
          Publications.
Kishwar, Madhu
  1986   "Pro-Women or Anti-Muslim? The Shah Bano Controversy." *Manu-
          shi* 32: 4–13.
  1993   "Call for Action: Law Commission's Report on Maintenance; Hu-
          mane Recommendations Ignored." *Manushi* 77: 27–31.
Kozlowski, Gregory C.
  1989   "Shah Banu's Case, Britain's Legal Legacy and Muslim Politics in
          Modern India." In *Law, Politics and Society in India,* ed. Y. Malik
          and D. Vajpay, pp. 88–111. New Delhi: Chanakya.
Lateef, Shahida
  1990   *Muslim Women in India: Political and Private Realities, 1890s–1980s.*
          London: Zed Books.
Lazarus-Black, Mindie, and Susan Hirsch, eds.
  1994   *Contested States: Law, Hegemony and Resistance.* New York: Routledge.
Masud, Muhammad Khalid
  1996   "Apostasy and Judicial Separation in British India." In *Islamic Legal
          Interpretation: Muftis and Their Fatwas,* ed. M. K. Masud, B. Mes-
          sick, and D. S. Powers, pp. 193–203. Cambridge, Mass.: Harvard
          University Press.
Merchant, Munira
  1992   "Indian Muslim Women: Post-Divorce Problems, Social Support
          and Psychological Well-Being." Ph.D. dissertation, Social Work,
          University of Illinois at Chicago.
Minault, Gail
  1997   "Women, Legal Reform, and Muslim Identity." *Comparative Studies
          of South Asia, Africa and the Middle East* 17, no. 2: 1–10.
Mines, Mattison
  1976   "Urbanization, Family Structure and the Muslim Merchants of
          Tamilnadu." In *Family, Kinship and Marriage among the Muslims in
          India,* ed. I Ahmad. New Delhi: Manohar Book Service.
Moog, Robert S.
  1997   *Whose Interests are Supreme? Organizational Politics in the Civil
          Courts in India.* Ann Arbor, Mich.: Association for Asian Studies.
Moore, Erin P.
  1998   *Gender, Law and Resistance in India.* Tucson: University of Arizona
          Press.
Muzumdar, P. V.
  1989   *The Law of Maintenance of Wives, Children and Parents.* Allahabad:
          Malhotra.
Nagasila, D.
  1991   "Family Courts: A Step Backward?" *The Hindu,* March 24.
  1992   "Family Courts: A Critique." *Economic and Political Weekly* 27:
          1735–1737.

Nair, Janaki
1996   *Women and Law in Colonial India: A Social History.* New Delhi: Kali for Women.
Natarajan, Subadra
1997   "A Study of Battered Women in Chennai." M.Phil dissertation, Madras School of Social Work.
1999   [See Subadra]
National Commission for Women, New Delhi
1994   *Justice Delivery through Family Courts: Proceedings of the National Conference.* New Delhi: National Commission for Women.
Pathak, Zakia, and Rajeswari Sunder Rajan
1989   "Shahbano." *Signs* 14: 558–582.
Ramaseshan, Geeta
1989   "Family Courts: Wide Gaps." *Indian Express,* 11 March.
Subadra [Natarajan]
1999   "Violence against Women: Wife Battering in Chennai." *Economic and Political Weekly* 34: WS 28–33.
Tiwari, Devendra Kumar, and Mahmood Zaidi
1997   *Commentaries on the Family Courts Act, 1984.* Allahabad: Alia Law Agency.
Vatuk, Sylvia
1990   "The Cultural Construction of Shared Identity: A South Indian Muslim Family History." *Social Analysis* 28: 114–131.
Verma, B. R.
1988   *Muslim Marriage, Maintenance and Dissolution.* Allahabad: The Law Book Co.
YMCA, Madras
1990   Unpublished Letter, Mrs. Vanjana Clement to Organizing Committee, Workshop on the Effectiveness of Family Courts. Office files.

PART IV

CROSS-CULTURAL PERSPECTIVES

Twelve

Affirmative Action in the United States and the Reservation System in India
Some Comparative Comments

Kevin Brown

Due to hereditary discrimination embodied by the Hindu caste system, many of the racial issues and conflicts that America addresses have counterparts in India. Indians, like Americans, find themselves dealing with issues of hereditary poverty, discrimination, subordination, and programs of benign discrimination to alleviate that legacy. India, however, is a different country from the United States. Her people have been shaped by a different history, a different culture, and a different philosophy upon which their culture is based. These influences have produced different ways of attacking India's legacy of hereditary subordination.

India is traveling on the road not taken by the United States. Unlike the United States, which rejected formal quotas as a means by which to dismantle repression and subordination of African Americans and other minority groups, India embraced them for government jobs and admissions to colleges and universities. India has a vast network of quotas and set-asides for members of certain depressed groups.

Part of the explanation for the different ways of attacking the legacy of hereditary subordination in India and in the United States are the disparate concepts of the person operating within their respective cultures and legal philosophies. I will elucidate the difference between these two concepts of the person by contrasting the justifications provided by the Supreme Courts of India and of the United States for their respective policies and programs of benign discrimination.

The ethos that dominates American society, particularly its legal institutions, can be called American secular individualism. This ethos underlies many of America's interpretations of individual rights that are enshrined in its Constitution. This belief system is based upon protecting the ability of autonomous, free-willed, and self-determining individuals to pursue their own plans and purposes, provided those plans do not interfere with their fellow citizens' ability to do the same. Within this belief system, the "true self" exists as a separate, unique, and distinct entity for every person. The "true self" of American secular individualism is the individual ego, which is to be developed and celebrated.

The Indian Supreme Court drew support from certain aspects of traditional Indian thought in interpreting the Indian Constitution's provisions for benign discrimination. Traditional Indian thought (Hindu, Buddhist, and Jain) tends to view the "true self" as being profoundly different from the external world of ordinary perception and difference, with Hindus and Jains focusing on the "true self" as pure contentless consciousness and Buddhists stressing the notion of "no-self" or a radical emptiness at the heart of existence. The individual ego is not the "true self." Rather it is a concept that must be overcome in order to come to recognize the "true self," which is part of an unmanifested pure consciousness, or in the Buddhist idiom, is an ultimate voidness that brings one to the threshold of *nirvana*. In other words, what American secular individualism seeks to develop and celebrate, traditional Indian thought seeks to overcome. This basic distinction is revealed in different types of benign discrimination programs instituted in India and justifications for those programs relied upon by the respective Supreme Courts.

The Traditional Indian Context

There are many stark contrasts between India and the United States, but the most striking is the difference between the orientation of traditional Indian thought and the orientation of American secular individualism. With the adoption of its Constitution fifty years ago, India declared herself a secular (though not necessarily individualist) nation, committed to modernization. There have certainly been dramatic changes in India since that time. But much of "Old India" continues to exert a strong influence on the modern Indian state. One aspect of Old India that modern India is trying to change is the Indian caste system, and even though Buddhist, Jain, and later Muslim traditions do not accept caste ideology in the same fashion as Hindus, the basic mind-set of caste tends to permeate all levels of social reality in India.

253

Caste System

The caste system is one of the major characteristics of Hindu social organization.[1] Caste membership is also one of the major forms of oppression in Indian society. The essence of the Hindu caste system is the arrangement of hereditary groups into a hierarchical social order.[2] The most significant aspect of the caste system, and perhaps its most unique aspect as well, is that it actually conceives of social superiority in terms of religious superiority. Under pressures of urbanization, nationalism, modernization, and globalization, the rigidity of the caste system is showing signs of weakening, especially in the cities. However, it continues to influence and regulate much of Hindu life.

The caste system is generally broken down into four major distinct castes or *varnas* and a fifth group that is seen as outside the caste system. The caste system, however, is far more complex than these five groupings. There are literally thousands of subcastes in India, usually referred to as *jatis* or "birth groups." It is actually these subdivisions that are important in daily life. These subcastes have their own separate *dharma*, or path of life, to follow. The *dharma* provides the rules of conduct and behavior for its members. Certain ideas of ceremonial and religious purity are peculiar to each subcaste. For many subcastes even the choice of occupation is dictated, and members of these subcastes are thereby prohibited from engaging in other types of callings, professions, or occupations.

The origin of the caste system can be traced back to the emergence into dominance on the Indian subcontinent of the lighter-skinned Aryans around 1500 B.C.E. The term "Aryan," while primarily a linguistic family designation, had a secondary meaning of "highborn" or "noble." The Caucasian Aryans brought their own religious traditions with a pantheon of gods and goddesses. According to Radhakrishnan, the original Aryans all belonged to one class, every one being a priest, soldier, trader, and tiller of the soil.[3] Each man could directly offer sacrifices to the gods. The increasing complexity of life, however, led to the division of labor, with certain families distinguished for learning, wisdom, and poetic and speculative gifts. This class was eventually freed from the necessity of laboring for existence in order to provide the rest of society with thoughtful reflections. Thus the highest caste, the Brahmins, came into existence as an intellectual aristocracy charged with molding the higher life of the people. They are also the custodians of the sacred knowledge and the arbiters of what is right and wrong in matters of religion. The next highest caste, known as Kshatriyas, composed of the kings, princes, rulers, soldiers, and administrators, became the patrons of the learned class. Kshatriyas are followed by the artisans and the commercial class, known as the Vaishyas. All of these castes are presumed to have accumulated religious merit from past lives that has led to their privileged births in this current life. Certain religious duties are common to the three higher castes, such as studying the sacred literature, performing religious rites, and making pious offerings.[4] Only members of the upper three castes are to undergo special initiation ceremonies which make them "twice born." Because of their dominance in the caste system, these three groups are also collectively referred to as "high-caste Hindus." The fourth caste, known as Shudras, or "low-caste Hindus," is composed of servant groups.[5] The religious duty imposed upon the Shudras is to serve the other three castes.[6]

This four-part division of caste society is usually linked to one of the most important creation myths contained in the Rig Veda, the most important sacred ritual text of the Hindus, namely, the "primal man" or Purusha hymn, Rig Veda X.90.[7] According to it, all that is in existence is derived from the division of an original "primal man" or *Purusha*. Three quarters of Purusha transcends the world we see, and one quarter appears on Earth. What became of the part on Earth? The head became the Brahmins, the priestly caste. The arms became the Kshatriyas, the princely and warrior caste. The stomach became the Vaishyas—the business and merchant caste. Purusha's feet became the Shudras, the peasants.

There is a fifth group within the Hindu religious system whose members have come to be called Dalits.[8] "Dalit" is a Hindi word meaning "oppressed" or "downtrodden." The term "Dalit" is not found in the traditional religious literature, but the notion of "outcast" or "untouchable" (*candala*) is very much present. They are not officially a caste under traditional Hinduism and are often referred to as "untouchables." When Gandhi embraced the cause of the Dalits, he referred to them as "Harijans," meaning children of God.

The Indian Reservation System

The caste system was not seriously disturbed until the colonization of India by the British.[9] In order to maintain dominance and control, the British instituted strategies to reinforce existing religious and caste divisions among the Indian people. The British encouraged the Indians to organize politically around ascribed identities. The primary nationalist organization challenging British rule was the Indian National Congress.

Founded in 1885, the Indian National Congress argued for a unified India based on a national identity. They recognized that there were many acute religious, cultural, and caste divisions in India. For the Indian National Congress, the solution to India's national problems lay not in perpetuating these existing distinctions, but in transcending them in favor of Indian nationalism.

The momentum for Indian nationalism generated during the independence struggle continued after independence. Several articles were included in the Indian Constitution, ratified in 1949, to attack centuries of subordination, discrimination, and oppression.[10] These not only included articles to forbid discrimination based on caste, but also articles encouraging affirmative measures for the alleviation of caste oppression.

India has developed a system of reservations that is both complex and massive. The concept of reservations in India represents what in the United States would be understood as a quota system. There are programs to assist Dalits and low-caste Hindus at the local, state, and national levels. These programs include fee concessions at schools, scholarships, land distributions, loans, relaxation of eligibility requirement for admission to educational institutions or appointment to services, and even reservations in legislative bodies.[11]

For the sake of simplicity I will focus only on the issue of reservations for jobs in the central government. Due to the compensation, fringe benefits, and great respect it is accorded in India, governmental service has always been treated as a matter of power, privilege, and authority.[12] The arguments for and against reservations in the central government based on caste could easily be replicated when discussing other programs of benign discrimination, including reservations at colleges and universities.

In the Indian Constitution, reservations were made for Dalits and Scheduled Tribes[13] (with some exceptions) in the lower House of Parliament known as Lok Sabha and in the state Legislative Assemblies. These electoral reservations were to equal the relevant proportion of Dalits and Scheduled Tribes to the total population of the state or the nation. After independence, these reservations were extended to include government employment and higher education as well.[14] The combined reservations for these two groups is 22.5 percent, which approximates their percentage of the population.

Article 340 of the Indian Constitution required the appointment of a commission to determine which groups—other than Dalits and Scheduled Tribes—should be considered socially and educationally backward, investigate the conditions of these groups, and make recommendations regarding what steps should be taken by the central government or any state to remove the difficulties encountered by them. While there was general agreement as to which groups constitute the Dalits and the Scheduled Tribes, which low-caste Hindu groups should be considered socially and educationally backward was more difficult. In current Indian legal parlance, the groups that are designated socially and educationally backward, but are not Dalits or members of Scheduled Tribes, are referred to as "Other Backward Classes" or "OBCs."

After the defeat of Indira Gandhi[15] and the Congress Party (the successor to the Indian National Congress in independent India) in March of 1977, the newly elected prime minister, Morarji Desai, and his coalition government appointed a backward class commission to carry out the duties set out in Article 340 of the Indian Constitution. The commission was chaired by a low-caste Hindu member of Parliament, B. P. Mandal.

The Mandal Commission delivered its recommendations on December 31, 1980. The Mandal Commission decided that the primary determinant of social backwardness in Indian society was caste membership.[16] Caste principally determined social, educational, and economic status.[17] The Commission went on to note that while there may have been a shift of emphasis that had occurred since independence, the caste system had lost very little of its vitality. It still remained as the basis of social organization in independent India. In its report, the Mandal Commission designated some 3,723 subcastes as Other Backward Classes, constituting 52 percent of the population. The Mandal Commission noted that 22.5 percent of the Indian population was classified as either Dalits or Scheduled Tribes and thus 22.5 percent of the government jobs and places of admissions to colleges and universities had already been reserved on their behalf. Even though OBCs constituted 52 percent of the population, a prior Indian Supreme Court opinion had limited the maximum percentage of reservations to 50 percent.[18] Thus, the commission felt that its ability to recommend reservations for OBCs was also limited. Among other things, the Mandal Commission recommended that 27 percent of the jobs of the central government be reserved for castes that it designated as Other Backward Classes. The report went on to recommend that the OBCs who obtained public employment through open competition should not be counted against the 27 percent reservation and that the reservations should apply not only to initial employment, but to promotions as well. The reservations would also apply to all private sector organizations that receive government financial assistance, including all colleges and universities.

By the time the Mandal Commission delivered its report, Indira Gandhi and her Congress Party were back in control of the government. Though the report was quickly accepted, the recommendations were largely ignored. The 1989 electoral defeat of Indira Gandhi's son, Rajiv Gandhi, and his Congress Party brought to power a coalition government headed by Prime Minister V. P. Singh. On August 7, 1990, Singh announced in a memorandum that he had accepted the Mandal Commission report and would immediately begin implementation of the reservations of central government jobs for OBCs.[19] Singh noted that while OBCs constituted 52 percent of the population, they made up only 4.69 percent of the decision-making governmental employees.[20] Candidates recruited on the basis of merit in an open competition were not to be considered in the reservation.[21]

A year later a second memorandum was issued by the central government. In this memorandum, the government stated that in determining which OBCs should receive government posts and services from the 27 percent reservation, preference should be given to the poorer sections of the castes.[22] Only if there were not enough candidates belonging to the poorer sections should the vacancies be filled by other OBC members. An additional 10 percent reservation for other economically backward sections of people who were not covered by any of the existing schemes was also included in this memorandum. Thus the total reservations of jobs at the central government was brought to 59.5 percent.

Mandal Commission Case

Both memoranda were met with legal challenges. The Indian Supreme Court addressed their validity in its 1992 opinion in *Indra Sawhney v. Union of India*[23] (also referred to as the Mandal Commission case). The Indian Supreme Court ruled that most of the recommendations contained in the Mandal Commission report—including the 27 percent reservation for government jobs—were constitutional. The Court, however, noted that to eliminate the possibility of advanced backward class members from unduly profiting from reservation schemes, a means test must be included for the list of designated eligible subcastes.[24]

The primary opinion in the Mandal case was written by Justice Chinnappa Reddy. Reddy noted that the Constituent Assembly that drafted the Indian Constitution had the difficult task of carving an egalitarian society out of a bewildering mass of religions, communities, castes, races, languages, beliefs, and practices. The Constituent Assembly was aware of the historic injustices and inequities afflicting Indian society and had taken into account the caste system. They also understood that the Hindu religion, as practiced, was not egalitarian.[25]

[The framers] were conscious of the fact that the Hindu religion— the religion of the overwhelming majority—as it was being practiced, was not known for its egalitarian ethos. It divided its adherents into four watertight compartments. Those outside this four-tier system were the outcastes, the lowliest. They did not even belong to the caste system—ugly as its face was. The lowliness attached to them (Shudras and Dalits) by virtue of their birth in these castes, unconnected with their deeds. There was to be no deliverance for them from this social stigma, except perhaps death. They were condemned to be inferior. All lowly, menial and unsavory occupations, generation after generation, century after century. It was their 'karma', they were told, the penalty for the sins they allegedly committed in their previous birth.[26]

Justice Reddy went on to note that the framers of the Indian Constitution knew that the alternative to addressing the legacy of the caste system was ignorance, illiteracy, and above all mass poverty. Justice Reddy noted that for "assuring equality of opportunity, it may well be necessary in certain situations to treat unequally situated persons unequally. Not doing so, would perpetuate and accentuate inequality."[27]

To justify the 50 percent limit on reservations, Justice Reddy only appealed to a general notion of fairness. Just as every power must be exercised reasonably and fairly, the power to make special provisions for depressed groups must also be exercised in a fair manner and within reasonable limits. "What is more reasonable than to say that reservation . . . shall not exceed 50% of the appointments or posts, barring certain extra-ordinary situations. . . ."[28]

In November of 1997, Justice Reddy appeared as a panelist at a symposium hosted by Washington University School of Law in Saint Louis, Missouri. In these remarks he commented:

Affirmative action (referring to India's reservation system) does breed some ill will. But the absence of affirmative action equally breeds ill will from other sections. The question is not whether it breeds ill will or resentment. The question is one of justice, fairness and what is called for in the national interest. The nation is comprised of several religions and/or racial and ethnic groups. . . . All these groups together constitute the nation. If so, all these groups must have some sense of participation in the governing structures. It cannot be the monopoly of one section or one group.[29]

Perhaps the words of Justice Pandian in his concurring opinion in the Mandal Commission case best expressed the way which the Indian Supreme Court conceptualized the conflict inherent in the reservation system.

The real conflict is between the class of people who have never been in or who have already moved out of the desert of poverty, illiteracy and backwardness and are entrenched in the oasis of convenient living and those who are still in the desert and want to reach the oasis.[30]

The American Context

America is a land of immigrants. Voluntary immigrants from all over Europe, with different national and religious traditions, came to settle in the United States. One of the ways to reduce the possibility of destructive religious and ethnic conflicts was to attenuate the attachment of these immigrants to the historical traditions of their countries of origin. Thinking of persons as individuals provided a solution to this important problem. Beginning in the 1950s, America began to try to solve its long-standing racial problem by expanding the notion of thinking of people as individuals.

Development of American
Secular Individualism

There are those who continue to think of America as a Christian nation. America was founded as a Christian nation and the founding fathers were deeply religious. While dedicated to individual freedom and self-determination, the founders still paid homage to a higher power. Ronald Dworkin has recently pointed out, however, that contemporary American culture does not share the same willingness to submit to a higher power that the American culture of the past did.[31] This modern version of individualism can be referred to as American secular individualism. This culture and its concomitant view of the person was the result of hundreds of years of intellectual development. The origins of this culture are rooted in Judeo-Christian theology, which presupposes the existence of a God that created humans and endowed them with separate and unique individual souls.[32] The Christian origins of American secular individualism perpetuated the fundamental belief in the existence of a unique individual person, but it was eventually realized that the notion of personal individuality could be applied without the accompanying notion of an almighty creator.

In seventeenth-century England, John Locke developed a defense of individual rights for political and legal purposes that was not rooted in classical or biblical sources.[33] The essence of Locke's philosophy was to view the rights of the person as prior to society.[34] In the state of nature, autonomous, free-willed, and self-determined individuals pursue their own plans and purposes. These individuals choose to form a society because it will aid them in the pursuit of their desires. Thus society comes into existence through the voluntary contract of individuals trying to maximize their own self-interest.[35] As a result, society and government are there to protect the natural rights of these individuals. What Locke's theory does is to make it possible to think about society as a collection of individuals that are ends in themselves and not as subjects of a divine being.

In America, thinking of persons as individuals provided the conceptual solution to a significant problem for a land of immigrants. Emigration to the United States was the largest single voluntary migration in human history. Between 1790 and 1920, more than 36 million people emigrated to the United States.[36] The character of American immigration changed drastically during the last part of the nineteenth century. A principally Protestant nation with immigrants from northern and western Europe began to see large influxes of Catholic and Jewish immigrants from southern and eastern Europe. Between 1900 and 1930 the Catholic population doubled to twenty-four million and the number of Jews increased from 229,000 in 1887 to more than 4,228,000 forty years later.[37]

One of the primary motivations—or at least one of the concerns—driving the conception of American society as a nation of individuals (especially as applied to white European men) was the desire to attenuate loyalties that were the result of historical traditions from the "old countries" of the immigrants. Preaching the sovereignty of the individual over ascribed traditions served as a means not only of attenuating the attachment of the individual to the old country, but of reducing the concerns about religious affiliation. By reducing the sense of ethnic and religious identity, the possibility of destructive and violent ethnic or religious conflicts that have so often flared up in other parts of the world were largely avoided in America.

Beginning in the 1950s, America began the process of trying to resolve another long-standing problem. In addition to voluntary immigration from Europe, America also had to contend with descendants of the sons and daughters of Africa. Beginning in 1619 when the first Africans disembarked from the first slave ship to arrive in North America, blacks were viewed as second-class citizens for an almost unbroken chain of more than 330 years. Blacks were never treated as individuals, but as members of an involuntary group. They were always an integral, though subordinated, part of American society.

In the 1950s, America began to dismantle its system of racial apartheid by striking down long-standing laws that separated black people from whites. Laws and customs that required blacks to attend separate schools, drink from separate water fountains, wait in separate areas, swim in separate pools, even be buried in separate cemeteries were ruled unconstitutional or made illegal. In the late 1960s, America went further and began to institute affirmative action programs that took account of race in order to desegregate American society. Through forced busing, public elementary and secondary schools became integrated. Colleges and universities began to institute affirmative action programs to increase the presence of minorities on their campuses. Governments and private corporations instituted policies and programs to channel business contracts to minority business enterprises. Employers, both public and private, made hiring and promoting minorities a priority.

As the concept of society as a collection of individuals could weaken religious and ethnic identity among whites, it was presumed that it would be able to accomplish the same objective with racial identity. The conceptual justification for the desegregation era was the idea that the problem of race in America could be ended if blacks were treated as individuals as well. A color-blind society where persons were judged on the content of their character and not the color of their skin could resolve the American dilemma created by race.

Regents of University of California v. Bakke

The case that first presented the United States Supreme Court with an opportunity to address the constitutionality of quotas was *Regents of University of California v. Bakke*. The application of a blue-eyed, blond-haired man of Norwegian ancestry,[38] Allan Bakke, was rejected by the University of California at Davis medical school. He brought suit challenging the legality of the school's special admissions program under which sixteen of the one hundred positions in the class were reserved for "economically or educationally disadvantaged applicants." The medical school viewed individuals who were African American, Chicano, Asian, or Native American as the only ones fitting the description of disadvantaged applicants.

When Allan Bakke presented his claim to the Supreme Court, the Court had to articulate the purpose animating the equal protection clause of the Fourteenth Amendment to the United States Constitution.[39] During the late 1950s, 1960s, and 1970s, the Supreme Court seemed to be on the side of the lowly, the despised, and the dispossessed. Many scholars argued that in America's governmental system of checks and balances, the Supreme Court functioned as a check against the majoritarian political process exploiting vulnerable minorities.[40] With this view of the position of the Supreme Court in mind, it was argued that the purpose of the equal protection clause was to protect discrete and insular minority groups from the ravages of the majoritarian political process. If the Supreme Court was not addressing a governmental program that discriminated against such minority groups, then it should generally defer to governmental officials.

Four of the nine justices in *Bakke* were prepared to strike down the special admissions program, arguing that any consideration of race or ethnicity in the admissions process violated the antidiscrimination provision contained in Title VI of the Civil Rights Act of 1964.[41] Four other justices were prepared to uphold the constitutionality of the University of California at Davis's special admissions program as written, including the use of quotas.[42] In an opinion for these justices, Justice Brennan noted that the assertion of human equality is closely associated with the proposition that differences in color, creed, birth, or status are neither significant nor relevant to the way in which persons should be treated and that this concept is summed up by the shorthand phrase "our Constitution is color-blind." He also indicated that the nation was founded on the principle that all men are created equal. Nevertheless, Brennan wrote, that principle was openly compromised in the very founding of the nation with its antithesis—slavery. Officially sanctioned discrimination is very much a current problem in America.

> Against this background, claims that law must be 'color-blind' or that the datum of race is no longer relevant to public policy must be seen as aspiration rather than as description of reality. This is not to denigrate the aspiration. . . . Yet we cannot . . . let color blindness become myopia which masks the reality that many "created equal" have been treated within our lifetimes as inferior by both law and by their fellow citizens.[43]

Brennan's opinion reflects the notion that animated much of the desegregation era. The goal of taking account of race and thereby approving quotas is actually motivated by a desire to convert America into a color-blind society, one where race is irrelevant. Thus, as paradoxical as it sounds, the justification for taking account of race is not to exalt racial and ethnic groups, but to eventually arrive at a society where all people are treated as individuals.

The controlling opinion in *Bakke* was delivered by a single justice—Lewis Powell. Powell traveled a middle ground between accepting a quota system and completely rejecting consideration of race or ethnicity. Powell concluded that while quotas are unconstitutional, race and ethnicity can be taken into account as a factor in the admissions process. Powell rejected the notion that the equal protection clause was there to protect discrete and insular minorities from the failures of the majoritarian political process. Powell noted that

> The Court's initial view of the Fourteenth Amendment was that its "one pervading purpose" was the "freedom of the slave race, the security and firm establishment of that freedom, and the protection of the newly-made freeman and citizen from the oppression of those who had formerly exercised dominion over him."[44]

This one pervading purpose, however, was virtually strangled in infancy and relegated to decades of relative desuetude by post–Civil War judicial reactionism. Decisions by the Supreme Court in the 1880s and 1890s emasculated the protections that were built into the Fourteenth Amendment for the freedmen and their descendants. Between the time the original purpose of the Fourteenth Amendment was strangled and the time new life was breathed into it in the 1950s, America had become a nation of minorities.

After discarding the original purpose of the Fourteenth Amendment, Powell noted that while many of the framers of the Fourteenth Amendment conceived of its primary function as bridging the vast distance between blacks and whites, the Amendment itself was framed in universal terms, without reference to color, ethnic origin, or condition of servitude. He went on to conclude that "the guarantee of equal protection cannot mean one thing when applied to one individual and something else when applied to a person of another color. If both are not accorded the same protection then it is not equal."[45]

Powell rejected a quota system because it treated applicants as members of racial and ethnic groups and not as individuals. That did not mean for him that race or ethnicity could not count at all. Rather, Powell noted that colleges and universities have a legitimate interest in providing an atmosphere that is most conducive to speculation, experimentation, and creation, an interest widely believed to be promoted by a diverse student body. Racial and ethnic diversity is one element in a range of factors such as unique work or service experience, leadership potential, area of the country that an applicant is from, or ability to communicate with the poor, that can be considered in attaining a heterogeneous student body.

According to Powell, each individual candidate is to be compared with other applicants. Race and ethnicity can be taken account of as a characteristic in assessing a given individual's ability to contribute to beneficial educational pluralism. Thus, taking account of race and ethnic membership is not for the purpose of advancing the interest of these groups, but for assessing the abilities of a given student.

Outside the context of higher education, the diversity rationale loses much of its appeal. As a result, in many opinions delivered since *Bakke*, the Supreme Court has generally opposed voluntary affirmative action programs sponsored by government.[46] In the 1995 opinion in *Miller v. Johnson*, the Court stated that the problem with "race-based classifications of citizens by government" is that it embodies "stereotypes that treat individuals as the product of their race, evaluating their thoughts and efforts—their very worth as citizens—according to a criterion barred by Government. . . . The idea at the heart of the Constitution's guarantee of equal protection lies the simple command that the government must treat citizens as individuals, not as simply components of a racial, religious, sexual or national class."[47]

Comparison of Judicial Treatment

It could be argued that the difference between the treatment of reservations and affirmative action by the Supreme Courts of India and the United States, respectively, is traceable to textual differences in the constitutions of the respective countries. While that might provide a partial answer, it clearly does not explain the entire difference. Arguments based on textualism ignore the flexibility that supreme courts vested with judicial review have in interpreting the words that make up the text of a given constitution. This flexibility was apparent in Justice Powell's opinion in *Bakke*. To find a more complete explanation of the justifications provided by the Supreme Courts of India and the United States for the treatment of benign discrimination requires an understanding that lies beyond the wording of the respective constitutional provisions. Looking at the different rationales put forth by each Supreme Court reveals something about different concepts of the person in operation in the two countries.

A major part of the difference lies in the fundamental intellectual orientations that have shaped the different countries. The main branches of traditional Indian thought, Hinduism, Buddhism, and Jainism, essentially all agree that the goal of life is liberation. The precise meaning of liberation may vary among the different branches of Indian thought and the different schools and subsystems within each branch. But all agree that the individual ego is not the "true self." In terms of social life, the separate individual is not as important as one's group identity. The modern Western notion of the "individual" is not as strong as a notion of the person as a member of the group. The anthropological theorizing of Louis Dumont (in his classic book *Homo Hierarchicus* [Chicago: University of Chicago Press, 1980]) and McKim Marriott (in *India through Hindu Categories* [New Delhi: Sage Publications, 1990]) has been instructive in this regard. Both have argued that the notion of the unique "individual" is not a primary value. Marriott speaks of the "dividual," rather than the "individual," as a primary value in India. There is a basic "fluidarity" in traditional Indian notions of social life that place a high value on hierarchical orderings of group-based life and that have come to be reflected in judicial thinking in India.

In contrast, the culture that dominates American society, particularly its legal institutions, is a firm commitment to the notion of the unique individual, or what I have called American secular individualism. This belief system is based upon protecting the ability of autonomous, free-willed, and self-determining individuals to pursue their own plans and purposes, provided those plans do not interfere with their fellow citizens' ability to do the same. Within this belief system, the person exists as a separate, unique identity. The "true self" of American secular individualism is the individual ego, which is to be developed and celebrated.

In limiting affirmative action, the justices of the United States Supreme Court drew upon the tenets embedded in American secular individualism. They articulate their positions primarily in terms of the individual. In contrast, the justices of the Indian Supreme Court generally express less concern about the impact of reservations on the individual and are more concerned about group identities. The concern about the individual expressed by the justices of the United States Supreme Court and the concern for group identities that flows from the justices of the Indian Supreme Court reflect the fundamentally different orientations toward the notion of individuality by American secular individualism and traditional Indian cultural notions.

Succinctly stated, what American secular individualism seeks to develop and celebrate, traditional Indian thought seeks to overcome. This basic difference in the concept and value of the person is revealed in the treatment of and justifications for benign discrimination programs to attack the respective legacies of hereditary subordination in the two countries.

Notes

1. Declan Quigley, *The Interpretation of Caste* (New York: Oxford University Press, 1993), p. 1.

2. M. N. Srinvas, *The Cohesive Role of Sanskritization* (Delhi: Oxford University Press, 1989), p. 5.

3. S. Radhakrishnan, *Indian Philosophy* (London: George Allen and Unwin, 1951), vol. 1, pp. 111–112.

4. Robert Lingat, *The Classical Law of India*, trans. J. Duncan M. Derrett (Berkeley: University of California Press, 1973), p. 30.

5. In current Indian legal parlance, the groups that are designated socially and educationally backward, but are not Dalits or members of Scheduled Tribes are referred to as "Other Backward Classes" or "OBCs." Collectively, this is the group I will refer to in this section as low-caste Hindus or Shudras.

6. Lingat, *The Classical Law of India*, p. 30.

7. *Sources Of Indian Traditions*, ed. Ainslie T. Embree (New York: Columbia University Press), vol. 1, pp. 30–31.

8. In the Indian Constitution and for purposes of actual programs, the term that is intended to include Dalits is Scheduled Caste. A Scheduled Caste is one that is designated by presidential order. India Constitution, pt. XVI, art. 341. Throughout this article, I will substitute the term "Dalit" for the legal term "Scheduled Caste." According to 1991 figures, India's population totaled 844,000,000 people. World Almanac and Book of Facts 1992, 767 (1991). There were 104,755,000 Dalits, which made up 15.8 percent of the Indian population.

9. Sunita Parikh, *The Politics of Preference: Democratic Institutions and Affirmative Action in the United States and India* (Ann Arbor: University of Michigan Press, 1996), pp. 33–34.

10. The main provisions dealing with equality and discrimination are contained in Articles 14, 15, 16, 17, 29(2), and 46 of the Indian Constitution.

11. C. L. Anand, *Equality, Justice and Reverse Discrimination in India* (Delhi: Mittal Publications, 1987), p. 1. The principle of reservations in the electoral process extends to Dalits and women but not to Shudras.

12. Justice Chinnappa Reddy appeared as a panelist at a symposium hosted by Washington University School of Law in Saint Louis, Missouri, in November of 1997. His remarks are reprinted in *Washington University Law Quarterly* 75, pp. 1561, 1594–1599 (1997).

13. Scheduled Tribes are Indians who are considered to be spatially and culturally isolated from the general Indian population, somewhat analogous to Native Americans in the United States. Their cultural, religious, and linguistic traits differentiate them from Dalits. There are 51,629,000 members in Scheduled Tribes constituting 7.8 percent of the Indian population. *Observer Statistical Handbook 55*.

14. Parikh, *The Politics of Preference*, p. 159.

15. The first prime minister of India was Jawaharlal Nehru. After his reign and an interim period, his daughter Indira Gandhi became prime minister

in 1966. Indira Gandhi was assassinated by her Sikh bodyguards in 1984. The assassination was widely believed to be in retaliation for an attack by the Indian Army that Prime Minister Gandhi ordered on the Golden Temple of Amritsar, the holiest shrine of the Sikh religion.

16. Anand, *Equality, Justice and Reverse Discrimination*, p. 146.

17. This link can be seen in the oldest Hindu legal codes, which date back to the laws of Manu. Under the laws of Manu, "Although able, a Sudra must not acquire excess riches, since when a Sudra acquires a fortune, he vexes the *Brahman*s with his insolence." *Indra Sawhney v. Union of India*, A.I.R. 1993 S.C. 477, 550.

18. *Balaji v. State of Mysore*, 50 A.I.R. 649, 663 (1963) (holding that the total percentage of reservations permissible under Article 15(4) of the Indian Constitution should generally be less than 50 percent). See also *Rajkumar v. Gulbarga University*, 77 A.I.R. (Kant.) 320, 332 (1990) (following the 50 percent limit for reservations).

19. One of the difficult issues the Mandal Commission had to address was the criteria for determining which groups constituted Shudras. The commission developed several indicators of social and educational backwardness. Indicators of social backwardness included whether most members of society considered their caste or class to be backward, whether they came from a region that was considered backward, whether they depended on manual labor for their livelihood, whether their source of drinking water was more than half a kilometer from their homes, the number of households who had taken out loans to pay for basic living expenses, and whether the percentage of females married at age seventeen or younger was more than 25 percent above the state average and the percentage of males married at age seventeen or younger was more than 10 percent above the state average (these figures were reduced to 10 percent and 5 percent in urban areas). See E. J. Prior, "Constitutional Fairness or Fraud on the Constitution? Compensatory Discrimination in India," 28 *Case Western Reserve Journal of International Law* 63, pp. 83–84 (1996).

20. *Indra Sawhney* at 514.

21. See reprint of the office memorandum on pp. 514–15 of the *Indra Sawhney* case.

22. *Indra Sawhney* at 515–16.

23. A.I.R. 1993 S.C. 477.

24. *Indra Sawhney* at 558–60. The Court directed the government of India to determine the basis of exclusion, which could be on the basis of income, extent of holding, or otherwise.

25. *Indra Sawhney* at 501–502.

26. *Indra Sawhney* at 510.

27. *Indra Sawhney* at 539.

28. *Indra Sawhney* at 565.

29. Justice Chinnappa Reddy's remarks are reprinted in *Washington University Law Quarterly* 75, pp. 1561, 1594–1599 (1997).

30. *Indra Sawhney* at 617 (S. Ratnavael Pandian, J).

31. Ronald W. Dworkin, *The Rise of The Imperial Self: America's Culture Wars in Augustinian Perspective* (New York: Garland Publishers, 1996), xiii. What Dworkin calls "Expressive Individualism" is similar to what I call "American secular individualism."

32. Reinhold Niebuhr, *The Nature and Destiny of Man: A Christian Interpretation* (New York: Charles Scribner's Sons, 1964), pp. 21–23.

33. The founding fathers were inspired by Locke's writings, and Locke's positions are evident in the Declaration of Independence. See, e.g., Richard Kluger, *Simple Justice* (Alexandria, Virginia: PBS Video, 1993), p. 35.

34. Despite Locke's philosophical writings that recognized the natural rights of men, in the Fundamental Constitutions of Carolina that he authored, he provided that "Every freeman of Carolina shall have absolute power and authority over his negro slaves, of what opinion or religion soever." 1 *Statutes at Large of South Carolina* 55, ed. David McCord (Columbia: A. S. Johnston, 1836). This wording of Locke's was used to justify slavery from the inception of the colony by planters who settled in South Carolina.

35. Robert N. Bellah, Richard Madsen, William M. Sullivan, Ann Swidler, and Steven M. Tipton, *Habits of the Heart: Individualism and Commitment in American Life* (Berkeley: University of California Press, 1985), p. 143.

36. Ibid.

37. Michael J. Klarman, "Rethinking the Civil Rights and Civil Liberties Revolutions," 82 *Virginia L. Rev.* 1, 49 (1996). Between 1850 and 1900 the number of Catholics increased from 1.7 million to 12 million. The number doubled again between 1900 and 1930.

38. This description of Allan Bakke comes from J. Harvie Wilkinson III, *From Brown to Bakke: The Supreme Court and School Integration, 1954–1978* (New York: Oxford University Press, 1979).

39. The equal protection clause in pertinent part states "No State shall deny any person the equal protection of the law." U.S. Constitution, Fourteenth Amendment.

40. This view animates Richard Kluger, *Simple Justice*. See also Richard B. Sobol, "Against Bakke," in *Racial Preference and Racial Justice: The New Affirmative Action Controversy*, ed. Russell Nieli (Washington, D.C.: Ethics and Public Policy Center, 1991), pp. 167–174.

41. *Bakke*, 438 U.S. at 408 (Stevens, J. concurring in judgment in part and dissenting in part).

42. *Bakke*, 438 U.S. at 324 (Brennan, J. concurring in judgment in part and dissenting in part).

43. Ibid. at 327.

44. *Bakke*, 438 U.S. at 292 (quoting *Slaughterhouse Cases*, 16 Wall. 36, 71, 21 L.Ed. 394 (1873)).

45. 438 U.S. at 289–90.

46. See, e.g., *Wygant v. Jackson Board of Education*, 476 U.S. 267 (1986) (striking down a collective bargaining agreement that provided protection against layoffs for certain minority teachers at the expense of majority teachers); *City of Richmond v. J. A. Croson*, 488 U.S. 469 (1989) (invalidating a program setting aside certain construction contracts for minority businesses enterprises).

47. Ibid.

Thirteen

Personal Law Systems and Religious Conflict
A Comparison of India and Israel

Marc Galanter and Jayanth Krishnan

Although India and Israel differ dramatically in size, population, and affluence, there are many important similarities. Each is the contemporary vehicle of an old and resilient culture or civilization that expresses a distinctive, influential, and enduring arrangement of the various facets of human experience.

Each of these cultures underwent a prolonged colonial experience in which its traditions were disrupted and subordinated to a hegemonic European Christian culture;[1] each had an earlier experience with victorious, expansive Islam;[2] each has reached an uneasy but flourishing accommodation with the secular, scientific modernity of the West.[3] In each case this was achieved by a movement that embraced "Enlightenment" values (Haskalah/Hindu renaissance) and in turn provoked a recoil from modernity to a rediscovery of tradition.[4] In each there is a conflict between those with "modern" secular views of civil society and those revivalists or fundamentalists who seek to restore an indigenous religious society. The secular nationalism that predominated in the struggle for independence and the formation of the state is now countered by powerful tides of conservative reaction.[5]

In the course of their long histories, Hindu and Jewish cultures had some contact, but each had been largely peripheral to the other; they were not the major presences in each other's arenas, but at most bit players. But now, in the new "global" setting at the turn of the new millennium, there is a proliferation of new connections. Each has successfully absorbed elements of the culture of the Christian West, which has supplied the idiom of intensified global communications. Each is a major participant in the global scholarly/intellectual exchange. Each has regained a political dimension and is now "represented" in the international arena by a state situated at the contested frontiers of Islamic militancy.

India and Israel are both new nations with multi-ethnic populations.[6] Each emerged as a nation-state in the first wave of de-colonization through a partition process that reduced the presence of its largest minority and increased the preponderance of its largest religious group.[7] Each has a Westminster-style parliamentary system—frequently populated by a fragmented coalition government.[8] Each has a legal system based on the British common law model (with an admixture of American-style constitutionalism, more in India, less in Israel) with many lawyers and strong higher courts that are major players in conflicts about the most fiercely controverted policy issues.[9] Each has a legal system that incorporates in a truncated form traditions of all-encompassing sacred law that, in their earlier forms at least, aspired to achieve both holiness and spiritual progress.[10] These truncated systems of sacred law are present as "personal law." In both India and Israel, the presence of these personal laws raises the question of reconciling their distinctive religious legacy with a convergent world of "universal" rights. Specifically, it involves reconciling claims for group integrity with claims for individual fulfillment and gender equality.

In this essay, we compare the way the administration of personal law systems reflects and shapes the social identities of religious communities within India and Israel. We also compare the way these personal law regimes affect the roles, rights, and burdens of women. We examine the evolution of personal law systems in India and Israel, and we focus on the way these systems affect the religious and ethnic communities they regulate.[11]

By systems or regimes of personal law, we refer to legal arrangements for the application within a single polity of several bodies of law to different persons according to their religious or ethnic identity.[12] Personal law systems are designed to preserve to each segment its own law.[13] In the last several centuries, the most prominent instances have been personal law regimes in the areas of family law (marriage, divorce, adoption, maintenance), intergenerational transfer of property (succession, inheritance, wills), and religious establishments (offices, premises, and endowments).[14] Such personal law typically co-exists with general territorial law in criminal, administrative, and commercial matters.[15] On occasion, some commercial or criminal rules may be included in personal law.[16]

As the new millennium begins, many countries that maintain such personal law systems are under increasing pressure to abandon these structures and adopt a universal set of rules and regulations that apply to all citizens. According to Bassam Tibi, globalization and the twentieth century's technological revolution have projected the concepts of fundamental human rights and freedom to even the most culturally traditional societies.[17] As a result, countries with personal law systems experience a clash between two ideological perspectives. Opponents of religiously based separate systems embrace a concept of universal human rights and freedom where "there is an urgent need for establishing globally-shared legal frameworks on cross-cultural foundations."[18] Those who favor maintaining personal law are suspicious of such (primarily Western-based) concepts as human rights and freedom, and they challenge the compatibility of human rights and freedom with their cultural traditions.[19]

We shall return to this conflict after we have examined the two different ways that personal law is institutionalized in India and Israel. Let us begin by first turning to the personal law system of India.

India: Division between Religious Communities

India and Israel represent very different systems of institutionalizing personal law. In India, the British raj established a general territorial law that operated in a common law style and was administered in a nationwide system of government courts.[20] Over time, through infusion of common law and codification, the substantive law came to resemble its British counterpart.[21] At the same time, the British preserved enclaves of personal law. The Bengal Regulation of 1772 provided that in suits regarding inheritance, marriage, caste, and other usages and institutions, the courts should apply "the laws of the Koran with regard to Mohammedans, and those of the Shaster with respect to the Hindus."[22]

Under the British, the personal laws of Hindus and Muslims were administered in the regular courts by judges trained in, and familiar with, the style of the common law.[23] Until about 1860, the courts had attached to them "native law officers," pandits and kazis, to advise them on questions of Hindu and Muslim law respectively.[24] To make the law more uniform, certain, and accessible to British judges—as well as to check the discretion of the law officers—the courts relied increasingly on translations of texts, on digests and manuals, and on their own precedents.[25] In 1860, when the whole court system was rationalized and unified, the law officers were abolished and the judges took exclusive charge of finding and applying the personal law.[26] These religious law systems were now reduced to texts severed from the living systems of administration and interpretation in which they were earlier embodied. Refracted through the common law lenses of judges and lawyers, and rigidified by the common law principle of precedent, there evolved distinctive bodies of Anglo-Hindu and Anglo-Muslim case law.[27]

These bodies of personal law were administered by the courts of British India and (later) independent India. The Constitution of 1950 appears to envision the dissolution of the personal law system in favor of a uniform civil code.[28] Article 44 directs the state to "endeavor to secure for the citizens a uniform civil code throughout the territory of India."[29]

After the Constitution came into force in 1950, the continued administration of separate bodies of personal law for the various religious communities was challenged as a violation of the right to equality guaranteed by the Constitution. The Indian courts upheld the continued validity of disparate personal law and the power of the state to create new rules applicable to particular religious communities. The judges in the leading case[30]—a Hindu and a Muslim, both distinguished legal scholars as well as prominent secularists—were sanguine about the continued existence of personal law, presumably in anticipation of its early replacement. The unwillingness, though, of the Muslim minority to relinquish the *Shari'at* (or the Anglo-Muslim amalgam administered in its name) sidetracked plans for a uniform code. Instead, the reformist forces within the Hindu community fashioned a major codification and modification of Hindu law, enacting in 1955–56 a series of statutes known collectively as the Hindu Code.[31] These acts modified the Anglo-Hindu law in important ways. They abandoned the *varna* distinctions, the indissolubility of marriage, the preference for the extended joint family, and for inheritance by males only and by those who can confer spiritual benefit.[32] In their place the new law emphasized the nuclear family, introduced divorce, and endorsed the equality of *varnas* and sexes.[33] Very few rules remained with a specifically religious foundation.

The Hindu Code was in large measure tutelary;[34] it mirrored "the values of [the] governing groups rather than those of . . . the congeries of communities that make up Hinduism."[35] While diluting if not effacing the traditional *dharmashastric* basis of Hindu law, the Hindu Code rearranged the relationship between the state and religious authorities. It marked the acceptance of the Indian Parliament as a kind of central legislative body for Hindus in matters of family and social life.[36] It discarded the notion, prevalent during the British period, that government had no mandate or competence to redesign Hindu society.[37] In contrast to earlier times when the absence of centralized governmental or ecclesiastical institutions rendered general or sweeping reforms impossible, the modern Indian state could now accomplish across-the-board changes.

While retaining the personal law system, independent India introduced a note of voluntarism. The Special Marriage Act of 1872 had provided a code of general law under which couples could choose to marry and divorce, but in order to utilize this option they had to affirm that neither was a Christian, Jew, Hindu, or Muslim.[38] In effect they had to renounce their religious and property relations with their families. In 1954, Parliament passed a new Special Marriage Act that eliminated the onerous renunciatory costs of availing of civil marriage.[39]

India retains a system that governs certain family matters of Hindus, Muslims, Parsees, and Christians by their respective religious laws. There is also a set of religiously differentiated public laws regulating religious endowments. While personal law in India covers issues of adoption, succession, and religious institutions,[40] marriage and divorce are the main focus of public attention. Twelve pieces of national legislation deal with particular issues of marriage and divorce for the various religious groups in the country.[41] The administration of these personal laws in India remains in the hands of state judges.

We submit that India's personal law system is not associated with much conflict within the several religious communities. Political conflict in India over personal law appears more prevalent between, rather than within, religious communities. This is not to say, however, that *intra*-religious dissension is entirely absent in India. Debate about women's rights in their respective personal law systems is present within the Hindu, Christian, and Muslim communities. Many Hindu women who champion equal rights for women support drastic reforms within (if not a complete abandonment of) Hindu personal law.[42] Many Indian Christian women, similarly, struggle and protest against the obstacles Christian personal law poses for women who seek divorce.[43] And there is a series of feminist critiques of Muslim law's treatment of women in divorce and maintenance.[44]

This intra-religious conflict, however, is overshadowed by the tensions between religious communities in India. Consider the current debate over whether or not India should adopt a uniform civil code and thereby abolish the various personal laws. Proponents of a uniform civil code (who typically are Hindus) point to Articles 14 and 15[45] of the Indian Constitution as well as to Article 44 as evidence that the "uniform civil code . . . [is] an ideal towards which the state should strive."[46] The Bharatiya Janata Party, the principal party in the ruling coalition at present, has been a supporter of a uniform civil code over the past eight years. During the 1996 and 1998 national election campaigns, the BJP, according to some observers, even made the enactment of a uniform civil code a tenet in its platform.[47] (Since coming to power in the spring of 1998, however, the BJP has not initiated any formal legislative proposals to alter the existing personal law structure.[48])

On the other hand, opponents of a uniform civil code (typically members of the minority religious communities) argue that the framers respected the fact that various religious communities deeply identified with their own personal laws and never intended for the country to implement one set of rules and regulations for its diverse population.[49] Many also contend that if a uniform civil code were adopted, the new laws would reflect the concerns of the majority Hindu population.[50]

Shah Bano

The fear that a uniform civil code would jeopardize the rights and integrity of minority religious communities manifested itself dramatically in response to the Indian Supreme Court's best-known and arguably most important decision on personal law—the now famous *Shah Bano* case.[51]

The story begins in 1975 with a Muslim woman, Shah Bano, who after forty-three years of marriage found herself divorced by her husband Mohammad Ahmed Khan.[52] In accordance with Islamic law, the divorce was performed by the procedure of *talaq*—that is the husband declaring (three times) that he ends the marriage.[53] Shah Bano had been a housewife who was financially dependent on her husband throughout the duration of the marriage.[54] With the marriage now ended, Shah Bano was left with no means to support herself. She sued her former husband for not providing her with adequate maintenance after the divorce under Section 125 of the Indian Code of Criminal Procedure. Section 125 states that maintenance, up to a maximum of five hundred rupees a month, must be provided for a former spouse who otherwise would be destitute.[55]

Shah Bano filed her case in a lower court in the state of Madhya Pradesh, where a magistrate ruled that her ex-husband was required to pay a continual monthly maintenance payment of twenty-five rupees a month (at that time about four American dollars).[56] Shah Bano, disheartened at the paltry amount awarded to her, appealed to the Madhya Pradesh High Court, which in 1980 ruled that the payment should be increased to approximately one-hundred eighty rupees.[57] Following this judgment, Mohammad Khan (a lawyer by profession) appealed to the Indian Supreme Court, reiterating the argument he made in the lower

courts: that because he satisfied Section 127 of the Indian Code of
Criminal Procedure, Section 125 did not apply to him. Section 127
states that Section 125 shall not apply where a divorced woman "has
received, whether before or after the date of the said order, the whole of
the sum which, under any customary or personal law, applicable to the
parties, was payable on such divorce."[58]

Mohammad Khan contended that under Muslim personal law he
had paid the "whole" sum to Shah Bano, and that as a result, he owed
her no further payment.[59] Because he had paid Shah Bano a dower
(*mahr*) of three thousand rupees prior to their marriage as well as having financially supported her for a three-month period after their divorce (*iddat*), Mohammad Khan claimed that he was no longer obliged
to maintain his former wife.[60] Furthermore, Mohammad Khan disputed
an additional argument made by Shah Bano that the Qur'an required, at
the very least, that she receive a *mataa*, or a lump-sum payment made
by the divorcing husband signifying the end of the marriage.[61] According to Mohammad Khan, *mataa* payments had to be made only by those
who were considered pious in the eyes of Allah (*muttaqeena*). This was
a personal description he claimed did not apply to him.[62]

The Supreme Court, in a bench comprised of Justices Chandrachud,
Desai, Venkataramiah, Chinnappa Reddy, and Misra, affirmed the Madhya Pradesh High Court ruling and held that Mohammad Khan was
still responsible to his former wife for maintenance payments.[63] Justice
Chandrachud, writing for the Court, rejected Mohammad Khan's interpretation of Muslim personal law. Relying on its own research and
understanding of the *Shari'at,* the Court opined that the principles of
Islam, in fact, require that a husband not "discard his wife whenever he
chooses to do so,"[64] without first ensuring that she is financially secure.

The Supreme Court's arrogation to itself of the power to ascertain
authentic Islamic law understandably elicited great anger within the
Muslim community.[65] Among many Muslims, there was a perception
that the *Shah Bano* judgment marked the beginning of the end of Muslim personal law in India.[66] Rather than judicially balancing the general
law against the personal law and then selecting the former as the basis
for its decision, the Supreme Court's attempt to interpret the *Shari'at,*
according to some observers, seemed to be a deliberate move to subvert
Muslim personal law in favor of the primarily Hindu-based Indian
Code of Criminal Procedure.[67]

Two earlier Supreme Court cases, involving facts similar to *Shah
Bano,* did not arouse the type of hostile reaction among Muslims that
was seen in 1985. In *Bai Tahira v. Ali Husain Fissalli*[68] and *Fazlunbi v.
K. Khader Vali,*[69] the Court twice upheld the rights of divorced Muslim
women to receive maintenance for a period beyond *iddat.* Why was there

no uproar by the Muslim community to either of these decisions? Perhaps the reason lies in the fact that the author of these two judgments, Justice Krishna Iyer, judiciously weighed the personal law against Section 127 of the Code of Criminal Procedure to arrive at decisions that appear to have been accepted and respected by the opposing parties. As Madhu Kishwar notes, Krishna Iyer resists making any normative judgment about the *Shari'at*, and in fact, "not once in the *Bai Tahira* judgement does he even mention the word 'Muslim.'"[70]

Following the *Shah Bano* decision, the Muslim lobby forced Prime Minister Rajiv Gandhi to push through the Muslim Women's Protection Act of 1986 which overturned the Court's decision and reinstated Muslim law, at least as previously understood.[71] Not surprisingly, "Rajiv's Law" further aggravated the conflict between many Hindus and Muslims over whether or not the country should impose a uniform civil code for all Indian citizens.[72] In fact, just recently the Bombay High Court ruled that "Rajiv's Law" actually entitles a divorced Muslim woman to maintenance payments for her "entire future."[73] Some observers predict that this Bombay judgment will rekindle the types of tensions between Hindus and Muslims similar to those seen after the 1985 *Shah Bano* decision.[74]

There are other examples of inter-religious tensions over personal law questions as well. For example, Indian Parsees argue that without separate personal law systems, the result would be a uniform civil code that would inevitably reflect mainly Hindu interests.[75] Many Christians also fear that their status and autonomy as a minority community may be in jeopardy without separate personal laws.[76] Christians in the state of Kerala are especially sensitive to this issue, as indicated by their reaction to a 1986 decision by the Supreme Court. In *Mary Roy v. State of Kerala*, the Court held that a 1916 statute known as the Travancore-Cochin Christian Succession Act violated women's constitutional rights to inherit property.[77] Christian protesters attacked this ruling as part of an effort to undermine a legitimate minority community.[78] Arguably, the current wave of violence against Christians may deepen this community's worries that without established personal laws their constitutionally recognized status might eventually fade, and that they may lose their identity as well as their ability to practice their religion freely.[79]

India: The "Second" Set of Personal Laws—Affirmative Action Benefits

In addition to its "traditional" personal law, India has a new body of rules which are a cousin to the personal laws and are also applied on the basis of personal identity; we might call this India's "second" system of personal law. Since independence, India has pursued a wide array of policies of preferential treatment intended to benefit disadvantaged caste and tribal groups.[80] These policies of "compensatory discrimination" include legislative set-asides, reserved places in government services, reserved educational admissions, scholarships, and other special benefits.[81] These benefits are for groups traditionally considered as "untouchables," who are classified as Scheduled Castes, and for tribal groups categorized as Scheduled Tribes. They constitute, respectively, some 15 percent and 7 percent of the population.[82] An even larger set of groups designated as Other Backward Classes (OBCs) are included within some of the reservation and benefit schemes; the vast bulk of these potential beneficiaries are Hindus.[83]

In the area of this "second" personal law, there is conflict on two levels. First, at the collective level, there is controversy over which groups are entitled to enjoy such benefits. Although the main contours of compensatory discrimination policies are determined by legislators, their decisions about which groups will be included as beneficiaries have frequently been reviewed by the courts, who have developed a jurisprudence of group standing and boundaries that draws on the jurisprudence of the personal law.[84]

Since its founding, the Supreme Court has been active in defining which groups qualify as OBCs. In *Venkataramana v. State of Madras,*[85] the Court ruled that underprivileged caste groups could be considered within the OBC category. In *Balaji v. State of Mysore,*[86] the Court, while condemning the use of caste as a means of classification for state reservations, nevertheless upheld the legislature's method of categorization on the basis of caste identity. Other cases from this period also demonstrate the Court's willingness to shape the parameters of the OBC category. In *Chitralekha v. State of Mysore,*[87] the Court reaffirmed the central tenet of *Balaji,* but qualified that decision by stating that factors apart from caste also must be considered.

The Supreme Court, more recently, has continued to maintain a similar approach. In a landmark 1992 decision (*Indra Sawhney v. Union of India*), the Court upheld the central government's response to the Mandal Commission report. The Mandal Commission was established by the Janata Party–led government following the defeat of Indira Gandhi's Congress Party in 1977. The purpose of the Commission, led by a retired civil servant named B. P. Mandal, was to ascertain which groups should be deemed backward classes and how to improve their socio-economic conditions.[88] In 1980, the Commission issued its report, in which it proposed affirmative action programs for a majority of India's population on the basis of their membership in lower castes. It called for the reservation of 27 percent of central government positions as well as seats in higher educational institutions for members of these groups.[89]

After a decade of lying dormant, the Commission's report was revived by Prime Minister V. P. Singh in 1990. In attempting to implement the report, Singh faced strong opposition both at the government and grassroots levels.[90] In response to a constitutional challenge to the government's implementation of the Mandal Commission report, the Supreme Court in 1992 ruled, in a nearly three-hundred-page opinion, that the state indeed had the prerogative to set aside government posts and educational seats on the basis of a group's caste status, so long as other factors were considered as well.[91] The Court ruled that Article 16 (4) provides the state with constitutional authority to continue pursuing compensatory discrimination schemes.[92]

Affirmative action benefits, thus, can be conferred on the basis of membership in designated groups. But courts are also confronted with cases where they must decide which individuals are members of the designated groups and therefore eligible for preferences. In these cases, judges face determinations of individual identity that closely resemble the questions of identity implicated in the administration of the personal law. For example, there has been an ongoing question over whether or not "untouchable" Hindus (*dalits*) who convert to Christianity should continue to qualify for compensatory discrimination benefits.[93] The courts have ruled fairly consistently that converts cannot claim such benefits.[94] "The general rule, is conversion [by an individual] operates as an expulsion from the caste. . . . [A] convert ceases to have any caste"[95] and thereby any grounds to claim compensatory discrimination benefits. The difficulty these "Christian *dalits*" have in obtaining benefits is particularly troubling for leaders in the Indian Christian community. As Dr. Godfrey Shiri, associate director of the Christian Institute for the Study of Religion and Society (CISRS), notes, "just because these dalits are now Christians does not mean their socio-economic status has improved."[96]

In an interesting elaboration on the conversion theme, however, the Supreme Court has ruled that converts to Christianity who reconvert back to Hinduism may qualify for compensatory discrimination benefits upon acceptance by that group.[97] Where an individual who otherwise would not qualify for compensatory discrimination benefits marries into a lower caste that is eligible for such preferences, the courts have ruled that sometimes (but not always) membership in the lower-caste group may be acquired by acceptance by the group.[98] Where an otherwise ineligible individual is adopted into a family that qualifies for benefits, however, the courts have considered other factors, including the adoptee's lifestyle prior to being adopted, instead of whether or not there is community acceptance.[99]

In 1996, the Supreme Court ruled that when an individual who enjoyed an "advantageous start in life" as a member of a "forward group" converts, marries, or is adopted into a group eligible for reservations, that individual does not become eligible for the benefits to which members of the group are entitled.[100]

> [w]hen a member is transplanted into the Dalits, Tribes and OBCs, he/she must of necessity also undergo same handicaps, be subject to the same disabilities, disadvantages, indignities or sufferings so as to entitle the candidate to avail the facility of reservation. A candidate who had the advantageous start in life being born in forward caste and had march of advantageous life but is transplanted in backward caste by adoption, marriage or conversion does not become eligible to the benefit of reservation.[101]

Judicial decisions about personal identity in the area of compensatory discrimination are influenced by, although do not necessarily conform to, the doctrines that prevail in the traditional personal law. Clearly, the "second personal law" in India remains highly salient and is slated to grow as affirmative action policies become more nuanced and more contested.[102]

Personal Law in Israel: Division within Religious Communities

In spite of this "second" personal law, most of the conflict over traditional personal laws in India is between religious communities. By contrast, conflict over the application of personal law in Israel occurs mainly within the majority religious community. Israel is a curious democracy. On the one hand, it was founded in order to be the national homeland of the Jewish people.[103] Judaism is not a state religion, but the state recognizes a special relation to it. As Martin Edelman observes, "religion in Israel is virtually synonymous with [Judaism, in particular] Orthodox Judaism."[104] On the other hand, Israel prides itself on treating all religious communities in a fair and equitable manner. While some 80 percent of the population is Jewish,[105] the state attempts actively to protect the religious freedom of the nearly one million non-Jewish Israeli citizens.[106]

In comparison to India, Israel exemplifies an entirely different system of administering personal law. The Israeli personal law structure descends from the *millet* system of the Ottoman Empire.[107] Under the *millet* system, each of the communities in the Empire—such as the Greek, Armenian, Jewish, Muslim, and Druze communities—had its own set of courts.[108] These courts were staffed by scholars of religious law who were empowered to apply their law to the respective communities. In instances of inter-communal conflict, matters were relegated to government courts. Since Islam was "the official religion of the Ottoman Empire,"[109] it was not uncommon for these courts to apply the *Shari'at*. The *millet* system conferred on the rabbinical courts full authority over all disputes among Jews,[110] including marriage and divorce, as well as maintenance, inheritance (succession), guardianship, legitimation, incompetency, adoption, and burial.[111]

With the arrival of the British Mandate, the rabbinical courts saw their jurisdictional authority shrink. The British administration of mandatory Palestine (1918–1948) established government courts (again in the common law style), but retained the *millet* system in matters of marriage, divorce, alimony, and succession.[112] Each of the religious communities had a court staffed by religious authorities who applied their respective religious laws.

When Israel achieved independence in 1948, there was a further transformation of the *millet* system. In a deal, known as the "status quo" agreement, struck between the secular Zionist government of David Ben Gurion and the religious parties of the time, it was agreed that the government would maintain the existing patterns of publicly enforced religious observance and recognition of religious authority.[113] The Israeli government, specifically, opted to maintain the general system of allowing religious groups to retain their respective religious laws to govern certain matters relating to the family. Later, in 1953, the status quo agreement was narrowed by the Knesset; rabbinical courts retained a monopoly only to regulate marriages and divorces.[114]

The present situation in Israel is that some questions within the "traditional" ambit of personal law are determined by religious judicial institutions while others are determined by state judicial institutions. This legal division does not ameliorate the social division within the Jewish population, for many Orthodox Jews believe that all personal law matters should be handled by rabbinical courts, while secularists and non-Orthodox Jews resent being subject to any Orthodox rabbinical control, particularly in matters of vital concern such as marriage and divorce.[115]

All Jews—regardless of whether or not they are Orthodox—fall under the jurisdiction of the rabbinical courts in matters of marriage and divorce.[116] In matters of marriage and divorce, there is no civil law for Israeli Jews.[117] Jews wishing to marry in Israel must seek the approval of the rabbinical courts that apply Jewish religious law, or *Halachah*.[118] Some observers note that since 1947 the rabbinical courts have interpreted the *Halachah* more strictly than before the creation of the state.[119]

What specifically is it about adhering to the *Halachah* and the authority of rabbinical courts that many non-Orthodox Jews find so objectionable? For one thing, in order for Jews to be married in Israel, the rabbinical courts must find that both the man and the woman are, in fact, Jews. The rabbinical courts thus prohibit marriage between a Jew and a non-Jew.[120] In order to be deemed a Jew, the individual must prove that he or she is a child of a Jewish mother, or that he or she was converted in a ceremony recognized by the rabbinical court.[121] Oftentimes, however, proving that an individual's mother was Jewish or securing agreement that a conversion conformed to the *Halachah* is not so simple a task.[122]

The rabbinical courts also bar *mamzerim* (Jews born of adulterous unions) from marrying Jews other than other *mamzerim*.[123] Jewish couples whose marriage ends without the approval of the rabbinical court are forbidden to re-marry. Jewish women who commit adultery are not permitted to divorce and marry the individual with whom they are having the adulterous relationship. Jewish law forbids *kohanim* from marrying divorcées.[124]

The imposition of such marital restrictions by the rabbinical courts pushes many Israeli Jews to marry outside the country. (Valid marriages performed outside Israel are recognized as legitimate by the Israeli government according to principles of private international law.[125]) Obviously, traveling abroad for marriage entails considerable trouble and expense. Much of the non-Orthodox community holds the rabbinical courts in contempt for causing them to incur such problems.

The hostility the non-Orthodox feel is not confined to the rabbinical courts wielding such power over Jewish marriages; the non-Orthodox are quite angry because these courts also control the process of divorce.[126] While divorce is allowable by Jewish law, rabbinical courts strongly favor preserving marriages. As observers note, contemporary rabbinical courts allow women to obtain divorces on many more grounds than in previous times.[127] But in form, the divorce is achieved only when the husband renounces the wife by delivering to her (under the supervision of a *bet din*, or rabbinical court) a *get* (divorce decree).[128] Rabbinical courts insist that the husband actually deliver a *get* to his wife in order to finalize a divorce.[129] Where a wife receives approval from the rabbinical courts to divorce her husband, but the husband refuses to grant a *get*, the rabbinical courts will not decree a divorce. Under Israeli state law, the wife may ask the Attorney General to demand that the husband appear in front of (state) district court to explain why he refuses to grant the *get*.[130] If the district court is dissatisfied with the husband's response, it can order the husband jailed until he delivers the divorce decree to the wife.[131] Sometimes the district court declines to jail the husband, and even if the husband is jailed, a *get* might still not be issued to the wife.[132] What results, then, is that the wife is left to live her life as an *agunah* (literally a "tied" woman). She cannot re-marry under Jewish law,[133] and if she were to do so under some other legal provision (say by obtaining a foreign civil divorce recognized in Israel), her children would be deemed *mamzerim* by the rabbinical courts. In light of these problems, it is not surprising that sentiment for revamping marriage and divorce laws exists in the non-Orthodox community within Israel.

The fact that Orthodox rabbinical courts possess the authority to decide "who is a Jew" for the purposes of marriage, as well "who may divorce," provides this religious institution with the capacity to shape the social identities of many Israelis. Individuals who have always thought of themselves as Jewish may learn that, in the eyes of the *dayyanim*,[134] they are actually not Jews. Women, likewise, who wish to end a marriage but are unable to do so are disabled from re-marrying or starting new families.[135]

The rabbinical courts are not the only legal institution that affects Jewish identity in Israel. State courts, too, play an important and, according to many in the Orthodox community, a damaging role in many aspects of Jewish life. As previously stated, prior to the creation of the state, the personal law jurisdiction included a number of matters in addition to marriage and divorce. For centuries these matters, and matters more generally relating to Jewish identity, were within the domain of the rabbis. But as Martin Edelman notes, since 1953 the state has reduced the jurisdiction of the rabbinical courts and allowed non-religious state courts to decide on many of these "personal laws" as well as on laws that more broadly affect "who is a Jew."[136] Those within the religious community see both types of involvement by state courts as a violation of the "status quo" agreement, and as contributing toward the further division of the Jewish people.

The encroachment by state courts upon the "turf" of rabbinical courts dates back to the 1960s. In the famous *Brother Daniel* case,[137] the Israeli Supreme Court decided in 1962 that it, not the rabbinate, would dictate who could qualify as a Jew for purposes of the country's "Law of Return."[138] "Who is a Jew?" thus was decided by a state, not religious, institution. Determinations of Jewish identity for application of public law resemble the "second personal law" of group identity that has arisen in the Indian setting.

In theory, "[i]n both its appellate and general equity capacities, the Supreme Court of Israel can consider matters relating to the various religious court systems only with regard to the *jurisdiction* of those courts to resolve a particular matter."[139] Nevertheless, the Supreme Court continues to venture into legal terrain that many within the Orthodox community believe is beyond the Court's domain. In early 1999, the Court was sharply attacked by ultra-Orthodox Jews who were upset not only with the Court's intervention in matters relating to marriage and divorce, but also with its involvement in other "second personal law" questions of Jewish identity.[140] The ultra-Orthodox were particularly angered by seventeen recent decisions that, in their view, undermined Judaism.[141] Since the Court is rarely subject to public challenge, the recent attacks on the Court by the ultra-Orthodox have been of grave concern to many in the government.

The tension between the Orthodox and non-Orthodox communities in Israel is a complicated issue. One thing, though, is certain: each side believes that the other is contributing to the "decay"[142] of Jewish society. The internal conflict is mirrored in the dual legal system within the country, in which certain questions of personal law and Jewish identity are decided by religious courts while others are decided by state courts. Abolishing this dual system would further anger and alienate the Orthodox side. Many Muslims and Christians would also oppose such a change. Even if it were politically feasible, which it is not at the moment, further abridgment of the power of the rabbinical courts is fraught with danger to the already strained fabric of civil life in Israel.

We have described how two personal law systems operate within two different religiously plural societies. We note six major differences that exist between the Indian and Israeli situations.

First, there is a difference in the location of the personal law courts. In Israel, personal laws are administered by qualified religious specialists in courts that are part of, or attached to, religious institutions. By contrast, in India, personal law is applied by common-law-trained judges in the regular state courts.

Second, both the Indian Supreme Court and the Israeli Supreme Court (especially in its capacity as the High Court of Justice) have intervened actively in human rights and public interest cases.[143] While the Supreme Court of India has been quite active in advancing the rights of many sorts of public interest claimants,[144] Indian judicial activism has not, with rare exceptions, addressed questions of personal law. In Israel, on the other hand, the personal law area has been an important site of judicial activism.[145]

Third, each country's personal law system contributes to different lines of conflict. In Israel, the rabbinical courts lend themselves to monopolistic control by more traditional elements unrepresentative of the wider Jewish community and are bitterly resented and resisted by a large segment of their constituents. In response, the rabbinate and its backers adopt a more rigidly orthodox stance and resist more adamantly any alteration of their status vis-à-vis the state.

By contrast, India's state-applied personal law system seems more resistant to traditionalizing elements and less provocative of conflict, at least among the Hindu population. The rise of the "second" personal law adds an element of conflict within the majority Hindu community, but this type of conflict remains overshadowed by the conflict between the country's differing religious communities.

A fourth major difference is the salience of the determination of membership in the majority community. In India, there is a general willingness on the part of Hindus to be expansive and inclusive; there is a lack of interest among Hindus in defining the details or boundaries of membership. In Israel, on the other hand, "who is a Jew" and who gets to decide who is a Jew are major foci of polarizing controversy.

This contrast is reflected in a fifth major difference regarding the way in which the majority religious law is seen to inform the character of the state. Although India has a sizable Hindu nationalist movement, there is no evident support for the restoration of traditional Hindu law.[146] Indeed, Hindu nationalists propose abolishing separate personal laws in favor of a general uniform law in matters relating to the family —and thus dissolving "Hindu law" as a living legal category. Although this position is asserted aggressively toward Muslims, it also amounts to an assertion that Hindu identity can be vouchsafed through the vehicle of the Indian state without specifically embracing the *dharmashastra* or empowering its exponents.

In Israel there is certainly disagreement over "who is a Jew," "who should decide whether or not an individual is a Jew," and "how much of a role Judaism should play in the Israeli state." But there is a general sentiment among the public that Israel should always remain the exclusive homeland of the Jewish people, that the state should be infused with a distinctive Jewish character, and that the Jewish law should be maintained and promoted by the state. As Martin Edelman puts it, "the controversy is about the *way* the status quo agreement is implemented, not about the basic arrangement itself."[147]

A final difference relates to the types of human rights and freedoms Indians and Israelis enjoy vis-à-vis their respective personal law systems. Both personal law systems offer their constituents what we might call a "comfortable shoe" brand of freedom. They are presented with a single, inalterable set of legal rules, but one that is an expression of a valued religious identity. For many or most of their constituents, the opportunity to have these doctrines and principles applied to them is embraced as valuable in itself. In both India and Israel, substantial populations uncomplainingly accept this personal law regime as giving them freedom to live as they wish. But personal law systems also may offer another sort of freedom by offering their constituents choices among alternative sets of rules. For instance, Indians can, in some circumstances, choose between religious-based marriage law and the law provided by the Special Marriage Act. This "menu" type of freedom is less available to citizens of Israel, where there is no escape from the legal monopoly of the various religious communities.[148]

Some scholars have proposed that one way to solve the tension between a system of personal laws and a democracy committed to equality is to introduce or enlarge the voluntary element in the personal law.[149] But by adding this menu feature, the state would elevate individual autonomy over group identity.[150] For many Muslims in India and for Orthodox Jews in Israel, expanding or introducing a system of volunteerism would shatter the sense that obligatory religious law is the defining feature of their collective sense of being. These groups view mandatory personal law as crucial for maintaining group identity, solidarity, and a continued existence. Thus the "comfortable shoe" and "menu" freedoms represent incompatible principles of human freedom. So, for most Indian Muslims and for Orthodox Jews in Israel, personal law trumps claims based on individual autonomy, while for most Hindus and non-Orthodox Jews (both of whom are the majority groups in their respective societies), these autonomy claims trump personal law.

We started with the notion that India and Israel represented distinct styles of administering personal law. We do not wish to suggest that such styles are unchanging and fated forever to run in parallel without any convergence. The career of the personal law in our two countries suggests otherwise. Although secularism, formally enshrined as an element of the Indian state, has been under attack from many quarters,[151] there is at least a slight leaning toward dissolution of the personal law system in favor of uniform territorial law, together with a "secularization" or de-sacralization of the law of the largest community, and there is no indication of any inclination to devolve the administration of personal law to the religious communities. In Israel, we see movement, fiercely resisted, from administration by religious authorities to administration by the state and a more pronounced movement toward more state supervision of what remains within the ambit of the religious courts (at least the Jewish ones). Like India, Israel seems to be moving in the direction of secularization or de-sacralization.

We may gain some perspective on these shifts from consideration of India's twin, Pakistan, which started in 1947 with the same personal law regime as India's. Pakistan's divergence from India flows from a characteristic that it shares with Israel. Pakistan and Israel are the only post-colonial new nations that were established to be religious homelands, respectively for the Muslims of the subcontinent[152] and for the Jews of the world. (In each case less than half of the group actually lives in the homeland.) Each nationalist movement put forth claims in the name of a religion that emphasizes the legal ordering of social life.[153] Yet in each case the state was founded by secular modernizers and at first regarded askance by traditional religious formations.[154] In Israel, the founders reconciled themselves to incorporating religious law and its traditional expositors in some sectors, but the scope of religious courts has been narrowed by the state and its courts. In Pakistan, unlike Israel, we see movement in the opposite direction—from state-administered personal law toward an expanded guidance of personal law and of public law by traditional religious expositors.[155]

Why has Pakistan moved toward de-secularization and sacralization of public life, while Israel and India have moved in the opposite direction? The contrast between Israel and Pakistan is stark: in Israel the majority of Jews are comfortable with modernity and want to confine religion to a restricted sphere of operation. The minority that wants to preserve or intensify religious control has a disproportionate say due to the electoral system in which cohesive minorities can demand concessions as coalition partners. In India, even with a "Hindu nationalist" government, we see no push for Hinduization of the law; indeed we see an undiminished willingness to attenuate further the connection of Hinduism, in its *dharmashastric* sense, with the law. In Pakistan, on the other hand, those who would separate religion from public life are a minority; the mainstream of politics has generated mass support for Islamicization and stifled opposition to it.[156] Why does India resemble Israel rather than Pakistan in turning away from the sacralization of personal law? Furthermore, how do we explain why the majority group in Pakistan resembles the insecure minorities we find in Israel and India? We leave these questions for another day.

Notes

1. Marc Galanter, "The Displacement of Traditional Law in Modern India," in *Law and Society in Modern India* (Oxford: Oxford University Press, 1989); Asher Arian, *The Second Republic: Politics in Israel* (Chatham: Chatham House Publishers, 1998), pp. 24–26.

2. Stanley Wolpert, *A New History of India* (Oxford: Oxford University Press, 1997), pp. 149–186; Arian, *The Second Republic*, p. 23; John L. Esposito, *Islam and Politics* (Syracuse: Syracuse University Press, 1991).

3. For an old, but still relevant, book on modernity in India, see Lloyd Rudolph, *Modernity of Tradition* (Chicago: University of Chicago Press, 1967); also see S. P. Gupta, *Modern India and Progress in Science and Technology* (New Delhi, Vikas, 1979); T. P. S. Nair (editor), *Modern India, Society and Politics in Transition* (New Delhi: Inter-India Publications, 1988); Yael Yishai, "Civil Society in Transition: Interest Politics in Israel," *The Annals of the American Academy of Political and Social Science* (1998), vol. 555, pp. 147–62.

4. For a discussion on the Haskalah, see Jacob Katz, ed., *Toward Modernity: The European Jewish Model* (New Brunswick: Transaction Books, 1987); Saul Goodman, ed., *The Faith of Secular Jews* (New York: Ktav Press, 1976). For a discussion on the Hindu renaissance and a literary review of important writers in this area, see David Miller, "Modernity in Hindu Monasticism," *Journal of Asian and African Studies* (1999), vol. 34, pp. 111–26.

5. Paul R. Brass, *Riots and Pogroms* (New York: New York University Press, 1996); David Landau, *Piety and Power: The World of Jewish Fundamentalism* (New York: Hill and Wang, 1993); Laurence Silberstein (editor), *Jewish Fundamentalism in Comparative Perspective* (New York: New York University Press, 1993).

6. Sunil Khilnani, *The Idea of India* (London: Hamish Hamilton, 1997), pp. 194–95; Arian, *The Second Republic: Politics in Israel*, pp. 28–41.

7. Wolpert, *A New History of India*, pp. 347–49; Arian, *Second Republic*, pp. 24–27.

8. Atul Kohli, "India," in Mark Kesselman, Joel Krieger, and William Joseph, eds., *Comparative Politics at the Crossroads* (Lexington: D. C. Heath, 1996), pp. 472–73; Samuel Krislov, "Israel," in W. Philips Shively, ed., *Comparative Governance* (New York: McGraw-Hill, 1997), p. 328; Deborah Sontag, "Barak Creates Wide Coalition with 7 Parties," in *The New York Times* (Internet edition), July 1, 1999.

9. Charles R. Epp, *The Rights Revolution: Lawyers, Activists and Supreme Courts in Comparative Perspective* (Chicago: University of Chicago Press, 1998), pp. 71–89; Granville Austin, *The Indian Constitution: Cornerstone of a Nation* (Oxford: Clarendon Press, 1966), pp. 164–84; H. E. Baker, *The Legal System of Israel* (Jerusalem: Israel University Press, 1967), pp. 197–

207, 232–43; Martin Edelman, *Courts, Politics, and Culture in Israel* (Charlottesville: University of Virginia Press, 1994), p. 46.

10. J. D. M. Derrett, *Essays in Classical and Modern Hindu Law* (Leiden: Brill, 1978), vol. 4, pp. 18–20; Izhak Englard, *Religious Law in the Israeli Legal System* (Jerusalem: Hebrew University), pp. 33–46.

11. For the most part, we focus on how personal laws affect the major religious community in each country: the Hindu community in India and the Jewish community in Israel. Because of the way the personal law system in India is structured, we see significant conflict between Hindus and Muslims. Hence, we devote some time to discussing how personal law in India affects not only the Indian Hindu community but also the Indian Muslim community. In Israel, because there is not the same degree of conflict *between* the various religious communities over issues involving personal status, we focus only on the country's majority Jewish population. The recognized minority religious communities in Israel are granted great autonomy to administer personal law matters. For example, the largest religious minority in Israel is the Muslim community. Muslims make up nearly 80 percent of the non-Jewish population, and this community is left almost entirely alone to handle issues relating to personal status. There are Muslim courts of first instance in which Muslim judges (*qadis*) apply Muslim law (*Shari'at*) to personal law cases. There is also a *Shari'at* court of appeals in Jerusalem. (There is no *'ulama'* or set of formal religious scholars who are affiliated with religious institutions in Israel. Nor is there a community of *muftis* or religious specialists in Islamic law. Thus, *qadis* are the main authorities who interpret and apply the *Shari'at* in Israel.) These Muslim courts are left to deal with various personal law issues including: dower for brides-to-be; maintenance for divorced women; unilateral divorces by men (*talaq*); and succession. The *qadis*, moreover, have a significant impact on these four areas. With respect to the first two issues, evidence indicates that the *qadis* have encouraged the curtailing of dower and promoted equitable maintenance payments to divorced women. With respect to the last two issues, evidence suggests that the *qadis* have been unwilling to abolish completely the practice of *talaq* and that women still have yet to be given the same rights to inherit as men. For further information on Muslim courts, see: Edelman, *Courts, Politics, and Culture,* pp. 77–88; Aharon Layish, *Women and Islamic Law in a Non-Muslim State: A Study Based on Decisions of Shari'a Courts in Israel* (New York: John Wiley & Sons, 1975); Nathan Brown, "Sharia and State in the Modern Muslim Middle East," *International Journal of Middle East Studies* (1997), vol. 29, pp. 359–76; Yitzhak Reiter, *Islamic Institutions in Jerusalem: Palestinian Muslim Organization under Jordanian and Israeli Rule* (Boston: Kluwer Law International and Jerusalem Institute for Israel Studies, 1997); Abdur Rahman I. Doi, *Shari'ah and the Islamic Law* (London: Ta Ha Pub., 1984); John L. Esposito, *Women in Muslim Family Law* (Syracuse: Syracuse University Press, 1982); Amira El Azhary Sonbol, *Women, the Family, and Divorce in Islamic History* (Syracuse: Syracuse University Press, 1996).

12. Edouardo Vitta, *The Conflict of Laws in Matters of Personal Status in Palestine* (Tel Aviv: S. Bursi, 1947), p. 14.

13. M. B. Hooker, *Legal Pluralism: An Introduction to Colonial and Neo-Colonial Laws* (Oxford, Clarendon Press, 1975); John H. Mansfield, "The Personal Laws or a Uniform Civil Code?" in Robert Baird, ed., *Religion and Law in Independent India* (New Delhi: Manohar Publishers, 1993), p. 139; M. P. Jain, *Outlines of Indian Legal History* (Bombay: Tripathi, 1981), pp. 369–70, 393–94.

14. Edelman, *Courts, Politics, and Culture,* pp. 52–53; Mansfield, "Personal Laws," p. 144; for more on the jurisdiction of personal law see: Galanter, "The Displacement of Traditional Law in Modern India," in *Law and Society; J. D. M. Derrett, *Religion, Law and State in India* (London: Faber & Faber, 1968); Derrett, *Essays in Classical;* Tahir Mahmood, *Muslim Personal Law, Role of the State in the Indian Subcontinent* (Nagpur: All-India Reporter, 1983); Tahir Mahmood, *Personal Laws in Crisis* (New Delhi: Manohar, 1986); Rajeev Dhavan, "Religious Freedom in India," *American Journal of Comparative Law* (1987), vol. 35, pp. 209–54; Izhak Englard, "Law and Religion in Israel," *American Journal of Comparative Law* (1987), vol. 35, pp. 125–208.

15. Mansfield, "Personal Laws," pp. 148–57.

16. Ibid., pp. 173–74.

17. Bassam Tibi, "Islamic Law/Shari'a, Human Rights, Universal Morality and International Relations," *Human Rights Quarterly* (1994), vol. 16, pp. 277–99.

18. Ibid., p. 285.

19. Ibid., pp. 277–99.

20. Mansfield, "Personal Laws," pp. 146–47.

21. Mahmood, *Personal Law in Crisis,* pp. 42–43; Galanter, "The Displacement of Traditional Law in Modern India," *Law and Society.*

22. Bengal Regulation of 1772. By 1793, the language was amended to 'Mohamadan Laws' and 'Hindu Laws.' Regulation IV of 1793, Section 15.

23. Mansfield, "Personal Laws," p. 163.

24. Ibid.

25. Derrett, *Religion, Law and State in India,* pp. 274–320.

26. On the transformation of Indian personal law, see Galanter, "The Displacement of Traditional Law in Modern India," in *Law and Society;* Derrett, *Religion, Law and State in India,* pp. 274–320.

27. *Ibid;* also see The Shari'at (Application) Act of India of 1937, which according to Derrett "was reactionary and tended entirely to the consolidation and unification of that [Muslim] community in terms of its personal law." Derrett, *Religion, Law and State in India,* p. 323.

28. Mansfield, "Personal Laws," pp. 148–50.

29. Art. 44, The Constitution of India. But see ibid. Mansfield makes the ar-

gument that the 7th Schedule of the Constitution (Item 5 List III), and Article 44 might also lend support for the continuation of personal laws in the country. In addition, Mansfield argues that the language in Article 372, Sections 1 and 3, along with Article 13 (19) indicates that the framers intended for "laws in force" prior to 1947 (which included personal laws) to remain valid so long as they did not conflict with the Fundamental Rights section of the Constitution.

30. *State of Bombay v. Narasu Appa Mali*, A.I.R. 1952 Bom. 84.

31. Galanter, "The Displacement of Traditional Law in India," in *Law and Society*.

32. Ibid.

33. Ibid. See also Derrett, *Religion, Law and State in India*, pp. 321–51. *Varnas* refer to the four great estates or divisions in Hindu socio-legal theory often mistranslated as caste. Anglo-Hindu law contained a number of rules that differed by "varna."

34. On the concept of tutelary laws, see Carl E. Schneider, "Moral Discourse, Bioethics, and the Law," *The Hastings Center Report* (1996), vol. 26, pp. 37–9; Luis Oropeza, *Tutelary Pluralism: A Critical Approach to Venezuelan Democracy* (Cambridge: Center for International Studies, Harvard, 1983); for a more general discussion, see Robert Dahl, *Polyarchy: Participation and Opposition* (New Haven: Yale University Press, 1971), p. 3.

35. Mansfield, "Personal Laws," p. 168.

36. Galanter, "The Displacement of Traditional Law in India," in *Law and Society*.

37. For a useful, extended discussion of this subject, consult Donald E. Smith, *India as a Secular State* (Princeton: Princeton University Press, 1963).

38. Special Marriage Act of 1872. Also see J. D. M. Derrett, *Hindu Law Past and Present* (Calcutta: A. Mukharjee & Co., 1957), p. 73.

39. Special Marriage Act of 1954; also see ibid., p. 74.

40. Derrett, *Religion, Law and State in India*, p. 328.

41. The laws include: The Converts' Marriage Dissolution Act, 1866; The Indian Divorce Act, 1869; The Indian Christian Marriage Act, 1872; The Kazis Act, 1880; The Anand Marriage Act, 1909; The Child Marriage Restraint Act, 1929; The Parsi Marriage and Divorce Act, 1936; The Dissolution of Muslim Marriage Act, 1939; The Special Marriage Act, 1954; The Hindu Marriage Act, 1955; The Foreign Marriage Act, 1969; and The Muslim Women's Protection Act, 1986.

42. Interviews by second author in 1995 with leaders of the Multiple Action Research Group, All-India Democratic Women's Association, and All-India Women's Association.

43. Shyamla Pappu et al., "Women and the Law," in B. K. Pal (ed.), *Problems and Concerns of Indian Women* (New Delhi: ABC Publishing, 1987), pp. 132–33; Epp, *The Rights Revolution*, p. 79.

44. Anika Rahman, "Religious Rights Versus Women's Rights in India: A Test

Case for International Human Rights Law," *Columbia Journal of Transnational Law* (1990), vol. 28, p. 473; S. Raj (ed.), *Quest for Gender Justice: A Critique of the Status of Women in India* (Madras: T.R. Publications, 1991); Asghar Ali Engineer (ed.), *Problems of Muslim Women in India* (London: Sangam, 1995).

45. These two articles propound the fundamental rights of equality. Article 14 states: "The State shall not deny to any person equality before the law or the equal protection of the laws within the territory of India." Article 15(1) states: "The State shall not discriminate against any citizen on grounds only of religion, race, caste, sex, place of birth or any of them."

46. Mansfield, "Personal Law v. Uniform Civil Code," p. 140.

47. Saba Naqvi Bhaumik, "Surviving Friends," *India Today* (Internet edition), January 19, 1998; Khilnani, *Idea of India*, pp. 189–90.

48. "Temple, Art. 370 not on Campaign Agenda: PM," *Times of India* (internet edition), August, 24, 1999. In this article there is a direct quote from BJP party leader, K. N. Govindacharya, who admits that the BJP "has not come out with its own manifesto" with regards to a uniform civil code.

49. Mahmood, *Muslim Personal Law*, pp. 118–125.

50. Rajkumari Agrawala, "Uniform Civil Code: A Formula Not a Solution," in Tahir Mahmood, ed., *Family Law and Social Change* (Bombay: M.N. Tripathi, 1975); Master-Moos, "The Personal Law of Parsees," in Namada Khodie, ed., *Readings in Uniform Civil Code* (Bombay: Thacker, 1975); Mahmood, *Personal Law in Crisis*.

51. *Mohd. Ahmed Khan v. Shah Bano Begum,* A.I.R. 1985 S.C. 945, 945–55.

52. A.I.R 1985 S.C. 946–47; also see Madhu Kishwar, "Pro Women or Anti-Muslim? The Shah Bano Controversy," in Madhu Kishwar, *Religion at the Service of Nationalism* (Delhi: Oxford University Press, 1998), p. 208; Robert Hargrave, "The Challenge of Ethnic Conflict," *Journal of Democracy* (1993), vol. 4, pp. 54–68.

53. A.I.R. 1985 S.C. 947. For a discussion on *talaq* see note 11. Note, a husband upon saying a phrase such as "I divorce you," or "You are divorced," three times may end the marriage. See Flavia Agnus, *Law and Gender Inequality: The Politics of Women's Rights in India* (Delhi: Oxford University Press, 1999), pp. 111–12; Bruce Lawrence, *Shattering the Myth* (Princeton: Princeton University Press, 1998), p. 131; Kishwar, *Religion at the Service*, p. 217.

54. A.I.R. 1985 S.C. 947.

55. Section 125, All India Code of Criminal Procedure.

56. A.I.R. 1985 S.C. 947.

57. Ibid.

58. Section 127 (3) (b), All India Code of Criminal Procedure. The purpose of this section was to accommodate dower or "mahr."

59. A.I.R. 1985 S.C. 950–52.

60. Ibid.

61. Ibid., p. 951.

62. Ibid.

63. Ibid., pp. 954–55. Although we attribute no causal importance to this fact, it is interesting to note that the five justices in this case were at least nominally Hindus.

64. Ibid., p. 947.

65. This was not the first instance of the Supreme Court attempting to define the essentials of a religious community. Cf. *Sastri Yagnapurushdasji v. Muldas Bhundardas Vaishya* (also known as the Satsangis case, A.I.R. 1966 S.C. 1119), where an earlier Supreme Court propounded its view of the essence of Hinduism to invalidate the practices of a Hindu sect. Galanter, "Hinduism, Secularism, and the Judiciary," in *Law and Society*.

66. Agnus, *Law and Gender*, pp. 100–06; Lawrence, *Shattering the Myth*, p. 163; Asghar Ali Engineer, "Forces Behind the Agitation," in Asghar Ali Engineer, ed., *The Shah Bano Controversy* (Hyderabad: Orient, 1987), pp. 39–41.

67. For a discussion on how Muslim law, in fact, may be more beneficial for women than is the Indian Code of Criminal Procedure, see Saleem Akhtar, *Shah Bano Judgment in Islamic Perspective* (New Delhi: Kitab Bhavan, 1994), pp. 243–61.

68. A.I.R. 1979 S.C. 362.

69. A.I.R. 1980 S.C. 1730.

70. Kishwar, *Religion at the Service*, pp. 206–207.

71. Epp, *The Rights Revolution*, p. 88; Daniel Latifi, "The Muslim Women Bill," in Asghar Ali Engineer, ed., *The Shah Bano Controversy*.

72. Since 1986 there have been two unreported cases, described by Flavia Agnes, in which an Allahabad High Court judge deemed *talaq* divorces unconstitutional. See, Agnes, *Law and Gender Equality*, pp. 112–116. The unreported cases are: *Rahmat Ullah v. State of U.P.,* Writ Petition no. 45 of 1993, and *Khatoon Nisa v. State of U.P.,* Writ Petition no. 57 of 1993.

73. Sultan Shahin, "Ulema to Launch Campaign for Personal Law," *Times of India* (Internet edition), May 6, 1999.

74. Ibid.

75. For a discussion of this position, see Agnes, *Law and Gender*, pp. 129–40; J. Hinnells, "Parsi Attitudes to Religious Pluralism," in Howard G. Coward, ed., *Modern Indian Responses to Religious Pluralism* (Albany: New York, 1987); also see more generally M. Shabbir and S. Manchanda, *Parsi Law in India* (Allahabad: Law Books Company, 1991).

76. For a discussion of this position, see Agnes, *Law and Gender*, pp. 141–63; Srimati Basu, *She Comes to Take Her Rights* (Albany: SUNY Press, 1999), p. 202.

77. A.I.R. 1986 SC 1011.

78. V. Menon," Mother Roy," *Rediff on the Net*, 1997 (*http://www.rediff.com/ news/oct/30arun.htm*). This news web site discusses how after the Court decision, there was a backlash by Christian community; also see Basu, pp. 201–02, 191–92.

79. The last half of 1998 and the first half of 1999 saw widespread reports of attacks on Christians in India. For a sample of articles, see: Dakshina Murthy, "Christian Prayer Service Attacked" *Hindustan Times* (Internet edition), November 24, 1998; "23 Million Christians to Protest Today," *Hindustan Times* (Internet edition), December 4, 1998; "CBI Accuses 18 in Staines Murder Case," *Times of India* (Internet edition), June 23, 1999; "Panel Presents Admission-Related Facts," *Times of India* (Internet edition), July 17, 1999.

80. Marc Galanter, *Competing Equalities* (Berkeley: University of California Press, 1984), pp. 41–42.

81. Ibid., pp. 43–44.

82. Ibid., p. 43.

83. Ibid., p. 42. OBCs may include non-Hindu, tribal, and nomadic groups as well.

84. Ibid., p. 534–35.

85. A.I.R. 1951 S.C. 229.

86. A.I.R. 1963 S.C. 649.

87. A.I.R. 1964 S.C. 1823.

88. Sunita Parikh, *The Politics of Preference* (Ann Arbor: University of Michigan Press, 1997), p. 186.

89. Ibid., p. 187.

90. Ibid., pp. 187–89. Parikh describes how Singh's policy decision sparked a chain of events that eventually led to the downfall of his government.

91. *Indra Sawhney v. Union of India*, A.I.R. 1993 S.C. 477.

92. Ibid., pp. 536–54. Note that the Court also stressed the importance of Article 16(1) of the Constitution, which guarantees "equality of opportunity in matters of public employment." The Court noted that in order eventually to arrive at a situation where there could be equal opportunity for all, the government's plan needed to be implemented.

93. Swami Agnivesh, "A Concept of Insecurity," *Hindustan Times* (Internet edition), January 23, 1999. In this article, Agnivesh is critical of converts to Christianity who "shout for government charity"; also consider, John Webster, *The Dalit Christians: A History* (Delhi: ISPCK, 1994).

94. Galanter, *Competing Equalities*, pp. 312–14.

95. Ibid., p. 312, quoting from *Michael v. Venkataswaran*, A.I.R. 1952 Mad. 478.

96. Jayanth Krishnan's interview with Dr. Godfrey Shiri, November 14, 1998, Bangalore, India.

97. *Rajagopal v. Armugam*, A.I.R. 1969 S.C. 101. But as Galanter (*Competing Equalities*, pp. 328–29) notes, consider the difficulty involved in the formula prescribed by the Supreme Court. Obvious questions emerge, including: What type of acceptance is necessary? What defines acceptance? Is acceptance required of the whole caste or just a section of it? Also see, *Guntur v. Y. Mohan Rao*, A.I.R. 1976 S.C. 1904.

98. *Wilson Reade v. C.S. Booth*, A.I.R. 1958 Ass. 128; *Horo v. Jahan Ara*, A.I.R. 1972 S.C. 1840. But see, *Urmila Ginda v. Union of India*, A.I.R. 1975 Del. 115, where the Delhi High Court ruled that a high-caste woman who sought membership into her husband's lower caste group for the purposes of seeking a reserved government post could not be admitted into this lower caste, even by the acceptance of its members. See also, *Mrs. Vaishali v. Union of India*, 1978 80 Bom. LR 182; *Smt. D. Neelima v. The Dean of P.G. Studies*, A.I.R. 1993 Andh. Pra. 299.

99. See, *Shantha Kumar v. State of Mysore*, 1971 Mys. L.J. 21; also see, Galanter, *Competing Equalities*, pp. 339–41; also see, *Natraja v. Selection Committee*, 1971 1 Mys. LJ 226; *R. Srinivasa v. Chairman, Selection Committee*, A.I.R. 1981 Karnataka 86; *A.S. Sailaja v. Kurnool Medical College Kurnoon*, A.I.R. 1986 Andh. Pra. 209; *N. B. Rao v. Principal, Osmania Medical College*, A.I.R. 1986 Andh. Pra. 196. But also see, *Khazan Singh v. Union of India*, A.I.R. 1980 Delhi 60, where the court ruled that an adoption alone into a Scheduled Caste family was enough to acquire benefits.

100. *Valsamma Paul v. Cochin University*, A.I.R. 1996 S.C. 1011.

101. Ibid., p. 1022.

102. Khilnani, *Idea of India*, p. 37.

103. Asher Arian, *Politics in Israel: The Second Generation* (Chatham: Chatham House, 1989), p. 18

104. Edelman, *Courts, Politics, and Culture*, p. 51.

105. Krislov, "Israel," p. 302.

106. Of the one million non-Jews, Muslims make up nearly 80 percent, Christians (of which there are ten state recognized communities) make up approximately 15 percent, and Druze make up 8 to 10 percent. Figures are from Israeli Central Bureau of Statistics. For further information please see: *http://www.cbs.gov.il*.

107. England, *Religious Law*, p. 13.

108. Vitta, *Personal Status*, sixth chapter, pp. 145–175. Also, according to Lewis, the formal *millet* system was extended to the Jewish community in the nineteenth century. Bernard Lewis, *The Jews of Islam* (Princeton: Princeton University Press, 1984).

109. Edelman, *Courts, Politics, and Culture*, p. 76; for a further discussion of

how Islam was the official religion of the state, also see Lord Kinross, *The Ottoman Centuries: The Rise and Fall of the Turkish Empire* (New York: Quill, 1977), p. 112.

110. Ibid., p. 52.

111. Informally, the scope of rabbinical and communal control extended further to regulation of property, employment, and consumption. As Shaw states, "Together Jewish law and custom, community regulations and customs and judicial decisions constituted what amounted to a code of law and jurisprudence which regulated in great detail all religious, social and economic areas of life in each Jewish community as well as in the millet as a whole. The *kahal* enforced them with a kind of policy surveillance to make certain that they were applied, whether in the temple, the school, the marketplace, or the home. Various penalties such as *herem* (excommunication) and *niddui* (bans) were imposed by the *bet din* courts and by rabbis against those who violated the laws and regulations or their provisions and instructions. Prisons were maintained in the synagogue buildings, usually on the ground floors directly beneath the sanctuaries, to punish members who violated the community regulations and laws, while violators of the Sultan's laws and those requiring execution and more severe or lengthy punishments were turned over to Ottoman police and prisons." Stanford J. Shaw, *The Jews of the Ottoman Empire and the Turkish Republic* (New York: New York University Press, 1991), p. 65.

112. Edelman, *Courts, Politics, and Culture*, p. 52.

113. Among other things, the status quo agreement provides for: the Sabbath as the official holiday for state institutions; *kashrut* in all state institutions; rabbinical control over family law; and a two-track educational system where Jews may opt to send their children to Orthodox religious schools that are only minimally monitored by the state. Ibid., p. 5; Asher, *Politics in Israel*, p. 238.

114. See Edelman, *Courts, Politics, and Culture*, pp. 52–53, for a useful discussion of this evolution of Jewish law from the time of the Ottomans through the time of the British Mandate and until 1955.

115. Yet, see ibid., 54–57, where Edelman argues that the debate over the jurisdictional authority of the rabbinical courts is just one source of tension between the Orthodox and non-Orthodox communities. Another source, he contends, may be in the overall interpretation of what political culture and national identity mean in Israel to these communities. For the traditional Orthodoxy, religion is inseparable from Israeli political culture and Israeli national identity, while for the less religious or non-religious segment of the population, religion is separable from these other two concepts.

116. Baker, *Legal System of Israel*, pp. 159–82.

117. Yael Yishai, *Between the Flag and the Banner: Women in Israeli Politics* (SUNY: Albany, 1997), p. 186.

118. Frances Raday, "Religion, Multiculturalism and Equality: The Israeli Case," *Israel Yearbook on Human Rights* (1996), vol. 25, pp. 211, 214–15.

119. Edelman, p. 53; also see M. Elon, "The Sources and Nature of Jewish Law and its Application in the State of Israel," *Israel Law Review* (1968), vol. 3, pp. 416–53.

120. England, *Religious Law*, pp. 62, 176

121. Ibid., p. 62.

122. Recently immigrated Ethiopians and Russians who have come to Israel under the Law of Return continually find that the rabbinical courts often refuse to recognize their Jewish identity for the purposes of marriage. Interviews with members from the Association for Civil Rights in Israel (October 1998); also for a sample of articles on this subject, see Aryeh Dean Cohen, "Russian Immigrants Believe PM Caves in to Haredim," *The Jerusalem Post* (Internet edition), May 12, 1999; Haim Shapiro, "Ministry Must Justify not Registering Ethiopian Family as Jews," *The Jerusalem Post* (Internet edition), June 22, 1999.

123. D. Sharfman, *Living Without a Constitution* (New York: M. E. Sharpe, 1993), p. 79.

124. Ibid., pp. 79–80. *Kohanim* are the "priestly caste"; membership passes patrilineally.

125. *Funk and Schlesinger v. Minister of Internal Affairs* (H.C.J. 143/62, 17 P.D. 222).

126. Raday, "Religion, Multiculturalism and Equality," p. 211.

127. Today, divorce most frequently occurs as a result of both parties mutually agreeing to end the marriage. (Jayanth Krishnan's interviews with lawyers from four of the country's most active women's organizations: Women's International Zionist Organization, Israeli Women's Network, Emunah, and Na'mat, October 1998).

128. Baker, *Legal System of Israel*, p. 210.

129. Ibid.

130. Edelman, *Courts, Politics, and Culture*, p. 64.

131. Baker, *Legal System of Israel*, p. 210.

132. Sharfman, *Living Without a Constitution*, p. 79. Also see Internet edition of the *Jerusalem Post*, March 1, 1999, where the article entitled "Chained Women to Picket Rabbinate Today" reports stories very similar to this scenario still currently occurring throughout the country.

133. Yishai, *Between the Flag*, pp. 186–87.

134. *Dayyanim* is the Hebrew word for rabbinical court judges. These particular judges are state officials. In order to serve they must take a competitive examination administered by the Chief Rabbinical Council. Members of a nomination committee within the Council then select the *dayyanim*. Edelman, *Courts, Politics, and Culture*, p. 53.

135. As opposed to restrictions on *agunot*, "the male divorce refusenik, on the other hand, can start a new family without fearing that the children born to the union will be bastards [mamzerim] (meaning that they can only marry other bastards [mamzerim])." Sharfman, *Living Without a Constitution*, p. 79. In addition, the problem of the *agunah* (the married woman who separates from her husband but cannot re-marry) is a classic and perturbing problem of Jewish law. Women whose husbands refuse a divorce are not the only *agunot*: the other major instance is the abandoned woman who is unable to prove that her husband is dead.

136. Edelman, *Courts, Politics, and Culture*, pp. 52–53, 62–63.

137. *Rufeisen v. Minister of the Interior* (Brother Daniel Case) (H.C.J. 72/62, 16 P.D. 2428).

138. The Law of Return is a statute passed by the 1950 Knesset. The law permits every Jew in the world to immigrate to Israel. As Asher Arian eloquently states, "the Law of Return is the concrete expression of the prophetic vision of the 'ingathering of the exiles'" (Arian, *Second Republic*, p. 10).

139. Edelman, *Courts, Politics, and Culture*, p. 32.

140. We define "second personal laws" as issues of education, conversion, burial, and exemption from military service that turn on the relation of public law to Jewish law and those who claim to interpret it.

141. The *Jerusalem Post*, in its February 12, 1999 Internet edition, entitled "A List of Haredi Grievances," summarizes the Court decisions that the Haredi are against. They include: two Court rulings that disallowed the withdrawal of a *kashrut* certificate in a public hall that displayed a Christmas tree as well as in another facility that held a New Year's Eve party; a Court ruling that prohibited military deferrals or exemptions for yeshiva students; a Court ruling that prohibited the Jerusalem Religious Council from setting the budget of a political party; a Court ruling that allowed for secular burial; a Court ruling that mandated that women be accepted in a course run by the Employment Service Board; two Court rulings stating that Religious and Conservative members be allowed to sit on religious councils; a Court ruling prohibiting the expulsion of a half-Jewish woman; a Court ruling that allowed a girl to return to a secular school after her father withdrew her; a Court ruling that prohibited *moshav* rabbis from engaging in certain political tactics; a Court ruling refusing to enforce the wearing of a *kippa* in a rabbinical court; a Court ruling allowing the registration of Reform conversions; a Court ruling prohibiting rabbis from distributing holy oil to voters; a Court ruling in favor of holding exams for women pleaders in rabbinical courts; and a Court ruling against giving double subsidies to Bnei Akiva. Also see the Internet edition of the *Jerusalem Post*, February 18, 1999, where the Court allowed women to hold the Torah and wear shawls as they pray at the Western Wall (article entitled "Women of the Wall Win High Court Hearing").

142. The term "decay" has been used by many scholars who study political culture. It refers to the destabilization or slow destruction of a political, social, or cultural community as a result of institutional in-fighting and instability. See, James Manor, "India," in Shively's *Comparative Governance*, p. 80. Also see Samuel P. Huntington, *Political Order in Changing Societies* (New Haven: Yale University Press, 1980).

143. Yoav Dotan demonstrates that the Israeli state judiciary has been an active policy-maker in range of rights-based matters. Article forthcoming in *Law & Society Review*.

144. Carl Baar, "Social Action Litigation in India: The Operations and Limitations of the World's Most Active Judiciary," *Policy Studies Journal* (1990), vol. 19, pp. 140–50. For a review of some of the general literature on public interest law in India, see: Rajeev Dhavan, *Litigation Explosion in India* (Bombay: M.N. Tripathi, 1986); Jamie Cassels, "Judicial Activism and Public Interest Litigation in India: Attempting the Impossible?" *American Journal of Comparative Law* (1989), vol. 37, p. 495; Madhava Menon, "Justice Sans Lawyers: Some Indian Experiments," *Indian Bar Review* (1985), vol. 12, p. 444; P. N. Bhagwati, "Judicial Activism and Public Interest Litigation," *Columbia Journal of Transnational Law* (1985), vol. 23, p. 561; Robert Moog, "Indian Litigiousness and the Litigation Explosion: Challenging the Legend," *Asian Survey* (1993), vol. 33, p. 1136; Upendra Baxi, *Courage, Craft, and Contention: The Supreme Court in the 1980's* (Bombay: M. N. Tripathi, 1985).

145. Edelman, *Courts, Politics, and Culture*, chapter 3. See also Dotan's forthcoming article in *Law & Society Review*.

146. For a detailed discussion, see Marc Galanter, "The Aborted Restoration of 'Indigenous' Law in India," in *Law and Society in Modern India*.

147. Edelman, *Courts, Politics, and Culture*, p. 61.

148. Our discussion on freedom draws on Isaiah Berlin's *Four Essays on Liberty* (Oxford: Oxford University Press, 1969), pp. 122–34.

149. Kishwar, *Religion at the Service*, pp. 245–46; Guido Tedeschi, *Studies in Israel Law* (Jerusalem: Hebrew University Students' Press, 1960), pp. 238–88; T. Mahmood, "Common Civil Code, Personal Laws and Religious Minorities," in Mohammed Imam (ed.), *Minorities and the Law* (Bombay: Tripathi, 1972), pp. 60–65; J. D. M. Derrett, "The Indian Civil Code or Code of Family Law: Practical Propositions," in N. Khodie, ed., *Readings in Uniform Civil Code*, pp. 28–30.

150. Mansfield, "Personal Law v. Uniform Civil Code," p. 169.

151. On the recent debate over secularism in India, see the various articles in Part IV of Rajeev Bhargava (ed.), *Secularism and its Critics* (Delhi: Oxford University Press, 1998); Brenda Cossman and Ratna Kapur, *Secularism's Last Sign: Hindutva and the (Mis) Rule of Law* (Delhi: Oxford University Press, 1999).

152. Lawrence, *Shattering the Myth*, pp. 56–64; Rashida Patel, *Socio-Economic*

Political Status and Women & Law in Pakistan (Karachi: Faiza Publishers, 1991), p. 2.

153. See ibid.; also see Rashida Patel, *Islamisation of Laws in Pakistan?* (Karachi: Saad Publishers, 1986), pp. 6–7.

154. See Lawrence, *Shattering the Myth,* pp. 54–64.

155. Patel, *Socio-Economic Political Status,* pp. 99–102; Rashid Ahmed, "Raise the Crescent," *Far Eastern Economic Review* (1998), vol. 161, no. 49, pp. 20–22; "Sharif's Sharia," *The Economist* (1991), vol. 319, p. 33.

156. Ahmed, "Raise the Crescent," pp. 20–22; Rashid Ahmed and Shiraz Sidhva, "Fundamental Pakistan," *Far Eastern Economic Review* (1998), vol. 161, no. 38, p. 20.

Fourteen

The Road to Xanadu
India's Quest for Secularism

Rajeev Dhavan

I

Too many centuries have passed by for India and Indians not to know the meaning of "secularism" or understand the importance of its implications for the subcontinent. India has been home to many people—some indigenous, some not. Some came to settle, others to conquer. Below the highest mountains of the world lie the fertile valleys of the many rivers of the subcontinent—each breeding in and around it a diversity of life and life forms, colors and seasons, and cultures and faiths that suffer no parallel. Its people have not always lived together amicably. But they have constantly devised ways and means to make living together in peace possible. Its history has been a tour de force—constantly adjusting to diversity and accommodating change. This process —of which the quest for secularism is a part—will undoubtedly go on.

Although there was always much to fight over, until recently there was a relative abundance to share. The dominant voice of Hinduism developed a complex hierarchical caste system to maldistribute resources and structure unequal relationships. Both its constitutive ideology and its over-structured prescriptions confronted opposition, defiance, and rebellion. Its endeavor was to catch people's imagination so that their lives would follow suit. It presented "life"—indeed, the universe and the cosmos—in its infinitude, locating people's lives in a hierarchic and cyclic understanding of where they belonged. Yet such a dispensation was not acceptable to skeptics and non-believers. Where wisdom failed, pragmatism followed. Yielding to people as much as it might have wanted people to yield to it, Hinduism preserved its hegemony precisely because it broke up into a plethora of sects, beliefs, interpretations, practices, and expressions—treating each variation as part of *dharma*, which adapted from place to place and *yuga* to *yuga* (epoch), but retaining an enviably tight control over resources and opportunities. In this plenitude grew rebel philosophies which abnegated "god," rebel sects which disclaimed adherence to the faith, and rebel faiths which turned their backs on Hinduism to flower in their own right.

New people brought new faiths to establish new empires and new bases for social and political governance. Many of these ideas found native root—transforming and adapting to the circumstances as they went along. New religious ideas and beliefs were invented—combining the diverse elements of many faiths and practices.[1] Inevitably, in the struggle for resources, opportunities, and supremacy, religion was subordinated to the struggles amongst peoples. Wars, battles, skirmishes, and tensions appropriated and exploited religion to lead the faithful into combat. This continues to happen. But each struggle—howsoever bitter—has made permanent additions to India's ever-increasing social diversity. The wisest of Indian rulers have not been those who have answered fanaticism with bigotry, but those who have looked for principles of governance which would bring people together rather than divide them. In our times, the subcontinent has been savagely dismembered along communal lines, leaving it to the rulers and peoples of the partitioned parts to pick up the pieces. A new quest for secularism began, which will carry over into the new millennium.

II

Even the most homogenous societies have to look for ideas to deal with differences between and amongst people. The quest for secularism begins when it is no longer possible or desirable to satisfy the demands emanating from diversity from within the conspectus of any one particular faith or tradition. Resisted by orthodoxy and supported by oppressed minorities, secular principles develop over time. Imposed coercively, they may fail to elicit support. Projected as consensus, they are as fragile as the forces that uphold or oppose them. We are concerned here not just with compromise solutions which will purchase peace, but with more lasting issues of principle to create justice amongst all peoples of all persuasions.

In all this, law plays a critical role in giving objective expression to secular practices, concretizing their existence in a seemingly autonomous status, stating them in explicit terms and rendering them enforceable. "Law" is indeterminably "Janus faced." It seeks to satisfy both the powerful forces which create it as well as the ideals of justice which it claims to fulfill and from which it derives legitimacy.[2] We are not just concerned with the "law" declared by the state, but also those innumerable rules in civil society which are clearly understood to be binding in their effect as a consequence of the many subtle and coercive mechanisms through which a society calibrates compliance to social norms.[3] Likewise, secularism is not just concerned with the triumphs and failures of the political state, but also of civil society. A state may be secular in form, but people in that state may be intolerant, tyrannical, and cruel to people not of their persuasion. Conversely, a state may be constitutionally linked with a church or faith, but located in a tolerant society. The secular capacity of a people needs to be tested at all levels. A secular state in an intolerant society is at best—and that too, not always—a progressive symbol. An intolerant state in a secular society is an aberration. Both situations can be volatile and can breed dangerous consequences for the future. Between these involuted extremes lie many variations of tolerance and intolerance.

There is a considerable difference between a merely tolerant society and a secular one. Toleration may simply be an act of necessity—a concession rather than an acceptance of another's right. The "toleration of difference" is writ large over many social and legal systems. The Hindu *dharmashastra* itself had no choice but to co-exist with stubborn customs *(sadachara)* and had to concede that *dharma* must change from *yuga* to *yuga*. Roman law distinguished *ius civille* (law for citizens) and *ius gentium* (law for others). Canonical law used the doctrine of *factum valet* to accept contrary customary practices as irredeemable facts from which there was no escape. Islamic jurists recognized the importance of *hadith* (tradition), *ijma* (consensus), and equity to mold the law.[4] Difference cannot be wished away. It has to be assimilated into law and social practice. We are still a considerable juristic distance away from an acceptance of the principle of equality which implicitly guarantees the right of people to be different, and not be discriminated against for being so. But although equality was an important breakthrough in the evolutionary quest for secularism, in some societies—not the least post-Civil War America—the acceptance of equality, too, may have been drawn out from necessitous circumstances. Toleration founded on necessity is concessionary in nature—not an entitlement, but a gift by the "them" to the "not-them." Beyond such necessitous circumstances lies the domain of secularism. A truly secular state or society is more than one which tolerates difference. It is one in which the right to be different is recognized and even encouraged, and, perforce, one whose identity is not overtly or covertly over-identified with or appropriated by the people of any one faith, persuasion, or community to the exclusion of others.

Diagram 14.1 attempts to typologize variations in secular and non-secular approvals to deal with differences between people.

Applicable both to states and civil society, this diagrammatic explanation does not necessarily seek to present a continuum along its two axes.[5] Thus, a state or society which is uncompromisingly conservative and wholly intolerant (i.e., Box A/1) has no place in a chart on secularism. Equally, it may be argued that a regulatory and reformist state or society (as that configured in Column F) does not belong at the end of a continuum of increasing tolerance toward religion. Yet, it receives a place at the end of that continuum precisely because intimations of such reform are supposed to enable a consensus for change by democratic dialogue under relatively non-coercive conditions. The distinction between "intolerant," "tolerant," "egalitarian" societies, and those which guarantee "religious freedom" does not merit further explanation. Some faiths require the positive help of the state to survive. Indeed, this is precisely how the institutions of the faith have been strengthened by land and other endowments by the state.[6] Along with respect for religious freedom and support for all faiths has also grown a new attitude toward religious faiths which "requires" them to respond—if not yield—to modernity, gender justice, and reform. States and societies have been broadly classified as "theocratic" and "non-theocratic." Theocratic societies have been broadly identified as those which are uncompromisingly fundamentalist, those with strong "church-state" links, and those where such links may be formal and ceremonial. Non-theocratic states may be "strictly neutral" and refuse to recognize religion in their dealings, or be generally supportive of all faiths but deal with all religions in a non-discriminatory way, or be strongly celebratory of each faith, affirming each as part of the social fabric of that society. The secularism of the American state veers in the direction of "strict neutrality"[7]—it being no business of any state authority, for example, to construct a Christmas tree during the festive season. Indian secularism claims to celebrate faiths with positive help and support where it is needed. Thus, several grants have been given to famous religious endowments which are allegedly part of India's heritage.[8] It was on this basis that the Delhi High Court defended the official state celebration of Lord Mahavir's 2500th birth anniversary, claiming that Lord Mahavir belonged to India and not just the Jain community.[9] Official public holidays are declared when there are important religious festivals. Yet there are limits to which this can be taken. It is difficult to accept the Su-

Diagram 14.1: Typologizing Various Kinds of Secular and Non-secular Societies

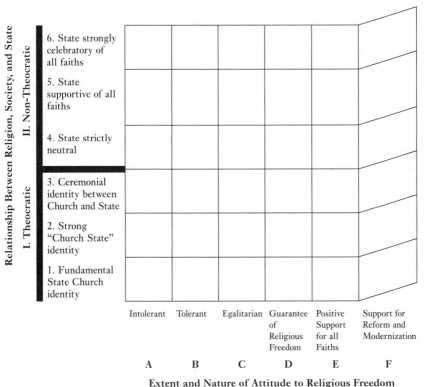

Relationship Between Religion, Society, and State

II. Non-Theocratic

6. State strongly celebratory of all faiths

5. State supportive of all faiths

4. State strictly neutral

I. Theocratic

3. Ceremonial identity between Church and State

2. Strong "Church State" identity

1. Fundamental State Church identity

Intolerant	Tolerant	Egalitarian	Guarantee of Religious Freedom	Positive Support for all Faiths	Support for Reform and Modernization
A	B	C	D	E	F

Extent and Nature of Attitude to Religious Freedom

preme Court's verdict that an electoral appeal to "Hindutva" was—in its context—not a religious appeal to Hinduism but a celebration of the wonder that was India.[10]

Is it enough for a secular state to guarantee religious freedom, or must it also display some element of neutrality and separation between religion and the state? Even though the Protestant Church is not disestablished in Britain and the coins of the realm continue to proclaim the Queen as the "defender of the faith," can Britain claim to be a "secular"—rather than simply a tolerant—society because the links between church and state are purely formal and confined to ceremonial occasions?[11] Can we accept a scholarly claim that because Israel permits freedom of religious belief and worship, it should be treated as a secular state and society even though the nexus between Israel's state and society and the Jewish faith is not only strong but heavily contested by the non-Jewish population as invidious?[12] Even if the theocratic links of the

British state are not put in issue on the mainland, such links are not acceptable to the Catholics of Northern Ireland under circumstances where their right to religious worship is not curtailed and discrimination against them is on the decline. It is not just the nature of the link between church and state that is important to determine the "secular" credentials of any society or state, but also the manner and extent to which such links are viewed by those who live in that society. The more such links are critiqued, contested, and rejected as unacceptable, the less plausible that society or state's claim to be considered a secular society or state is.

All this is of considerable significance to contemporary Indian debates. In their best restatement for a tolerant India, the Bharatiya Janata Party (BJP) and its conservative allies project a future Indian *ram-rajya* (the perfect reign of Lord Rama) in which Hinduism would be the official religion of the realm but equality of treatment and opportunity and religious freedom would be guaranteed to all. Such a projection is heavily contested and discounted by minorities and secularists as both a false promise as well as unacceptable. India's Muslim population is now over 100 million—making India's Muslim contingent the third largest in the world after Indonesia and Bangladesh. Its Sikh, Buddhist, and Jain populations have important shrines in India. Indian Christianity falls in a unique class of its own. Hinduism itself is not a monolithic or homogenous faith but one which breaks into thousands of faiths and practices, each distinct from the other. The idea that India or the Indian state belongs exclusively to a group or entity called the Hindus, or any one sect or section of them, is eminently unacceptable. A secular India is not just one in which there is a genuine non-discriminatory toleration of the religions of others, but one which is not appropriated by one faith to the exclusion of others.

The colonial and imperial expansion of the Western nations of the last four centuries was inextricably linked with an arrogant, racist, and condescending attitude in which Christianity was politically transformed and appropriated to serve the purposes of empire. More than half the peoples of the world were liberated from imperialism on the basis of the right to self-determination. It would be wholly unsatisfactory if the aftermath of that liberation was to clothe the "liberated" nations with immutable religious identities. Using the same demand of the right to self-determination, various peoples and groups within the new nation-states could, and do, demand independence and the right to secede. The extent to which they succeed depends on the extent of support they get from the powerful nations of the world. Thus, German and European support had a lot to do with Croatia's demand for independence in 1991. If this pattern is followed anywhere and everywhere, the map of the world would be in constant flux, at the mercy of those who are economically and politically strong enough to contrive change. States would be constantly partitioned amidst conditions of chaos. Going beyond the minimalist agenda that the rights of minorities should be protected, secularism is an alternative to the continuous politically inspired religious balkanization of the world. While such a re-drawing of the political map may be necessary in some cases, rather than continue the imperialist agenda of continuously re-drawing the political map of the world along religious lines, the secular approach is to increase religious toleration, maximize religious and cultural diversity, and preserve the neutrality of the state and governing processes of a society. Eventually, this must be a goal for the whole world—the practice of which must commence and take root in the sovereign states which compose the family of nations. The world and the state do not belong to any one group; nor should that be permitted. In a choice between "balkanization" and "secularism," the latter is to be preferred.

It is very easy to view the future of the world as a "clash of religious civilizations"[13] and leave it at that. It is infinitely more difficult to preserve the pluralistic diversity of the world, increase religious tolerance and equality toward all faiths, and seek to separate church and state from the dangerous propensities that have made the twentieth century one of the bloodiest centuries of all time. However, secularism is not a stagnant ideal, but a vector along which a society will move in its own way. Each society has to view its circumstances and evolve its own answers along this vector.

III

India's contemporary quest for secularism is firmly located in its post-colonial predicament following the aftermath of the empire. Too much can be made of the policy of "divide and rule" of the British, too little may have been learned from its implications. As trade gave way to empire and revenue collection to governance, the British devised a common administration to exact revenue and keep the peace and a unified court system culminating in provincial High Courts in India and the Privy Council in London to provide for civil and criminal justice.[14] Convinced that they were dealing with a lesser "oriental" people who needed to be introduced to Christianity, modernity, and the "occidental" way of life, the British burdened the Indian psyche with a self-reinforced bias against itself and its own ways.[15] To the burden of "occidentalism" was added the influence of Benthamite utilitarianism.[16] Within the limits and needs of the empire, India soon became the laboratory of many modernist experiments.

From a legal point of view, a seemingly contradictory policy was developed. On the one hand, it was decided that it was more consistent with "justice, equity and good conscience" that natives should be governed by their own personal and customary laws as recognized and modified by British Indian courts.[17] On the other hand, it seemed more convenient and progressive to create a uniform civil and criminal code by which all persons in India would be governed. The products of this all-embracing codification were the Anglo-Indian codes of the nineteenth century, which continue to govern Indians today and will continue to do so in our new century.[18] However, while these codes covered civil and criminal procedure and the law relating to property, contract, trust, and fiduciary and commercial relations, they kept clear of the personal law and social practices of the natives. Although several successful and unsuccessful attempts were made by the British to reform various invidious social practices (such as *sati*, dowry, child marriage, infanticide, and the like), such social reform was later left to be devised by Indians for themselves. In time, the British Raj settled for a holding operation to keep the "Imperial" peace, and amended their criminal law and censorship to enable this.[19] This tri-focal legacy—to (1) recognize and give effect to traditional laws, practices, and customs, (2) develop a powerful system of modern law courts and administration, and (3) assume a superior reformist posture within the framework of a "holding" operation to keep the peace—continues to maintain a basic ambiguity in the policies of India's present rulers.

If the law of British India entrenched identities, the policies of the Raj politicized them. As the movement to gain "independence" gathered ground, it was more conducive to the British to give a political identity to various communities by promising them separate representation. This began by "communal" nomination to government councils under the Indian Councils Act 1892 and continued until India was partitioned in 1947. A policy of "separate representation," founded on distinct and "separate electorates," was readily included in the Indian Councils Act 1909. Once the ball was set rolling, Indians themselves negotiated with each other in these terms. The Lucknow pact of 1916 accepted a division of spoils on the basis of communal electorates. By 1928, the Nehru report's proposal of joint rather than separate electorates was rejected by leading Muslim politicians. Despite Gandhi's interventions, the Communal Award of 1932 was accepted as the basis for the Government of India Act 1935 whereby separate electorates were guaranteed to Muslims, Europeans, Sikhs, Indian Christians, and Anglo-

Indians.[20] The politicization of religious communities was complete. The leaders of various communities, as indeed the communities themselves, were drawn into the vortex of claiming political power for themselves.[21] The British knew that what they were doing was wrong. The Montagu-Chelmsford Report protested that such an approach was invidious. In 1930, the Indian Statutory Commission (better known as the Simon Commission) recalled the words of the Montagu-Chelmsford Report, which they paraphrased as follows: "Such communal electorates . . . were opposed to history. . . . [T]hey perpetuated class division. . . . [T]hey stereotyped existing relations . . . [and] constituted a very serious hindrance to the development of the self governing principle."[22]

Yet the lessons of history gave way to the politics of empire. No number of speeches, resolutions, and protests were of any avail. The moving finger of imperial politics had written and, having writ, moved on. It is idle to speculate on the counter-factual possibilities of history to ask whether the cabinet plan of a quasi-confederal government was workable or whether it was Nehru or Jinnah who irritated "partition" into being.[23] One thing was clear: the politicization of religious communities paved the way for new kinds of warring demands which often did not admit to consensus solutions or compromise. It was under those brittle circumstances, and under the shadow of the cataclysmic events of partition, that the Constituent Assembly drafting India's Constitution was confronted with the task of resolving the highly charged demands of overtly politicized communities into a Constitution. Since tragedy stalked the events of partition, the tone of the demands was initially less full-throated than it might have been. Yet the undercurrent behind the demands was comparatively clear. The minorities sought a constitutional compensation for their loyalty. This "compensation" consisted of comprehensive guarantees to protect the individual and group rights of the minorities.[24]

Although the Constituent Assembly is correctly revered for its insight, pragmatism, and sagacity, it had a seamier side which has been glossed over by those who have written about its deliberations, and, no less, by the small cabal which guided its deliberations. If the Drafting Committee was cheekily referred to as the "Drifting Committee," it was to express the angst with which some members viewed it.[25] Looked at from this angle, its deliberations were like a political auction in which bids were made, accepted, rejected, or ignored. At the very initial stage when three drafts were made of the proposed chapter on fundamental rights, K. M. Munshi's draft was skillfully prioritized over the Ambedkar and Harnam Singh versions. The record of the Constituent Assembly displays a tussle between many factions. The compromises are self-evident from the text of the Constitution.[26] Proceeding from the universally sublime to the strangely particular, the religious freedom articles contain a specific provision that "(t)he wearing and carrying of *kirpans* shall be deemed to be included in the profession of the Sikh religion." The same Article throws open "Hindu religious institutions of a public character to all classes and sections of Hindus" and sweepingly includes the "Sikh, Jaina [and] . . . Buddhist religion(s)" as "part of the Hindu religion."[27] The Swaminarayans were justly annoyed with the Supreme Court's attempt to declare that they were in fact Hindus even though they protested that they were not![28] The Constitution abolishes "untouchability" and makes it a punishable offense. The "socialist" lobby was able to include the prohibition of *begaar* or forced labor as an enforceable fundamental right, but the rest of the socialist agenda was relegated to the unenforceable Directive Principles. Unable to resolve the hotly contested issue of cow slaughter, a compromise was evolved that this issue be housed in the chapter containing the Directive Principles of State Policy which were unenforceable in a court of law but allegedly important to the business of the nation.[29] A similar exercise was undertaken over the vexed issue of the "uniform civil code," which, in the Indian context, is concerned solely with the reform of personal laws and, more often than not, is in our times politically pointed in the direction of the Muslims to embarrass them over the reform of Muslim personal law.[30] It was only on 16 June 1949 that the contentious issues over separate or joint communal electorates were resolved by declaring that there would be a common electoral roll. But, while special electorates were abolished for the imperially selected Muslim, Christian, and Sikh communities, such electorates were retained for the Anglo-Indians, Scheduled Castes (SCs), and Scheduled Tribes (STs).[31] Provisions were also made for ameliorative programs for the SCs and STs, but, as if to concede to the caste-based demands of the "Other Backward Classes" (OBCs), the possibility of preferential treatment for the OBCs—who were primarily identified on the basis of caste—was left open.[32] Years later, the demands of the OBCs were politicized in the 1980s to wholly alter and de-stabilize Indian politics.[33] At the end of the Constitution-making process, the "minority" faiths were not entirely appeased even though cultural and linguistic demands of the "Urdu"-speaking people and others, as well as the autonomy of the Christian schools, were duly protected as enforceable cultural and educational rights. Special areas—including Kashmir—were demarcated for special treatment.[34] What emerged from these constitutional endeavors was an accommodating secular compromise at a time when—in the aftermath of partition—such a compromise seemed improbable. Today, even the possibility of such compromises evolving is doubtful. Contemporary India has not been able satisfactorily to quell disputes over a medieval mosque which was ignominiously destroyed in 1992.[35] If India were to start a new Constitution-making process afresh today, it is doubtful that a common text would emerge.

The Constitution makers had done well. It would be a tremendous disservice to their efforts to point to their compromise solutions without acknowledging the overall secular design of the Constitution which can be summarized as articulating three salient principles:

First and foremost is the principle of "religious freedom," which expansively covers not just the right to religious thought and belief, but every aspect of the faith, including its beliefs and rituals, and also freedom from discrimination on grounds, *inter alia*, of religion, race, caste, place of birth, or gender.[36]

The second secular principle of "celebratory neutrality" and the depoliticization of religion underlying the Constitution was devised to create a participatory secular state which would neutrally assist and celebrate all faiths and generally not discriminate amongst them. Accordingly, there was nothing to prevent the state from giving financial and other assistance to all faiths, but no person could be compelled to pay taxes which were specifically appropriated "for the promotion or maintenance of any particular religion or religious denomination." Such assistance could also be given to religious denominational schools who, in turn, could not then compel anyone to partake in religious instruction or refuse to admit persons not of that denomination.[37]

The third salient feature of India's secular state was social welfare and reform, with an accent on a "regulatory and reformative justice." The Constitution was self-professedly regulatory and reformative in nature. Apart from the usual statements that religious freedom could be curtailed on grounds of "public order, health and morality" and that the "economic, financial, political or other secular activity" of a religion could be regulated, there was a strong specific and general reformatory element. The Constitution specifically permitted the state to provide for "social welfare and reform" and, more specifically, abolished untouchability. It threw open all Hindu, Jaina, and Sikh temples for all castes and sections of that community, prohibited discrimination by the state and those financially assisted by, or linked to, the state on grounds of religion, and generally pointed in a reformatory direction in matters of gender justice, the uniform civil code, and cow slaughter, by placing these and other issues in the Directive Principles of State Policy.[38]

What do we make of these three principles underlying the secularism of the Indian Constitution? Are they not contradictory? Is not the "third" principle (which espouses the regulation and reform of religion) contrary to the "first" principle of religious freedom? And, if the "third" principle unfurls its agenda of regulation and reform, will this agenda not run foul of the "second" principle of celebratory neutrality toward all faiths? If all faiths are to be celebrated, which parts within these faiths are to be undermined to enable regulation and reform? Jumbled up as opposing and contradictory, these questions can never yield satisfactory answers. The initial pride of place must be given to the "first" principle so as to maximize genuine claims to religious freedom, ensure equality of all faiths, and increase and expand toleration of plural diversity. But this "first" principle does not stand on its own to the exclusion of all else. It has never been the case anywhere that religious freedom should be unlimited in its scope and design. The usual limit below which no faith can go is the time-honored formula of "public order, health and morality." The contours of such a formula are—in our times—usually eventually determined by judges. However, in the Indian context, the Constitution makers specifically empowered the state to generally ordain or assist in the reform of many unjust religiously sanctioned social practices, customs, and laws. This is the essence of the regulation and reform-oriented "third" principle, which was intended to be much more cautious in its emphasis as it was wide in its empowerment. The "third" principle did not represent some demoniac deification of modernity which would eclipse all religions into obsolescence.[39] Both state and society were enjoined to develop a consensus for social change. The "third" principle of secularism was certainly not devised to arm political Hindu fundamentalists to chastise Muslims for not making their law "gender just," or vice versa. It was expected that a sense of fraternity would animate the interpretation of the "third" principle and guide its implementation.

India's Constitution was an elegant response to its sensitive and somewhat unparalleled post-colonial solution. The guarantee of religious freedom was broad, but included an invitation to evolve a consensus for reform, while placing the Indian state in a positively neutral, benign position to provide support for and celebrate all faiths.

IV

Although it is fashionable to criticize Prime Minister Nehru for the many ills that plague us today, in 1950 there were few doubts that the way forward was to transform Indian society through planned development. The goals of this projected change were technological transformation, modernization, economic growth, and poverty alleviation through a powerful state machinery to liberate people from the bondage of their past and fulfill their future "tryst with destiny."[40] Nehru was not really saying anything new. This was happening all over the world. Modernity was held up as the Holy Grail, indicting Indians and others for lagging behind.[41] "Salvation" was alleged to lie in instrumenting change through a powerful model of "law and development." New laws would replace old traditions. New bureaucracies would create plans. The people for whom such plans were to be made were expected to do their bit and change their lifestyles, social practices, and attitudes. This is not the place to enter into controversies over the naive instrumentalism[42] of this approach or its crippling effect of forcing Indians to look down upon themselves. All this was avidly accepted by India's "Western"-educated middle class who thought they had an edge over others because they were already halfway there. Neither Nehru nor anyone else thought that these prescriptions meant—or could ever mean—that India would give up its colorful diversity. But there was a fear that casteism, communalism, and traditional linguistic and other identities could tear India apart. The pain of partition was too fresh to elude memory.[43] No less, the new Republic of India had brought people from various provinces and princely states together into a single political entity after a very long time—if not for the first time. Consequently, a broad and strongly reformist and vastly overwritten Indian secularism may have been brought into play to declare "war" on all or any forms of divisiveness.

The reality was more forbidding than the posture. Although Nehru made strong Cassandra-like warnings about the fissiparous tendencies that plagued India's future, his discourse on "change" was democratic —seeking to move toward reform through consensus. Nehru's government first tackled those areas of reform directly ordained by the Constitution (e.g., the abolition of untouchability) and then moved on to the wider goal of creating a more integrated and modern society. When a demand was made to create the state of Andhra Pradesh on a linguistic basis, Nehru strongly opposed it—ostensibly because it would lead to the balkanization of India, but no less because it concerned the Nizam's dominions in Hyderabad where a strong communist movement was gaining ground. Yet, Nehru succumbed to this demand eventually, realizing that a claim of linguistic diversity strengthened rather than weakened the polity.[44] When the Hindu Code Bill ripened for its final rites of passage through Parliament, Nehru's government encountered strong resistance and backed off to enact an incomplete codification of Hindu law in which the property relations of the joint family were left relatively untouched.[45] Although various Congress state governments of Nehru's era set about to control religious endowments, this was done with a lightness of touch. The social reform legislation of the period used criminal law techniques and penal measures to exact social change. It had too many design faults to be wholly effective.[46] Nehru's regime extolled diversity but was fearful of too much of it. Its policies had inadvertently adopted, willy nilly, a strong and seemingly uncompromising reformist posture which was later misunderstood, attacked, and ridiculed as pseudo-secularist.

Nehru's approach to secularism was a political response to confront India's contemporary challenges. Proud of India's diversity, which he portrayed in his *Discovery of India* and *Glimpses of World History,* Nehru had not even imagined that this plural richness would be put at risk by his more general project to modernize India.[47] India was both colorfully diverse as well as modern. Any concept of secularism had to be built around this vision. It was for the courts to develop a juridical concept of secularism and define its content.

The Supreme Court was already at loggerheads with Nehru's government over political censorship and land reform.[48] At first, it also appeared to be resistant to some of the other initiatives of the government of the day. In 1951, it refused to allow a distribution of seats along caste lines to masquerade as affirmative action.[49] In 1954, in the *Srirur Math* and connected cases, justice B. K. Mukerjea, an expert on the law relating to Hindu religious endowments, tried to give the widest possible meaning to freedom of religion to protect all the essential practices of a faith, striking down insensitively intrusive regulatory provisions.[50] But this "essential practices" test was double-edged. It was left to the court to decide what an "essential practice" was and who could claim to be its custodian. After some sensitive decisions, including upholding a religion's power to excommunicate its adherents,[51] many questionable decisions emerged from the Court. In this, a leading role was played by Justice Gajendragadkar, who was determined to extend the regulatory control of the state over religious endowments and practices. Without abandoning the "essential practices" test, the courts—especially the Supreme Court—deprived the Khadims of the Durgah Committee of Ajmer of many of their traditional rights,[52] refused to accept the rights of those traditionally linked with the Nathdwara temple in Rajasthan,[53] threw open both temples and mosques for worship, told the Swaminarayans that they were, in fact, Hindus even as they protested they were not,[54] permitted the exclusion of non-Gowda Saraswat brahmins from certain ceremonies of a public temple,[55] proclaimed that the Jains had lost their right to manage a temple which had been taken over by the Raja of Udaipur and enabled its statutory takeover,[56] made the role and functions of the traditional *archakas* of a temple purely secular in nature,[57] informed the Muslims that, on the basis of the Court's reading of the texts and the advice of a Hindu pandit, "cow sacrifice" was not an essential practice of the Muslim faith,[58] pronounced that the "tandava" dance was not a significant part of the faith of the Anand Margis,[59] found that the practice of *pinda* and *shraddha* were integral to the Hindu faith,[60] and stated that praying in a mosque was not crucial to the Muslim faith because they could pray anywhere, "even in the open."[61] A similar pattern followed in the Court decisions on state control of schools and colleges run by religious denominations.[62] Slowly but surely, such institutions have been brought under a rigorous state and statutory control. At times, the Court has been called upon to defuse difficult situations such as those concerning the shifting of Muslim graves,[63] cow slaughter,[64] the right to proselytize for a faith, or to resolve the aftermath of the destruction of the Babri Masjid in 1992.[65] Some of its solutions—including the reasoning underlying them—have been questionable, insensitive in their formulation, and excessive in permitting more regulation of religious institutions and practices than should be expected in a secular society which guarantees religious freedom.

State control of Hindu religious endowments can be traced back to a British formula of 1863 by which the custodians of these endowments were declared to be "trustees," and the state had the limited rectificatory "default power" to issue instructions, or temporarily take over, where there was mismanagement of the institutions and embezzlement of funds.[66] However, since 1950, there has been an increasing tendency in India to take over important temples and run them through bureaucrats and statutory boards, while including some of the adherents of the denomination in the management of the endowment. The most widely publicized among them was Governor Jagmohan's takeover of the temple at Vaishno Devi in Kashmir.[67] The "Jagmohan" model—if it can be called that—is defended on the basis of a belief that the state manages such institutions much better than those who have traditionally managed them. On this basis, the famous Vishwanath Temple at Varanasi has also been placed under the control of a board. In a series of recent judgments,[68] the Supreme Court has not just condoned such takeovers, but defended them as being consistent with the true interpretation of Hinduism. What is happening is not the temporary intervention of regulatory control by the state. Religious endowments are being nationalized on an extensive scale. The affairs of the Sikh community were placed within a statutory framework in 1925, with awkward results.[69] Several statutes of various states have brought many religious and charitable trusts and societies under state ownership and strict bureaucratic control.[70] The concept of state-run religious institutions sits uneasily with either the idea of religious freedom or the concept of a positive and supportive secular state. The strength and continuity of religious faiths rests on such faiths creating viable institutions which keep the faith alive and responsive to pressures, demands, and challenges from both within and without the faith. No doubt, crooks, thieves, and layabouts have lumpenized many religious institutions; however, it is not for the state to take over institutions, but for the communities to find the appropriate answers.

But if the regulation of religious institutions has been one part of the state program, reform has been the other. One important area of reform has been the issue of the uniform civil code.[71] Many of the religious personal laws of various communities are unjust and discriminatory—especially to women. What is to be done about them? Involved here are delicate issues of marriage, divorce, children, guardianship, adoption, succession, and the multiple ownership of many forms of property. One possible solution is to codify all personal laws and merge them under a uniform civil code. A small step in this direction was to provide a "secular" law of marriage, divorce, guardianship, and succession which could be opted for by adherents of any or every faith.[72] This preliminary optional solution is not enough. Society and its pressures take over. The social status quo remains. The second alternative is the "Fundamental Rights" (or the Article 13) solution. If we accept that "personal laws" are laws (under Article 13 of the Constitution), they have to be subjected to rigorous scrutiny under the Fundamental Rights chapter. Thus, if personal laws are discriminatory to women, they would have to be tested against the doctrine of equality, and then struck down if found to be discriminatory or unreasonable. But this "Fundamental Rights" (or the Article 13) solution is pre-eminently a court-oriented solution, leaving it to the judges to determine what is fair and what is unfair and should be eliminated from the personal laws. Unfortunately, the judges have lost courage and backed away from this "Fundamental Rights" (or Article 13) solution. Finding technical refuge in the impossible distinction that "personal laws" were not like other "customary laws" and therefore outside the ambit of the Fundamental Rights chapter,[73] the courts shied away from being lumbered with the responsibility of making personal laws fair, just, and non-discriminatory. This takes us to the third or "statutory" solution, which seeks to reform all or any of the personal laws by enacting legislation to that effect. Few religions like to be told that they need to be reformed—still fewer by outsiders. Perhaps that is why the goal of "personal law" reform was more neutrally described in Article 44 of the Constitution in terms of achieving a "uniform civil code" (UCC). But reference to the "uniform civil code" complicates rather than clarifies the issue. It grows out of a nineteenth-century dream to codify all laws in the manner of the later Justinian of Roman law or of the Napoleonic Code. But codification may simply be consolidatory rather than reformative. A reformative uniform civil code of personal laws does not just require all personal laws to be stated in the form of a statute, but seeks radically to transform—and not just rewrite—them. Such a goal sets up a competition among personal laws, with the state asking: "Which is the fairest of them all?" Nor is the task of finding a common denominator from all of them any easier. The British Raj made an elaborate codification of all but the personal laws. After some evangelical attempts to reform some practices such as *sati, thugee,* infanticide, and child marriage, the British administration backed off—acceding to native Indian requests to change the Muslim law relating to *waqfs* or the Hindu law on the Gains of Learning to correct unacceptable decisions of the Privy Council.[74] It was under pressure from Muslims that the government enabled the *Shari'at* to displace the application of customary laws in certain areas in 1937,[75] even though support was not forthcoming for the legislation which made "dissolution of marriages" possible under circumstances outside the *Shari'at.*[76] Under the British regime, tentative steps were taken to initiate the enactment of a reformist Hindu Code. After independence, the legislation to create a Hindu Code was confronted by political controversy. Eventually a truncated "code" was enacted, amidst opposition, in 1955–56; this dealt with the laws related to marriage, adoption and maintenance, guardianship, and succession.[77] But the law relating to the joint family remained intact. So India today portrays the position that a woman can be prime minister of India but not the head of a Hindu joint family!

If the "uniform civil code" was once a serious constitutional objective, it has now been trivialized into becoming a tragic farce. Politics has taken over. Hindu politicians, who are not really concerned about personal law reform, use the idea of the uniform civil code to chastise Muslims for not emulating the Hindu example. The accusation concentrates on "sexual" matters, and in particular the right of the Muslim male to have four wives and divorce them at will. That Muslim jurisprudence is a lot more delicate in its response to such issues is overlooked. The cause celebre came when the Supreme Court subjected Muslim spouses to the "secular" law of maintenance in the Code of Criminal Procedure,[78] and Rajiv Gandhi's Congress government promptly responded with a separate legislation exclusively for Muslims.[79] This initiative was seen as preferential treatment for Muslims and inimical to secularism. Matters became more highly charged than necessary. In the end, the solution was awkward, but not entirely unsatisfactory. The issue of the "uniform civil code" will remain with us for a long time. The political arm of the state is as paralyzed as the powers that control it. The judiciary refuses to be drawn into finding a solution. It is for the various communities to devise appropriate reforms for their adherents under non-contentious conditions. When they are persuaded to do so, they will no doubt be aware that they are free to draw inspiration from their own inventive and rich traditions as well as those of others. But politics has perversely blocked and obviated such a simple solution. As long as the issue of the "uniform civil code" remains a Hindu weapon to beat the Muslim and other communities into embarrassment, no further progress can take place.

Over the last twenty years of this century, India's politics has been intensely communalized along religious lines. This is an offshoot of the general "lumpenization" of all aspects of India's politics and social life generally, whereby, according to the official Vohra Report, governance has been taken over by hoodlums—no less disguised as politicians than as anyone else.[80] It is these lumpen elements in various social groups and political parties who have whipped up Hindu sentiment as political emotion. Once in power, governments elected on such platforms have been as inept and corrupt as any other. But a politically nurtured communalism has gained ground as a tactic—exploiting every possible event as an issue to excite and exact support. The story of the Babri Masjid, alleged to have been built on Lord Rama's birthplace, is only one such story which resulted in the four-century-old Masjid being razed to the ground in 1992, with the connivance of the BJP in power in the state of Uttar Pradesh and the Congress in power at Delhi. Even after the Masjid was destroyed, Prime Minister Narasimha Rao established a pro-Hindu status quo which was unfortunately validated and blessed by a split decision of the Supreme Court.[81] While the Supreme Court has made brave declarations on secularism and validated the imposition of emergency rule on BJP state governments after the chaos that followed in those states following the destruction of the Masjid,[82] it has been skillful, but irritatingly vague, in its non-elucidation of the meaning of secularism.[83] Meanwhile, in 1998–99, attacks were made on Christians in Gujarat, Orissa, Maharashtra, and other states.[84] While commissions and committees have been appointed to investigate the problem, most governments and political parties have been slow to defend the minorities for fear of electoral repercussions.[85] No state can be neutral or aloof in these circumstances. To do so is itself violative of the most elementary principles of tolerance in a civilized society. Populism of this nature which feeds on religious mal-sentiment gets caught in its own frenzy to excite awkward situations into brinkmanship and violence.

V

"Secularism" has been declared part of the basic structure of the Indian Constitution and was inserted along with socialism into the preamble of the Constitution during the emergency in 1976.[86] But what does it mean? We must return—as inevitably as we started—to the various debates on Indian secularism. Some doubt whether it exists. Others proclaim that it is no more than a spurious invitation to an over-rationalized modernity.[87] Others ask: "What is wrong with this kind of modernity?"[88] After all, the resistance to modernity is itself born out of the discourse on modernity. It has been argued that Indian secularism clumsily rests on an imperial concept of communities which is outmoded, subversive, and irrelevant.[89] Conversely, a plea had been made to retain a framework of communities[90] between, among, and around those for whom an egalitarian justice must be created. Indian secularism has been found wanting as not effecting a proper separation of state from church when compared with its American counterparts.[91] If some governments and political parties have been criticized for not protecting innocent religious communities, others have been assailed for being over-partisan in extending help to disempowered minorities for political reasons. The discussions on secularism continue—more often than not as unsavory exchanges rather than in the spirit of democratic dialogue.

Yet, more than simply a word which invites esoteric academic discourse, secularism is an important aspect of the discourse on power on states and society in India. To begin with, it has a special significance as a response to the problems of post-colonial India. The makers of India's Constitution did not intend secularism to be seen as a modernizing whirlwind—sweeping away all "irrational" beliefs and practices that lay in its path. Nor did they intend to create a state which stood wholly aloof from the rich cultural diversity of India. Molded as a positive and participatory entity, India's secular state was designed to celebrate all faiths and also enjoined to eliminate some especially invidious practices sanctioned by the religions in question. The larger questions of social reform had been left open to be worked out as they emerged. The carnage that followed partition, when social fervor was diverted to communal savagery, is a reminder of what has happened, and can happen. We live in no less unsettled times. New conservative political pressures have tried to cash in on and exploit raw communal nerves for political, social, and economic advancement. The BJP's White Paper on Ayodhya[92] declared that some kind of historical revenge was due to Muslims. And if such a stance is taken, can the Buddhists complain about Hinduism? What form will such a revenge take? Will it be the destruction of "Muslim" monuments? Will Muslims, along with many other communities in India, remain second-class citizens within a Hindu India? Or will India be partitioned again along politically communalized religious lines? Where will all this end? Abjuring such derisive and vicious alternatives, the Indian answer seems to lie within a yet-to-be-fully-explored concept of "secularism" which goes beyond tolerance to guarantee equality and freedom of religion, and to deny the appropriation of state and society by any one particular faith. This is only a framework that requires many inconsistencies and contradictions to be worked out.

India's quest for the basis of a viable secularism, however, cannot just be located in the tawdry politics of our time. Not just a nation-state, the subcontinent of India houses a complex civilization, with a dazzling array of cultures and traditions. It is a kind that does not exist anywhere else in the world. Like Europe, it has many languages. Like the rest of the world, it houses many faiths and traditions. Yet it eludes description precisely because it is large and contains multitudes. How does one script a Constitution for a civilization? Or devise principles of governance for a singularly unique and varied people? It is like devising a Constitution for the world. The concept of secularism as it is evolving in India is not just an answer to the problems created by an imperial legacy, but is a more global response to the predicament of a veritable civilization which eludes self-definition. The three ingredients of India's secularism—religious freedom, celebratory neutrality, and reformatory justice—have a universal significance. If there be a Xanadu, the road to Xanadu must surely lead to peace and justice, of which secularism is a part. In a shrinking world, all societies have to strive to be secular, but some societies, like ours, have to be more secular than others. And, in a sense, they lead the way for the rest.

Notes

1. In this essay, I am not really concerned with the creation of new "syncretic" faiths which are abstracted from the existing one; see C. Stewart and R. Shaw, eds., *Syncretism, Anti Syncretism* (London, 1994). India is replete with genuine examples of such abstractions. Akbar's attempts to create a new faith (*Din-i-ilahi*) is a political—as opposed to a social—example of the attempt to create such a syncretic faith. But syncretic faiths are not

born just out of a conscious desire to "sink" differences; they also emerge as practices of various faiths merge with each other.

2. The phrase "Janus faced" is taken from D. Washbrook, "Law, State and Agrarian Society in Colonial India," *Modern Asian Studies 7* (1981). But I am suggesting that such a "double"-faced system of laws does not just exist in colonial societies, but all societies where a "law" or legal system seeks to simultaneously speak for its political masters in the language of justice. This contradiction creates "indeterminacy" in the law and leaves open the possibility that the "rule of law" will become what E. P. Thompson (in *Whigs and Hunters* [London, 1975]) calls a "mixed blessing" and the possible situs of struggle.

3. I take this expanded view of law from B. Malinowski's *Crime and Custom in a Savage Society* (London, 1959), pp. 55, 67–68. India's *dharmashastra* is very much a "social law" supported and enforced by a range of social mechanisms.

4. On the *dharmashastra* see generally R. Lingat, *The Classical Law of India* (Berkeley, 1973), pp. 176–206, on custom and the changing nature of law; on custom in the *dharmashastra* see also P. V. Kane, *History of the Dharmashastra* (Poona, 1941), vol. III, pp. 825–55; on the doctrine of *factum valet* see J. D. M. Derrett, "Factum Valet: Adventures of a Maxim," *International and Comparative Law Quarterly* 7 (1958): 280–302. On the development and sources of Muslim law see J. Schacht, *An Introduction to Islamic Law* (Oxford, 1964); *Mulla's Principles of Mahomeddan Law* (Bombay, 1994), pp. 22–24.

5. Some may—as we shall see—demur that religious freedom cannot co-exist with a reforming modernism (column F). Nor, arguably, should the state distort faiths by positively supporting all faiths (column E). By the same logic the most secular state may not be celebratory in nature (row 6). I have indicated my sense of the range and deliberately placed column F on a differently angled trajectory.

6. Grants have played a great role in the development of all faiths throughout the world. In a secular state, grants would have to be given evenhandedly to all. This could become a difficult exercise. Since 1950, Indian dispensations in this regard have been sporadic rather than systematic. Note the converse situation of religious institutions being asked to pay for their upkeep by the state or to charge pilgrims a "fee" (see Ram Chandra v. West Bengal, AIR 1966 Cal. 164; Modi Das v. Sahi, AIR 1959 SC 942) on the basis that such a levy is for a secular activity.

7. The concept of "neutrality" stems from the non-"establishment" clause in the United States Constitution. See generally L. Tribe, *The Constitutional Protection of Individual Rights* (New York, 1976), pp. 812–885; G. R. Stone, Louis M. Seidman, Cass R. Sunstein, and M. Tushnet, *Constitutional Law* (New York, 1996), pp. 1531–1626.

8. Grants have been given for the restoration of religious monuments which

suffered riot damage (see K. Raghunath v. Kerala, AIR 1974 Ker. 48). But even outside the exigencies of riots, restorative or renovative grants have been made to temples, such as Lord Jaganatha's temple in Orissa (see Bira Kishore Deb v. Orissa, AIR 1975 Orissa 8).

9. Suresh Chandra v. Union of India, AIR 1975 Delhi 162.

10. Ramesh Yeshwant Prabhu v. Prabhakar, (1996) 1 SCC 130.

11. For interesting examples which tax British ingenuity see S. H. Bailey, D. J. Harris, and B. L. Jones, *Civil Liberties: Cases and Materials* (London, 1995), pp. 578–612.

12. See Gary J. Jacobson, "Three Modern Examples of Secular Constitutional Development: India, Israel and the United States," *Studies in American Political Development* 10 (1996): 1–58.

13. Samuel P. Huntington, *The Clash of Civilizations and the Remaking of the World Order* (New York, 1996).

14. On the "modernization" of the Indian legal and administrative system and its displacement of the traditional system see M. Galanter, *Law and Society in Modern India* (Oxford, 1989), pp. 15–53, 92–100. By this process the personal law was transformed to suit "modern" "imperial" needs (on which see R. Dhavan, "Dharmasastra and Modern Indian Society: A Preliminary Exploration," *Journal of the Indian Law Institute* 34 [1992]: 515–540).

15. Cf. James G. Carrier, ed., *Occidentalism: Images of the West* (Oxford, 1995).

16. For a glimpse of the Benthamite influence see Eric Stokes, *The English Utilitarians in India* (Oxford, 1957).

17. On the origins and use of this formula in India, see J. D. M. Derrett, "Justice, Equity and Good Conscience in India," *Bom L.R.* 64 (Journal) (1962) 129 and 145.

18. See Whitely Stokes, *The Anglo India Codes*, vol. 1: *Substantive Law;* vol. 2: *Procedural Law* (Oxford, 1887).

19. Once again, the "rule of law" came into play to project a "neutral" image of colonial aims. Under the aegis of keeping the peace, a powerful system to control public order and impose censorship was built up—especially to deal with religious tension and to put down dissent (see R. Dhavan, *Only the Good News: On the Law of Censorship in India* [Delhi, 1987], pp. 25–91, 274–339). On British attempts at social reform through law and Indian reactions see C. H. Heimsath, *Indian Nationalism and Hindu Social Reform* (Princeton, 1964).

20. For the constitutional background see B. Shiva Rao, *The Framing of India's Constitution: A Study* (Delhi, 1968), pp. 459–472.

21. Indeed, it has been powerfully argued by Benedict Anderson (in *Imagined Communities* [London, 1991]) that "nationalism"—as we know it—is a modern phenomenon, using modern methods to create "imagined" communities by drawing inspiration from the past. *A fortiori,* "communal"

identities flow from similar efforts (see G. Pandey, *The Construction of Communalism in Colonial North India* [Delhi, 1990]). Both Muslim and Hindu identities came to discover and use "nationalism" for self-definition (see C. Jaffrelot, *The Hindu Nationalist Movement in India* [New York, 1996]; Mushirul Hasan, ed., *Islam: Communities and the Nation—Muslim Identities in South Asia and Beyond* [Delhi, 1998]; and more generally the many views in G. D. Sontheimer and H. Kulke, eds., *Hinduism Reconsidered* [Delhi, 1987]). This is not to detract from the wider argument that "nationalist" thinking is inextricably linked to colonial discourse (see P. Chatterjee, *Nationalist Thought and the Colonial World* [London, 1986]).

22. *Indian Statutory Commission* (known as the Simon Commission) (1930) Cmd. 3568; Vol. 1, pr. 147, p. 137.

23. This controversy was awakened with fervor with Ayesha Jalal's *The Sole Spokesman, Jinnah: The Muslim League and the "Demand for Pakistan"* (Cambridge, 1985). This thesis finds support from a distinguished Indian jurist (see H. M. Seervai, *Partition of India: Legend and Reality* [Bombay, 1989]). What principle of "causation" do we use to analyze these events? The best that can be said is that Nehru did not create the situation that led to partition, but may have blundered in his tactical diplomacy.

24. See B. Shiva Rao (supra n. 20), particularly Chapter 25 at pp. 741–780 (on minorities). Indeed, many matters shuffled back and forth from the "Fundamental Rights" Committee to the "Minorities" Committee, and vice versa (infra n. 26).

25. Comment of N. Ahmed: (1949) XI Constitutional Assembly Debates 973 (25 Nov)—see generally R. Dhavan, *The Constitutional Assembly and Human Rights* (forthcoming).

26. See B. Shiva Rao (supra n. 20), pp. 107–118 (on how the Constituent Assembly worked) and pp. 257–281 (on the discussion on religious and minority rights in the Assembly). More generally, on the practice exploited out of the constitutional text, see R. Dhavan, "Religious Freedom in India," *American Journal of Comparative Law* 25 (1987): 209–254.

27. See Constitution of India, Article 25 (2), Explanation I and II.

28. Yagnapurushdasji v. Muldas AIR 1966 SC 1119; and note the comments of M. Galanter, *Law and Society in Modern India*, Delhi, 1989, pp. 237–258; J. D. M. Derrett, "The Definition of a Hindu," 2 *Supreme Court Journal* (1966) 67.

29. See Constitution of India, Article 48 (on animal husbandry and cow slaughter). The status of the Directive Principles of State Policy is that they are unenforceable in a court of law but fundamental to the governance of the nation (see Article 37 of the Constitution). In the fifties, the court merely used the Directive Principles as an aid to interpretation. After the Fundamental Rights case [Kesavananda v. State of Kerala, (1973) 4 SCC 225], their presence has been greatly emphasized to include some of them as part of the enforceable right to "life and liberty" of the Constitution.

324

By this route, the Directive Principle on "universal education" until the age of fourteen years has been rendered enforceable. However, the controversial Directive Principles dealing with cow slaughter (Article 46) or the uniform civil code (Article 44) have been less emphatically stressed for judicial implementation.

30. Constitution of India, Article 44.

31. See Constitution of India, Article 325 (on the general electoral roll) and Articles 330–334 (on reserved seats for Scheduled Castes, Scheduled Tribes, and Anglo-Indians—initially for ten years, but decennially extended until the year 2000).

32. See Constitution of India, Articles 15 (3), (4); 16 (3), (4), (4A); 335.

33. A great controversy started in 1990 over reservations for jobs and posts in the central government. This affirmative action was resisted by the privileged who held the posts. Riots ensued, resulting in the fall of Prime Minister V. P. Singh's government and the famous Mandal case [Indra Sawhney v. Union of India, (1992) Supp. 3 SCC 217]—see further R. Dhavan, "The Supreme Court as Problem Solver: The Mandal Controversy," in V. P. Panandiker, *The Policies of Backwardness* (Delhi, 1997), pp. 262–332. Attention is drawn to other articles in the book as well.

34. See Constitution of India, Articles 370 (on Kashmir), 371 (on Gujarat and Maharashtra), 371A (on Nagaland), 371B (on Assam), 371C (on Manipur), 371F (on Sikkim), 371G (on Mizoram), 371H (on Arunachal Pradesh), 371I (on Goa). Indian federalism has thus yielded to regional considerations and India's plural diversity.

35. Neither the courts (see M. Ishmail Faruqui v. Union, infra n. 61) nor legislation [see the Religious Institutions (Prevention of Misuse) Act 1988, which generally prohibited politicizing religions, and the Places of Worship (Special Provisions) Act 1991, which tried to defuse the Babri Masjid and other temple controversies] has had even a symbolic effect. In the future, it may not be possible to even pass legislation of this nature.

36. See Constitution of India, Articles 14 (equality), 15 (2), (3), 16 (2) (non-discrimination), 17 (abolition of untouchability), Articles 25–26 (religious freedom, subject to limitations), Article 29–30 (right to language and culture).

37. The fact that the state may have to be involved in religious matters is foreshadowed in Article 16(5) of the Constitution. Neutrality is maintained to assure non-discrimination where the state gives a grant to an educational institution [Articles 28 and 29 (2)]. The clause dealing with non-taxation for specific religious purposes (Article 27) does not prohibit grants by the state to religious institutions and causes.

38. More specific to religious freedom and secularism, the reformist element can be seen in the Constitution of India, Articles 14 (equality); 15 (1), (3), 16 (2) (gender equality); 15 (2), 25 (2) (non-discrimination in public places); 17 (abolition of untouchability); 25 (1), 26 (regulatory control of

religious affairs); 25 (2) (general and specific empowerment for reform); 44 (uniform civil code); 45 (compulsory education for all women including presumably "the girl child"); 48 (animal husbandry and cow slaughter); 15 (4), 16 (4) (affirmative action); 330–342 (special provisions for certain communities).

39. There has been a tendency in recent discussions on secularism (as, for example, by Ashis Nandy and T. N. Madan, infra n. 87) to lay a far greater emphasis on the reformist modernity of the secular dispensation of the Constitution than is warranted. Such a construction reinforces a fundamentalist approach.

40. Taken from Nehru's famous speech on the night of 14 August 1947 when India got independence.

41. Foreign scholars seem to have tried to assuage Indian sentiments by paying tribute to the modern inventiveness of Indian "tradition" (see L. Rudolph and S. Rudolph, *The Modernity of Tradition: Political Development in India* [Chicago, 1967]). E. Said's *Orientalism* (New York, 1979) is surely right in drawing attention to the emotional and intellectual effect of people being disparagingly portrayed as inferior orientals.

42. For a summary of the literature on the "instrumental" dimensions of law and development and how the standard American export models of law and development came to be abandoned, see R. Dhavan, "Law as Concern: Reflecting on Law and Development," in Y. Vyas, *Law and Development in the Third World* (Nairobi, 1994), pp. 25–50.

43. The fear of India not being able to hold together may, in hindsight, seem exaggerated, but was a genuine fear at the time. We have just to turn to contemporary accounts of partition to range its impact; for an example see Mushirul Hasan, *India Partitioned: The Other Face of Freedom* (Delhi, 1995).

44. See S. K. Agarwala, "Jawahar Lal Nehru and the Language Problem," in R. Dhavan, ed., *Nehru and the Constitution* (Delhi, 1992), pp. 134–60.

45. For an account of Hindu codification see Archana Parashar, *Women and Family Law Reform in India* (Delhi, 1992), pp. 134–60.

46. See R. Dhavan, "Kill Them for Their Bad Verses: Criminality, Punishment and Punishing Social Crimes in India," in R. Shankardass, ed., *Punishment in India* (Delhi, 1999).

47. I have taken a much more charitable view of Nehru's secularism in my long "Introduction" to R. Dhavan, ed., *Nehru and the Constitution* (Delhi, 1992). Even if Nehru's *Glimpses of World History* (Oxford, 1981) and *Discovery of India* (Oxford, 1981) appear to be greatly overwritten, Nehru was genuinely committed to celebrating India's diversity.

48. See State of Bihar v. Kameshwar Singh, AIR 1952 SC 252; and more generally H. C. L. Merrillat, *Land and the Constitution* (Bombay, 1970) (on land reform); and Romesh Thapar v. Madras, AIR 1950 SC 124; and Brij Bhushan v. Delhi, AIR 1980 SC 129 (on the early censorship cases). Both

these cases gave rise to constitutional amendments to reverse the Supreme Court's decisions.

49. Madras v. Champakam Doraijan, AIR 1951 SC 226; Venkaratarmana v. State of Madras, AIR 1951 SC 229. Later the court was concerned about "caste" being the basis of affirmative action (see the eclectic decision in Balaji v. Mysore, AIR 1963 SC 1649; Chitralekha v. Mysore, AIR 1964 SC 1823), but realized in the Mandal case (supra n. 33) that caste could not be ignored in any determination of the beneficiaries of affirmative action schemes in India.

50. Commissioner HRE v. Sri Lakshmindra, (1954) SCR 1005; Mahant Sri Jagannath v. Orissa, (1954) SCR 1046; Ratilal v. Bombay, (1954) SCR 1055. Justice B. K. Mukedee's Tagore Law lectures were on the *Hindu Law of Religious and Charitable Endowments* (Calcutta, 1952).

51. Saifuddin Saheb v. Bombay, AIR 1962 SC 853; and note the comments of J. D. M. Derrett, *International and Comparative Law Quarterly* 12 (1963): 693.

52. Durgah Committee Ajmer v. Syed Hussain, AIR 1961 SC 1402.

53. Tilkayat Shri Govindlalji Maharaj v. State of Rajasthan, AIR 1963 SC 1638.

54. This arises out of the provisions of Article 25 (2) of the Constitution. It was in this context that the Swaminarayans protested they were not "Hindus" (see the Yagnapurushdasji case supra n. 28); on the opening up of Muslim mosques see Sarwar Hussain v. Additional Civil Judge, AIR 1983 All. 251.

55. Venkararamanna v. Mysore, AIR 1958 SC 255.

56. Rajasthan v. Sulanmal, AIR 1975 SC 706, where the Court also went into pronouncing on tenets of Jainism.

57. E. R. J. Swami v. Tamil Nadu, AIR 1972 SC 1586.

58. Mohd. Hanif Qureshi v. Bihar, AIR 1958 SC 231, A.H. Qureshi v. Bihar, AIR 1961 SC 448.

59. Jagdhishwaranand v. Police Commissioner, Calcutta, AIR 1984 SC 51. But note the courageous stance of the High Court in Commr. v. Jagdishwaranand, AIR 1991 Cal. 263, where Justice Ruma Pal took the view that the Supreme Court had not explored the issue adequately.

60. See R. M. K. Singh v. State, AIR 1976 Patna 198. *Quaere.* Are those who do not perform those essential rites not "Hindus" in the eyes of the law? Can the Court say—as it did in S.P. Mittal v. India, AIR 1983 SC 1—that followers of Sri Aurobindo do not adhere to a faith but only a philosophy?

61. M. Ishmail Faruqui v. Union of India, (1994) 6 SCC 360 (the Babri Masjid case); see further R. Dhavan, "The Ayodhya Judgement: Encoding Secularism in the Law," *Economic and Political Weekly* 29 (1994), pp. 3034–40.

62. Denominational schools have had to struggle to defend their constitutional viability. Note the leading judgments in Bombay v. Bombay Educational

Society, AIR 1954 SC 561; In Re Kerala Education Bill, AIR 1958 SC 956; St. Xaviers Colleges v. Gujarat, AIR 1974 SC 1389; St. Stephens College v. University of Delhi, AIR 1992 SC 1630. See generally R. Dhavan (supra n. 26) 231–245. The extent of protection and autonomy to be given to such schools is now before the Supreme Court of India.

63. Ghulam Abbas v. Uttar Pradesh, AIR 1983 SC 1268; Abdul Jalil v. Uttar Pradesh, AIR 1984 SC 882.

64. Supra n. 58.

65. On the right to proselytize for a faith see the controversial decision in Stanislaus v. State of Madhya Pradesh, AIR 1977 SC 908. For details of the Babri Masjid case see M. Ishmail Faruqui v. Union, supra n. 61.

66. For the background see R. Dhavan, "The Supreme Court and Hindu Religious Endowments: 1930–1975," *Journal of the Indian Law Institute* 20 (1978): 52–102, especially pp. 57–63.

67. On aspects of the Vaishno Devi case when it reached the Supreme Court see Bhumi Nath v. State of JK, (1997) 2 SCC 745.

68. Sri Adi Visheswarn of Kashi Nath v. Uttar Pradesh, 1997, 4 SCC 606 (on the takeover of the Vishwanath temple). For the other important recent cases which consolidate the state's regulatory control and takeovers of religious endowments, see also Sri Lakshmanna v. Andhra Pradesh (1996) 2 SCC 498; A.S. Narayana v. State of Andhra Pradesh (1996) 9 SCC 548, and by way of follow up at (1997) 5 SCC 376; Pannalal v. State of Andhra Pradesh (1996) 2 SCC 498; Shri Jagannath Puri Management Committee v. Chantamani Khuntia, (1997) 8 SCC 422.

69. The Sikh Gurdwara Act 1925 was designed by the British to keep the Sikhs apart. Instead, for decades the statutory framework proved to be a cementing force; see Rajiv Kapur, *Sikh Separatism: The Politics of Faith* (London, 1984).

70. The sweep of control is increasing—see for example the Andhra Pradesh Charitable and Hindu Religious Endowment Act 1996 (as amended) which virtually takes over crucial aspects relating to the working of all public charitable trusts.

71. The objective of a "uniform civil code" is to be found in Article 44 of the Constitution. For the background to this controversy see Archana Parashar, supra n. 45, pp. 201–263.

72. The "secular option" is provided by the Special Marriage Act 1954, the Indian Succession Act 1956, and the Guardianship and Wardship Act 1890, in addition to provisions like Section 125 of the Code of Criminal Procedure 1973 for providing maintenance to wives and children—on which see Shah Bano's case (infra n. 78). In some areas the personal law obviates the exercise of the secular option.

73. Ahmedabad Women's Action Group (AWAG) v. Union Government.

74. The Gains of Learning Act 1930 was passed when the Privy Council de-

clared in Gokul Chand v. Hukam Chand, (1921) 48 IA 162, that the salary of a civil servant belonged to the "joint family" which invested in his education. Likewise after the Privy Council ruled in Abul Fatah v. Rusumoy, (1994) 22 IA 76, that *waqfs* (trusts) which were ultimately dedicated to God were invalid in Muslim law, the Mussalman Waqf Validating Act 1913 was passed to reverse this decision.

75. See Muslim Personal (Shari'at Application) Act 1937.

76. See the Dissolution of Muslim Marriage Act 1939.

77. Thus, the truncated "Hindu" code consists of the Hindu Marriage Act 1955, the Hindu Succession Act 1956, the Hindu Adoption and Maintenance Act 1956, and the Hindu Minority and Guardianship Act 1956. For an interesting review of Hindu law immediately following this codification, see J. D. M. Derrett, *A Critique of Modern Hindu Law* (Bombay, 1970).

78. See Mohd. Ahmed Khan v. Shah Bano Begum, AIR 1985 SC 943.

79. Rajiv Gandhi's government successfully introduced the Muslim Women (Protection of Rights on Divorce) Act 1986 which grants maintenance rights for larger sums to divorced Muslim women from the husband and his family. The view that a summary procedure is not available under this Act is also, perhaps, incorrect [Noorjahan (1988) Cr.L.J. 2826 (Bom.)].

80. The Vohra Committee's report was an internal report on the extent of extra-constitutional control over Indian governance. For details, and on the litigation that followed, see Dinesh Trivedi v. Union of India, (1997) 4 SCC 306.

81. M. Ishmail Faruqui v. Union, (1994) supra n. 61.

82. S.R. Bommai (infra n. 83).

83. The Supreme Court's statements on secularism are collected in S. R. Bommai v. Union of India, (1994) 3 SCC 1; and M. Ismail Faruqui (the Babri Masjid case, supra n. 61). These statements are ambiguous, equivocal, and without any centrality and direction.

84. Christian communities have been mercilessly attacked in Gujarat, Maharashtra, and Orissa in 1998–99. The murder of Reverend Staines and an Australian priest led to the appointment of the Justice Wadhwa Commission to investigate the incident.

85. Do government commissions make a difference? In 1998, the eminently sensible report of the Srikrishna Commission on the Bombay riots was rejected. Justice Ranganatha Mishra's report on the riots of 1984, following Prime Minister Gandhi's assassination, was pro-Congress and pro-government. Various other reports including those on Mallegaon (1967), Ranchi-Hattia (1967–68), Gorakhpur (1967 and 1969), Ahmedabad (1969), Bhiwana (1970), and Jamshedpur (1979) have been ignored.

86. This was done during the emergency (1970–71) by the Constitution (Forty-Second Amendment) Act 1976. More generally on the spurious nature of this Amendment see R. Dhavan, *The Amendment: Conspiracy or Revolution?*

(Allahabad, 1976). The Indian debates on "secularism" are legion and range from India's deviation from the true "secularism" (infra n. 91) to attacks on its modernity (infra n. 87). If secularism is a site for plural diversity (see Rustom Bharucha, "The Shifting Sites of Secularism: Cultural Politics and Activism in India Today," *Economic and Political Weekly* [24 January 1998]: 167–80), it is also a vehicle for a strong reformism, if not a political ideology (infra n. 88). In this essay, I have projected secularism as an eminently sensible "consensual" basis for governance with justice.

87. See Ashis Nandy, "The Politics of Secularism and the Recovery of Religious Tolerance," in Veena Das, ed., *The Mirrors of Violence* (Delhi, 1990), pp. 69–93. T. N. Madan, "Secularism in Its Place," *Journal of Asian Studies* 46 (1987): 747–59.

88. Achin Vanaik, *Communalism Contested: Religion, Modernity and Secularism* (New Delhi, 1997). But Vanaik seeks both to gather the political faithful to fight for the new "political ideology of secularism" as well as advance the superior normative claims of this ideology. This is a plea to liberate people to move toward the "secular city" (see H. Cox, *The Secular City* [New York, 1990]).

89. For an interesting and insightful approach see Kumkum Sangari, "Politics of Diversity: Religious Communities and Multiple Patriarchies," *Economic and Political Weekly* 30 (1995) (23 and 30 December): 3287–3300; 3381–3389. Apart from this distinctive approach, there is a more general view that the "majority-minority" framework generates invidious politics, undermines equality between and amongst communities, and creates a vested interest in entrenched identity and a "communal" identity. Equally, identification with a community should not obviate the quest for a just order (see A. G. Noorani, "Muslim Identity: Self Image and Political Aspirations," in Mushirul Hasan, supra n. 21, pp. 121–138).

90. Approaching this question from another angle see Rajeev Bhargava, "Why Must We Retain the Majority-Minority Framework?" (*Economic and Political Weekly* 1997).

91. For this earlier approach which sought to compare "our" secularism with "theirs," see V. P. Luthera, *The Concept of the Secular State and India* (Oxford, 1964); D. E. Smith, *India as a Secular State* (Princeton, 1963).

92. See BJP's White Paper on Ayodhya (Delhi, 1993).

Some Continuing Issues

William D. Popkin

The essays in this volume about law and religion in India attest to the overwhelming challenges confronted by the Indian legal system as it tries to work out the proper balance between the secular and the religious. It could hardly be otherwise. Law is an integral part of any country's social and political fabric, anchored in both its realities and aspirations. In a country like India, where secular and religious realities and aspirations are so contested, the pitfalls and opportunities for law are numberless, and the continuing issues confronted by law are as varied as the country itself.

The assumption pervading this volume is that the major challenge for law and religion in India is to achieve a secular-religious balance that undermines some, but only some, traditional religious practices; and, further, that the goal to be achieved by this balance is the enhancement of individual dignity and human rights (e.g., eliminating caste barriers to advancement, protecting women, preserving religious liberty) without undermining religious identity—an oxymoronic task that only the law would attempt. Daunting as this seems, this assumption provides the appropriate starting point because it is built into the Indian Constitution. Balanced legal reform is part of the warp and woof of India's basic legal document, although the pattern that this reform should take is rigorously unclear. This is nowhere more apparent than in the conscious decision of the founders to place the goals of secular modernity associated with a uniform civil code in the Constitution's *non*mandatory Directive Principles (Art. 44). It is not surprising, therefore, that efforts to achieve a secular-religious balance sometimes seem more like a dangerous high-wire act than the systematic unfolding of social and political change through law.

The rise of a strong Hindu political movement has made this balancing act even more precarious by raising the possibility of a nonsecular conception of law. At the very least, the search for a uniform civil code looks different today than when uniformity was obvious shorthand for modern secular goals. The possibility that India will embrace nonsecularism will not detain us here, however, because that is still not the Indian constitutional vision. If nonsecularism carries the day, disputes about law will become the province of those who argue about religious detail, not those who struggle with the larger constitutional tensions produced by the clash of modernity and tradition. In these remarks, I assume (optimistically) that this latter task will occupy Indian law in the future.

The first section offers some thoughts about the continuing challenges that India faces as it tries to work out a secular-religious balance in a variety of settings—specifically, the development of a conception of secularism and the role of law in achieving a secular-religious balance.[1] The second section notes the differences between how the United States and India approach the problem of law and religion and raises the provocative possibility that, instead of religious India becoming more like the secular United States, the United States might eventually become more like India.

The Challenges for India

The Concept of Secularism

What concept of secularism will animate India's efforts to achieve a secular-religious balance? Briefly put, the issue is whether secularism is (1) a mandate for uniform law drained of religious content (the secularism-as-uniformity version) or (2) the absence of a dominant state religion (the no-dominant-religion version). The legal conception of secularism in India is important because the Indian Supreme Court has enshrined secularism in the Constitution's "basic structure," which cannot be amended away,[2] and which serves as a background consideration for interpreting the constitutional text.[3] This entrenchment of secularism has taken on added importance in light of the creation of a Constitutional Review Commission by the current ruling government led by a Hindu-oriented political party.

The secularism-as-uniformity version was a response to the centripetal forces that have been part of the Indian social and political fabric. It was a dominant theme in the framing of the Constitution in the late 1940s, responding to intense fears that national disintegration would result from the varieties of language, religion, and caste. The original national trauma of partition and the integration of the princely states shaped the national psyche and reinforced fears for the survival of the nation. Unlike the United States, where independence from England was followed belatedly by constitutional integration after a decade-long experience with the perils of multiple independent states, India needed no such tutelage about the hazards of national disintegration in a modern world of military vulnerability and economic opportunity.

As it turned out, the survival of the Indian nation is not the problem it originally appeared to be. Early redrawing of the state map along linguistic lines defused some of the most serious threats to national unity. To be sure, Kashmir remains an issue and instability in the northeast persists, but the Khalistan movement is now quiescent and the nation seems secure. In this environment, neither the reality nor the symbolism of a secular uniform civil code seems necessary to glue the country together. Indeed, Hindu conservatives are now wary of what a uniform civil code might do to traditional Hindu religious law (which contains far more variety than the label "Hindu law" implies), and the Hindu party that heads the current government coalition is sufficiently concerned with attracting Muslim votes that a uniform civil code is now out of the question.

The preferred version of Indian secularism is now the no-dominant-religion approach, which precludes establishing a single state religion and assures that government involvement with the numerous religions of the subcontinent will be nondiscriminatory and will be based on respect for religious freedom. The no-dominant-religion version best serves a nation like India whose multiple religious-cultural traditions and indistinct boundary between state and society inevitably lead to *some* relationship between religion and government (e.g., through aid to religious schools), as long as that relationship remains rigorously neutral.

The adoption of the no-dominant-religion version of secularism creates a dilemma for those interested in achieving the kinds of substantive legal reforms that were once the goal of secularism generally and a uniform civil code in particular. The most promising approach for legal reform, given the historical baggage associated with the term "secularism," would be to focus on particular reforms for which secularism has been the rallying cry, rather than use that term as a banner around which to rally political support. This theme is strongly suggested by a number of papers in this volume—most dramatically and prominently in concern for the status and rights of women, less dramatically in providing special treatment (e.g., educational and job reservations) for members of disadvantaged groups, and, even less dramatically, in the evolution of the law dealing with religious endowments. In a country where modernity can be associated with religious intolerance (for example, by helping Muslim women), and where violent religious discord lies near the political surface, it is important to disaggregate the issues that have traditionally clustered under the secular banner and to address them separately with as little appeal to either secular or religious ideology as possible.[4] With apologies to Arundhati Roy, we might call this the law of small things—and it is to that possibility that we now turn.

The Role of Law: Large- vs. Small-Scale Change

What role can law play in the evolution of the secular-religious balance in India? In the following discussion, I distinguish between two roles—grand bold measures and small incremental steps. A further distinction, which partially tracks the grand/small distinction, is between legislation and judicial decisions (including judicial interpretation of uncertain statutory law).

LEGISLATION

Large-scale. In the modern legal world, major legal changes usually occur through legislation, and bold judicial decision making is usually confined to placing constitutional limits on what legislatures can do—e.g., blocking land reform or limiting affirmative action. Moreover, major legislative change tends to be associated with revolution and political upheaval (as evidenced by the Napoleonic civil code), or colonial imposition of law (such as the Indian penal code and various Indian civil codes in the second half of the nineteenth century). This suggests that successful large-scale legislative changes in the secular-religious balance are unlikely in modern India. For that to occur, there would have to be a seismic political upheaval or overwhelming governmental power comparable to the early days of the Republic (the 1950s) when the Congress Party dominated Parliament. (Even in that early period, a radical uniform civil code could not be passed over the objections of conservative Hindu and Muslim opposition.) Moreover, if the legal environment existed today for large-scale legislative change, that would have serious negative consequences for secularism, because the only current prospect for such change is a conservative Hindu-oriented government.

Small-scale. If we shift our attention to small-scale legal change, we

William D. Popkin

can readily envision both a legislative and a judicial role. Historically, Indian legislation frequently made small changes in the secular-religious balance (as explained in the essay by Rudolph and Rudolph in this volume). For example, statutes adopted during British rule outlawed *sati* and child marriage, chipping away at selected practices deemed seriously objectionable. And a more Western conception of individual property rights in contrast to joint family ownership was adopted to preserve the rights of converts from Hinduism to inherit joint family property, to allow testamentary wills to override joint family claims, and to permit a son educated by a family to keep subsequent income rather than share it with the joint family. Muslim law was also altered, although (significantly) the pressure for change often came from within the Muslim community (e.g., allowing women to obtain divorce to discourage conversion from Islam).[5]

In independent India, the conglomerate of statutes known as the Hindu Code sponsored by a dominant Congress Party in the 1950s made some significant changes in the family law applicable to Hindus, defined expansively to include Sikhs, Jains, and Buddhists. The Hindu Code permitted divorce, raised the marriage age, and allowed women to inherit in the case of intestacy, although the practical implementation of these changes outside the urban areas is unclear. These changes, however, stopped well short of radical family law reform, e.g., by omitting Muslims, exempting agricultural land from intestate inheritance by women, and not permitting women to be the head of a Hindu joint family.

Small-scale legislative reforms in personal religious law have been sanctioned by Indian courts against a charge that they deny equal treatment to those not benefiting from selected changes. This result rests on the conclusion that personal laws are not "law" for purposes of the Constitution's equal protection clause, so that the personal laws of different religions can be unequal.[6] Thus, a statute outlawing bigamy by Hindus, but not providing similar rules for Muslims, is not unconstitutionally discriminatory.

JUDICIAL DECISIONS

When we turn our attention to judicial decisions, we observe numerous examples of the courts achieving small-scale change in the secular-religious balance through the interstitial application and interpretation of personal law, legislation, and the Constitution. This occurred repeatedly in British India (as discussed in the essay by Kunal Parker in this volume). For example, (1) criminal statutes were interpreted to give voice to perspectives that were sometimes hostile to Hindu tradition (e.g., in the definition of temple dancing as prostitution); and (2) English judges implemented a classicized and homogenized Anglo-Hindu approach that overlooked the variety in Hindu legal practice and had a tendency to incorporate Victorian morals in the guise of applying the "spirit" of Hindu law (e.g., allowing a Hindu woman to leave her husband and remarry was against the "spirit" of Hindu law). The same process of small-scale adjustments in the secular-religious balance occurs in independent India as well, except that the judge must now paint on a broader and more complex canvas that includes constitutional issues that were not relevant during the British period. In this complex legal environment, the judge in independent India can respond to a variety of different legal cultures—both modern/secular and traditional/religious—but the one constant in these cases is the judge's involvement in the process of small-scale legal change. Judges find a legal space within which to influence the secular-religious balance without (in most instances) engaging the most volatile and divisive issues that would undermine the judge's ability to contribute to incremental change.

I will look at some continuing issues involving judicial influence on the secular-religious balance in India in three major settings: (a) the determination of membership in traditional religious groups eligible for modern secular-oriented government assistance to the disadvantaged; (b) the application of family law, both regarding membership to take advantage of specific rules (as when a convert claims the law of the newly adopted religion), and to determine internal family matters (e.g., the right of maintenance for a divorced woman); and (c) constitutional law regarding government involvement in religion and regulation that burdens religious practices.

Traditional religious group membership and modern secular-oriented government policy. Membership in certain religiously defined traditional groups—specifically, Scheduled Castes (Untouchables or Dalits) and Other Backward Classes (defined primarily by caste)—is no longer just a traditionally defined low social status associated with religious tradition. It is also a ticket to a government job and educational preferences for the disadvantaged group. Although it is impossible to generalize about the galaxy of practices associated with Hinduism, birth was traditionally the way to determine a person's caste membership. While a caste might have some limited mobility, individual choice was not a traditional way to become a member of a Hindu caste, even though conversion is now recognized by certain subcategories of the capacious Hindu religion. What then should an Indian court do when a person exercises the modern secular right of personal choice to opt into a Hindu caste (by conversion, marriage, or adoption), claiming thereby to become a member of a group eligible for government assistance?

The complexity of this legal environment—involving older and newer religious traditions and modern secular reform—opens up a space for judges to work out a secular-religious balance that is sensitive to the claims of modern secularism without being dismissive of traditional religious law. Although the cases have not always been consistent (as explained in the essay by Galanter and Krishnan in this volume), the courts have not generally recognized conversion, adoption, or marriage as a way to achieve status in a group eligible for preferential treatment. More recent cases seem especially hostile to voluntary efforts to obtain government assistance. For example, a person born of Christian parents who had converted from being Hindu Scheduled Caste could not convert to Hinduism and claim government benefits (Christians cannot legally be members of a Scheduled Caste).[7] And a "forward" woman who married an Other Backward Classes (OBC) man did not become an OBC member eligible for government assistance.[8] The judge in the latter case, despite praising inter-caste marriage as an aid to secularism, referred generally to marriage, adoption, or conversion as examples of "voluntary mobility" that could constitute a "fraud on the Constitution,"[9] if exploited to qualify for government preferences.

These decisions about caste and class membership are classic examples of disaggregating an issue with religious significance to take account of the various ways it may impinge on secular concerns. Although the cases making it difficult to choose group membership appear to be traditional—by depriving the individual of the benefits of personal choice and insisting on membership by birth—they implement modern secular goals of delivering government assistance to their intended beneficiaries. At the same time, they do not adopt a traditional monolithic view of caste membership, because a person who cannot choose group membership for purposes of obtaining government benefits can still rely on new caste membership to determine other legal consequences (such as inheritance).

The legal relevance of caste in modern law arises not only when courts determine eligibility for government assistance, but also when the courts review the government's use of caste itself as the fundamental principle for distributing such benefits. The secular goals of providing equal treatment and opportunity without entrenching caste rigidities opens up a judicial space for working out a secular-religious balance. The Indian judicial response has been to permit the government to use caste for distributing benefits preferentially as long as it does not overwhelm the political system and is not an all-encompassing criterion.

Thus, in a 1963 decision, the Court held that reservations for disadvantaged groups can be made for no more than 50 percent of available government benefits,[10] stating that more than 50 percent would be a "fraud" on the Constitution. And more recently, in 1993, the Court held that Other Backward Class status can be determined by caste, as long as caste is a suitable proxy for class distinctions.[11]

In these cases, the secular goal of preventing caste from completely defining the distribution of government benefits puts some limits on the government's use of traditional religious categories, although the use of these categories is still allowed to dominate government decisions. Those familiar with United States constitutional law will recognize this judicial tightrope act as an effort to allow the government to achieve the modern secular goal of helping disadvantaged groups without completely entrenching traditional religious groups in the political and social system. Not surprisingly, in a traditional group-oriented religious society, the Indian courts have far less space to advance the secular goal of undermining group identity while allowing traditional group identity to be used to promote modern secular goals. The only way for judges to retain some space for readjusting the entrenchment of caste in Indian society is to insist on careful scrutiny of claims of a factual correlation between backwardness and traditional caste membership.

Family law. The secular-religious balance is relevant for family law in two situations—determining who is eligible for a particular body of family law (e.g., after conversion), and determining family law for people whose religious status is not in question.

As in the case of government reservation of benefits, conversion can create a conflict between the secular and religious that opens up a space for judging. For example, when a Hindu man becomes a Muslim in order to divorce his wife without difficulty, secular concerns with protecting women's rights clearly arise. In such cases, the courts protect the woman by not allowing the conversion to terminate her rights as a divorced Hindu woman, even though the man's conversion may be valid for other purposes.[12]

When there is no question of identifying group membership and the judges must determine the content of a person's family law, the challenge to the judge's role in determining the secular-religious balance is most acute. If a person chooses his religion or caste, the effort to manipulate the law is often apparent and the act of choice is itself a challenge to traditional practice. Absent choice, the courts must determine the meaning of family law without an obvious judicial space into which secular concerns can intrude.

The variety of Hindu sub-traditions increases the likelihood that family law decisions will impinge on members of the "majority" religion. These decisions are likely to cause resentment among some Hindus and are one reason why a homogenizing uniform civil code has lost some of its political momentum.[13] But when the decisions regard minority religions, the risks of imposing unwelcome modern secular views on traditional religious practices threatens political disruption.

Indian judges learned about the pitfalls of both the rhetoric and practice of judicially imposed secularism in the aftermath of the landmark Shah Bano case.[14] This 1985 decision expanded a Muslim woman's rights to maintenance after divorce. What most irked the Muslim community was not necessarily the specific result, but the claim that this was already Muslim law and the court's dictum regretting that "Article 44 [the Directive Principle for a uniform civil code] . . . ha[d] remained a dead letter," and asserting that "the role of the reformer ha[d] to be assumed by the courts" in the absence of legislation.[15] The Court could have reached the same result as a "small-scale" interpretation of the Indian Criminal Code under which the maintenance suit was brought, but the breadth of the holding carried portents of imposing major legal change through an interpretation of Muslim law by secular courts that was unacceptable to the Muslim community (or at least those elements with political clout in the mid 1980s).

This decision spawned a 1986 legislative response—the Muslim Women (Protection of Rights on Divorce) Act (1986) (MWA)—which appeared to override the Shah Bano result. However, the scope of a divorced Muslim woman's rights under this 1986 statute was unclear and the Indian newspapers have reported a Bombay High Court ruling in July 2000 that provides more substantial changes in the Muslim man's maintenance obligations to a former wife than many people anticipated. It remains to be seen whether this decision will be upheld on appeal and whether it will be viewed as a small-scale legal change or a major threat to the Muslim minority. There is every possibility that the Bombay court's interpretation will stand up politically as a small adjustment to Muslim law, given the fact that the opinion relies solely on the statute and does not purport to dictate Islamic law to Muslims.

Constitutional law and religion. Indian judges must also address the sensitive secular-religious balance when the legislature takes action that appears to support or burden a particular religion. This occurs in two situations: first, in determining if the law is religious or secular in the first place; and second, in determining whether a secular law improperly interferes with religious practices.

Not surprisingly for a country with deep religious traditions that make prohibition of cow slaughter a Directive Principle in Article 48 of the Constitution, the Indian courts have sought secular justifications for religiously oriented legislation. For example: (1) an appeal to "Hindutva" in a political election did not necessarily constitute electoral malpractice; the Court said that "Hindutva" was a term denoting Indian civilization or culture—a "way of life of the people of the subcontinent";[16] (2) a court overruled objections by the minority Jain religion to government celebration of the 2500th birth anniversary of the founder of the Jain religion (Mahavir), on the ground that this tradition belonged to all of India;[17] and (3) the courts have upheld the governmental takeover of various aspects of Hindu temple administration on the ground that only secular practices were assumed by the state.[18] Clearly, an Indian court will uphold significant government involvement in religion under the guise of secularism.

The secular-religious balance must also be addressed when secular law burdens religious practices. These cases raise issues at least as sensitive as those that arise when the courts determine personal law. The sensitivity arises because courts specifically embrace a balancing test to decide whether government regulation is permissible—taking into account not only the constitutional grant of legislative power to regulate in the interest of public order, morality, and health in Article 25 of the Constitution, but also determining whether the burden falls on "essential" religious practices. Determining what is "essential" to a religion carries with it the same potential to offend as when a court determines the content of religious law.

For example: (1) an Allahabad High Court decision upheld an antipolygamy statute against a Hindu man's claim that his religion required him to have a male child, for which purpose he wanted to take a second wife; the court said that polygamy was not essential for this purpose because he could adopt a male child;[19] (2) a Calcutta High Court decision struck down a prohibition of street dancing by a Hindu sect on the ground that it was essential to the sect's religion, taking account of evidence supporting that conclusion that had not been presented in an earlier Supreme Court decision; this evidence enabled the High Court to reach a different conclusion than the Supreme Court, which had previously upheld the prohibition;[20] (3) the Supreme Court upheld a statute maintaining the status quo at the disputed Babri Masjid site, in part on the ground that Muslim law in India does not establish a mosque as an "essential part of the practice of the religion of Islam" because prayer can be offered anywhere, even in the open;[21] and (4) the Supreme Court held that a government prohibition of proselytizing (aimed primarily at Christian missionary work) was permissible; the justice concluded that there could "be no such thing as a fundamental right to convert any person to one's own religion," because any such religious freedom would interfere with the freedom of the person being converted.[22]

The occasions for constitutional judgments about the secular-religious balance will probably increase if a Hindu majority attempts to legislate practices that favor the dominant religion or disfavor a minority. And these concerns will reach a fever pitch if the Constitutional Review Commission set up by the current ruling party coalition (the National Democratic Alliance) succeeds in amending the Constitution to reconfigure the secular-religious balance to favor the majority religion (a remote possibility as of this writing because a two-thirds parliamentary majority is needed to amend the Constitution). If that occurs, the courts will have to decide what part of the existing secular-religious balance is part of the unamendable basic structure of the Constitution. Or, more indirectly, the courts may have to decide whether the threat to secularism is great enough to justify the central government's taking over a state government by invoking President's Rule under Article 356 of the Indian Constitution. (In the Bommai case, the Court held that a state government's inability to preserve secularism was a permissible reason for President's Rule.[23])

In making all these judgments, there is nothing remotely close to an easily implemented formula, and the Indian courts must eke out the answers case by case. The opportunity exists for diligence in protecting secular values—in the sense of preventing a dominant religion from becoming paramount and in protecting majority and minority religions from undue state interference—but the effort is also fraught with danger. Judges can act or speak too boldly, attracting an intensely hostile reaction that prevents them from making incremental contributions to achieving the specific goals that sometimes cluster under the banner of secularism.

Who Are the Judges?

Working out a secular-religious balance requires judicial statesmen and stateswomen of the highest order, jurists who are sensitive both to the nuances of law and political realities. This is especially important in a country like India where the judges have at times been very bold in making broad pronouncements about the content and role of law—e.g., declaring the basic structure of the Constitution to be unamendable,[24] affirming that judges do in fact make law,[25] and urging the legislature to adopt a uniform civil code.[26] India has been fortunate to have distinguished High Court and Supreme Court judges who are aware of the delicate balance between tradition and change, but the future method of judicial appointment is in doubt.

The Constitution provides for appointment of Supreme Court justices by the president after consultation with the chief justice. In recent practice, the consultative function has been transformed into a process of appointment by the chief justice and a collegium of fellow Supreme Court justices. (A roughly analogous transformation has occurred with appointments to the High Court, except that the participating officials are the state governors and chief judge of the High Court.) There are presently proposals for creation of a judicial appointing commission consisting of five people: the chief justice or his nominee from other Supreme Court justices; a nominee from among High Court chief justices; the prime minister or his nominee from the Union Cabinet; the leader of the opposition or his nominee in consultation with other opposition parties; and a nominee from the state advocates-general, the attorney general for India, and the solicitor general. This proposal would allow neither the government in power nor Supreme Court justices to control judicial appointments and appears to provide a balanced input of legal and political considerations.

The implications of the judicial appointment process in India are unclear. Like most institutional arrangements, it is hard to generalize *a priori* about their political consequences, and certainly not in the long run. A total separation of law from politics could insulate judges from undesirable religious influences, but it could also break a link that has helped to produce judges that are sensitive to what courts can and cannot do. Moreover, appearances are important. Explicit recognition of a judicial political link is clearly suspect in India, not only because the British tradition rejects such practices, but also because law is often spread thinly over a cauldron of potential social unrest. For law to have a chance, there must be rigorous adherence to the appearance of separation between law and politics.

The appointment process must therefore be sensitive both to the appearance of judging (separating law and politics) and the reality of judging (acknowledging political realities). This demands of judges a high level of sophistication regarding the judicial role. I leave it to others more familiar with the Indian legal system to pass judgment on which appointment process best suits the complex needs of the Indian judiciary.

The Indian Experience and United States Law

The first reaction of an American who reads about law and religion in India is likely to be one of relief at not having to confront the same intense pull of traditional religion in working out the secular-religious balance. Certainly, India's religious traditions are so strong that religion

William D. Popkin

intrudes far more into Indian law than is possible in the United States, where a strong tradition of separating religion and government prevails. In the United States, for example, the definition of minorities eligible for government benefits has no religious implications, and the problems of working out personal law with religious overtones are completely absent.

Even the apparent similarities between Indian and United States approaches—which occur primarily in constitutional law—are misleading. The Indian courts' willingness to allow legislation based on religious traditions appears similar to the U.S. Supreme Court's acceptance of Sunday closing laws[27] and state-financed Christmas creches[28] as secular observances. But this judicial reasoning makes more sense in the United States than in India, where holidays with a religious tradition are more truly experienced as secular. When an activity in the United States retains strong religious implications, such as school prayer, U.S. courts carefully restrict the extent of government involvement.[29]

Indian and United States courts have also differed in the way they deal with laws burdening religion, or at least that is the traditional point of view. In India, courts forthrightly balance public interest against religious concerns, openly examining whether religious practices are "essential." By contrast, the traditional view of U.S. courts is that they do not have the power to decide what religious practices are essential, because that would excessively involve the courts in religious matters.[30] U.S. doctrine still appears to insist that U.S. courts focus on whether laws burdening religion are supported by a public interest; if they are, the burden on religion is allowed. The only qualification is that a higher level of state interest is needed if the burden is not imposed neutrally on all religious and secular activity.[31] Thus, polygamy,[32] the use of peyote by Native Americans in a manner analogous to the sacramental wine and wafer in Christianity,[33] and wearing head covering in the armed forces can all be forbidden.[34] And the impact of Sunday closings on those who must also close their businesses on another day of the week for religious reasons is irrelevant once the secular objective of Sunday closing is identified.

I am not suggesting that United States laws have not confronted conflicts between secular and religious views of life. For example, legal efforts to protect gay rights bump up against traditional religious values, some of which arouse the kinds of violent reactions that we encounter in India. And the reaction of courts to legislation dealing with women has a vaguely religious and certainly traditionalist tone of protecting family values. For example, in the late nineteenth century, married women's acts (intended to give a wife control of her property independent of her husband) were viewed by some judges as assaults on the traditional family. Consequently, these statutes were sometimes interpreted to prevent the legislative changes from having more than a modest effect. In one case,[35] the court refused to interpret the law generously in the wife's favor, stating that "[i]t is impossible that a woman can use and enjoy her property as fully and separately after marriage as before" because "[t]he husband is still the head of the family" and, therefore, the court would "presume that no innovation on the old law was intended further than was absolutely required."[36] But usually, conflicts in the United States that involve group identity are nonreligious. Thus, efforts to help racial and ethnic minorities through affirmative action sometimes seem to threaten group (but not religious) identities in both majority and minority communities. And English-only laws have obvious roots in a nonreligious sense of national identity.

Unlike India, Western historical experience associating the combination of government and religion with violence produced a reaction, seen in the United States Constitution in the late eighteenth century and in the state constitutions in the early decades of the nineteenth century, against government involvement with religion. This is an unfair irony of history that haunts a traditional society seeking to become a modern nation. Modern political India was born in a religious conflagration that did not, however, lead to a wholly secular political society, and the persisting interaction of government and religion continues to resonate throughout India's politics in ways that are not experienced in the United States. Of course, the United States had its own conflagration— the Civil War—whose legal implications were not resolved until many decades later. Although the Thirteenth, Fourteenth, and Fifteenth Amendments to the United States Constitution were passed soon after the Civil War—providing former slaves with the vote, equal protection of the laws, and due process of law—the reality was a long period during which the promise contained in those Amendments was not realized. Perhaps the promise of a selective "secularism" in India will take as long to materialize.

If India's religious traditions seem remote from the contemporary United States, it remains to be seen what the future will bring. At present, India's religious traditions allow the legislature to support religion more readily than in the United States, and they require the courts to balance the impact of government regulation against "essential" religious practices in a way that would draw U.S. courts too deeply into rendering religious judgments. But is United States secularism as secure as we think?

Whether we admit it or not, our history as a Christian nation has successfully marginalized claims of many religious minorities. Historically, the practices of diverse religious traditions in the United States—e.g., polygamy (Mormons) and Sabbatarianism (Jews)—have not stood up well against majority rule. And a nineteenth-century Supreme Court case also used statutory interpretation as a vehicle for adopting religious values. The Court held that a law making it a crime to import "labor or service of any kind" could not possibly mean that bringing a pastor into the United States was criminal, because "[t]his is a Christian nation."[37] But the pressure for amalgamation into U.S. society that has been so strong in the past (at least, in our ideology) seems to be on the wane. How will the U.S. react, for example, to a Muslim population growing both through immigration and internal conversion? Will laws disadvantaging any Sabbath except Sunday survive and will a prayer in the legislature limited to the Judaeo-Christian tradition still be permissible?[38] How will the U.S. react to customs brought by immigrants from Asia regarding a marriage age that does not fit our "secular" rules about the age of consent (as if consent had anything to do with marriage in many communities)?

First, there are signs that United States courts will permit a breach of the wall between religion and the state, as evidenced by a more hospitable reception toward nondiscriminatory public aid to private religious and nonreligious schools.[39] Second, there are strong hints that U.S. courts will insist on accommodating minority religions by engaging in the kind of balancing of "essential" religious practices against governmental interests that Indian courts have accepted. For example: (1) the Supreme Court struck down a prohibition of animal slaughter, not only on the ground that the government policy was not neutral regarding the minority religion, but also by taking into account that this practice was "central" to the complainant's religion;[40] (2) the Supreme Court held that Amish children could not be required to attend public high school, given that Amish beliefs about education played a "vital role" in their religion; this decision is especially controversial because the state law was neutral in regard to religion, aimed generally at educating students, and yet the Court still forced the law to yield to religious practice;[41] and (3) the Court held that a state could not deny unemployment insurance to a worker who refused to work on Saturday for religious reasons; the decision is difficult to understand except on the ground that it forces the state to subordinate its otherwise neutral policies to those practices that are essential to a person's religion.[42]

There remain strong voices insisting that U.S. decisions which appear to balance neutral government regulation against practices that are "essential," "central," or "vital" to a particular religion can be explained on narrower grounds. Thus, the case dealing with the Amish involved important parental rights over their children's education, and the unemployment insurance case involved particularized judgments about an individual's reasons for making work decisions.[43] But these efforts to insulate U.S. courts from making sensitive decisions about the relationship of government regulation to religious practices seem less and less like maintaining a clear separate wall between government and religion and more and more like putting a judicial finger in a crumbling dike.[44]

As Rajeev Dhavan points out in his essay in this volume, the world is more like India than like the United States. The nation-state is a recent creation, currently under pressure from groups below and across national boundaries: the Welsh and Scottish in the United Kingdom; the Sicilians and some northern Italians; linguistic groups in a variety of countries; the Pan-Islamic movement. Whether a sense of group identity not tied closely to the nation will take root in the secular United States, and if so how that will affect its law, is an open question.

Notes

I must acknowledge in more than routine fashion the efforts of Rajeev Dhavan and Dan Conkle in educating me regarding the legal complexities of law and religion in India and the United States respectively. They are most definitely not responsible for my inability to grasp the sensitivities and subtleties that run through the legal cultures of these two countries.

1. Although the 42nd Amendment to the Indian Constitution added the word "secular" to the Constitution's preamble in 1976, it did not add anything new. Secularism, whatever it means in the Indian Constitution, has been part of the constitutional structure from the start. See S. R. Bommai v. Union of India, AIR 1994 SC 1918,1951. The 42nd Amendment was an element in the Congress Party's platform to help justify the declaration of emergency (suspending many fundamental rights), by aligning the party with the poor (it also added the word "socialism" to the preamble) and in opposition to the Hindu-oriented Jan Sangh party.

2. See Kesavananda v. State of Kerala, AIR 1973 SC 1461.

3. See S. R. Bommai v. Union of India, AIR 1994 SC 1918, 2004, 2020, 2066.

4. Some such idea underlies efforts in the United States to provide gay partners with benefits analogous to those available to married couples, without necessarily allowing gay partners to marry.

5. Muslim Personal (Shari'at Application) Act of 1937.

6. See Ahmedabad Women Action Group v. Union of India, AIR 1997 SC 3614 and cases discussed therein.

7. S. Swvigaradoss v. Zonal Manager, F.C.I., AIR 1996 SC 1182.

William D. Popkin

. Valsamma Paul v. Cochin Univ., AIR 1996 SC 1011.

9. AIR 1996 SC, at pp. 1021–1022.

10. Balaji v. State of Mysore 1963 AIR SC 649.

11. Indra Sawhney v. Union of India, AIR 1993 SC 477.

12. Sarla Mudgal v. Union of India, AIR 1995 SC 1531.

13. The "museum of beliefs" that constitute Hinduism led one court to determine that a group was Hindu despite its denial, thereby requiring the group to provide temple access to untouchables. Yagnapurushdasji v. Muldas Bhundardas Vaishya, AIR 1966 SC 1119, 1128. The case invoked the capacious Hindu tradition for modern secular purposes—ending discrimination against Dalits.

14. Mohd. Ahmed Khan v. Shah Bano, AIR 1985 SC 945.

15. AIR 1985 SC, at p. 954.

16. Ramesh Yeshwant Prabhu v. Prabhakar, 1996 AIR SC 1113, 1130.

17. Suresh Chandra v. Union of India, AIR 1975 Delhi 168.

18. See, e.g., Bira Kishore Deb v. State of Orissa, AIR 1964 SC 1501, 1507–10.

19. Ram Prasad v. State of U.P., AIR 1957 All. 411, 413.

20. See Commissioner of Police vs. Jagadiswarananda, AIR 1991 Cal. 263, and cases discussed therein.

21. Faruqui v. Union of India, AIR 1995 SC 605, 641.

22. Rev. Stanislaus v. State of Madhya Pradesh, AIR 1977 SC 908. See also the case discussed by Rajeev Dhavan in his essay in Part IV of this volume.

23. S. R. Bommai v. Union of India, AIR 1994 SC 1918.

24. Kesavananda v. State of Kerala, AIR 1973 SC 1461.

25. Fuzlunbi v. K. Khader Vali, 1980 AIR SC 1730, 1731.

26. Indian judges, at least in the past, have issued very bold statements affirming the virtues of a uniform secular civil code and the importance of the judicial role in advancing this cause. See, e.g., Sarla Mudgal v. Union of India, AIR 1995 SC 1531, 1538.

27. McGowan v. Maryland, 366 U.S. 420 (1961).

28. Lynch v. Donnelly, 465 U.S. 668 (1984).

29. Santa Fe Independent School District v. Doe, 120 S.Ct. 1266 (2000).

30. See Suresh Chandra v. Union of India, AIR 1975 Delhi 168,171.

31. Church of Lukumi Babalu Aye, Inc. v. City of Hialeah, 508 U.S. 520, 531 (1993).

32. Reynolds v. United States, 98 U.S. 145 (1878).

33. Employment Division, Dept. of Human Resources of Oregon v. Smith, 494 U.S. 872 (1990).

34. Goldman v. Weinberger, 475 U.S. 503 (1986).

35. Walker v. Reamy, 36 Pa. 410, 415–16 (1860).

36. The Court is unsure what to do about modern legislation that adopts a traditional paternalistic attitude toward women. In Rostker v. Goldberg, 453 U.S. 57 (1981), it upheld a law keeping women out of combat, but in Craig v. Boren, 429 U.S. 190 (1976), the Court struck down a law providing that the drinking age for women was 21, but only 18 for men.

37. Church of Holy Trinity v. United States, 143 U.S. 457, 471 (1892).

38. In Marsh v. Chambers, 463 U.S. 783 (1983), the Court held that a prayer in the legislature was constitutional because it was an entrenched tradition when the Constitution was adopted, even though the prayer was always based on the Judaeo-Christian tradition.

39. Agostini v. Felton, 521 U.S. 203 (1997); Mitchell v. Helms, 120 S.Ct. 2530 (2000).

40. Church of Lukumi Babalu Aye, Inc. v. City of Hialeah, 508 U.S. 520, 534 (1993) (animal sacrifice is "central element" of the religion).

41. Wisconsin v. Yoder, 406 U.S. 205, 235 (1972).

42. Sherbert v. Verner, 374 U.S. 398 (1963).

43. 494 U.S., at pp. 1601–06.

44. See also Bollard v. California Province of the Society of Jesus, 211 F.3d 1331 (9th Cir. 2000) (dissenting opinion discusses cases refusing to apply Title VII—prohibiting gender discrimination—to church ministers).

Bibliographical Note

Gerald James Larson

The literature on law and specifically "personal law" is extensive, as the many references in the notes in the present collection of essays indicate. There are, however, some basic sources for anyone wishing to get started in reading in these areas, and it may prove useful to provide a brief bibliographical guide to some of the more well-known discussions in the literature.

By far the most important name is that of J. Duncan M. Derrett and his important study, namely, *Religion, Law and the State in India* (New York: The Free Press, 1968). See also J. Duncan M. Derrett, *Essays in Classical and Modern Hindu Law* (Leiden: E. J. Brill, 1978). Derrett is also the translator of another major work, Robert Lingat's *Classical Law of India* (Berkeley: University of California Press, 1973). In terms of classical literature, there is the massive work of P. V. Kane entitled *The History of Dharmaśāstra* (5 volumes, Second Edition, Poona: Bhandarkar Oriental Research Institute, 1968–1974), a work that must be consulted by anyone seriously interested in issues of personal law in India.

Other important discussions in the field of personal law include the work (in alphabetical order) of Marc Galanter, M. P. Jain, Tahir Mahmood, John H. Mansfield, and Ludo Rocher. Marc Galanter's *Competing Equalities* (Berkeley: University of California Press, 1984) is the definitive study of affirmative action issues in Indian law. Galanter's most recent collection of essays on issues of law and personal law is entitled *Law and Society in Modern India* (edited by Rajeev Dhavan, Delhi: Oxford University Press, 1989; and see also the excellent "Introduction" to that collection by the editor, Rajeev Dhavan, pp. xiii–c). M. P. Jain's *Outlines of Indian Legal History* (4th ed., Bombay: N. M. Tripathi, 1981) and Tahir Mahmood's *Muslim Personal Law: Role of the State in the Indian Subcontinent* (2nd ed., New Delhi: Vikas Publishing, 1983) and *Studies in Hindu Law* (2nd ed., Allahabad: The Indian Press, 1986) are standard treatments of personal law issues in India. John H. Mansfield's essay, "The Personal Laws or a Uniform Civil Code?" is a valuable overview of most of the relevant issues and, in fact, was used in our Colloquium as a basic working paper (in Robert D. Baird, editor, *Religion and Law in Independent India* [Delhi: Manohar, 1993], pp. 139–177). Finally, Ludo Rocher's "Hindu Conceptions of Law" (*The Hastings Law Journal* 29 [1978]: 1284–1305) and "Indian Reactions to Anglo-Hindu Law" (*Journal of the American Oriental Society* 92, no. 3 [July–September 1972]: 419–424) provide helpful historical analysis of many of the issues raised in this volume.

For helpful discussions regarding the issue of India as a secular state and the manner in which issues of personal law relate to India's secular identity, the work (again, in alphabetical order) of Robert D. Baird, P. N. Bhagwati, Gerald J. Larson, T. N. Madan, Ashis Nandy, Lloyd I. Rudolph and Susanne H. Rudolph, and Donald Eugene Smith should be noted. Robert D. Baird's "Religion and the Legitimation of Nehru's Concept of the Secular State" (in *Religion and the Legitimation of Power in South Asia*, ed. Bardwell L. Smith [Leiden: E. J. Brill, 1978], pp. 73–86) is still one of the best treatments of the notion of the secular state at the time of India's independence. P. N. Bhagwati's "Religion and Secularism under the Indian Constitution" (in *Religion and Law in Independent India*, ed. Robert D. Baird [Delhi: Manohar, 1993], pp. 7–21) provides a helpful analysis of the concept of Indian secularism from the perspective of a former Chief Justice of the Supreme Court of India. A more recent discussion of many of the same issues may be found in Gerald J. Larson's *India's Agony over Religion* (Albany: State University of New York Press, 1995, and Delhi: Oxford University Press, 1997). Two essays that have sharply called into question the validity of India's identity as a secular state are T. N. Madan's "Secularism in its Place" (*Journal of Asian Studies* 46, no. 4 [November 1987]: 747–759) and Ashis Nandy's "An Anti-Secularist Manifesto" (*Seminar* 314 [October 1985]: 14–24). A useful discussion of the manner in which India's political economy relates to the notion of the secular state may be found in Lloyd I. Rudolph and Susanne H. Rudolph's *In Pursuit of Lakshmi* (Chicago: University of Chicago Press, 1987), and there is, of course, the classic discussion of India as a secular state, namely, Donald Eugene Smith's *India as a Secular State* (Princeton: Princeton University Press, 1963). Finally, for a general theoretical discussion of the problem of secularism, see William E. Connolly, *Why I Am Not a Secularist* (Minneapolis: University of Minnesota Press, 1999).

For the definitive studies of the history of the Indian Constitution, see Granville Austin, *The Indian Constitution: Cornerstone of a Nation* (Delhi: Oxford University Press, 1966, Oxford India Paperbacks, 1999), and *Working a Democratic Constitution: The Indian Experience* (New Delhi: Oxford University Press, 2000).

Contributors

Granville Austin is an independent historian in Washington, D.C.

Robert D. Baird is Director of the School of Religion, University of Iowa, Iowa City.

Srimati Basu is Assistant Professor, Women's Studies and Anthropology, Depauw University, Greencastle, Indiana.

Kevin Brown is Professor, School of Law, Indiana University, Bloomington.

Paul B. Courtright is Director of the Asian Studies Program, Emory University, Atlanta, Georgia.

Rajeev Dhavan is a practicing attorney before the Supreme Court, New Delhi, India.

Marc Galanter is John and Rylla Bosshard Professor of Law and Professor of South Asian Studies, University of Wisconsin, Madison.

Namita Goswami is Lecturer in Women's Studies, Emory University, Atlanta, Georgia.

Laura Dudley Jenkins is Assistant Professor, Political Science, University of Cincinnati, Cincinnati, Ohio.

Jayanth Krishnan is a doctoral candidate in Political Science, University of Wisconsin, Madison.

Gerald James Larson is Rabindranath Tagore Professor of Indian

Cultures and Civilization, and Director, India Studies Program, Indiana University, Bloomington.

John H. Mansfield is John H. Watson, Jr. Professor of Law, Harvard University Law School.

Ruma Pal is Justice, Supreme Court of India, New Delhi.

Kunal M. Parker is Assistant Professor, Cleveland-Marshall College of Law, Cleveland.

William D. Popkin is Walter W. Foskett Professor of Law, School of Law, Indiana University, Bloomington.

Lloyd I. Rudolph is Professor, Political Science and South Asian Studies, University of Chicago.

Susanne Hoeber Rudolph is Professor, Political Science and South Asian Studies, University of Chicago.

Sylvia Vatuk is Professor, Anthropology and South Asian Studies, University of Illinois at Chicago.

Arvind Verma is Assistant Professor, Criminal Justice, Indiana University, Bloomington.

Index

Index

and British administration of personal law, 16–17, 52
and communalism, 18–19, 115–116
compared to Jewish culture, 270–272, 280–287
and criminal law, 125–128
and cultural federalism, 38–40
denominations of, 16
and eldercare, 177
and endowment of images to deities, 28–29
and feminism, 221–222
and the Hindu Code Bill, 147–151
and Hindu Undivided Family, 28, 179
and inheritance laws, 167–172
and intercaste marriage, 106–109
and issues of volition, 109–110, 113–114
Kshatriya, 254
legislation affecting, 27–28, 64n55
and marriage, 41, 149–150, 153–154, 193–195, 202–203
Marriage Act of 1955, 27, 71
Minority and Guardianship Act of 1956, 27
and modernity, 312–313
nationalism among, 53–54, 193–195, 285, 322–323n21
and personal law, 15, 21–23, 94n1, 147–148, 163–167, 272–275, 289n11
and pluralism *versus* universalism, 37
and polygamy, 28, 149–150
and the practice of Sati, 201–207, 212–215
and religious and charitable endowments, 70–72, 74–76, 102n111
schools of law, 16
and secularism, 301–302, 304–306, 330–331
Shiva, 16
Shudra, 254
Sikh, 16
and societal divisions, 19–23, 49–50

and superstition, 214–215
in the United States, 220–221
Vaishya, 254
Vishnu, 16
Homo Hierarchicus, 265

Identity
and ethnicity, 16
group, 47–49, 104–106
and intercaste marriage, 110–111
and Judaism, 283–284
and religion, 16, 37
and religious and charitable endowments, 90–94
and religious conversion, 116–118
and reservations, 104–106
Ilbert, Courtney, 43
Impact of Social Legislation on Social Change, 147, 159n6
Independence movement, Indian, 17, 36, 47–49, 55–56, 254–255, 272–273, 307–309
India through Hindu Categories, 265
Indian National Congress, 254–255
Indian Penal Code of 1860 (IPC), 124–125
Indian Slavery Act of 1843, 126
Indian Succession Act, 77, 78–80, 88, 96n16, 99n53
Indian Trusts Act, 78, 82, 99n53
Indra Sawhney v. Union of India, 120n19, 257, 267nn17,20–28, 268n30, 278, 294n91
Inheritance laws, 167–172. *See also* Endowments, religious and charitable
Islam. *See* Muslims
Israel
British rule of, 281
compared to Pakistan, 287, 300nn152–153
divorce in, 282–283, 297n127, 298n135
and human rights, 286
marriage in, 282–283